The Laws & Customs Of Erev Shabbos
And Motzei Shabbos

Includes the Laws of Shnayim Mikra & Kiddush Levana

Based on the Alter Rebbe's Shulchan Aruch
Includes summaries and hundreds of practical Q&A.

Compiled by Rabbi Yaakov Goldstein

The Laws & Customs of Erev Shabbos and Motzei Shabbos
Revised Edition
Published and copyrighted © by
Yaakov Goldstein
Rebbe Akiva 44/7 Beitar Elite, Israel
For orders, questions, comments contact:
Tel: 050-695-2866
E-mail: rabbiygoldstein@gmail.com

5773 • 2013

Approbation for the Authors "A Semicha Aid For Learning The Laws of Shabbos"

ב"ה

RABBI MENACHEM M. GLUCKOWSKY
CHABAD RECHOVOT
12 HAGANA ST. RECHOVOT ISRAEL
Tel: 08-9493176 Fax:08-9457620 Cel: 050-4145770

מנחם מענדל גלוכובסקי
רב קהילת חב"ד ברחובות
מען : רח' ההגנה 12/1 רחובות 76214
שרד 08-9493176 פקס. 08-9457620 נייד 050-4145770

Elul 577

I have seen the valuable Sefer "A Semicha Aid for Learning The Laws of Shabbos" written by Rabbi Yaakov Goldstein. The purpose of this Sefer is to assist students learning Semicha in learning the material from the Alter Rebbe's Shulchan Aruch, as well as for them to come out with a valuable and large database of knowledge in practical Halachic questions dealt with in contemporary authorities. It excels in its clear presentation, concise language and thorough summaries in all the relevant laws covered in the Shulchan Aruch of Admur.

It can also serve the general English public in giving them the opportunity to learn the Laws of Shabbos faithful to the opinion of the Alter Rebbe.

Mention must be made, as writes the author in his foreword, that one is not to use this Sefer, amongst all Sefarim of Melaktim, to Pasken for himself. One must rather address all matters which require clarification to a qualified Rav.

I bless the author for his work and wish him much success.

Menachem Mendel Gluckowsky.

בס"ד

RABBI B. YURKOWICZ

CHABAD LOD

ברוך בועז יורקוביץ

רב ומר"א דשיכון חב"ד לוד

אה"ק ת"ו

The book "The laws of Shabbos" written by Rabbi Yaakov Goldstein is a comprehensive compilation of the laws and customs of Shabbos, up until the many Poskim of today's time, which discuss the practical applications of the laws. Sefarim of this nature are very important and will certainly strengthen the proper observance of Shabbos.

I thus come here with words of blessing and praise to my dear acquaintance, the author, who brings merits to the masses through this important work.

As the author himself has mentioned in his foreword I reiterate that which is known that the layman cannot use this Sefer to Pasken for himself even after learning it in whole, but must rather address all their questions to a qualified Rav.

I am confident that in the merit of this spreading of the laws of Shabbos, on which the Sages state "If the Jews guarded Shabbos they would be redeemed", it will hasten the coming of our righteous Moshiach speedily in our days.

Rabbi Baruch Jurkavitch

SHIKUN CHABAD 1/25 LOD. TEL:08-9256070 FAX:08-9204770   פקס 08-9256070 :לוד טל 1/25 שיכון חב"ד

Warning

The Halachas provided in this book are intended to serve as an aid in understanding Halacha, and as a resource of practical Halachic questions and sources for the English reader. It is not meant at all to take the place of a competent Rav, Moreh Horaah or one's own personal research of a Halacha. Hence one should not Pasken based on this book without either discussing the matter with a Rav or verifying the matter in the many resources provided by author.

Foreword

Acknowledgement:
First and foremost I give thanks to the Almighty which has blessed me to be able to compile this work. I thank my wife, My Eishes Chayil, Shayna, which if not for her support this book would have been impossible to accomplish. I thank all the Rabbanim and Rosheiy Yeshivas which have given me advice and support regarding the project, and of course my students in which through teaching them many insights have been added to the laws written here, following the dictum of the Sages "And from my students more than all".

The importance of learning Halacha:
It is known and evident the importance that the study and knowledge of Halacha plays in the role of the life of a Jewish man and woman. As is known the Rebbe lived and preached that one must be a Shulchan Aruch Yid, a Jew which every movement of his life is dictated by the directives of the Shulchan Aruch. To such extent was the knowledge of Halacha in the forefront of the Rebbe's eyes, that he pleaded and suggested in a talk of Yud Shvat 1955 that in today's time, the Yeshivas are not to begin the accustomed deep analytical studies in Talmud until the students have been taught the fundamental principles of Jewish belief and the laws which are written in Shulchan Aruch. The Rebbe continued, "If the situation continues the way it is, then in a number of years from now there will not be a Rabbi which will know a simple law regarding a Jew's daily life, such as a law in the laws of Muktzah. Yes, he will know maybe a law in Nezikin or Choshen Mishpat from the Talmud which he learned, but he will be ignorant to the simplest of laws brought down in Shulchan Aruch". This statement of the Rebbe follows the ruling of the Alter Rebbe in Hilchos Talmud Torah [2/3] that one is to learn and become expert in the practical laws prior to learning anything else. Likewise, in letters the Rebbe suggests that one is not to pass a day without studying some section of practical Halacha. In Chassidus we also find a greater emphasis given to the study of Halacha over the other sections in the Torah. [See Tanya Igeres Hakodesh 1/26; Lekutei Torah Mamar "Lo Sashbis Melach"]

Understanding the format of the Halachas provided within this Sefer and which Poskim they are based on:
In general the rulings provided in the Sefer are faithful to the rulings of the Shulchan Aruch Harav otherwise known as the Alter Rebbe's Shulchan Aruch. When there are other opinions applicable, such as the opinion of the Michaber, or Mishneh Berurah, or other opinions, they are mentioned in the footnotes. The Halachas provided are split in to three sections:

1. The Halacha Section: The Halacha section is the main section written in the non-boxed area. Only those rulings recorded in the Shulchan Aruch Harav are brought and summarized within this section. Many times there are additional explanations, stipulations and clarifications of a Halacha in Admur which is brought in other Poskim. All these additions are brought in brackets or footnotes. This allows the reader to maintain an understanding of the Halacha as written by Admur without the additional comments of later authorities, but at the same time gain from their necessary additions. Thus the rulings in the non-boxed areas which are not in brackets are all sourced in the Alter Rebbe's Shulchan Aruch.

2. The footnotes: The footnotes provide the reader with a number of different points of information. They provided the sources for each statement written, as well as additional explanations and opinions of a given Halacha. Many footnotes serve to delve into the wording of Admur in a given Halacha, his intent and the background of his rulings.

3. The boxed area: The boxed area which follows each Halacha serve to provide a concise summary of the Halacha and additional practical Q&A that have been dealt with in contemporary Poskim and relate to the given subject. The Q&A section does not include Halachas that are explicitly ruled in the Shulchan Aruch of Admur, as these Halachas have already been written in the Halacha section of the book.

➤ *The Q&A:* The Q&A section lend the learner a greatly needed base knowledge for practical application of the resulting law learned within a topic. Many times even after one has sifted and comprehended the final ruling of Admur, its influence within practical cases remain obscure. This is besides for the fact that researching a question amongst the sea of Poskim is both time comprising as well as not always practical. We therefore have compiled many major practical Halachic questions which connect with a given Halacha that was learned. The answers given have been compiled from various sources, including Piskeiy Teshuvos, Shemiras Shabbos Kehilchasa as well as the many resources of Poskim brought within these Sefarim. Mention must be made that effort was placed in verifying the sources of the rulings found within these Sefarim by looking into their sources and verifying their ruling. In cases where a dispute amongst Poskim is recorded we have not given final rulings, being that we are not in a position to rule for the public like which Posek one is to follow. In these cases one is to consult with his personal Rav and receive guidance for what he is to do. **It is of importance to note that the ruling of one's personal Rav takes precedence over any dissenting opinion brought in the book, whether or not this opinion is known to the Rav. Furthermore, even those which are in Rabbinical position of giving rulings are not to base their rulings on opinions brought in this book without first studying and verifying its source.** As is known that one may not base a ruling on summarized Halachas [Melaktim a compiler of opinions] but is rather to discern this for himself in the sources that are brought. [See Piskeiy Teshuvos Vo. 3 in the approbations of Gedolei Yisrael, and the introduction there.]

About the author:

Rabbi Yaakov Goldstein teaches Semicha in Yeshivas Beis Menachem, Jerusalem. The Yeshiva provides a unique Semicha program with focus on bringing down the learned laws into practical Halacha.

Rabbi Goldstein received Semicha from Rabbi Shnear Zalman Labkowski of the Tomchei Temimim headquarters in 2005. He has since served as a chaplain in an elite unit within the Israeli army. There he dealt with various Halachic issues relating to soldiers in his unit. Since then he has become a certified Shochet, and teaches Semicha in the Beis Menachem Yeshiva run by Rabbi Gershon Mendel Avtzon.

Rabbi Goldstein is currently on Shlichus with his wife Shayna and seven children in Beitar Elite, Israel in which he serves through his classes to spread the knowledge of Nigleh and Chassidus to the Chareidi public.

Other works by the Author

The present author has written books on various subjects in Shulchan Aruch. Some of these sections are not yet available to the public in a published format although are currently available **free of charge** as a PDF document which can be sent via E-Mail. To receive the PDF documents on any of the subjects listed below please contact the author at rabbiygoldstein@gmail.com. In order for these subjects to become available on the bookshelf we are in need of funding. If you or anyone you know would like to sponsor a Halachic section to become available in print, please contact the author and the merit of spreading Halacha and the merit of the Alter Rebbe will certainly stand in your favor!

The following is a list of other subjects currently available:

1. A Semicha Aid for Learning The Laws of Shabbos Vol. 1 [available on Amazon.com]
2. A Semicha Aid for Learning The Laws of Shabbos Vol. 2 [available on Amazon.com]
3. The Laws of Shabbos Volume 3 [available on Amazon.com]
4. The Laws and Customs of Erev Shabbos and Motzei Shabbos [available on Amazon.com]
5. A Semicha aid for learning the laws of Basar Bechalav [available on Amazon.com]
6. A Semicha aid for learning the laws of Taaruvos [available on Amazon.com]
7. A Semicha aid for learning the laws of Melicha [available on Amazon.com]
8. The laws of Rosh Hashana [available on Amazon.com]
9. The Laws of Yom Kippur
10. The Laws of the Three Weeks
11. The Laws of Chanukah
12. The Laws of Shavuos
13. The Laws of Purim

To subscribe to receive a free copy of Halachic topics as they become available by the author, please contact the author at the above e-mail.

Home Learning Semicha Program

The Semicha Aid Series in collaboration with Yeshivas Beis Menachem, Jerusalem runs an international Home Learning Semicha program catered for those which desire to study the Semicha curriculum and receive Semicha certification although do not have the ability to do so in a Yeshiva setting. A home study program is hence available for students of all ages to become efficient in Halacha and receive Semicha certification from the comfort of their home in accordance to their time and leisure. For more information on the program and other available Semicha programs in Jerusalem please contact rabbiygoldstein@gmail.com.

Table of Contents:[1]

❖ The Laws & Customs of Erev Shabbos 11
❖ The Laws & Customs of Motzei Shabbos 79
❖ The Laws & Customs of Kiddush Levana..159

Topics included in our previous publication "The Laws of Shabbos"

List of Topics included in Volume 1:
❖ The Laws of Shehiyah
❖ The Laws of Chazara
❖ The Laws of Hatmanah
❖ The Laws of Bishul
❖ The Laws of Muktzah

List of Topics included in Volume 2:
❖ The Laws of Building and Destroying
❖ The Laws of Cutting and Tearing
❖ The Laws of Smearing
❖ The Laws of Ohel
❖ The Laws of Trapping/Killing
❖ The Laws of Tying and Untying
❖ The Laws of Borer
❖ The Laws of Winnowing
❖ The Laws of Squeezing
❖ The Laws of Melting
❖ The Laws of Molid Reiach
❖ The Laws of Dyeing
❖ The Laws of Salting
❖ The Laws of Grinding
❖ The Laws of Kneading
❖ The Laws of Bathing
❖ The Laws of Medicine

List of Topics included in Volume 3:
❖ The Laws of Shearing
❖ The Laws of Writing & Erasing
❖ The Laws of Meameir
❖ The Laws of Sewing, Gluing & Taping
❖ The Laws of Reading
❖ The Laws of Music, Clapping & Dancing
❖ The Laws of Home Cleaning
❖ The Laws of Games
❖ The Laws of Plants, Trees and Garden Produce
❖ The Laws of a Shabbos Bris
❖ The Laws of International Dateline, Time Zones

---

[1] A detailed Table of Contents with the subtopics and Q&A is brought prior to each subject.

Laws and Customs pertaining to Erev Shabbos

Based on Shulchan Aruch Harav Chapters 242, 249-252, 260

Erev Shabbos Checklist[1]

*Suggested use: For easy use photo copy this page numerous times and hang one copy in a public area of the house every Erev Shabbos. After each chore is done the person who did the chore is to highlight the task hence signifying its completion. This is one more step in making Erev Shabbos preparations less stressful and more organized.

Thursday
✓ On Thursday buy the foods that require cooking in order so one has enough time to prepare them.

Home Preparations
✓ Begin preparing for Shabbos in the morning of Erev Shabbos.
✓ Tidy the home
✓ Sweep and mop dirt from the floors
✓ Remove cobwebs from the walls and ceiling
✓ Sharpen the knives
✓ Set the Shabbos table
✓ Open all cans needed for Shabbos such as cans of tuna, corn, olives, pickles.
✓ Open all closed bags of food and paper ware, such as cake wrappers, plastic plates, potato chips etc
✓ Polish silverware, Kiddush cup, candlesticks
✓ Separate garbage bags for Shabbos if they are attached
✓ Cut tablecloths for each meal if they are attached or are one large roll.
✓ Place tissues in the bathroom. Open the tissue bag.
✓ Cut toilet paper, if no tissues are available.
✓ Tape or cover light switches if necessary.

Food Preparations
✓ Begin preparing for Shabbos in the morning of Erev Shabbos.
✓ The father of the house is to personally prepare his favorite Shabbos dish. At the very least he should prepare one thing for Shabbos.
✓ Bake Chalas on Erev Shabbos
✓ Freeze ice cubes if needed
✓ Prepare dips or salads for the first course
✓ Cook at least two foods which will be eaten during the meal
✓ Boil water
✓ Invite guests

Bodily Preparations
✓ Begin your Erev Shabbos meal before the 10th hour of the day. [three Zmaniyos hours before sunset]
✓ Cut your nails
✓ Get a haircut if needed.
✓ After cutting nails recite Shnayim Mikra after midday
✓ Bathe entire body in hot water
✓ After Shnayim Mikra immerse in a Mikveh

---

[1] The checklist for Erev Shabbos has been compiled based on the Halachos discussed within the Sefer and also on simple matters of practicality that are relevant to Pre-Shabbos preparations. For further information on the details of an item on the checklist, refer to its Halachic section. Also refer to "The Shabbos Primer" p. 49-55

✓ Wear fresh clothing for Shabbos. One is to try to arrange that every piece of his clothing that he wears is designated to be worn only on Shabbos.
✓ Polish Shoes
✓ Brush hat
✓ Untie any double knots in clothing or shoes that will be worn on Shabbos
✓ Apply necessary creams, deodorant, makeup before Shabbos
✓ Brush teeth

Close to Shabbos checklist

✓ Taste the Shabbos foods to see if they need anything added.
✓ Prepare the Blech:
Prepare Blech with enough time for the food to become hot before Shabbos if it were to be cold. [This applies even if the food is currently hot.]
✓ Prepare the Shabbos clock.
✓ Put away all Muktzah items, such as phones etc
✓ Verify the refrigerator light is off.
✓ Verify your water boiler is on Shabbos mode.
✓ Check your pockets to verify they do not contain Muktzah, or any item if there is no Eiruv.
✓ Give charity prior to lighting candles or leaving to Shul for Mincha.
✓ Accept Shabbos with joy!
✓ Daven Mincha with extra concentration.

Good Shabbos!

Table of Contents

Chapter 1: The Shabbos preparations

1. A Mitzvah and obligation upon each person:

2. When on Erev Shabbos is one to begin the preparations for Shabbos?

3. Shopping for Shabbos:

4. The mitzvah of Kavod and Oneg Shabbos:

5. What matters are included within the Mitzvah of Kavod and Oneg Shabbos?
Q&A
Why is no blessing said over the fulfillment of the Mitzvah of Oneg Shabbos?
Is there a Mitzvah of Simcha applicable on Shabbos?
Should one do "Iskafya" on Shabbos and refrain from delving into lavish delicacies?

6. How much should one spend in order to enhance Shabbos and what should be part of the Shabbos menu?

7. Borrowing money and taking money from charity for the sake of the Shabbos meals:

8. Baking Chalas:
Q&A
Why today are not all women particular to bake Chalas for Shabbos and rather buy them from the store?
May one bake only a few Chalas and buy the remainder from bakery even according to the above custom?
Is one try to bake the Chalas specifically on Erev Shabbos?
Separating Chalah:

9. Food designated for Shabbos

10. Cleaning the house for Shabbos:
Importance of cleaning the house for Shabbos:
When on Erev Shabbos is one to tidy the home?
May one remove cobwebs on Shabbos if he forgot to do so before Shabbos?

11. Not to dirty one's floor by the Shabbos meals

12. Sharpening knives on Erev Shabbos:

13. Setting the table for Shabbos:
Q&A
Who should set the table the husband or the wife?
Should one cover other tables of the house?
Should one eat specifically on a four legged table?

14. Tasting the foods on Erev Shabbos:

15. Bathing on Erev Shabbos:
Q&A
Does one fulfill the Mitzvah if he bathes in warm water rather than hot water?
What is one to do if he will not have time to bath or shower on Erev Shabbos?
Going to Mikveh on Erev Shabbos:
Not to bathe too close to Shabbos:

16. Getting a haircut

Q&A

May a woman shave body hair other than the head on Erev Shabbos which is also Rosh Chodesh?
When should one have a haircut on Erev Shabbos?
May a gentile give one a haircut?
Must one wash his hands after cutting someone else's hair?

17. Cutting ones nails:

A. Cutting nails during the week, prior to Erev Shabbos?
B. Not to cut the toe and hand nails on same day:
C. The order of cutting the nails:
D. What is one to do with the nails after they are cut?
E. Washing ones hands after nail cutting:

Q&A

When on Erev Shabbos are the nails to be cut?
May one cut his nail when Rosh Chodesh falls on Erev Shabbos?
May one cut his nails on Erev Shabbos Chol Hamoed, or Erev the last day of Yom Tov?
If one will not have time to cut his nails on Friday may he be lenient to do so on Thursday?
If Yom Tov falls on Friday may one cut his nails on Thursday?
May a Chasan and Kalah cut their nails on Thursday if their wedding is taking place that night?
May one cut his toe nails at night and his hand nails the next day?
If one did not cut his toe nails prior to Erev Shabbos, may he cut them on Erev Shabbos together with his hand nails?
May one cut his toe nails on Thursday?
Must one skip a nail also when cutting the toe nails?
What is one to do if a nail dropped and became lost?
May one throw the nails into the sink or toilet rather than burn or bury them?
May one learn Torah while cutting his nails?
Must one wash his hands after cutting another person's nails, such as one's children?
Must one wash their hands if another person cut his nails?

18. Shabbos clothes:

Q&A

Should one buy shoes specifically for Shabbos?
Should one make a point of wearing Shabbos clothes if he is spending Shabbos alone, or amongst gentiles?
What is one to do if he does not have any Shabbos clothing to wear?
Color of Shabbos attire:
If one is bathing early for Shabbos when should he put on his Shabbos clothes?
When are women to dress in their Shabbos clothes?

19. Laundry:

May one today do laundry on Erev Shabbos using a washing machine?
May one launder his Shabbos clothes prior to Thursday?

20. Reminding ones household that Shabbos is near

21. Carrying an object close to the start of Shabbos:

22. Checking ones pockets close to Shabbos:

Q&A

If on Shabbos one desires to walk past the area of the Eiruv must he check his pockets prior to leaving?

23. Accepting Shabbos with joy:

Doing Teshuvah on Erev Shabbos:
Not to quarrel on Shabbos:

24. Mincha on Erev Shabbos:

Q&A

If the Minyan has begun Ashreiy and one has not yet recited said Hodu and Patach Eliyahu what is he to do?

If one's Shachris prayer continued past midday is he to recite Tachanun?

Is an Avel to be Chazan by Mincha of Erev Shabbos?

The greatness of Mincha Erev Shabbos:

25. Shnayim Mikra:

Chapter 2: Learning and doing other activities on Erev Shabbos:

1. Doing work on Erev Shabbos and Erev Yom Tov:

2. The forms of work that are forbidden to be done past Mincha:

3. Examples of activities that may be done after Mincha:

Q&A

It is forbidden to do work 2.5 Halacha hours prior to sunset on Erev Shabbos unless:

Until what time on Erev Shabbos may a store be left open?

List of activities that may be done past Mincha of Erev Shabbos:

May an employee work past 2.5 hours before sunset if his boss requests him to do so?

If a gentile pays one a monthly payment in exchange for him receiving a haircut whenever he wishes, may one do so if the gentile desires a haircut on Erev Shabbos within 2.5 hours before sunset?

May one begin an activity, such as giving a gentile a haircut, prior to 2.5 hours before sunset, if he knows it will continue into the 2.5 hours?

May a Sofer write Mezuzas, Tefillin, or Sifrei Torah past 2.5 hours prior to sunset?

May one perform cleaning help for Shabbos past 2.5 hours before sunset, in exchange for payment?

May one work in cleaning Shtreimals for Shabbos past 2.5 hours before sunset?

May one work to collect payment for Mikveh past 2.5 hours before sunset?

May one build his Sukkah on Erev Sukkos past the 10th hour?

4. Learning and doing other activities on Erev Shabbos:

Chapter 3: Reading Shnayim Mikra

1. The obligation:

Q&A

Are women obligated to read Shnayim Mikra?
Is an Avel obligated in Shnayim Mikra?

2. What is one obligated to read?

Q&A

Is one who cannot read Hebrew obligated to read Shnayim Mikra in translation to his language?
May one read Shnayim Mikra of Vezos Habracha prior to Hoshana Raba?
Must one read Shnayim Mikra of the Maftir of the four Parshiyos or Rosh Chodesh?
If one traveled from Eretz Yisrael to the Diaspora in a week that the Diaspora is reading the Parsha that was read the previous Shabbos in Eretz Yisrael, must he re-read Shnayim Mikra?
If one will be traveling from Eretz Yisrael to the Diaspora in a week that in Eretz Yisrael the weekly parsha is read while in the Diaspora that Shabbos coincides with Yom Tov, is he to read Shnayim Mikra of the Parsha of Eretz Yisrael?
If one traveled to Eretz Yisrael in a week that Eretz Yisrael is reading a different Parsha than the Diaspora which Shnayim Mikra is one to read?

3. When is one obligated to read Shnayim Mikra?
A. The custom:
B. The letter of the law:

Q&A

Is one to read Shnayim Mikra before or after going to Mikveh on Erev Shabbos?
Is one to cut his nails prior to Shnayim Mikra?
Is one to begin reading Shnayim Mikra immediately after midday of Erev Shabbos, or may it be delayed?
May one make Kiddush and eat a snack prior to reading Shnayim Mikra by Shabbos day?
When is the Haftorah to be read?
May one read Shnayim Mikra of next week on Shabbos after Mincha?
If one read Shnayim Mikra of a Parsha prior to the week of that Parsha must he repeat the reading when that weeks Parsha arrives?
If a certain Parsha will not be read on Shabbos that coming week due to Shabbos coinciding with Yom Tov, when one may begin reading Shnayim Mikra of that Parsha?
By what time on Simchas Torah should Shnayim Mikra of the previous year's Parshiyos be completed?
When making up Parshiyos of previous weeks should any specific order to be followed?
If one is in doubt as to whether he said Shnayim Mikra of a certain Parsha must he now say it?
May one read Shnayim Mikra at night?
Can one fulfill his obligation of Shnayim Mikra through hearing someone else read it?

4. How is it to be read?

Q&A

Is one to read the Pasuk of Shema Yisrael twice?
Is one to read the Parsha with the tune of the Torah reading [Taamim]?
Must the verses be read in order?

Chapter 4: Traveling on Erev Shabbos:

1. Traveling On Erev Shabbos:

Q&A

What is defined as the beginning of the morning from which one begins counting the 4 hours and 48 minutes?

If one does not have a prearranged meal [or a host to eat by] at his destination and it is already past the beginning of morning, how much time does he have to travel?

How close to Shabbos may one travel in a case that he has already informed the host of his arrival?

May one travel on a plane which will be arriving close to Shabbos?

If one already cooked all his meals, must he still reach his destination prior 5 hours into the day?

If one is traveling to a hotel for Shabbos and will be eating his own food, must he arrive at his hotel within 4 hours and 48 minutes from the morning?

May one travel close to Shabbos on a bus or taxi driven by a Jew, if doing so may cause him to travel back to his destination on Shabbos?

Chapter 5: Eating On Erev Shabbos:

1. Eating On Erev Shabbos:

A. Arranging a large feast:

B. The law by a Seudas Mitzvah/Mitzvah meal:

C. Pores Mapa Umikadeish-Continuing the Friday meal into Shabbos:

D. Eating a small meal on Erev Shabbos:

E. Eating snacks:

F. Eating on Erev Yom Tov:

Q&A

May one celebrate a Siyum Mesechta on Erev Shabbos?

May one celebrate a Bar Mitzvah on Erev Shabbos?

If one began a small meal prior to the 10th hour may he continue to eat after the 10th hour has arrived?

May one eat less than a Kebeitza of bread [less than 55 grams] after the 10th hour?

Is there a limited amount of fruits that one may eat past the 10th hour?

May one drink alcohol past the 10th hour?

2. May one fast on Erev Shabbos:

Chapter 6: Beginning a Melacha before Shabbos which will continue into Shabbos

1. May one begin a Melacha before Shabbos if it will continue into Shabbos?

Q&A

May one light incense before Shabbos having its smell burn on Shabbos?

May one place water under his candles to prevent the possibility of a fire occurring on Shabbos?

May one close the water of his sprinklers on Shabbos?

May one arrange for his sprinklers to go off on Shabbos?

May one place clothing in the washing machine or dryer before Shabbos, having them be washed or dried into Shabbos?

May one arrange that his Shabbos clock turn on a radio, television, or tape on Shabbos?

May one leave a radio, television, or tape on into Shabbos?

May one listen to the radio of a neighbor which is on?

May one have a wake up service call on Shabbos?

May one set up a recorder from before Shabbos to record on Shabbos?

May one leave a microphone on into Shabbos and use it?

May one leave his answering machine active on Shabbos?

May one leave his fax machine active on Shabbos?

May one set up a timer to activate machines which work on electricity? May one set up a timer to activate or shut off his lights at home?

May one set up a timer to activate a fan or air conditioner?

May one on Erev Shabbos place food on his electric plate which is not yet on but will later turn on with the timer?

Chapter 1: The Shabbos preparations

1. A Mitzvah and obligation upon each person:[1]

Best to personally perform all the Shabbos preparations: Even if one has many servants he is to endeavor to personally prepare [all[2] or as much as possible of] his Shabbos needs.[3] [This applies even if doing all the Shabbos preparations will come in expense of his Torah learning.[4]]

Obligation to personally perform one act of preparation: Even if the person is a very prestige figure and great Torah scholar, of which it is unusual for him to purchase items in the marketplace, or do certain labors in the home, nevertheless he is **obligated**[5] to endeavor to personally perform at least some of the Shabbos preparations.[6] [Practically although it suffices for him to perform even one act of preparation[7] nevertheless it remains a Mitzvah for him to engage in many acts of preparations, even if this will come in expense of his Torah learning[8]. In such a case that one will only be performing one act of preparation it is best that he involve himself with the preparations of the food that is most enjoyed by him, in order so he also benefit from the Mitzvah of "better to perform a Mitzvah personally then through a messenger".[9]]

Best to personally prepare the food one enjoys most:[10] It is best that one personally involve himself with the preparations of the food that is most enjoyed by him.[11]

Performing even belittling acts for the sake of Shabbos: One is not to hesitate performing even belittling acts for the sake of honoring Shabbos, as honoring Shabbos is itself one's reason for honor[12], and so did the greatest of our Sages[13] of which each person is to emulate.

---

[1] 250/4

[2] Ketzos Hashulchan 70 footnote 14 and so is implied from Admur. In any event the more Shabbos preparations one personally performs the greater the Mitzvah.

[3] As it is better for one to personally fulfill a Mitzvah rather than do so through an emissary. This concept is a general rule which applies by all Mitzvos.[ibid]

[4] *Mishneh Berurah* 250 in *Shaareiy Tziyon* 9. This unlike the understanding of *Ketzos Hashulchan* 70 footnote 14 [and *Kitzur Hilchos Shabbos* 250 footnote 3], which understands from Admur that one who is able to learn is rather to do so and have another do the remaining Shabbos preparations [besides for the one which he must personally perform]. Likewise the *Kaf Hachayim* 251/22 and *Aruch Hashulchan* 251/3 rule that one who has someone else available to prepare his Shabbos needs for him, is to do have them do so if he plans to spend his time learning..
Defense of the ruling of the Mishneh Berurah in accordance to Admur: It is evident from Kuntrus Achron 2 that the above ruling applies even by a Torah Scholar, as Admur there explains that only by the Amoraim **which were Toraso Umnaso** did they have to suffice with one act of preparation and not more, being that they had to follow the dictum [Yoreh Deah 246/18] that learning Torah pushes off a Mitzvah which could be fulfilled through others. This wording of Admur implies that today being that the Halachic concept of Toraso Umnaso no longer applies, seemingly the Mitzvah remains upon all to increase in their Shabbos preparations even on expense of their Torah learning. Now, although following the above dictum is not limited to one who is on the level of Toraso Umnaso, and rather all Jews which are learning are to continue learning if the Mitzvah is able to be preformed through another, [as explained in Yoreh Deah ibid], nevertheless preparing for Shabbos is considered like a Mitzvah Shebegufo, in which the above dictum does not apply. [Shaareiy Tziyon ibid] This too is possibly hinted in Admur which regarding the above dictum referenced the reader to chapter 240/8, which is not the source of the dictum, as there it is explained that only by a Mitzvah Overes is one to precede the Mitzvah to serving his father, thus implying here too that by this type of Mitzvah of preparing for Shabbos [which is no less than serving ones father] one only gives up its extra preparations if he has to do a Mitzvah Overes, and the idea of Torah learning being defined as a Mitzvah Overes only applies by one who is Toraso Umnaso.
Accordingly the footnote of the Ketzos Hashulchan [70/14] which understood the M"B to be contradicting the Kuntrus Achron of Admur, is inaccurate and in truth the explanation of the Mishneh Berurah compliments it.
However based on this, that today even learning is to be pushed off, a question would arise on the ruling of Admur in 250/2 that there is no need to diminish in ones learning sessions or other activities if others are doing the preparations for them. In truth however this question would regardless apply as according to all there is a Mitzvah to personally prepare all or many of one's needs of Shabbos, as Mitzvah Bo Yoser etc., thus why does Admur in 250/2 not require diminishing other activities even if someone else will be preparing for Shabbos on his behalf. Hence one must conclude that in 250/2 Admur was referring to the letter of the law while in 250/4 he mentions the preferred method of one doing as much as he can personally.

[5] There is an obligation upon every person to do some preparation for the honor of Shabbos, as is evident from the fact that many Tzadikim even though they would learn torah without stop (תורתו אומנתו), on Erev Shabbos they would stop to do this mitzvah. [250 Kuntrus Achron 2]

[6] As this is required out of respect and honor for Shabbos [which is an obligation upon all, and thus at least some act of honor in preparing for Shabbos must be done by all]. [ibid]

[7] Meaning that at the very least one is obligated to perform one act to fulfill the Mitzvah of honoring Shabbos, which is a Mitzvah that cannot be fulfilled through another person. However to personally perform more than one act is not an obligation, but nevertheless is a Mitzvah, as said earlier, that it is better to perform a Mitzvah personally than through an emissary. [Kuntrus Achron 2]

[8] This follows that which was explained above that it is better for one to personally perform a Mitzvah then for one to send an emissary to so for him. See footnote there!

[9] Kuntrus Achron 2. There Admur explains that when the Amoraim would salt the fish, which was their greatest delicacy, they fulfilled, in addition to the obligation to assist in preparing for Shabbos, as well the Mitzvah of "Mitzvah Bo Yoser Mebishlucho"

[10] Kuntrus Achron 2.

[11] This is done in order so one also benefit from the Mitzvah of "better to perform a Mitzvah personally than through a messenger" in the item of which the actual Mitzvah of Oneg Shabbos is being performed with. [ibid]

[12] Thus there is no room to say "How can I belittle my honor with doing such a belittling task", as in truth by doing so he is really gaining the respect that his honor demands.

Summary-Each person is to personally help prepare for Shabbos:

It is an obligation upon every person to personally perform at least one act of preparation for the honor of Shabbos. The more preparations that one personally performs the greater the Mitzvah, and one is thus to strive to personally prepare all his Shabbos needs, even if he has many servants.

Sparks of Chassidus: [14]

It is written in the name of the Arizal that the sweat which one breaks due to preparing for Shabbos is auspicious for erasing one's sins, just as are tears. Therefore one needs to exert much effort in honor of Shabbos.

---

2. When on Erev Shabbos is one to begin the preparations for Shabbos? [15]

Begin the preparations in the morning: One is to always wake up early on Erev Shabbos in order to begin working and preparing for the needs of Shabbos in the morning of Erev Shabbos. [16]

Add in preparations also by Bein Hashmashos: Aside for the preparation done in the morning one is to also add in preparation during twilight [after sunset]. [17]

Summary:

It is a mitzvah to begin preparing the food in the early morning, and then later during Bein Hashmashos.

---

3. Shopping for Shabbos:

When to go shopping[18] It is best to purchase foods which require further preparation[19] on Thursday, as opposed to Erev Shabbos. [20] Readymade foods, such as beverages and different readymade desserts and the like, are better to be purchased on Friday.

If the store will close and one has not yet Davened what is he to do?[21] If one has not yet recited the Shachris prayer and will be unable to purchase his Shabbos needs after completing his prayer, then he is to first say Shema within its proper time [if applicable] and then purchase his Shabbos needs[22], delaying his prayer until after the purchase. This applies even if it is possible[23] that due to the purchase he will miss praying within Zman Tefila, nevertheless he is to first make his purchase. [24] If however delaying the prayer until after his shopping will cause one to fail to pray with a

---

[13] They themselves would perform tasks which were beneath their dignity. Rav Chisda would chop vegetables very thin; Raba and Rav Yosef would chop wood; Rav Zeira would ignite the bonfire; Rav Nachman would tidy the house. [It requires further analysis why Admur omitted the names of the Sages, in contrast to the Michaber which lists them as written in the Gemara.] This was all done to show their respect for Shabbos, emphasizing the importance it had to them, and that they were in awe of its honor. This is just like a servant who is hosting his master in his home in which case the servant endeavors to show that the master is of importance to him and he awes his honor to go out of his way and do preparations for his arrival. [ibid]

[14] Shaareiy Teshuvah 250, brought in Ketzos Hashulchan 70 footnote 14

[15] 250/1

[16] This is hinted to in the verse [Exodus 16/5] regarding the gathering of the Man of which it states that the Man was gathered in the morning of each day, and regarding Erev Shabbos the verse states "And it was on the 6th day that they prepared that which was brought". This implies that they immediately began preparing the Shabbos foods after gathering the Man, which, as said, took place in the morning. Hence today we too begin the Shabbos preparations in the morning. [ibid]

[17] This is hinted to in the above verse which states "and there will be **double** of that which they gather each day". This implies that the preparation should be done twice, once by morning of the 6th day and once towards the 7th day. [ibid]

[18] 250/7

[19] Meaning they require cooking or grinding etc in order to become edible or in order to be served.

[20] This is in order to give one enough time to prepare these foods as well as the other Shabbos needs. [ibid]

[21] 250/3

[22] He must say the Shema prior to shopping even if there may be time left to say it after shopping, as we suspect that perhaps it's time will pass prior to him finishing shopping. [ibid]

[23] But not definite, as will be explained.

[24] We do not suspect that one will come to pass the time for Davening [which is the 4th hour of the day], as we do by Shema, as Davening contains one more hour then does the Shema. Now, although there is room to suspect that this time will too pass until the shopping is complete, nevertheless since the Mitzvah of preparing for the Shabbos meals will definitely be not fulfilled if one Davens first, due to the closing of the stores, while it is possible that he still be able to Daven on time if he go to the store first, therefore he is to first go to the store. [ibid]

Minyan, then he is to first pray [see footnote[25]]. [Likewise if doing the purchase will **definitely** cause him to fail to pray within Zman Tefila then he is to first pray.[26]]

Verbalizing that the bought produce is for Shabbos:[27] It is proper[28] for one to say on every item of purchase "This is for the honor of Shabbos".[29] Likewise on all matters that one does it is good to think that he is doing so for the honor of Shabbos.

Designating food for Shabbos as one buys it during the week:[30] Living with the verse "Remember Shabbos and sanctify it" if one sees a nice portion of food during the week he is to designate it for Shabbos. If he then finds a nicer portion, he is to eat the previous portion during the week and designate the nicer portion for Shabbos. This was the custom of Shamaiy, and so agreed Hillel that it should be the practical directive for others. However Hillel himself, as a result of his great trust in G-d would wait [until Friday] to designate food for Shabbos, saying that certainly G-d will grant me the greatest portion [on Friday] in honor of Shabbos.

Summary:
When to go shopping for Shabbos: Shopping for Shabbos should be done on Thursday for those foods that require preparation. However ready to eat foods are better to be bought on Friday. One should say upon anything he buys that it is being bought Likaved Shabbos.

May one shop before prayer on Erev Shabbos:
One is only to first shop and then pray if all the following apply:
1. He will be unable to go shopping afterwards.
2. He says Shema prior to the shopping.
3. It is not definite that he will miss Zman Tefila due to the shopping.
4. He will not questionably miss Zman Tefila and also definitely miss Davening with a Minyan due to the shopping. If he will certainly not miss Zman Tefila but will definitely miss Davening with a Minyan he is first to make his purchases, unless he is needed for the Minyan.[31]

---

[25] Admur ibid writes that one is to first purchase his groceries and then pray even if there is doubt that he may not be able to pray within Zman Tefila due to this. Nevertheless "if the congregation is praying he is not to separate himself from the congregation". This implies that if one will miss the Minyan due to the shopping he is to first Daven and then shop.
Other Opinions-Mishneh Berurah: The *Mishneh Berurah* [250 *Biur Halacha* "*Yashkim*"] questions how could the Rabbinical Mitzvah of Davening with a Minyan push off the Mitzvah and obligation to prepare for the Shabbos meal, which is a Biblical command of Oneg Shabbos. Furthermore, even if Oneg Shabbos is only of Rabbinical origin, since one can Daven in private how can we allow Davening with a Minyan to completely nullify the Mitzvah of Oneg Shabbos. He thus concludes that one is to first go shopping, even on expense of missing the Minyan, and then Daven in private.
Opinion of Ketzos Hashulchan: The *Ketzos Hashulchan* [70 footnote 11] suggests that in truth everyone agrees that Davening with a Minyan alone is not enough to nullify the Mitzvah of Oneg Shabbos, and one is to thus first go shopping in such a case. When however do we say that Davening takes precedence? In a case that in addition to one losing out in praying with a Minyan, there is also possibility that if he shops before Davening, he will miss Zman Tefila, and in such a case that there is possibly two transgressions involved in first going shopping, one is to forgo the shopping and first pray. However if one knows for certain that he will not miss Zman Tefila then he is to first go shopping, even on expense of missing the Minyan. [This opinion of the Ketzos Hashulchan does not contradict the ruling of Admur or the ruling written above, as whenever one goes shopping in the morning there seemingly is doubt he will lose Davening within Zman Tefila, as there is no prediction of how long the shopping will take.]
Vetzaruch Iyun on the above distinction of the Ketzos Hashulchan, as Admur in 90/17 rules that the Mitzvah of Davening with a Minyan which contains the greatest positive command of sanctifying Hashem's name in public, pushes off even a negative command of not freeing a slave. [This is in contrast to other Poskim, such as Michaber Yoreh Deah 267/79 which do not view any special advantage in Davening with a Minyan regarding pushing off this negative command, and rather rule that all Rabbinical Mitzvos may push off this command of not freeing a slave.] Thus certainly in our case that a) there is a dispute if Oneg Shabbos is Biblical or Rabbinical, and b) It is possible for one to eat at someone else's house or borrow food, that Davening with a Minyan would push off shopping, even on expense of Oneg Shabbos.
However perhaps one can differentiate between the Halacha here and in 90/17, as perhaps only in a scenario that there will not be a Minyan at all do we say that making a Minyan overrides even a Biblical command. However if there will be a Minyan regardless of if one joins this Minyan, then Davening with a Minyan does not override even a Rabbinical command. This distinction can also be proven from the law that one may not delay praying within Zman Tefila even if he needs to use the bathroom, if he can withhold himself for a Shiur Parsa. However one is to delay praying with a Minyan if he has to use the bathroom even if he can withhold himself for Shiur Parsa. Likewise the law states that if Zman Tefila is passing he is to begin Davening Shemoneh Esrei before the Minyan even though he will miss Davening with the Minyan due to this.
In any event one can deduce from here that if one is the 10th man for a Minyan he may not leave the Minyan and go shopping even if the store will be closing, and even if he will be able to Daven later, after shopping, within Zman Tefila.
[26] So is implied from Admur and so rules Ketzos Hashulchan 70/5
[27] 250/6
[28] Lit. good
[29] As by doing so the holiness of Shabbos befalls onto that food. [Machatzis Hashekel, brought in Ketzos Hashulchan 70 footnote 13]
[30] 242/10
[31] Based on footnote above.

4. The mitzvah of Kavod and Oneg Shabbos:[32]

A Biblical or Rabbinical precept: There are two matters regarding Shabbos that were expounded on by the prophets. These are the Mitzvah to honor Shabbos [i.e. Kavod Shabbos] and Oneg Shabbos.[33] These two Shabbos obligations [to honor and enjoy it] are in truth rooted in a Biblical precept.[34] However there are opinions[35] which learn that these two above obligations contain no Biblical root and are rather of Rabbinical origin.[36] Nevertheless, even according to the latter opinion one must be very careful to fulfill these two obligations of honor and enjoyment on Shabbos, as Rabbinical precepts are of more severity than even Biblical precepts. [Practically in the laws of Yom Tov[37] Admur rules plainly like the latter opinion that the Mitzvos of Oneg and Kavod are Rabbinical precepts which have been explained by the prophets.[38]]

The reward: Whoever fulfills the Mitzvah of Oneg Shabbos his reward is explicitly mentioned in the Prophets that he will merit "basking in pleasure of G-dliness". Furthermore, the sages state that whoever performs the Mitzvah of Oneg Shabbos all his sins are forgiven and he is saved from the judgment of Gehenom.

5. What matters are included within the Mitzvah of Kavod and Oneg Shabbos?

➢ **Oneg Shabbos**: Eating delicacies of food and beverages[39] was defined by the Sages as the requirement of the Mitzvah of Oneg Shabbos[40] and it is the main aspect of Oneg.[41] The following sub-categories are included within this Mitzvah:

- Eating 3 Shabbos meals with bread, as bread is the main part of a meal.[42]
- Eating hot foods on Shabbos is included within honoring Shabbos and within Oneg Shabbos.
- Lighting candles on the table in which one eats.[43]
- Sleeping on Shabbos is included within Oneg Shabbos.[44]
- Marital relations on Shabbos is included within the Mitzvah of Oneg Shabbos.[45]
- Not to have any thoughts regarding mundane activities, and rather viewing all of one's needs and worries as already taken care of by G-d, is included within Oneg Shabbos.[46]

➢ **Kavod Shabbos**: Wearing clean [and elegant] clothing was defined by the Sages as the requirement of the Mitzvah of honoring Shabbos. The following sub-categories fall under this Mitzvah:

- Baking Chalas for Shabbos, as opposed to buying them from a bakery, is included in Kavod Shabbos and Yom Tov.[47] (Likewise even those which generally are lenient to eat Pas Akum bread are not to do eat it on Shabbos as this too is included in the Mitzvah of Oneg Shabbos. Rather they are to eat from bread baked in their homes.[48])
- Bathing: Bathing one's body in hot water is included within the Mitzvah of honoring Shabbos.[49]
- Removing cobwebs from walls and roofs is included within the Mitzvah of honoring Shabbos.[50]

---

[32] 242/1

[33] As says the verse "And one calls enjoyment onto Shabbos, to sanctify the honored G-d".

[34] As Shabbos is included within the group of days called "Mikraeiy Kodesh" or "A calling of holiness", and the Sages have learned that the term "A calling of holiness" is coming to teach that one is to sanctify and honor the Shabbos with clean clothing, and to enjoy the day through pleasurable foods and drinks. [ibid] So rules Sefer Chareidim chapter 4

[35] Tosafos; Mahril

[36] As they learn that the wording of "A calling of holiness" is coming to teach that one is to sanctify the Shabbos through refraining from doing forbidden labor. [ibid]

[37] 529/5

[38] The Mishneh Berurah in Biur Halacha [250 "Yashkim"] sides that the eating of bread during the meal is Biblical while other delicacies are Rabbinical.

[39] Such as meat, fish and wine

[40] 242/1

[41] 288/3

[42] 529/3-4 regarding Yom Tov that this is the definition of Oneg. It requires further analyses why this was not mentioned regarding Shabbos, neither in 242 [which simply defines Oneg as eating delicacies] or in 274 1-4 which discusses the laws of having three meals on Shabbos. There it is mentioned that the obligation of eating bread is hinted to from verses in the Torah and no support for its obligation is brought due to it being considered part of Oneg Shabbos. Furthermore, the reason mentioned for ones obligation to eat bread is because of the verses discussing the "*Mon*" eaten in the desert and not because of the Mitzvah of Oneg Shabbos. Vetzaruch Iyun. To note that in 249/10 and 254/8 Admur mentions that eating bread is the main part of the Shabbos meal, although this does not necessarily connect to the idea of Oneg.

[43] 263/1

[44] 281/1

[45] 280/1

[46] 306/21

[47] 242/12

[48] 242/13; For the innovation of this ruling and as for why it was placed in parentheses-see Chikreiy Halachos 3 p. 30

[49] 260/1

- Cutting ones hair and nails on Erev Shabbos is included within the Mitzvah of honoring Shabbos.[51]
- Not to eat a meal on Erev Shabbos past the 10th hour, in order to be able to eat the Shabbos meal with an appetite, is included within the Mitzvah of honoring Shabbos.[52]
- Setting the Shabbos table on Erev Shabbos for the Friday night meal is included within the Mitzvah of honoring Shabbos.[53]
- Preparing on Erev Shabbos all the matters of one's house that require preparation for Shabbos so that when one arrives from Shul it is already all arranged.[54]
- Having a tablecloth cover ones table throughout the entire day of Shabbos is included within the Mitzvah of honoring Shabbos.[55]
- Preparing Melaveh Malka after Shabbos is done in honor of Shabbos.[56]

Summary:
Is disputed if Kavod and Oneg Shabbos is a Biblical or Rabbinical obligation. Nonetheless according to all one must be very careful in fulfilling the Mitzvah, and one who does so basks in G-dliness in the future, has all his sins forgiven and is saved from the judgment of Gehenim.

Q&A
Why is no blessing said over the fulfillment of the Mitzvah of Oneg Shabbos?
Various answers have been given towards this question:

- As there is no specific food that one is required to eat in order to enjoy Shabbos.[57]
- It is included in the blessing said over the lighting of candles.[58]
- It is included in the blessing said over Kiddush.[59]
- No blessing is said over the eating of the three Shabbos meals as we never say a blessing over a Mitzvah which is not fulfilled in one timeframe.[60]

Is there a Mitzvah of Simcha applicable on Shabbos?
There is no Mitzvah of Simcha explicitly mentioned regarding Shabbos.[61]

Should one do "Iskafya[62]" on Shabbos and refrain from delving into lavish delicacies?[63]
It is clear that both on the Halachic[64] and esoteric[65] aspects of the Torah it is a Mitzvah to embellish in Oneg Shabbos, by eating delicacies and drinking fine beverages, and the concept of sanctifying oneself with that which

---

[50] 262/2
[51] 260/1; 529/2 that this is included in the honor of Yom Tov
[52] 529/2 regarding Yom Tov that it is included in the honor of Yom Tov.
[53] 262/1
[54] 262/1
[55] 262/1
Rambam [30/2] mentions that wearing Tzitzis on Erev Shabbos and waiting for the coming of Shabbos is included in honoring Shabbos,
[56] 300/1
[57] Toras Shabbos 263/7
[58] Toras Shabbos 263/7
[59] Keren Ledavid 61
[60] Sdei Chemed Asifas Dinim Brachos 1/16
[61] 529/8; and so is proven from 242/1 that Shabbos does not have a Mitzvah of Simcha. However the Rebbe in Shaareiy Halacha Uminhag 1/127 writes that the reason that the Mitzvah of Simcha was not written regarding Shabbos is because it is nullified to the Mitzvah of Oneg applicable on Shabbos. However this requires further analysis as by Yom Tov there is also a Mitzvah of Oneg [Rabinically (529/5 as is the second opinion in 242/1), and if the Oneg involves Simcha-Biblically (242/1 KU"A 2)] and nonetheless Admur mentions also the Mitzvah of Simcha by Yom Tov. Thus omitting the Mitzvah of Simcha by Shabbos seems to imply it does not exist, as writes Admur explicitly in 529/7.
[62] Iskafya is a Chassidic term used to describe self control from indulgent in pleasures.
[63] For a full analysis on this see Kitzur Hilchos Shabbos Miluim p. 7; Piskeiy Teshuvos 242/3-5
[64] As explained above in the Shulchan Aruch
[65] **Tanya chapter 7** "One who eats fatty ox meat and drinks tasty wine…., when done for the sake of fulfilling the Mitzvah of Oneg Shabbos and Yom Tov, its divine sparks become elevated." This is in contrast to during the week that one who eats for the sake of fulfilling his desires descends the Divine sparks to impurity.
The Mitzvah is likewise stated in **Igeres Hakodesh 26** "However on Shabbos that there is an elevation of the Kelipas Nogah itself together with the external aspects of all worlds, **therefore it is a Mitzvah to eat all the delicacies on Shabbos and to increase in meat and wine**, even though that during the week one would be considered a gluten for doing so." This matter of difference between the eating on Shabbos and weekday is discussed in various Mamarim in Torah Oar and Lekutei Torah. [See Torah Oar Chayeh Sara 15b; Torah Oar Beshalach 65b; Siddur 200-203; Sefer Hasichos 5703 p. 142-146]
In the **Mamarim Haketzarim** of Admur Hazakein [p. 59] he writes that in essence Shabbos is meant to be a day without eating or drinking, as it

is permitted does not apply on Shabbos. Nonetheless the above is contingent on that one eats and drinks the delicacies for the right intentions, which is mainly for the sake of fulfilling the Mitzvah of Oneg Shabbos.[66] One who however does not have such intentions, but rather is simply doing so in order to fulfill his animalistic desires, such eating is no better than eating during the week, of which the concept of "sanctify yourself with the permitted" applies.[67] Such a person is considered not to be honoring Shabbos but to be honoring himself on Shabbos.[68] Hence it has been found that Chassidim in general[69] as well as certain Tzadikim[70] would diminish their amount of embellishment contained within their fulfillment of this Mitzvah. One is certainly to avoid over eating if this will refrain him from spending his time in learning Torah, which is the purpose of Shabbos.[71]

6. How much should one spend in order to enhance Shabbos and what should be part of the Shabbos menu?

The foods eaten to fulfill the mitzvah of Oneg Shabbos vary in accordance to each countries definition of a luxurious food. Thus those foods and beverages which considered delicacies in ones area are to be eaten on Shabbos.[72]

Meat and wine:[73] Although there is no obligation to specifically eat meat and drink wine on Shabbos, nevertheless since in general most people have greater pleasure in consuming meat and wine over other foods and beverages therefore they are to increase in eating meat and drinking wine in accordance to their affordability.

Fish:[74] Eating fish is included in the Mitzvah of Oneg Shabbos. In the times of the Talmud Oneg Shabbos was fulfilled through eating large fish.[75] Fish should be eaten in every meal, unless it is hazardous for his health or he despises eating fish to the point that he does not receive pleasure in eating it but rather pain.[76] It should especially be eaten by the third meal.[77]

At the very least-two cooked dishes:[78] Even one who cannot afford to buy many varieties of foods for Shabbos, nonetheless it is proper to beware to have at least two cooked[79] foods [by each meal]. [This applies for the first two Shabbos meals but not for the third meal, in which case having less than two dishes suffices.[80] If one generally has

---

is similar to the world to come, however since it is impossible to receive the G-dly pleasure of Shabbos without a physical vessel for this pleasure, therefore one is obligated to eat on Shabbos in order to receive the spiritual pleasure which is contained within it.

[66] Kaf Hachayim 529/45; *Kesav Sofer* 107/16 writes that one who does not eat for the sake of the Mitzvah then that meal is considered Seudas Reshus and does not contain a Mitzvah. So is also evident from Tanya chapter 7 from the words "for the sake of Oneg Shabbos";

Shlah [Shabbos Neir Mitzvah] writes: Those which eat and drink to their hearts content and due to the great amounts of foods fall into slumber are not considered to be pleasuring Shabbos but to be pleasuring themselves on Shabbos.

Sefer Hamamarim Samech Vav p. 154 "Eating on Shabbos is not a physical pleasure but a spiritual pleasure."; Rebbe in Sichas 1951 Chayeh Sarah 18 states that even the scrupulousness of eating on Shabbos needs a measurement, and that measurement is in accordance to the amount one is scrupulous by other Mitzvos, especially Mitzvos that are painful to accomplish. To note from a story of the Baal Shem Tov who showed his students on Shabbos a man with Shabbos clothes and he appeared like an ox due to his over involvement in eating his meat.

To note also from *Mateh Efrayim Alef Hamagen* 581/3 which writes that one may delay eating a Shabbos delicacy in middle of his meal, for the sake of Iskafya, and one who does so is considered that he has fasted the entire day.

Reishis Chochmah Shaar Hakedusha 15/53 states: It is proper that one not satiate himself with coarse foods, and he should not fulfill his desires for good foods even on Shabbos.

Elya Raba 293/2 brings in name of Abudarham that one is not to eat too much on Shabbos as this will refrain him from having an appetite for the coming meal. Thus one is to control his inclination and push away the next food even if he desires it.

[67] So is evident from Ksav Sofer ibid

[68] Shlah ibid

[69] Kitzur Hilchos Shabbos ibid states that this is a tradition amongst Chassidim.

[70] Rav Moshe, the son of the Alter Rebbe would diminish his eating throughout the week including Shabbos and Yom Tov. [Igros Hakodesh Rebbe Rayatz 7 p. 18]; Magid Meisharim end of Bo states that the Magid commanded the Beis Yosef to diminish in eating food even on Shabbos and Yom Tov.

[71] See Shlah ibid

[72] 242/2

[73] 242/2

[74] 242/7

[75] 242/2

[76] Thus in such a case he should not eat fish, as Shabbos was given for pleasure. [ibid]

[77] Siddur. Sefer Chareidim [chapter 33] states it is a mitzvah to eat fish by all the meals, especially by third meal in order to elevate the souls that have been reincarnated into the fish. In the writings of the Arizal it is taught that the souls of the Tzadikim are reincarnated into fish. [See Piskeiy Teshuvos 242 footnote 63] In Kuntrus Achron 242/4 Admur mentions an opinion which rules that eating fish on Shabbos is a Biblical command. However Admur rejects this ruling saying there is no legal basis to say that the Sages instituted specifically fish to be eaten.

[78] 242/7

[79] Lit. Tavshilin. This refers to two cooked foods. [see Peri Megadim 242/1; 527/12] As for the definition of cooked foods in this regard the Peri Megadim [242 A"A 1] refers the reader to chapter 627/3-4 [Admur 11-12] in which the definition of Tavshilin, cooked foods, is discussed regarding the Mitzvah of Eiruv Tavshilin. There cooked foods are defined as follows: Any food which is cooked, fried, baked, pickled and is eaten together with bread is defined as a cooked food. Thus one may use meat, fish or eggs. A raw food is invalid.

[80] Nimukeiy Orach Chaim 242

two cooked dishes for his weekday meal then he is to increase on Shabbos and have three cooked dishes. If one is accustomed to have three cooked dishes during the week he is to have four on Shabbos.[81]]

Increasing in ones Shabbos expenditure-making many dishes of foods:[82] Besides for the basic Shabbos foods listed above, whoever increases in his expenditure of Shabbos foods [and other Shabbos needs[83]] in accordance to the amount he can afford, is praised. The money spent for one's fulfillment of Oneg Shabbos is not included in the budget decreed on Rosh Hashana.

List of the basic foods that are to be eaten during the Shabbos meal:
- Chalah
- Meat and wine
- At least two <u>cooked</u> dishes.
- Fish
- Increase in foods as much as one can afford.

Q&A

If one has a dislike for meat and wine must he nevertheless make an effort to eat it on Shabbos?
No.[84]

---

7. Borrowing money and taking money from charity for the sake of the Shabbos meals:

Borrowing money to enhance Shabbos:[85] If one does not have money for Shabbos expenses he is to borrow money if he has an item which is able to be given as collateral to the lender[86].[87] Nonetheless, although collateral is needed, Chazal say that Hashem will arrange for him to be able to pay the lender back the money which he borrowed. This is consistent with the saying of the Sages that Shabbos expenses do not come out of one's Heavenly ordained budget which is annually decreed on Rosh Hashana. If one does not own any collateral then he should not borrow the money in order to enhance Shabbos on the basis relying that G-d will reimburse him, as there is no obligation to spend for Shabbos more than one can afford.

Borrowing money with interest/Ribis:[88] It is permitted to borrow money under terms of Rabbinical interest[89] [Ribis Derabanan] for the purpose of enhancing the Shabbos and Yom Tov meal, as well as any Seudas Mitzvah. This however only applies if one is unable to borrow under a no interest rate.

Using money from a charity fund to enhance Shabbos: If one can afford two basic daily meals for every day of the week it is forbidden[90] to take money from a charity fund for the purpose of having food for the third Shabbos meal, or for the purpose of buying Shabbos delicacies.[91] However if one cannot afford two daily meals for every day of the week and is thus in need of receiving money from the charity fund for these two meals then he is to also be given money for the third Shabbos meal as well as for the Shabbos delicacies such as fish and vegetables.[92] Similarly if one already received money from the community charity fund he may use some of that money for enhancing

---

[81] Kaf Hachaim 242/9

[82] 242/3

[83] So is implied from Admur's wording of Shabbos expenditures and making lots of foods.

[84] As there is no obligation to eat specifically meat or drink wine on Shabbos, and since to this person eating or drinking the above is not enjoyable, he does not have to make an effort to eat or drink it.

[85] 242/3

[86] From which the lender can collect the money from just in case the borrower cannot find the money to pay him back.

[87] However other Poskim [Aruch Hashulchan 242/44] rule that one is to only borrow money if he has a business, or other means, in which he can expect an income that he can then use to repay the loan. According to Admur however this is unnecessary as we have absolute trust that Hashem will pay him back.

Chasidic Explanation: The Rebbe explains that money used for Shabbos is considered similar to Mon which is heavenly bread that derives from G-dliness that is above nature. One thus does not need to have available a proper vessels within nature that can bring him back the money, and rather Hashem compensates him on His own. This is further seen from the fact that the money spent for Shabbos is not included in ones yearly budget allotted to him on Rosh Hashana. Nonetheless this is only to be done if one owns collateral, as the blessing of G-d must be invested in some form of action. [Shaareiy Halacha Uminhag 1/128]

[88] 242/9

[89] It is forbidden to lend or borrow money from a Jew with interest. However certain forms of interest are Biblical while others are only Rabbinical. It is permitted to pay interest which is only Rabbinical to the lender for the sake of enhancing Shabbos.

[90] Regarding asking for extra delicacies Admur writes it is forbidden, while regarding asking for a 3rd meal he writes "not to do so".

[91] 242/4; As in such a case we apply the saying of Chazal: "Make your Shabbos like a weekday and do not become needy unto the public." [ibid]

[92] As once a person is in need and thus may receive from charity he has to be given all that he lacks, including what he lacks for Shabbos. [ibid] Meaning that to originally be eligible for charity one must lack his necessities, however once is eligible then he is given all that he lacks, even things that are not necessities.

Shabbos. However in such a case he must make sure that this will not cause him to need to ask for more money for his daily needs.[93] If one is unable to do so, then if he has some of his own money, he should push himself to use that money for honoring Shabbos to the best of his ability.

Asking for a present from a friend in order to enhance Shabbos:[94] There is no obligation for one to ask to be given money as a gift in order to enhance Shabbos as the Sages have stated "Make your Shabbos like a weekday and do not become needy unto the public". One must budget himself properly so he is able to enhance Shabbos at least a minute amount. It is better for one to do so then to become needy onto the public [and ask for gifts to be able to enhance Shabbos].[95]

Proper budgeting-What is one to do if he does not have any extra money to enhance Shabbos and cannot borrow or take from the charity fund?[96] Even in a case where one has just enough money for daily meals and lacks money to enhance Shabbos, in which case he cannot receive from charity, nevertheless he is still obligated to budget himself during the week in a way that he will be able to enhance Shabbos a minute amount at the very least.[97] Likewise it is proper for him to have at least two dishes, as stated above.

Summary:
One may only borrow money in order to enhance Shabbos if he owns collateral which can be used to repay the loan. One may even borrow money under terms of Rabbinical interest if he is unable to borrow money on a interest free rate.

If one has two meals worth of food for Shabbos he may not take money from charity to buy extra delicacies for Shabbos or even in order to have food for the third meal. If however he does not have two meals of food for Shabbos he may take money from charity for all the Shabbos meals and delicacies. It is better that one budget his money during the week in a way that he will be able to afford the Shabbos foods rather than ask others for money as a gift for Shabbos expenses.

---

8. Baking Chalas:[98]
It is customary for every household to bake *Chalas* for Shabbos which are used for Lechem Mishneh and not to buy them at the bakery as is done during the week. This matter of baking one's own Chalah is included in the honoring of Shabbos and Yom Tov and one is not to divert from this custom.

How much is one to bake? One is to bake at least the amount that requires one to remove Chalah from the dough.[99]

Pas Akum[100]:[101] (For those which are accustomed to eat Pas Akum throughout the week it is proper for them to refrain from eating it on Shabbos and Yom Tov. Rather they are to eat from the Kosher breads which have been kneaded in their homes, as this is included in the Mitzvah of honoring Shabbos and Yom Tov.[102])

Summary:
One is to bake Chalas for Shabbos as opposed to buying them from a store.

Q&A
Why today are not all women particular to bake Chalas for Shabbos and rather they buy Chalas from the store?

Some Poskim[103] rule that today being that fresh and tasty Chalas are available in all bakeries it is not necessary for every woman to bake Chalas in their home. This especially applies if there is much work needed to be done for Shabbos in the home and it is a short Friday. Other Poskim[104] however argue that even today one may not divert from the custom of baking Chalas in the home.

---

[93] 242/5; As in such a case he has ended up placing the burden of his honoring Shabbos expenses onto the community, which negates the saying of the Sages that one is to have a weekday Shabbos rather than be needy onto the public. [ibid]

[94] 242/6

[95] Its implied that nevertheless if one chooses he may ask others for help, although he is not obligated to do so, and perhaps is even shunned.

[96] 242/6

[97] As he too must fulfill the Mitzvah of Oneg Shabbos. [ibid]

[98] 242/12

[99] See also Shach Yoreh Deah 324/25 that the women are scrupulous to specifically bake enough to separate Shiur Chalah on Erev Shabbos.

[100] Gentile baked bread

[101] 242/13

[102] As for why this law was placed in parentheses by Admur, see Chikreiy Halachos 3/30

[103] Oar Letziyon 2/47; Mishnes Yosef 5/63

[104] Mishneh Halachos 15/95

May one bake only a few Chalas and buy the remainder from bakery even according to the above custom?[105]

Yes. One may use some home baked Chalas and some bakery Chalas even according to the above mentioned custom.

Is one to bake the Chalas specifically on Erev Shabbos?

Yes.[106] It is proper to bake the Chalas specifically on Erev Shabbos.[107] If however one is unable to do so, he may also bake them on Thursday or Thursday night.

Separating Chalah:[108]

The amount of dough needed to separate with a blessing: One may only separate Chalah with a blessing if he has 1,666.6 grams of flour.[109] If one has less than this amount but more than 1,250 grams[110] he is to separate Chalah without a blessing.

How much dough is one to separate:[111] One is to separate one Kezayis [approximately 28 grams[112]] of dough. If one separated less than this amount it is nevertheless valid.

Saying the blessing? One is to designate an area from the dough that the Chalah will be separated from. Then one is to say the blessing "Lehafrish Chalah[113]". One then separates[114] a Kezayis of dough and says "Hareiy Zu Chalah" or "This is Chalah". If one separated the Chalah prior to the blessing one may still say the blessing if he [or she] has not yet said "Hareiy Zu Chalah".[115]

What to do with the Chalah:[116] The separated piece of Chalah is to be wrapped in tinfoil and burnt in the oven [or on the stove].[117] It is to be wrapped well to the point that the dough will not become revealed while being

---

[105] Chelkas Yaakov 1/59

[106] Seder Hayom ; Siddur Yaavetz; Machatzis Hashekel 242/10

[107] As amongst the reasons for baking Chalas for Shabbos is because it resembles the showbread which were baked on Erev Shabbos as well as that it rectifies the sin of Adam which was the Chalah of the world.[See Siddur Yaavetz; M"B 242/6]

[108] For a general summary of the order of Hafrashas Chalah see Hakashrus 14/18-22; Piskeiy Teshuvos 242/11; Spice and Spirit Lubavitch cookbook p. 47-50 [The Halachas in Spice and Spirit were edited by Harav Y.K. Marlow OBM]; Hiskashrus 731

[109] Shiureiy Torah Chapter 3/3-4; This follows the ruling of Rav Avraham Chaim Naah the noted Chabad Posek, author of Shiureiy Torah. So is also the custom of the Sefaradim [see Yechaveh Daas 4/55], and is the vintage custom of Jerusalem Jewry. However some [Chazon Ish] are stringent to require there be 2,250 grams of flower to be allowed to separate with a blessing.
While in Shiureiy Torah he records the amount with a blessing is 1666.6 grains in Piskeiy Teshuvos 242/11 and Hakashrus 14/7 they record in the name of Grach Naah 1660 grams. Seemingly this is a typing error. In "Spice and Spirit" they record 1666.6 grams.
The old Ashkenazi custom: The vintage custom of Ashkenazi Jewry was to separate Chalah with a blessing from three Kvartin of flour. [This equals approximately 3 Russian liters which is 1213 grams. If one measures three American pounds then it is 1363 grams. See Koveitz Zalman Shimon p. 77.] Thus they would separate with a blessing from this amount and higher. The source for this custom is Harav Yaakov Viyal in his Sefer Mahriy Viyal chapter 153. There he writes that the Shiur of Chala is a vessel that holds three Kvarton of flour. The Shach [324/3] brings down this opinion and writes that this is the custom. The Aruch Hashulchan [324/10] writes that this is the custom amongst all Jewry and one should not question this ruling.
The Chabad custom: The Tzemach Tzedek [Yoreh Deah chapter 323] writes that "It is known that by us the Shiur of Chalah is approximately three Liters [1213 grams]". This is also recorded to be the practical directive given to people who asked Rav Z.S. Dworkin regarding how much flour is needed to separate Chalah with a blessing. [Koveitz Zalman Shimon p. 77] The Ketzos Hashulchan however claims that this Teshuvah printed in the Shut of the Tzemach Tzedek is not truly from the Tzedek Tzedek, as is known that many Teshuvos of other Geonim found their way into the Teshuvos of the Tzemach Tzedek. The Ketzos Hashulchan's final ruling is as stated above that one is not required to separate from this amount at all and only if there is 1250 grams is it good [but not an obligation] to separate without a blessing. Practically the widespread custom amongst Chabad Chassidim follows the ruling of the Ketzos Hashulchan printed above to separate with a blessing from 1666.6 grams. Nevertheless there are Chabad Rabbanim which rule that one is to separate from three pounds [1363 grams- Koveitz Zalman Shimon p. 77] or 1230 grams [Hiskashrus 731]

[110] Shiureiy Torah ibid writes one is to separate from 1615.3 without a blessing and less is exempt from separation. However one who is scrupulous separates from even 1,250 grams without a blessing. In however Piskeiy Teshuvos 242/11 they record that one is to separate without a blessing from 1,200 grams according to all opinions. This is the opinion of the Chazon Ish. In Hakashrus 14/7 they record 1,150 grams. In "Spice and Spirit" they record 1,230. Vetzaruch Iyun.

[111] Rama 322/5

[112] Following the ruling of Rav Avraham Chaim Naah. However according to the Chazon Ish one separates 55 grams.

[113] Some have the custom to add "Min Haisa" [see Taz Yoreh Deah 328/1]

[114] As applies by all Mitzvahs that the blessing is said prior to the Mitzvah. [So writes Hakashrus 14/20; "Spice and Spirit"] However Piskeiy Teshuvos 242/11 records that one is to only say the blessing after completely separating the Chalah from the rest of the dough in order so no part of the Chalah remains on the dough if one were to separate it after the blessing.

[115] Hakashrus 14/21

[116] See Hakashrus 14/22; Piskeiy Teshuvos 242/11

[117] Yoreh Deah 322/5

burnt, as Chalah is forbidden to be eaten and thus burning it in the oven is similar to cooking a non-kosher food in one's oven.[118] Due to this reason one is to never bake any other foods in the oven until the Chalah is burnt or removed. Alternatively rather than burning the Chalah, one is to wrap[119] the Chalah and discard it in the garbage. Practically today this is the more preferred custom to follow due to a Kashrus worry that the tinfoil of the Chalah may open prior to the Chalah becoming fully burnt hence causing a Kashrus issue for the oven.[120] Furthermore today most garbage is burnt and hence one regardless fulfills the Mitzvah of burning the Chalah when discarding it in the trash, and there is thus no need to burn it in one's Kosher oven.

9. Food designated for Shabbos:[121]
If one was given food for Shabbos it should not be eaten during the week. This is an act of piety, although from the letter of the law there is no prohibition in the matter.[122]

Household preparations for Shabbos

10. Cleaning the house for Shabbos:[123]
One is to clean and tidy all matters of his house so that when he comes home from Shul the house is found clean and organized.[124] [The floors are to be swept and cleaned.[125] When cleaning the house for Shabbos one should mention that he is doing so in honor of Shabbos.[126]]

Removing cobwebs: It is proper[127] for one to clear his house of cobwebs before Shabbos in order so one's house is clean in honor of Shabbos.

Importance of cleaning the house for Shabbos:[128]
The Sages mentioned[129] that every person is escorted by two angels upon returning from Shul, one good and one evil. If the house is found tidy and prepared for Shabbos the evil angle is forced into blessing the home. If however the opposite is found then the good angle ends up giving the opposite of blessing. [Mishneh Berurah 262/3]

Q&A

When on Erev Shabbos is one to tidy the home?
Some Poskim[130] mention that the tidying of the house should be done close to Plag Hamincha, as opposed to the morning or too close to Shabbos.

May one remove cobwebs on Shabbos if he forgot to do so before Shabbos?
Cobwebs are considered Muktzah[131] and thus may only be removed using an irregularity.[132] If they have become repulsive to oneself or to guests in the room they may be removed even regularly.[133] Some Poskim[134] however rule that one is to avoid removing cobwebs at all on Shabbos, even with an irregularity due to suspicion that this may involve the destroying prohibition.[135]

---

[118] If the Chalah became revealed in the oven prior to becoming burnt one is to contact a Rav. The answer to this question depends on whether the dough touched the oven floor, walls or oven grates.

[119] Some write the Chalah is to be doubly wrapped. This is done for purposes of respect so the Chalah not be discarded as regular trash. [See Hakashrus ibid] Others however make no mention of this requirement and as long as it is wrapped once it suffices. [Piskeiy Teshuvos ibid]

[120] See Koveitz Mibeiys Leivi 3 p. 22; Avnei Yishpeh 3/72; Hakashrus ibid

[121] 242/8

[122] This can be learned from the law in Rama 494/2 that a pauper may decide to do whichever he wants with the charity money that he receives, even though the donors gave it with a specific intent. [So is implied from Admur's reference to this chapter].

[123] 262/1

[124] As coming home to a clean and organized home is included within the honor of Shabbos. [ibid]

[125] Aruch Hashulchan 262/1

[126] Kaf Hachayim 262/19

[127] Lit. good

[128] Mishneh Berurah 262/3

[129] Shabbos 119b

[130] Shaareiy Teshuvah 262/1; Kaf Hachayim 262/20 in name of Bircheiy Yosef

[131] Tehila Ledavid 328/79

[132] Betzeil Hachachmah 5/18

[133] They may be removed even normally as then they are considered a Graf Shel Reiy. [SSH"K 23 footnote 34 in name of Rav SZ"A]

[134] Kaf Hachayim 328/270; SSH"K 23/9

[135] Betzeil Hachachmah ibid and Rav SZ"A ibid both argue that this prohibition does not at all apply.

11. Not to dirty one's floor by the Shabbos meals:[136]

It is proper[137] to beware at the night and day meal from dirtying one's floor by throwing food remnants onto it.[138] Rather one is to throw the remnants onto the tablecloth which is on the table and after the meal one is to shake it [into the garbage] or outside of the house. If however one is accustomed to sweep the floor, in a permitted way, after each meal[139], then it is allowed to throw the remnants onto the floor.

12. Sharpening knives on Erev Shabbos:[140]

One is to beware to sharpen the [kitchen] knives every Erev Shabbos, as preparing oneself for eating is included within the honor of Shabbos.[141] In addition [at times] one needs to sharpen the knives for the sake of *Shalom Bayis* [marital harmony], such as if the blade has dulled and one is unable to cut with it.[142]

Summary:
One should be careful to sharpen the knives on Erev Shabbos. This is done for honor of Shabbos and for purposes of *shalom bayis*.

---

13. Setting the table for Shabbos:[143]

When to set the table: One[144] is to set the Shabbos table [including its chairs[145]] on Erev Shabbos in preparation for the Friday night meal.[146] [The silverware and china are to be clean and polished for the meal.[147] There is no need however to set one's bed on Erev Shabbos.[148]]

Placing a tablecloth on the table: It is customary for there to be a tablecloth spread over one's table throughout the entire Shabbos. One may not swerve from this custom.[149] There are those which have the custom to spread two tablecloths over the table.[150] [Some[151] write one is not to remove the Shabbos tablecloth until after Havdala.]

---

[136] 362/2

[137] Lit. good. This is in contrast to the ruling of the Magen Avraham 262/1 which rules that it is **forbidden** to throw remnants on the floor if one does not plan on sweeping the floor immediately after the meal. Admur in Kuntrus Achron 1 proves that there is no prohibition involved and it is a mere matter of scrupulousness.

[138] The Darchei Moshe [brought in M"A 262/1] explains that the reason for this avoidance of dirtying the floor is due to that it may cause the escorting Shabbos angel to desire to leave the home.

[139] If however one only sweeps after the day meal, then one is to beware against dirtying the floor by the night meal. [ibid]

[140] 250/5

[141] This is further hinted to in the words "And prepare *Es*/that which you brought" and a knife is alluded in the word "Es", from the wording of "Lesim Ulemizmoros". Thus implying in the verse that one is to prepare the knives before Shabbos. [ibid]

[142] This is learned from the verse "And you shall know that your tent is in harmony" and the Sages expounded this to be referring to the sharpening of a dull knife for the sake of Shalom Bayis. [Ibid]

[143] 262/1

[144] See Q&A regarding who is preferably to set the table, the husband or the wife.

[145] Aruch Hashulchan 262/1
The ruling brought in Shulchan Aruch regarding setting up the beds on Erev Shabbos was referring to the table seats of back then which were in essence beds which the diners lied on while eating. [Admur 262/1; M"A. See Aruch Hashulchan 262/1] There is thus room to learn that today there is no longer a need to set up the chairs being that they do not entail much work as do setting up the sitting beds of back then. The Aruch Hashulchan however learns differently.

[146] This is done out of honor for Shabbos so that when he returns from Shul he finds everything already set and organized. [ibid]
Background:
This follows the ruling of the Michaber. The Rama writes on this ruling of the Michaber that one is to keep his table set throughout the entire Shabbos. He concludes that so is the custom and it is forbidden to swerve from it. Admur learns that the Rama [and so learns Kaf Hachaim 262/22] was not referring to leaving the table set with its dishes and the like but rather to leave it covered with a table cloth, and on this Admur rules that it must be covered throughout the entire Shabbos and one may not swerve from this custom.

[147] Aruch Hashulchan 262/1

[148] Admur ibid, based on M"A, specifically mentions setting the beds of the dining room, and omits adding the beds of sleeping, despite that the Bach adds as well the beds of sleeping. [See Peri Megadim A"A 262/1] The M"B [262/2] however adds that one should also set the beds of one's room, and so seems to be the leaning opinion of the Peri Megadim ibid, and so rules Kaf Hachaim 262/18; Aruch Hashulchan 262/1.

[149] See previous footnotes

[150] This is besides for the cloth which covers the bread. The reason for this custom is because they want to ensure that the table remains constantly covered throughout the entire Shabbos, and hence even when they need to shake the [upper] tablecloth to remove crumbs from it, the table will still remain covered. [ibid] There is however no Ohel prohibition involved in having only one tablecloth which one shakes and replaces on Shabbos, as is explained in Vol. 2 "The Laws of Ohel". [Admur in 315 and M"A 262/1 unlike Bach]

[151] M"B 262/4 in name of Elya Raba and Aguda

Q&A

Who should set the table the husband or the wife?[152]
Some[153] write the husband[154] is to set the table on Erev Shabbos. Others[155] write it is to be done by the wife.[156]
One who comes home and sees the table is not yet prepared:[157] Even in families that it is the custom of the wife to set the table on Erev Shabbos, if one comes home to see that the table is not set extra care must be taken not to voice anger at one's wife, and one must rather judge her favorably to the point he feels no resentment in his heart.

Should one cover other tables of the house?[158]
One is to cover all the tables that are within the room that the meal is eaten in. It is likewise proper to cover the tables of the other rooms of the house. [159]

Should one eat specifically on a four legged table?
The Arizal was very careful to only eat on a four legged table, to emulate the table of the Tabernacle.[160] This law however was omitted by Admur.

14. Tasting the foods on Erev Shabbos:[161]
One is to taste the Shabbos foods on Erev Shabbos [to see if they need anything added to them in order to ensure their tastiness[162]]. [Nevertheless this was not seen to be the custom of the Previous Rebbe.[163]] It is proper to taste each and every dish of food.

15. Bathing on Erev Shabbos:[164]
It is a Mitzvah[165] [upon both men and women[166]] to initially bathe one's entire body[167] in hot water[168] on Erev Shabbos [and Erev Yom Tov[169]] in honor of Shabbos [and Yom Tov]. If one is unable to do so then he is at the very least to wash his hands, feet[170] and face in hot water.[171]

---

[152] Kaf Hachaim 262/21

[153] Chesed Leavraham 2

[154] As it is his Mitzvah to prepare for the meal [ibid]

[155] Ben Ish Chaiy Vayeira 17

[156] This is based on Kabala. [ibid]

[157] Kaf Hachaim 583/1

[158] Biur Halacha, brought in Ketzos Hashulchan 73 footnote 13; Peri Megadim M"Z 262/1

[159] Aruch Hashulchan 262/2 rules that all the tables of the house are to be covered throughout the entire Shabbos, and it is considered a great shame for the Shabbos if the table becomes uncovered. However see Kaf Hachayim 262/22 which brings that there is no need to cover the other tables of the house which one is not eating on, as the Divine blessing only rests on the table which one eats on and says Birchas Hamazon.

[160] Brought in Magen Avraham 262/1. See Kaf Hachayim 262/1

[161] 250/8

[162] Kaf Hachaim 250/5 in name of Mateh Moshe 308

[163] Shaareiy Halacha Uminhag 1/130

[164] 260/1

[165] This bathing [even of the face feet and hands] is not an actual obligation, but rather one who fulfills it is rewarded, while one who does not is not punished. [ibid]

[166] Mishneh Berurah 260/2 brought in Ketzos Hashulchan 73 footnote 2

[167] The *Michaber*, based on the custom of *Rav Yehuda Bar Elay* in the Talmud, rules that the Mitzvah is to wash only ones hands feet and face. The *Rama* extends this Mitzvah to one's entire body, and so rules *Admur* here.
Ruling of Yaavetz-Not to enter entire body into hot water: The *Yaavetz* in his Siddur rules that one is to bathe his hands, feet and face in hot water. One is not however to enter into a bathhouse as doing so can cause difficulty in marital relations which is supposed to be performed on Friday night, as is written in the laws of Derech Eretz.
Practically, Admur does not mention this ruling of the Yaavetz, despite him mentioning other matters [i.e. eating garlic] which are to be done to enhance Tashmish, and we thus see he does not suspect for this at all. Therefore it remains a Mitzvah upon all to bathe their entire body in hot water on Erev Shabbos as rules Admur.
Furthermore, even according to the Yaavetz if one's wife is not pure he too would agree that one is to bathe his entire body in hot water. Furthermore, even when she is pure it is likely that the Yaavetz was referring to the bathhouses of the past which consisted of an entire lengthy bathing ritual of sauna, steam room and hot tub. Thus mere showering in hot water was not being referred to, and hence remains a Mitzvah upon all to perform. To note however from Kitzur SH"A 72 which states that the Yaavetz rules one is not to **bathe his entire body in hot water** without mentioning the idea of a bathhouse, as is the original words of the Yaavetz.

[168] One does not fulfill his obligation with bathing or showering in cold water. It requires further analysis if even warm water is valid. [Biur Halacha "Bechamin"]

[169] 529/2

[170] The M"B 260/4 notes that washing the feet is no longer an obligation, as it was only require to be done in times that people walked barefoot as

Washing one's hair: It is a Mitzvah for one to [shampoo[172],] scrub[173], and wash the hair of his head on every Erev Shabbos.

When on Erev Shabbos should one bathe:[174] It is proper[175] for one to bathe himself as close to Shabbos as possible[176], and then immediately put on his Shabbos cloths.[177] [This however only applies when bathing in one's home. If however one is bathing in a bathhouse, as is customary when going to Mikveh on Erev Shabbos, then one should visit the Mikveh with plenty of time still left in the day.[178] If one however plans to merely [rinse and then] immerse in the Mikveh, he is to visit the Mikveh as close to Shabbos as possible.[179]]

Miscellaneous laws associated with bathing:

The order in bathing:[180] When bathing ones entire body one begins with washing his head, as the head is the king of all the other limbs. Regarding the rest of the body one first washes his right side[181] and then his left, [thus honoring the right].[182]

Avoiding scorching water:[183] One who is accustomed to pour very hot water on his skin [should avoid doing so as it] can lead to leprosy.

Drying one's face:[184] One should dry his face thoroughly after washing them as not drying the face properly can cause his skin to crack or break out with boils. If one did not do so then his cure is to wash his face *many times*[185] in water that had *beets/spinach*[186] [cooked[187]] in it.

Drying one's feet: One who washes his feet and places his socks[188] or shoes on prior to drying them, can bring him to become blind r"l.[189] [Therefore one needs to dry his feet prior to putting on his [socks or] shoes[190] as is the law regarding all matters which endanger a person.] [Nevertheless the populace, including Rabbis and other G-d fearing Jews, are not accustomed to dry their feet, and nevertheless G-d protects them from danger[191]. Thus being that this is the custom, and G-d prevents the danger from occurring, one may even do so initially.[192]]

Q&A
Does one fulfill the Mitzvah if he bathes in warm water rather than hot water?

It requires further analysis if one fulfills the Mitzvah of bathing if he bathes in warm water.[193] Regarding the definition of hot water versus warm:[194] The Tehila Ledavid[195] learns that all water which is warmer than body temperate [98.6], or its heat is felt in it is considered hot water. So is implied also from other Achronim[196].

---

opposed to today.

[171] Hence in the winter when the days are short and not much time remains for the mother of the home to shower, she can simply wash her hands face and feet in hot water. [M"B 260/2]

[172] Biur Halacha 260 Lachof.

[173] So is implied from Yoreh Deah 199/2 that Chafifah means to scrub.

[174] 262/5

[175] Lit. good.

[176] Lit. near sunset.

[177] This is done in order so one only begins dressing himself in Shabbos clothes in close proximity to Shabbos. The advantage of doing so is that it is now apparent that it is in honor of Shabbos that one is wearing them. [ibid]

[178] As we suspect he may come to take his time and come to transgress Shabbos.

[179] Ketzos Hashulchan 73 footnote 23

[180] Kama 2/6, Basra 2/4

[181] In the Mahdurah Basra Admur writes to wash the right hand first. However in the Mahdurah Kama it implies the entire right side of the body is to be washed first.

[182] The Aruch Hashulchan 260/3 writes that after the head one is to wash the heart, right hand, left hand, right leg, left leg. The same applies regarding the order of applying soap. So rules also Kaf Hachayim 260/1 based on the teachings of the Arizal.

[183] Admur in Hilchos Shemiras Haguf Vehanefesh 9

[184] Kama 4/20-21

[185] Lit. "Harbeh"

[186] Lit. Tradin. This is also called silka as mentioned in The Laws of Rosh Hashana 583. It is defined as either spinach or beets.

[187] So is implied from Rashi Berachos 39a "Meiy Silka"

[188] To note that there are opinions which hold that there is no need to dry the feet if he is putting on socks, however this is not the ruling of Admur. [Rebbe in Shaar Halacha Uminhag Yorah Deah page 43]

[189] Admur Choshen Mishpat Hilchos Shmiras Haguf Vihanefesh Halacha 9

[190] Ketzos Hashulchan 2/10

[191] Machatzis Hashekel Shulchan Aruch chapter 260. Brought also in Ketzos Hashulchan 73 footnote 1.

[192] Based on Teshuvah of Tzemach Tzedek, elaborated on by Rebbe in Shaar Halacha Uminhag Yorah Deah page 42.

[193] Biur Halacha 260 "Bechamin"

[194] See Ketzos Hashulchan 133 footnote 1, and SS"K chapter 14 footnote 3

[195] 326/3

[196] The Aruch Hashulchan [326/3] writes that although the measurement of hot water is not brought anywhere, it most likely refers to all waters

However there is room to learn from Admur[197] that so long as the water is less than Yad Soledes then it is not considered hot.

What is one to do if he will not have time to bath or shower on Erev Shabbos?[198]
In such a case then he should bathe on Thursday, or the closest day possible to Shabbos.

Going to Mikveh on Erev Shabbos:[199]
It is a great Mitzvah to immerse in a Mikveh on Erev Shabbos[200], and so is the Chabad custom.[201] Immersing before Shabbos draws down the holiness of Shabbos onto one's soul.[202] Regarding Erev Yom Tov, even one who is not particular to go to Mikveh on Erev Shabbos is obligated to immerse on Erev Yom Tov.[203]
Preparation for Mikveh: One is to clean his body with hot water and comb through his hair prior to immersion.[204]
When on Erev Shabbos is one to go to Mikveh? One is to only go to Mikveh after midday[205], or at the very least past the 5th hour of the day.[206] If one cannot immerse at that time then he may immerse anytime in the morning.[207] One is to cut his nails[208] and complete the saying of Shnayim Mikra prior to immersing.[209]
The amount of times one is to immerse:[210] It suffices to immerse one time for purposes of cleansing oneself from emission of seed [Baal Keri]. One is to immerse three times for purposes of Teshuva.[211] There are numerous opinions[212] mentioned in regards to additional immersions[213].
Taking a shower after Mikveh: It is permitted to shower after Mikveh[214], although some are stringent not to do so.[215] Nevertheless, on Erev Shabbos according to all it is better not to do so, in order so one not completely wash off the Mikveh water from his body, as will be explained next.[216]
Drying oneself after Mikveh: Based on the teachings of the Arizal one should not dry the Mikveh water off his body after immersing.[217] Practically we are particular to dry ourselves with a towel after immersion and one who

---

that people call hot. This ruling is also found in the Chacham Tzevi 11 which forbids for women to immerse in water on Shabbos that is called hot, rather it must be cold or slightly warm.

[197] In Halacha 4 [brought above in Halacha 1C] regarding water heated on Shabbos Admur mentions "even if it will not be heated to Yad Soledes", implying that before Shabbos only water that is heated to Yad Soledes is forbidden. [Ketzos Hashulchan ibid]

[198] Ketzos Hashulchan 73 footnote 2

[199] Ketzos Hashulchan 73 footnote 1

[200] Immersing before Shabbos is a tradition which was handed down from the Baal Shem Tov.

[201] Sefer Haminhagim p. 50 [English edition]

[202] Aruch Hashulchan 260/1

[203] In order to purify oneself for the holiday. [Mateh Efrayim 625/15]

[204] This is also required based on the teachings of the Arizal. [Kaf Hachayim 260/4]

[205] Kanfei Yona 1/95; Mishnes Chassidim Yom Hashishi 7/1; Shlah p. 138a last line in name of Kanfei Yona

[206] As from that time and on the radiance of Shabbos begins to shine. [Mateh Efrayim 625/14, in name of Shaar Hakavanos and Peri Eitz Chaim]

[207] Mateh Efrayim 625/14

[208] See Kaf Hachayim 260/1 and Mate Efrayim 625/13; Shlah 138 that the nails are to be cut prior to Mikveh.

[209] M"A 285/1; This was the custom of the Arizal [Brought in Kaf Hachayim 260/7; M"A ibid] and so writes Shalah p. 138 explicitly in Hagah that one is to read Shnayim Mikra prior to immersing. So rules also Oar Tzadikim 28/18 stating that if one immerses prior to Shnayim Mikra he does not have the ability to receive the holiness of Shabbos.
This is unlike what is written in the Peri Megadim 260 A"A 1 in name of Eliyah Raba [260/4] **in name of Shalah** that one is to immerse prior to Shnayim Mikra. After researching this seeming contradiction the following was discovered: The Eliyah Raba [260/4] himself never makes such a claim and rather simply states in name of Shalah that one is to cut his nails prior to Shnayim Mikra, and does not discuss immersion in that regard. Furthermore, in some prints of the Peri Megadim the entire novelty of immersion after Shnayim Mikra was placed in brackets hence lending suspicion as to the accuracy of what in truth the Peri Megadim wrote. Due to all above seemingly there was a misprint in some versions of the Eliyah Raba or the Peri Megadim. This seemingly occurred due to a misreading of the word "Yitol" [take the nails] which was read "Yitvol" [immerse] and hence this caused the change. In any event the ruling of the Shalah is clear as written in his Sefer Shlah Hakadosh, that one is to immerse after Shnayim Mikra! In light of all the above there is no room for the ruling brought in Piskeiy Teshuvos 260/1 or 285/1. [In the new edition of Piskeiy Teshuvos 260/4 they fixed the ruling and wrote as we stated above.]
Other Opinions: Siddur Yaavetz rules one is to immerse prior to Shnayim Mikra.

[210] Shaareiy Halacha Uminhag 1/131

[211] Admur 606/11-12

[212] 2, 4, 5, 13, 14, 39 [Shalah]. The Arizal would immerse 2 times on Erev Shabbos, once to remove the mundane garments of his soul, and the second to attain the holy garments of Shabbos. If one is a Baal Keri then he is to dip three times in total according to the Arizal. [Kaf Hachayim 260/6]

[213] The Rebbe concludes "Who am I to arbitrate between all these opinions". [ibid]

[214] Sheivet Halevy 7/33; Even regarding a Nida the Rama Yoreh Deah 202/75 rules that only <u>some</u> opinions are stringent and so is the custom. However others argue on Rama and rule doing so is permitted even by a Nida. [See Gr"a ibid; Darkei Teshuvah 202/332; Lechem Vesimla 122]

[215] Piskeiy Teshuvos 260/1 in name of Sheivet Halevy that so is the custom of the world to avoid doing so despite it being allowed from the letter of the law. See also Tiferes Adam which rules one should never shower after Mikveh.

[216] Based on Kaf Hachayim 260/5

[217] As the water is considered holy with the spirit of Shabbos and it is thus proper for the body to absorb it. [ibid] However see Kaf Hachayim

desires to follow the directive of the Arizal is to leave some part of his body not dried.[218] It suffices for one to leave his feet wet in order to fulfill this directive.[219]

Going to Mikveh on Shabbos day: See Volume 2 "The laws of Bathing" Halacha 5 Q&A!

Not to bathe too close to Shabbos:[220]
One is to be careful, and warn others against bathing too close to the beginning of Shabbos, as even if one will be able to finish bathing before sunset, he may come to squeeze water from his towel or hair and come to transgress.

16. Getting a haircut?[221]

If one has long hair it is a Mitzvah to cut it [any day prior to Shabbos] in order so one not enter into Shabbos in disgrace. Furthermore, it is a Mitzvah Min Hamuvchar to cut the hair specifically on Erev Shabbos and not beforehand.[222] If however one will not have time to get a haircut on Erev Shabbos[223] then he is to do so on Thursday[224].

Rosh Chodesh which falls on Erev Shabbos: It is customary not to cut one's hair on Rosh Chodesh.[225] This applies even when Rosh Chodesh falls on Erev Shabbos.[226] [Thus in such a situation one is to get a haircut on Thursday or Wednesday.]

Washing ones hands after a haircut:[227]
One is to wash his hands [immediately[228]] after cutting his hair.[229]

The danger involved in not washing the hands:[230] If one does not wash his hands after getting a haircut, then he will have inner fear for three days.

How one is to wash: One must use water to clean his hands. It does not suffice to clean his hands in other ways [such as to rub them on something. The reason for this is because an impure spirit resides on ones hands after these actions are done[231]. Thus one needs to wash his hands even if he does not plan to pray or learn Torah afterwards.[232]] However one does not need to pour the water on his hands three times as is required when washing upon awakening. [The entire hand is to be washed until ones wrist, or at least until ones knuckles.[233] The above washing is only in order to remove impurity, and does not prevent one from studying Torah or praying beforehand.[234]]

260/8 which writes that this only applies if one did not immerse more than once, otherwise he has already washed away the main Mikveh water. Nevertheless he concludes that even these second waters of the Mikveh has some holiness and is thus not to be dried.

[218] The holiness of that leftover water from the Mikveh will then subsequently spread to the rest of the body. [Rebbe Shaareiy Halacha Uminhag 1/131]

[219] Shaareiy Halacha Uminhag 1/131

[220] Ketzos Hashulchan 73 footnote 2

[221] 260/1

[222] In order so it be evident that one is doing so for the honor of Shabbos. [ibid]

[223] Due to being involved in the Shabbos preparations. [ibid]

[224] As one is to proximate the haircut as much as possible to Shabbos in order so it be evident that it is being done for the sake of Shabbos. [ibid] There is no custom against cutting the hair on Thursday, as there is with nails, being that hair grows back the same day as it is cut. [*Kuntrus Achron* 260/1]
However the *Taz* [260/1] rules that hair also begins growing back on the 3rd day as do nails and one is to thus avoid cutting them on Thursday. The *Kaf Hachayim* 260/15 argues on this ruling.

[225] This custom is based on a warning of Rav Yehuda Hachasid which stated that one is not to take a haircut on Rosh Chodesh due to worry of danger. [ibid]

[226] Admur writes that the custom to avoid haircuts even on Rosh Chodesh which falls on Erev Shabbos is only followed in certain communities. Today however this is the common widespread custom, and thus no diversion of the custom has been mentioned above.

[227] Kama 4/18-19

[228] Magen Avraham and Peri Megadim 4/18. Vetzaruch Iyun as Admur omitted this.

[229] Kama 4/19; It requires further analysis why washing after a haircut was not listed in 4/18 together with all the other matters listed there.

[230] Kama 4/19

[231] Ketzos Hashulchan 2/11. See also Admur 97/3 and Peri Megadim Ashel Avraham 227/2. However see Kaf Hachayim 4/90 which brings an opinion which holds that not all of the following actions bring an impure spirit. Admur however seems to hold that they all do, being that he rules that only washing with water helps.

[232] Ketzos Hashulchan 2/11

[233] Ketzos Hashulchan 2/11

[234] As is evident from chapter 6, see there. Seemingly this impurity is not the same type as that which resides when one awakens from sleeping at night, and thus it does not hold the restriction mentioned prior to washing hands in the morning.

Q&A
May a woman shave body hair other than the head on Erev Shabbos which is also Rosh Chodesh?
Yes.[235] The warning of Rav Yehuda Hachassid only applies to the hair of the head and not to body hair.

When should one have a haircut on Erev Shabbos?
Some[236] rule it is best to get a haircut after midday in order that it is evident that the haircut is being done in the honor of Shabbos. If however one desires to do so beforehand he need not refrain. The Arizal however would always refrain from cutting his hair after midday, and hence would always initially cut it before midday on Erev Shabbos[237], and so conclude some Poskim.[238] However according to the rulings of Admur in Hilchos Shabbos[239] it is evident that this is not required.

May a gentile give one a haircut? [240]
Based on Kabala there those which avoid receiving a haircut from a gentile.

Must one wash his hands after cutting someone else's hair?[241]
Yes.[242]

---

17. Cutting ones nails:
It is a Mitzvah to cut one's [hand[243]] nails <u>every</u> Erev Shabbos.[244] **[See Q&A]**

A. Cutting nails during the week, prior to Erev Shabbos?[245]
Although it is a Mitzvah top cut the nails on Erev Shabbos as stated above nevertheless if one does not desire to wait until then, the question arises whether he may cut them during other days of the week. There are two customs recorded in this regard:
First Custom-Only cut on Erev Shabbos and Yom Tov: Some are cautious to avoid cutting their nails on any day other than Erev Shabbos or Erev Yom Tov. They thus cut their hand nails only on Friday and toe nails on Thursday[246]. However on other days they do not cut their nails at all due to reasons known to them [based on Kabala].

---

[235] Tzavas Rav Yehudah Hachasid ibid: "A person is not to shave his **head** or beard on Rosh Chodesh"
[236] Aruch Hashulchan 260/6; See also 251/3
[237] M"A 251/5; Kaf Hachayim 260/13
[238] Kitzur SHU"A 128/15;
[239] 251/4
The Arizal would not get a haircut past the time of Mincha Gedola [midday], based on Kabalistic reasons. This is brought in Magen Avraham 251/5. Admur however omitted this custom of the Arizal. See Shaareiy Halacha Uminhag 1/130 that the Rebbe concludes regarding the time of cutting nails, which is similar to the time of the cutting of the hair, that he did not receive a directive in how to follow.
<u>Opinion of Gr"a:</u> The Gra is stringent against allowing haircuts past midday, although this is not the worldly custom. [Aruch Hashulchan 251/3]
[240] Kaf Hachayim 260/13; Mateh Efrayim-Alef Hamagen 581/105
[241] Kaf Hachayim 4/92
[242] As it is common for the barber to touch the persons hair which is full of sweat.
[243] As the hand nails look repulsive when they are long. However the toe nails which are not visible are not considered a Mitzvah to be cut Erev Shabbos. [Ketzos Hashulchan 73 footnote 4] However see Kaf Hachayim 250/17 which states that the Arizal would cut both his hand <u>and toe</u> nails in honor of Shabbos.
[244] 260/1
Elya Raba 260/4 records a Midrash which states "There was once a Rabbi who passed away and appeared to his students in a dream with a blemish on his forehead. He told them this is due to his negligence in speaking in middle of the blessing of Meiyn Sheva and Kaddish, and due to him not being careful to **cut his nails Erev Shabbos**".
[245] 260/2
Although it is a Mitzvah to cut ones nails specifically on Erev Shabbos, as stated above, the question here is may one cut them on other days if he so chooses.
[246] Being that the hand and toe nails are not to be cut the same day, as will be explained, therefore they cut the toe nails on Thursday rather than Friday. Thus this custom seemingly does not hold of the custom to avoid cutting nails on Thursday. [Kitzur Hilchos Shabbos 260] Perhaps however one can say that this custom of avoiding cutting the nails on Thursday only applies to the hand nails being that they are visible. However the toe nails which are not visible, and thus there is no Mitzvah to cut them before Shabbos, then likewise there is no issue if they are cut on Thursday. Practically the M"B 260/6 rules that this is the custom that one is to follow.

Second Custom-Only avoid cutting on Thursday: Some[247] [are accustomed to allow one to cut nails on other days of the week[248] if he chooses not to wait until Friday[249], although they] are particular to not cut the nails on Thursday.[250] [**See Q&A**] [Thus beginning from Wednesday night one should not cut his nails.]

B. Not to cut the toe and hand nails on same day:[251]

Some[252] are cautious to avoid cutting the hand and toe nails on the same day, due to worry of danger.[253] [However one may cut one during the day and the other that night.[254] Some also allow to cut one of them at night and the other the next day however others rule this is not to be done, and so seems to be the opinion of Admur.[255]]

C. The order of cutting the nails:[256]

Which hand is one to begin with? One first cuts the nails of his left hand and then the right.[257]

Skipping a nail in between each cut: It is proper to initially be careful[258] not to cut the [hand[259]] nails one finger after the other, in the set order of the hand[260]. Rather one is to skip the finger that is adjacent to each finger that is cut, and cut the finger which is adjacent to the skipped finger. Hence one is to begin with his left hand cutting first the index finger closest to the pinky and skipping one finger each time. One then cuts the nails of the right hand beginning with the index finger closest to the thumb, skipping one finger each time. Hence the number order of the cutting beginning from thumb to pinky [thumb is #1 pinky is #5] is for the left hand 4,2,5,3,1. By the right hand it is 2,4,1,3,5.

---

[247] The Aruch Hashulchan [260/6] argues against this custom. Likewise he writes that all these cautions mentioned by nails are not required by the letter of the law, and one who is not particular in them, has not done any transgression.

[248] It is implied that this opinion is only particular regarding Thursday, however they allow one to cut the nails on Wednesday or another day of the week. See however Peri Megadim 260 M"Z 1 which brings the Elyah Raba which learns that this opinion holds that even before Thursday the nails are not to be cut, as then certainly one will have grown nails by Shabbos. This understanding however requires further analysis as if so then what is the dispute between this opinion and the previous opinion. Accordingly they both hold the nails are to only be cut on Erev Shabbos. This is besides the fact that this is not the simple implication of Admur, and does not fit in with the explanation of the Machatzis Hashekel [260-brought in the footnotes to follow] behind the stringency.

[249] However according to all if one is able to delay cutting his nails on Friday, it is a Mitzvah to do so in honor of Shabbos, as explained above.

[250] As the nails begin growing on the 3rd day after being cut and hence if they are cut on Thursday they will begin growing on Shabbos, thus some avoid cutting it on Thursday. [ibid] Now, although there is no prohibition involved if the nails begin growing back on Shabbos, nevertheless it is not respectful that the nails which one ridded himself of in honor of Shabbos begins growing back on Shabbos. [Machatziz Hashekel 260/1] The above applies only to nails however a haircut may be given on Thursday being that hair begins to grow back that same day. [Kuntrus Achron 260/1]

Regarding if also the toe nails are not to be cut on Thursday according to this opinion: Perhaps one can say that this custom only applies to the hand nails being that they are visible. However the toe nails which are not visible, and thus there is no Mitzvah to cut them before Shabbos, then likewise there is no issue if they are cut on Thursday. Practically the M"B 260/6 rules that one is to cut the toe nails on Thursday. However the wording of Admur seems to imply that they avoid cutting all nails on Thursday. Vetzaruch Iyun.

[251] 260/2

[252] The Arizal was not careful to avoid cutting the nails on the same day. Practically the Mateh Efraim rules that one is to be stringent in this matter. [Ketzos Hashulchan 73 footnote 5]

[253] However women which are preparing for Mikveh may do so being that Hashem guards those which are observing a Mitzvah.

[254] Ashel Avraham Butshatch, brought in Ketzos Hashulchan 73 footnote 4.

[255] See Ashel Avraham ibid which suggests at first that the night has no relation to the day in this regard. However later he mentions that the night goes after the next day and not the previous day. So rules also Ashel Avraham Tinyana in 260 that the night goes after the day and one is to beware from cutting on Thursday night as well as on Thursday. So is also implied from Admur 260/2 that does not mention to cut the toe nails on Thursday night rather than Thursday. However see Piskeiy Teshuvos 260 footnote 84 for opinions that rule that the night does not follow the previous day or the following day.

[256] 260/3

[257] Although in Admur there seems to be a slight discrepancy [see below] regarding which hand one is to begin with, the Ketzos Hashulchan [73/2] rules to begin with the left hand, and so rules Kalbo [brought in Aruch Hashulchan 260/6], Eliyahu Raba and Peri Megadim based on Rama which mentions the left hand first.

Other Opinions-Begin with right: The Aruch Hashulchan himself [ibid] rules that one is to begin with the right hand and then the left, and so rules Ashel Avraham [Butchatcher] 260, based on the Talmudic ruling that the right is always to be given precedence over the left.

Discrepancy in Admur: Admur began the law of cutting nails with the left hand and then the right, and then concluded with the right and then the left. This is especially puzzling being the Rama concluded also first with the left and then with the right, and hence for what reason did Admur change from the order of the Rama. Some desire to explain that Admur in truth holds there is no preference as to which hand one cuts first. Vetzrauch Iyun.

[258] Admur 260/3 records a difference of opinion regarding this matter: Some are cautious to skip a nail when cutting their nails. Others [Arizal/Tashbatz brought in Taz 260/2 and M"A 260/1] however belittle this custom. Admur concludes: Nevertheless it is good for one to initially be cautious in this matter. [ibid as rules M"A 260/1]

[259] However by the toe nails there is no need to be careful to skip a nail in between. [Ketzos Hashulchan 73 footnote 7]

[260] As they believe that doing so brings one towards forgetfulness, causes one to bury his children, and brings one to poverty. [ibid]

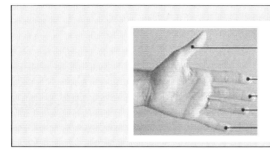

1. Thumb
2. Index finger, also called 'pointer finger', or 'forefinger'
3. Middle finger, often the longest
4. Ring finger, also known as fourth finger
5. Little finger, also known as 'pinky'

D. What is one to do with the nails after they are cut?[261]

Nails contain a certain impurity which can be lethal for the fetus of a pregnant woman, and cause miscarriage, if she steps on it. For this reason it is necessary to discard one's nails properly to assure that a pregnant woman will not come to step on it. There are three different ways of discarding the nails relative to three types of characteristics.

- *Chassid:* A Chassid burns his nails.[262] [The Rebbe Rashab would mix some wood together with the nails before burning it.[263]] [**See Q&A**]
- *Righteous person*: A righteous person buries his nails.[264]
- *Rasha*: A Rasha discards his nails on the floor.[265]

Throwing one's nails in a Beis Hamidrash: It is permitted for one to throw his nails in a Beis Midrash and places of the like in which women are not accustomed to enter.

Nails which have been swept to a different area: The nails are only considered a danger while in the original area[266] that they were thrown in after they were cut. If however they are swept to another area then they are no longer a danger.[267]

E. Washing ones hands after nail cutting:[268]

One is to wash his hands [immediately[269]] after cutting his nails. [This applies to both one's hand and toe nails, and applies whether one cut his nails with a nail cutter or with his teeth.[270]]

The danger involved in not washing the hands:[271] If one does not wash his hands after cutting his nails, then he will have inner fear for one day. In addition if he is a Torah scholar, he will forget his learning, while if he is a layman, he will lose his mind[272].

How one is to wash: One must use water to clean his hands. It does not suffice to clean his hands in other ways [such as to rub them on something. The reason for this is because an impure spirit resides on ones hands after these actions are done[273]. Thus one needs to wash his hands even if he does not plan to pray or learn Torah afterwards.[274]]

However one does not need to pour the water on his hands three times as is required when washing upon awakening.

---

[261] 260/4

[262] In order so they are destroyed from the face of the earth and there is no longer any possibility for them to become uncovered and cause potential damage to a fetus. One who does so is called a Chassid being that burning part of one's body, even one's nails, is damaging for oneself, hence he is called a Chassid as he overrides his own health in order to fully protect his friend. [Machatzis Hashekel 260/1]

[263] Hayom Yom 16 Iyar

[264] This is however of less righteousness then is a Chassid, as it is possible for the nails to resurface.

[265] He is considered a Rasha as he is causing a potential hazard if a pregnant woman were to walk on it.

[266] It requires further analyses with regards to the definition of "area"? Bircheiy Yosef 260/6 rules like the Perisha that as long as the nail has moved from the exact area it fell it is no longer considered dangerous, even if it remains in the same room. So rules also Aruch Hashulchan 260/6. The Elya Raba rules that "area" means a room, thus only when the nail has been swept to another room is it considered to have switched areas. [brought in M"B 260/6] However if placed into another area within the same room the Elya Raba questions whether this suffices to remove the danger. [see Peri Megadim A"A 260]

[267] The Aruch Hashulchan 260/6 notes that if one cut another item with the nail cutter after the nails were cut, the danger is no longer applicable.

[268] Kama 4/18-19

[269] Magen Avraham and Peri Megadim 4/18. Vetzaruch Iyun as Admur omitted this.

[270] Ketzos Hashulchan 2/11, and Badei Hashulchan 2/12

[271] Mahadurah Kama 4/18

[272] Meaning that he will come to sin, as one does not sin unless a spirit of insanity enters him. [Kaf Hachayim 4/89]

[273] Ketzos Hashulchan 2/11. See also Admur 97/3 and Peri Megadim Ashel Avraham 227/2. However see Kaf Hachayim 4/90 which brings an opinion which holds that not all of the following actions bring an impure spirit. Admur however seems to hold that they all do, being that he rules that only washing with water helps.

[274] Ketzos Hashulchan 2/11

[The entire hand is to be washed until ones wrist, or at least until ones knuckles.[275] The above washing is only in order to remove impurity, and does not prevent one from studying Torah or praying beforehand.[276]]

Summary and practical guideline:

It is a Mitzvah to cut one's finger nails on Erev Shabbos. When cutting during other days of the week one is to avoid cutting the nails on [Wednesday night through] Thursday. One is to avoid cutting the hand and toe nails the same day.

One is to begin cutting the nails of his left hand starting with the index finger closest to the pinky. One skips a finger between each nail. On his right hand one first cuts the index finger closest to his thumb and then skips a finger in between each nail. One is to discard the nails properly, such as in the toilet or through burning them. One is to wash his hands after cutting the nails.

Q&A

When on Erev Shabbos are the nails to be cut?[277]

The nails are to be cut prior to bathing for Shabbos or going to Mikveh.[278] Regarding when they are to be cut prior to Mikveh or bathing there are various opinions mentioned: Before Midday, [after midday before Mincha[279]], after Mincha, before Shnayim Mikra, after Shnayim Mikra but before Mikveh.[280] We have not accepted any final ruling. [Practically many have the custom to cut the nails prior to Shnayim Mikra.]

May one cut his nail when Rosh Chodesh falls on Erev Shabbos?

Yes and so is implied from Admur.[281] However there are Poskim[282] which are stringent and forbid doing so.

May one cut his nails on Erev Shabbos Chol Hamoed, or Erev Yom Tov Achron?

If one cut his nails on Erev Yom Tov:[283] One who cut his nails on Erev Yom Tov [or in close proximity to Erev Yom Tov to the point there was nothing to cut before Yom Tov[284]] is permitted to cut his nails during Chol Hamoed.[285]

If one did not cut them Erev Yom Tov:[286] Some Poskim[287] rule it is forbidden to cut nails on Erev Shabbos, or Erev Yom Tov of the last days, if he did not cut them on Erev Yom Tov of the first days. So is also implied to be the opinion of Admur.[288] Others[289] however rule it is permitted to cut nails on Erev Shabbos [or Erev Yom

---

[275] Ketzos Hashulchan 2/11

[276] As is evident from chapter 6, see there. Seemingly this impurity is not the same type as that which resides when one awakens from sleeping at night, and thus it does not hold the restriction mentioned prior to washing hands in the morning.

[277] Shaareiy Halacha Uminhag 130

[278] Kaf Hachayim 260/1 as was the custom of the Arizal; Mateh Efrayim 625/13; Shlah ibid

To note however of the custom of the Rebbe Maharash which would cut the nails after Mikveh. His reasoning was because at this time the nails are softer. [Story heard from Rav Zalmon Shimon Dworkin]

[279] Aruch Hashulchan 260/5-6

[280] The *Magen Avraham* brings in the name of the *Shlah* [p. 138] that one should cut the nails on Erev Shabbos prior to saying Shnayim Mikra [which is then followed by Mikveh]. However in *Peri Eitz Chaim* it states to cut them after Shnayim Mikra, prior to immersing in the Mikveh. Elsewhere it is brought in the name of the *Arizal* to cut them prior to midday. This however contradicts that which is brought in *Shaar Hakavanos* that the *Arizal* would cut his nails after *Mincha*.

[281] *Shaar Hakolel in Nesiv Hachayim 48/3;* Opinions brought in footnotes on Tzavah Rav Yehuda Hachassid]. see *Kitzur Halachos Shabbos-*Supplements; *Ketzos Hashulchan* 72 footnote 4 leaves this matter as a Tzaruch Iyun.

Background of ruling: If Rosh Chodesh falls on Erev Shabbos, although some have the custom not to cut their hair, despite the fact that this is usually a mitzvah to do on Erev Shabbos, nevertheless regarding cutting ones nails it seems that no such custom exists and they should therefore be cut in honor of Shabbos. This is based on the law written in Admur regarding Rosh Chodesh which falls on Shabbos, in which Admur only writes that cutting hair is refrained while cutting nails is omitted. To note that this omission of cutting nails is also within the Magen Avraham and Kneses Hagedola which is the source of the ruling regarding haircuts.

[282] M"B 260/7; Aruch Hashulchan 260/6; Kaf Hachayim 260/12 allows only cutting the nails that stretch past the skin.

[283] M"A 532/1; Chayeh Adam 109/3; M"B 532/2; Kitzur SH"A 104/12; Chol Hamoed Kehilchasa 4/5; Kaf Hachaim 532/7

Other Opinions: The Elya Raba 532/1 rules one may only remove the nails with a knife and not with scissors.

[284] Aruch Hashulchan 532/2

[285] The reason for this allowance is because even regarding a haircut there are Poskim which allow it to be done on Chol Hamoed if one cut his hair on Erev Yom Tov. Thus regarding cutting nails which is itself disputed whether it is at all forbidden during Chol Hamoed, one may certainly be lenient if he cut his nails on Erev Yom Tov. [M"A 532/1; P"M 532 A"A 1]

[286] See Shaareiy Teshuvah 468/1; Kaf Hachaim 532/5

[287] Shvus Yaakov 1/17; Koveitz Mibeis Levi 1/47 that so is the custom; Piskeiy Teshuvos 532/1

[288] 468/6 from the fact he forbids cutting the nails on Erev Pesach past Chatzos even though it is Erev Yom Tov. See Shvus Yaakov ibid. It is thus a wonderment that Chol Hamoed Kihilchasa 4/6 rules plainly that it is allowed despite this clear ruling of Admur.

[289] Nachalas Shiva 2/57; Shulchan Gavoa 532/2; Chol Hamoed Kihilchasa 4/6; Kaf Hachaim 532/5 concludes one who is lenient has upon whom to rely.

Tov[290]] if one is accustomed to do so on every Erev Shabbos throughout the year.[291] According to all it is forbidden to cut the nails on Erev Shabbos if he is not accustomed to always do so.

If one will not have time to cut his nails on Friday may he be lenient to do so on Thursday?[292]
Yes.

If Yom Tov falls on Friday may one cut his nails on Thursday?[293]
Yes. It is a Mitzvah to do so.

May a Chasan and Kalah cut their nails on Thursday if their wedding is taking place that night?
If they did not cut the nails beforehand and will be unable to cut the nails on Thursday night, they may be cut on Thursday.

May one cut his toe nails at night and his hand nails the next day?
Some Poskim rule this is not to be done. Others rule it is allowed.[294]

If one did not cut his toe nails prior to Erev Shabbos, may he cut them on Erev Shabbos together with his hand nails?[295]
Yes.

May one cut his toe nails on Thursday?
It is unclear if those which avoid cutting nails on Thursday are only particular regarding the hand nails.[296]

Must one skip a nail also when cutting the toe nails?[297]
No. This cautiousness is only relevant to the hand nails.

What is one to do if a nail dropped and became lost?[298]
He is to sweep the dirt of that area into another room.[299]

May one throw the nails into the sink or toilet rather than burn or bury them?[300]
Yes. Throwing the nails into the sink or toilet is similar to burying them. Nevertheless one who wishes to follow the practice of a Chassid is to specifically burn them rather then throw them in the toilet.

May one learn Torah while cutting his nails?[301]
Yes.

Must one wash his hands after cutting another person's nails, such as one's children?[302]
No. One is only obligated to wash his hands after cutting his own nails.[303]

---

[290] Chol Hamoed Kihilchasa 4/6

[291] As it is permitted to cut nails for the sake of a Mitzvah and cutting them on Erev Shabbos in honor of Shabbos is a Mitzvah. [ibid]

[292] Aruch Hashulchan 260/6

[293] Aruch Hashulchan 260/6

[294] Ashel Avraham Butshatch, brought in Ketzos Hashulchan 73 footnote 4 suggests at first that the night has no relation to the day in this regard. However later he mentions that the night goes after the next day and not the previous day. So rules also Ashel Avraham Tinyana in 260 that the night goes after the day and one is to beware from cutting on Thursday night as well as on Thursday. So is also implied from Admur 260/2 that does not mention to cut the toe nails on Thursday **night** rather than Thursday. However see Piskeiy Teshuvos 260 footnote 84 for opinions that rule that the night does not follow the previous day or the following day.

[295] Mateh Efrayim 625/14-Alef Lamateh 21

[296] Perhaps one can say that this custom only applies to the hand nails being that they are visible. However the toe nails which are not visible, and thus there is no Mitzvah to cut them before Shabbos, then likewise there is no issue if they are cut on Thursday. Practically the M"B 260/6 rules that one is to cut the toe nails on Thursday. However the wording of Admur seems to imply that they avoid cutting all nails on Thursday. Vetzaruch Iyun.

[297] Ketzos Hashulchan 73 footnote 7

[298] M"B 260/6

[299] As once it has switched rooms, the nail is no longer of danger.

[300] Beir Moshe 6/133-12

[301] Mahrsham 4/148 brought in Shearim Hametzuyanim Behalacha 2/5

[302] Ashel Avraham Buchacher Mahdurah Tinyana 4/18

[303] So is also implied from Admur 4/18 "Cutting **his** nails" and not plainly "cutting nails".

Must one wash their hands if another person cut his nails? [304]
Yes.

Sparks of Kabala-Meaning behind nails: [305]
The nails are rooted in a very high spiritual source. Prior to the sin of eating from the tree of knowledge Adam was completely covered by nails which protected him from evil. The sin then caused the nails to leave and only remain on the tips of the fingers, in which there also resides the impurities of the sin. Due to this the nails must be removed, and doing so brings peace to the world. However they may not be belittled by throwing them away as they derive from a high source and on them is dependant the fixing of the world.
It is also for this reason that they are dangerous for women. This is measure for measure as the woman caused Adam to lose his sublime revelation contained within the nails, therefore the nails cause her danger.

---

18. Shabbos clothes: [306]

Every person is obligated to strive based on his affordability, to have elegant clothing for Shabbos. [307] These clothing are to be designated specifically [308] for Shabbos (and are to be nicer than the clothing he wears during the week). [309] [Hence one is to avoid wearing these clothing at all during the week. [310] Furthermore, even on Shabbos itself one is to avoid doing activities that can dirty the clothing. For this reason one should not hold a child (which can cause one to become dirty) unless he places a covering over his clothes. [311]]

A Shabbos Tallis: One who is able to afford a second Tallis should have a second Tallis specifically designated for wearing on Shabbos.

Not to wear any weekday garments: There are scrupulous men which are meticulous not to wear any weekday clothing on Shabbos. [312] They thus have an entire wardrobe of clothing designated to be worn only on Shabbos. [313] This includes even a belt, pants, undershirt, [under garments, Yarmulke, socks, shoes, Tzitzis, hat].

Wearing a different article of clothing : It is proper for one to wear a piece of clothing or jewelry which is different than the clothing or jewelry worn during the week. [314] This is done in order that one constantly remembers that it is Shabbos and not come to desecrate it. [Hence the custom of Jerusalemites is to wear a Shtreimal which is a completely different type of hat then the hat worn during the week, as it serves as a reminder of Shabbos. [315]]

When on Erev Shabbos should one put on his Shabbos clothes: [316] It is proper [317] that one garb himself in Shabbos clothes immediately after bathing himself for Shabbos. For this reason it is proper [318] for one to bathe himself as

---

[304] Ashel Avraham Buchacher Mahdurah Tinyana 4/18

[305] Shalah Hakadosh p. 138 in name of Tolas Yaakov

[306] 262/3

[307] As one is obligated to honor Shabbos through clean clothing as was explained in chapter 242. [ibid]

[308] Lit. One is to switch his clothing for Shabbos to nicer clothing.

[309] This is learned from the words of the prophets "And you shall honor Him from doing your ways". The Sages expounded this verse to mean that one shall honor Him by designating different clothing for Shabbos in contrast to clothing worn during the week. The reason why the Sages specifically learned that one is to honor Shabbos through nicer clothing is because one's clothing is also referred to as one's honor, as clothing dignify a person as seen from the fact that when one arrives to an unknown community in elegant clothing, then he receives respect from the community. [ibid]
Why the above law was placed in parentheses: As for the reason that Admur places the ruling of "nicer clothing" in parentheses- See Aruch Hashulchan 262/3 which explains that only on Yom Kippur is there an obligation to wear nicer clothing than that of the week, however on Shabbos one merely has to wear a fresh pair of even weekday style clothing.

[310] So is implied from Admur and so explains Minchas Shabbos 72/71, based on M"A 262/2, that one is not to wear any of these clothing during the week. See Kitzur Halachos Miluim p. 57

[311] Sefer Chassidim brought in Bier Heiytiv 262/4; Mishneh Berurah 262/6.

[312] To note that the wording of the Magen Avraham 262/2 is in opposite order "One should not wear during the week any of the clothes which he wore on Shabbos".

[313] So is implied from Admur and so explains Minchas Shabbos 72/71, based on M"A 262/2, that one is not to wear any of these clothing during the week.

[314] Seemingly the novelty in this ruling in contrast to the ruling brought above is that not only should one's clothing be more elegant [such as a nicer white shirt], but one of those article of clothing should be of completely different style, such as a frockcoat or Shtreimal.

[315] Ketzos Hashulchan 115 footnote 47

[316] 262/5

[317] Lit. good

[318] Lit. good

close to Shabbos as possible[319], and then immediately put on his Shabbos cloths.[320] [This however only applies when bathing in one's home. If however one is bathing in a bathhouse, as is customary when going to Mikveh on Erev Shabbos, then one should visit the Mikveh with plenty of time still left in the day.[321] If one however plans to merely [rinse and then] immerse in the Mikveh, he is to visit the Mikveh as close to Shabbos as possible.[322]]

When after Shabbos may one remove his Shabbos clothing? It is proper to wear at least some of one's Shabbos clothing until after Havdala on Motzaei Shabbos. [Some however have the custom to not remove their Shabbos clothes until after eating Melaveh Malka.[323] Others only remove them prior to going to sleep.[324] It is told of the Rebbe Rashab that he would remove his Shabbos clothes immediately after Shabbos, not wanting at all to wear them during the weekday. However of the Rebbe Rayatz it is told that his father the Rebbe Rashab told him to follow the custom of Chernobyl to not change his Shabbos clothing on Motzaei Shabbos, and so is the custom of the Rebbe.[325]]

Q&A

Should one buy shoes specifically for Shabbos?
Yes[326], although there are Poskim[327] which write that there is no need to do so.[328]

Should one make a point of wearing Shabbos clothes if he is spending Shabbos alone, or amongst gentiles?[329]
Yes, as the clothing are not out of respect for the observers but out of personal respect for Shabbos.

What is one to do if he does not have any Shabbos clothing to wear?[330]
He should change to freshly laundered weekday clothing. If he does not have any laundered clothing available, then he should launder them on Thursday.

Color of Shabbos attire:
There remains a difference of customs regarding the desired color of the Shabbos attire.[331] Many wear all white[332], others black[333] and others wear colored clothing. One is to follow the custom of his community.[334]

Wearing a silk garment/Kapata:[335]
The Rebbe stated that married men are to strive to wear a silk Kapata/Frockcoat on Shabbos and Yom Tov. Those which do so are praised.[336]

---

[319] Lit. near sunset.

[320] This is done in order so one only begins dressing himself in Shabbos clothes in close proximity to Shabbos. The advantage of doing so is that it is now apparent that it is in honor of Shabbos that one is wearing them. [ibid]

[321] As we suspect he may come to take his time and come to transgress Shabbos.

[322] Ketzos Hashulchan 73 footnote 23

[323] So rules Kaf Hachaim 262/28 as the extra soul does not depart until after Melaveh Malka. [300/106]

[324] Brought in Leket Yosher that so was the custom of his teacher the Terumas Hadeshen.

[325] See Kitzur Halachos Miluim p. 56

[326] Kaf Hachaim 262/25

[327] Rav Poalim 4/13

[328] The Kaf Hachaim [ibid] however explains that even Rav Poalim holds this way only from the letter of the law, however as an act of piety he too agrees that one should have shoes designated to be worn only on Shabbos.

[329] Chayeh Adam 5 brought in Ketzos Hashulchan 73 footnote 20

[330] Ketzos Hashulchan 73 footnote 24

[331] The Kaf Hachaim 262/24 and 26 brings that the color of clothing which one wears on Shabbos in this world one will as well wear in the next world. He then goes on to suggest based on this that one is to only wear white clothing.

[332] This is based on the writings of the Arizal which says that one is to wear 4 white garments. [Beir Heiytiv 262/4] The Kaf Hachaim [262/24] strongly writes that one is to only wear white clothing on Shabbos and not other colors. He brings a story from his teacher which once had the soul of a deceased Sage reveal himself to him and tell him that he was being punished in the next world for wearing black clothing on Shabbos. Some Poskim however discourage wearing white if it appears as an act of extra haughtiness. [Peri Megadim A"A 262] The Kaf Hachaim [ibid/26] however rules that even when there is appearance of haughtiness, such as no one else wears white clothing in that community, one may nevertheless do so, as on this is dependant his wardrobe of the world to come.

[333] Peri Megadim A"A 262; brought in Biur Halacha

[334] Shaareiy Halacha Uminhag 1/240

[335] Shaareiy Halacha Uminhag 5/29; Hisvadyus Purim 1955

[336] The concept of wearing a silk Kapata on Shabbos and Yom Tov is brought in Mamarim of the Rebbe Rashab [1902 p. 231; 1911 p. 328; 1912 Vol. 2 p. 872]. There it is explained that the reason we wear silk on Shabbos is because Shabbos receives from the world of Beriya and since silk comes from an animal which corresponds to the world of Beriya it is therefore proper to wear silk on Shabbos. Now although wool also grows on an animal, nevertheless wool is considered the level of Tzomeiach Shebichaiy, however silk is Chaiy Shebichaiy. [Toras Menachem 13 p. 309]
Wearing a coat over one's silk Kapata: It is worthy to note the Rebbe's custom of wearing a coat in public over his silk Kapata, whenever it was worn, even in the summer. Some write this is because it is improper for gentiles to view one wearing silk. [See "Hashabbos Bekabala

---

If one is bathing early for Shabbos when should he put on his Shabbos clothes?[337]
In such a case one is to switch his underclothes, pants and shirt to fresh Shabbos clothes right after bathing even though there is still plenty of time left before Shabbos. However his upper clothes [such as a jacket, hat etc] he is to only put on right before Shabbos.[338]

When are women to dress in their Shabbos clothes? [339]
Women, just like men, are to dress in their Shabbos clothes immediately after they shower close to Shabbos. They are to be wearing Shabbos clothes before candle lighting.

---

19. Laundry:[340]

It is an institution of Ezra for one to do laundry on Thursday in honor of Shabbos, in order so he have clean white clothing to wear on Shabbos. This is in contrast to one doing laundry on Erev Shabbos, as on Erev Shabbos there is no time to do laundry due to the need for one to deal with the Shabbos preparations.

Q&A
May one today do laundry on Erev Shabbos using a washing machine?
Although today it is possible to wash clothes with much less effort and time then was required back in the times of the Sages, nonetheless one is to still fulfill their decree to not push off the laundry to Friday.[341] Nevertheless there is no prohibition to do laundry on Friday if one needs. Furthermore some Poskim[342] rule that today with the use of washing machines there is no restriction at all in doing laundry on Friday rather than Thursday.

May one launder his Shabbos clothes prior to Thursday?
Yes.[343]

---

20. Preparing the Blech:

❖ *For the full Halachic background of this section, explanations and sources refer to The Laws of Shabbos Volume 1 "The Laws of Shehiyah". Below is provided a quick summary of the Halachas explained there.*

It is forbidden to leave less than half cooked food on an open flame into Shabbos. This law created the use of a Blech. The blech effectively covers the fire and allows one to leave even less than half cooked foods on the fire into Shabbos. In most cases the foods are in any event fully cooked and a blech is hence not needed. It is customary however to place a blech over the fire even in such a case, as this allows one to be allowed to return foods to the fire on Shabbos in case of need. [See The Laws of Shabbos Volume 1 "The Laws of Chazara" for more information!]
Covering knobs: It is proper to cover the knobs of the stove in addition to covering the fire. Today there are blechs available that contain a side metal addition which is used to cover the knobs. Alternatively one can place tinfoil over the knobs.
Electric plates: If one uses an electric plate to keep his food hot over Shabbos then if the electric plate does not have alternate settings of heat, it does not need to be covered even if the food will not be half cooked before Shabbos. If it

---

Ubichassidus" p. 235]
Wearing a mixed material Kapata of wool and silk: Some quote the Rebbe to have spoken against wearing a mixed material Kapata of wool and silk. Practically a source is needed to verify this claim.
[337] Ketzos Hashulchan 73 footnote 24
[338] Vetzaruch Iyun as the implication from Admur is that placing on one's Shabbos clothes immediately after bathing is of more importance then wearing them close to Shabbos.
[339] M"B 262/11; Kaf Hachayim 262/31
[340] 242/11
[341] So rules Mishneh Halachos, brought in back of Piskeiy Teshuvos Shabbos, and so rules Rav SZ"A [SSH"K 42 footnote 13] on the basis that today we are accustomed to wash clothing for many days worth. However earlier on in the footnote there a suggestions is given that the decree perhaps no longer applies today. It seems from Ketzos Hashulchan 73 footnote 22 that he too learns that the decree of the Sages is applicable at all times.
[342] SSH"K 44 footnote 13; Oar Letziyon 2/16; Yechaveh Daas 7/18; See Piskeiy Teshuvos [new edition] 242/10
[343] Rav SZ"A in SSH"K 42 footnote 13.

does have alternate settings of heat then it must be covered for one to be allowed to leave less than half cooked food on it into Shabbos.

Ovens: One may leave food which is at least half cooked in a lit oven into Shabbos. One may not leave less than half cooked foods in an oven unless the inside of the oven is properly covered. [See "The Laws of Shehiyah" Halacha Q&A 3 for details!] One must beware not to open an oven while it is off if it is temperature based. [See *The Laws Of Cooking*" Halacha 15]

When to set up the blech: The blech is to be set up together with the food with enough time for the food to heat up if the food were to be cold. Meaning even if the food is currently hot it is to be placed on the Blech with enough time for it to become hot if it were to be cold. In a case of need one may set up the Blech any time before Shabbos even if the food is cold.

If one does not have a blech or electric plate: If one does not have a blech or electric plate for Shabbos he may still leave all his food on an open flame before Shabbos, so long as the food is half cooked by the time Shabbos enters.

21. Reminding ones household that Shabbos is near:[344]

Slightly[345] prior to sunset, one is to caution his household that they should light the candles and cease from doing any forbidden work. Likewise, if one's wife baked Chalah [as is required due to the custom] then slightly prior to sunset it is [an obligation in Eretz Yisrael[346], and even] in the Diaspora, it is good[347], to ask her if Chalah was removed.[348] If one is not at home at this time then he must [call or] send a messenger to remind his household of the above.

How to speak to ones wife and kids: The above reminders and questions must be said in a soft tone in order so they accept his words.[349]

22. Carrying an object close to the start of Shabbos:[350]

The public area is defined as a Reshus Harabim: It is forbidden for one to carry an object in his hand [or pocket[351]] into a public domain which is defined as a *Reshus Harabim* very close to the start of Shabbos.[352] This is due to a decree that one may come to forget to rid himself of the object[353] prior to the start of Shabbos, and he will come to

---

[344] 260/5

[345] However one is not to hurry and remind his family while there is still much time left during the day, as they will not adhere to the reminder, as they will assure themselves that there is still plenty of time remaining. [ibid]

[346] Ketzos Hashulchan 73 footnote 10, as in Eretz Yisrael one may not eat bread if one did not separate Chalah from it before Shabbos. Thus it is an obligation. However in the Diaspora being that one may still eat bread even if one did not separate Chalah from it before Shabbos, as will be explained in the coming footnotes, it therefore is not an obligation to ask one's wife if she separated Chalah but is merely a good thing to do.

[347] But not an obligation.

[348] As Chalah may not be removed on Shabbos. (Now although in the Diaspora from the letter of the law one may eat un-tithed bread so long as he leaves over some bread which he will remove the Chalah from later on, [and thus the above reminder should not be needed in the Diaspora], nevertheless initially the custom is to remove Chalah before eating the bread due to suspicion that one may come to forget to remove later on, and in retrospect it happened that he ate Tevel.) [Ibid] The M"B [260/13] however concludes that today the custom is no longer to ask if the Chalah was removed.

Asking if the food was tithed in Eretz Yisrael: From the letter of the law in Eretz Yisrael it is also necessary for one to ask his wife if she removed the tithes from the other produce needed for Shabbos. [ibid] Nevertheless today being that the Kashrus organizations deal with these separations, this question is irrelevant. [Ketzos Hashulchan 73 footnote 9]

Asking on Eiruv Chatzeiros: Likewise it was required back then to ask if Eiruv Chatzeirus has been done, however being that today this Eiruv is done once a year on Erev Pesach, there is no longer any need to ask. [ibid]

[349] The Magen Avraham 260/2 writes that one is to speak softly being it is forbidden to enter too much fear into one's household. This itself is due to that if they fear the father too much they may come to lead him to transgress eating a forbidden food, or that they themselves will transgress Shabbos due to fear of not serving him his needs promptly.

[350] 252/17-18

[351] Mishneh Berurah 252/52; as is also evident from Admur 252/18 regarding a pin stuck in ones clothes that it was only allowed to walk with it outside on Erev Shabbos because it is only a Rabbinical prohibition to carry it on Shabbos.

Accordingly it requires further analysis why Admur wrote that it is specifically forbidden to carry an item in ones hand and does not also write in one's clothes, as we wrote above. Now, although the Michaber himself wrote "hand" that is because he is dealing with a case of a needle, of which when on ones clothes is allowed. [See Biur Halacha 252 "Beyado"] However Admur mentions generally "an item" and thus why does he use the words "in ones hands" at all, if in truth the same law would apply if the object is on one's clothes.

[352] This prohibition however only applies to items which carrying them on Shabbos is Biblically forbidden. However it is permitted to carry close to Shabbos an item which on Shabbos itself is only Rabinically forbidden to carry, such as a needle pinned to ones clothes. As although it is Rabinically forbidden to carry this item on Shabbos itself, the Sages did not decree against doing so near Shabbos due to worry that he may forget and carry it, as this would be a decree made to protect a matter which is itself a decree, of which the Sages do not make. [ibid]

[353] Such as to hide the object if it is of value. [ibid]

For this reason this prohibition does not apply to Tefillin which one is wearing in a *Reshus Harabim* close to Shabbos being that one must always be conscious of Tefillin when they are on him and he will certainly remember to remove them prior to the start of Shabbos. [252/19] However if one is not wearing the Tefillin and is merely carrying them, then the above decree applies to it as well. [Mishneh Berurah 252/54 in name of M"A]

transgress the laws of carrying.[354] [Furthermore, this prohibition applies even while one is still in his own house, and thus he may not take hold of an object near the start of Shabbos with intent to exit with that object to a *Reshus Harabim*.[355]]

The public area is defined as a Karmalis: If the public domain of one's area is defined as a *Karmalis*, then there is no prohibition to carry items into it, even in ones hand, very close to Shabbos [even if there is no Eiruv in the area].[356]

Practically are our public areas defined as Reshus Harabim or as a Karmalis? Today the custom has spread to follow the opinion which considers all public areas as a Karmalis[357], and accordingly there is no longer any prohibition to carry an item very close to Shabbos into the public domain. [**see footnote**[358]]

Summary:
It is forbidden to carry an object into a *rishus harabim* close to the beginning of Shabbos, as this may lead to one carrying it on Shabbos. This prohibition does not apply to carrying into a *Karmalis* or to carrying something that is only Rabinically forbidden to carry on Shabbos.
Practically today being that all areas are considered a Karmalis, there is no longer a prohibition to carry items close to Shabbos into a public area.

---

23. Checking ones pockets close to Shabbos: [359]

It is a Mitzvah[360] upon every person to check his clothing[361] on Erev Shabbos, in close proximity to the beginning of Shabbos. This is done in order to verify that he is not carrying anything which is forbidden to carry[362] on Shabbos.[363] [This applies even in an area with an Eiruv, in order so one verifies whether or not he is holding a Muktzah object.[364]]

If one forgot to remove the item before Shabbos: [365] If one forgot and did not remove the item from his pockets before Shabbos, then he is to remove it on Shabbos [immediately] upon remembering. [Regarding how to remove the object if it is Muktzah- See Vol. 1 "The Laws of Muktzah". Regarding if one noticed that he is carrying the object on Shabbos while in an area without an Eiruv-See Vol. 3 "The Laws of Carrying".]

---

[354] Either by carrying the object into a private domain, or by carrying it four Amos within the Reshus Harabim.
This transgression however is only Biblically applicable if, after Shabbos began, one remembered that he was holding the object and despite this continued to carry it [such as he forgot that Shabbos began]. If however one did not become aware of the object after Shabbos began then he does not transgress a Biblical command by carrying it, as the Torah only forbade doing a Melacha which one is aware of its occurrence, which means that the person intends knowingly to do that Melacha, and it is only that if in such a case he did not remember that it was already Shabbos, or that this Melacha is forbidden that he would be liable to bring a sin offering. [ibid]

[355] So is implied from Admur which mentions that "he may come to carry it from a private domain into a public domain" hence clearly implying that the person is currently standing in a private domain, and it is nevertheless still forbidden. So rules also Peri Megadim 252 A"A 26, based on the wording of the Michaber.

[356] As carrying in a Karmalis is itself only a Rabbinical prohibition, and the Sages do not make a decree upon a decree. [ibid]

[357] As they hold that a true Reshus Harabim is no longer in existence today. [ibid]

[358] Vetzaruch Iyun if according to Admur there is any need for one to be stringent, if he so chooses, to suspect for the opinion which rules that even today there is a *Reshus Harabims*. On the one hand if there were no need to be stringent at all, then why did Admur mention the entire lengthy discussion in this matter rather than simply stating that today the prohibition does not apply. On the other hand the Ketzos Hashulchan [73] completely omits this entire discussion, seemingly learning that there is no longer any need to suspect for this at all today.
Opinion of Mishneh Berurah: The M"B [252/52] concludes that according to many Poskim one is to be stringent.
Requires Analysis: To note from 266/15 that Admur states that one who carried a wallet into Shabbos was negligent that he took it with him. This is not understood in light of the above ruling of Admur that today we hold all areas has the status of a Karmalis, and thus what negligence is there. [Glosses of Tzemach Tzedek on Admur, printed in Shulchan Aruch 2 p. 836].

[359] 252/20

[360] Tzaruch Iyun on this Lashon, which is the Lashon of the Michaber, as opposed to the wording of the Gemara and Rambam which is "obligated". See glosses of Tzemach Tzedek printed in Shulchan Aruch 2 p. 836 which asks this question. See also Biur Halacha 252 "Mitzvah" which explains this wording.
To note that in the Kuntrus Achron [252/14] Admur explains that in truth this is not a Rabbinical decree, but rather is an obligation which comes as a result of the prohibition of carrying into a Karmalis, as it is very possible that one already has an item in his pocket, as is commonly done during the week.

[361] This refers to his pockets and all other areas of which one commonly uses to place items into. [Mishneh Berurah 252/55]

[362] Whether it being an item which is forbidden to carry in a Karmalis, or whether it being a Muktzah item which is always forbidden to carry [as explains M"A]. Now although as said before the Sages did not make a decree as a precaution against carrying into a Karmalis, being that this is a decree upon a decree, nevertheless since one always accustomed during the week to place things in his pocket, and this is something which can be easily verified, it therefore is not even considered a Rabbinical decree but rather a true doubt. [Kuntrus Achron 252/14]

[363] This applies even according to the custom today to consider all public areas as a Karmalis. [ibid]

[364] Kuntrus Achron 252/14 in name of Magen Avraham.

[365] 303/23

May one place items in his pocket on Shabbos itself?[366] It is forbidden to place any object into ones pockets on Shabbos, even at home, if one lives in a community that does not have an Eiruv [**see footnote**[367]] which allows them to carry.[368] However in a case of need one may be lenient to place things in his pocket while in his house.[369]

Q&A

If on Shabbos one desires to walk past the area of the Eiruv must he check his pockets prior to leaving?[370]

Even in an area that has an Eiruv, if one plans to walk past the Eiruv area then he is to check and remove all the items from his pockets prior to doing so.

---

24. Accepting Shabbos with joy:[371]

One is to wear elegant clothing and rejoice in the coming of Shabbos like one is going to greet the king, and like one who is greeting a bride and groom. This was the custom of the greatest of our Sages which would garb themselves in elegant clothes and say to each other "Let us go out to greet the Shabbos queen". They would then proclaim "Greetings Oh Bride Greetings Oh Bride". In some places they would leave the Shul and enter the courtyard and then make this proclamation. Others were accustomed to go to the field.

Doing Teshuvah on Erev Shabbos:[372]
One should have thoughts of Teshuvah and make an accounting of his soul on every Erev Shabbos.[373]

Not to quarrel on Shabbos:[374]
The Kabalists strongly warned against there being any quarrelling on Shabbos, especially amongst husband and wife. It is brought[375] that the Satan tries to ignite a quarrel especially near the entrance of Shabbos, hence extra care must be taken at that time.

---

25. Mincha on Erev Shabbos:

Saying Hodu:[376] It is a custom established from the Ball Shem Tov to recite psalm 107 prior to the Mincha prayer.[377] Hodu is omitted prior to Mincha Erev Shabbos which is also Yom Tov or Chol Hamoed.[378] [Some communities are accustomed to recite Hodu together with a Minyan.[379] This is not the Chabad custom, and rather every congregant recites Hodu on his own and the Chazan then begins from Ashreiy.[380]]

---

[366] 303/23
This matter is disputed there, and the following is Admur's final ruling which states to be stringent unless it is a case of need.
[367] In parentheses Admur adds that this prohibition applies **even in an area which has an Eiruv**, and thus accordingly it would be always forbidden to place items in ones pockets, in any community in the world, even while in one's home. Practically though since even by a community which does not have an Eiruv it is disputed whether it is allowed or not, and Admur himself placed this ruling in parentheses, which represents his own personal doubt in whether it is even correct according to the stringent opinion, one may therefore be lenient. So rules Ketzos Hashulchan 115 footnote 44, and so is the worldly custom. Nevertheless one who desires to be stringent even in a city with an Eiruv, basing himself on the strict wording of Admur that one is to follow the stringent opinion, seemingly may do so.
[368] This is due to worry that one may come to forget about the item if he places it in his pocket, and will then come to carry it. [ibid]
[369] As there are opinions which hold that there was never a prohibition made against placing items in ones pockets while in one's home.
[370] Mishneh Berurah 252/56
[371] 262/4
[372] Mishneh Berurah brought in Ketzos Hashulchan 73 footnote 25
[373] As it is improper to accept the Shabbos queen when dirty with the filth of sin.
[374] Mishneh Berurah 262/9
[375] Shabbos 113; Aruch Hashulchan 262/5
[376] Siddur; This custom is brought in Maor Eiynayim Beshalach in name of the Baal Shem Tov
[377] This psalm is said as a thanks to G-d that our body and soul have not been injured during the work of the week. [Shaar Hakolel , brought also in Ketzos Hashulchan 77 footnote 1; See Piskeiy Teshuvos 267 footnote 10 for other reasons mentioned.]
[378] As it is belittling of Yom Tov to recite a thanks to Hashem for removing us from the mundane activity of the week to Shabbos when Yom Tov is likewise not a time of mundane activity. [Ketzos Hashulchan 77 footnote 2]
[379] So is the custom of Polisher Chassidim. [Ketzos Hashulchan 77 footnote 1] Shaar Hakolel writes it is to be said with a Minyan in order to thank Hashem in a public forum.
[380] Ketzos Hashulchan 77 footnote 1

Saying Patach Eliyahu: After Hodu one recites Patach Eliyahu. [Patach Eliyahu is recited even when Hodu is omitted such as Erev Shabbos Chol Hamoed.[381]]

Tachanun:[382] It is customary to omit Tachanun by Mincha of Erev Shabbos. [This applies even when Davening Mincha early by Mincha Gedola.[383] Likewise, for this reason one who ate bread after midday does not recite Al Naros before Birchas Hamazon but rather recites Shir Hamaalos.[384]]

Wearing a Tallis: Many communities are accustomed that the Chazan wear a Tallis for Mincha of Erev Shabbos.[385] This is not the Chabad custom. Nevertheless if not wearing a Tallis will cause strife in the Shul one is to compromise on his custom and wear the Tallis for Mincha. However one is not to wear a Tallis for Kabalas Shabbos.[386]

Q&A

If the Minyan has begun Ashreiy and one has not yet recited said Hodu and Patach Eliyahu what is he to do?[387]

One is to Daven Shemoneh Esrei with the Minyan and recite Hodu and Patach Eliyahu after Mincha.

If one's Shachris prayer continued past midday is he to recite Tachanun?

Some Poskim[388] rule Tachanun is not to be recited.

Is an Avel to be Chazan by Mincha of Erev Shabbos?

An Avel may be Chazan by Mincha of Erev Shabbos and so is the Chabad custom. However there are communities which are accustomed to not have an Avel Daven as Chazan by Mincha due to its extra holiness.[389]

The greatness of Mincha Erev Shabbos:[390]

According to the teachings of the Arizal the revelation of the holiness of Shabbos begins from the 5th hour of Erev Shabbos. This revelation intensifies with the prayer of Mincha. It is an auspicious time for the elevation of the soul, and for repenting on actions done during the previous week.

It is customary to Daven Mincha close to the entrance of Shabbos, after immersing in a Mikveh and wearing Shabbos clothing. One is to Daven Mincha with extra concentration due to its great level.

---

26. Shnayim Mikra:

Shnayim Mikra is to be read on Erev Shabbos past midday. See chapter 3 for the full details of this topic.

27. Candle Lighting:

G-d willing a full section on the laws of candle lighting will appear in one of our later volumes in our series of Hilchos Shabbos.

---

[381] Ketzos Hashulchan 77 footnote 3
[382] 267/1
[383] Peri Megadim 267 M"Z 1
[384] M"B 267/1
[385] Piskeiy Teshuvos 267/1
[386] Shaareiy Halacha Uminhag 1/57
[387] Ketzos Hashulchan 77 footnote 1
[388] Az Nidbaru 11/1
[389] Likutei Mahrich, brought in Piskeiy Teshuvos 267/1
[390] Kaf Hachaim 267/2; Piskeiy Teshuvos 267/1

Chapter 2: Learning and doing other activities on Erev Shabbos:

Important note:
Although one may do work on Erev Shabbos until the time to be mentioned below, he nevertheless is to prepare for Shabbos prior to this time, as explained in the previous chapter[1] and as is evident from the story told by Rav Yehuda Hachasid[2].

---

1. Doing work on Erev Shabbos and Erev Yom Tov:

The law:[3] The Sages forbade[4] one to do [certain forms[5] of] work on Erev Shabbos and Erev Yom Tov beginning from the time of Mincha and onwards.[6]

The reason:[7] As the sages desired that from this time and onwards one is free from his duties so he can deal with his Shabbos needs. (Even if one does not need to prepare for Shabbos at all, it still remains forbidden for him to do work from Mincha and onwards as the Sages did not want to differentiate in their decree.[8])

If one transgresses and does forbidden work pass the above mentioned time:[9] One who does forbidden work after Mincha will not see blessing from that work which was done.[10] However one is not punished for doing work past this time, neither through excommunication or lashes although this is usually done for one who transgresses a Rabbinical command.[11] Nevertheless he is to be admonished, and forcibly prevented from doing the work.

When is considered the "time of Mincha":[12] It is disputed as to whether the prohibition of doing work past Mincha refers to *Mincha Gedola* [i.e. half hour past midday[13]] or *Mincha Ketana* [i.e. 3.5 minutes past midday[14]]. Practically one who is lenient to do work up until Mincha Ketana does not lose any blessing from the work done[15]. [The above hours are calculated in accordance to *Shaaos Zmaniyos,* in which one divides the total amount of day hours by 12 in order to calculate the amount of each hour.[16]]

Stopping the people from work from after Mincha Ketana:[17] A messenger is to be sent in order to stop the working people from doing work [of physical labor], beginning from Mincha and onwards, which is two and half hours before Shabbos.[18]

---

[1] That one is to prepare for Shabbos in the morning.

[2] The Sefer Chasidim [122] [brought in Kaf Hachaim 251/4] writes how a woman was severely punished for having spent her time on Erev Shabbos sewing instead of preparing for her Shabbos needs. The Kneses Hagedola explains on this that although the woman had done the sewing prior to midday, she was nevertheless punished as due to this she refrained from preparing properly for Shabbos. He then explains that one is required to prepare his Shabbos needs even before the time of Mincha and the prohibition to do work after Mincha was made even when one has already completed all his Shabbos preparations.

[3] 251/1. See Aruch Hashulchan 251/4 who brings a Limud Zechus for those which are not careful in this set of laws and continue to work past the prohibited mentioned time.

[4] The wording of some Poskim [Michaber and others] does not mention a prohibition but rather simply states that work past Mincha will be fruitless. Admur [as does other Poskim] however rules that it is an actual prohibition. [See Kaf Hachayim 251/7]

[5] The forms of work which remain permitted will be discussed below.

[6] The *Reishis Chachmah* writes based on the Zohar that after going to Mikveh, which is likened to accepting Shabbos, one is forbidden to do any work with exception to work done in preparation for Shabbos, and rather one is to spend his time learning Torah. [Kaf Hachayim 151/3]

[7] 251/3

[8] See above footnote in story with Rav Yehuda Hachasid, in which the Kneses Hagedola explains on this that one is required to prepare his Shabbos needs even prior to the time of Mincha and the prohibition to do work after Mincha was made even when one has already completed all his Shabbos preparations. However see Aruch Hashulchan 251/4 suggests as a defense for those which are lenient to do labor past Mincha, being that their wives prepare for them all their Shabbos needs.

[9] 251/1

[10] This means that whatever profit he has gained from the work done, he will accordingly lose out that same amount on a different occasion. [Ibid]

[11] As the Sages were not that strict regarding this prohibition. [Ibid]

[12] 251/2; Both opinions are brought by the Michaber in 251/1.

[13] Mincha Gedola begins from 6 hours and 30 minutes into the day, which is a half hour past midday. [ibid] This opinion of Mincha Gedola is the opinion of Mordechai and Tur, and so rules the Bach and Levush.

[14] Mincha Ketana begins from 9.5 hours into the day, which is 2.5 hours prior to sunset. [ibid] This opinion of Mincha Ketana is the opinion of Rashi.

[15] As by a dispute in a Rabbinical matter one may be lenient. [ibid]. So rules Taz 251/1. However the *Magen Avraham* 251/4 plainly sides like the opinion that it refers to *Mincha Ketana* [and thus according to him there is no need to be stringent, unlike the implication from the wording of Taz/Admur which would hold that one that is stringent has what to be stringent on]. To note that *Admur* plainly rules like the lenient opinion in 256/1, which is brought next regarding the community announcement of stopping to do work. However see footnote there.
The *Ketzos Hashulchan* [69/6] plainly rules in accordance to the opinion which holds of Mincha Ketana, which is 2.5 hours prior to sunset, and does not mention any need to be stringent if one wishes to.

[16] Mishneh Berurah 251/3

[17] 256/1

2. The forms of work that are forbidden to be done past Mincha:[19]

The Sages only forbade one to do forms of work which fulfill all the following conditions:

1. *Melacha Gemura*: The work is a complete form of work. [Meaning that it involves laborious activity, as opposed to a job which involves mere buying and selling, as will be explained below.]

2. *Kavua Work*: It is only forbidden to do work past Mincha if the work requires one to settle himself over it, and takes a lot of one's time.[20] It is however permitted to do an activity, even if laborious, which is temporary and does not take much time, such as to write a greetings letter to a friend and activities of the like.[21] [One may do temporary work on behalf of another even for the sake of receiving payment.[22]]

3. *The work is not being done for the sake of Shabbos or a Mitzvah*: Settling oneself into doing a laborious activity was only forbidden if this activity is not being done for the sake of Shabbos or a Mitzvah. If however he is doing so for the sake of Shabbos, such as to sew clothing for Shabbos[23], then it is permitted for him to do so throughout the entire day. This applies whether one is working on behalf of himself or on behalf of someone else, [so long as he is doing so free of charge, as will be explained next]. Likewise, if one is doing the activity for the sake of a Mitzvah[24], such as to write Sefarim [and Chidushei Torah[25]], it is permitted to be done throughout the entire day, whether for himself, or for another free of charge.

   One is doing so for the sake of Shabbos or a Mitzvah but is receiving payment: It is forbidden for one to settle himself into a laborious activity, such as sewing a garment, on behalf of another in exchange for payment, even if one is doing so for the sake of Shabbos or a Mitzvah.[26] It is permitted to do so free of charge as explained. The above is with exception to giving a haircut to another Jew which may be done even for payment as will be explained later on.

   One is doing a laborious job for the sake of using the money for Shabbos expenses: One who is poor and wishes to work a laborious job in order to use the money to buy his Shabbos needs[27], may do so throughout the entire day of Erev Shabbos[28] [even if the labor is not needed for the employer for the sake of Shabbos, and even if it is a professional labor[29]].

4. *The work is forbidden on Chol Hamoed*:[30] In all situations that work is permitted to be done on Chol Hamoed it is likewise permitted to be done past Mincha of Erev Shabbos.[31]

3. Examples of activities that may be done after Mincha: [32]

- **Business-Buying and selling**:

   It is permitted for one to do business past the time of Mincha as such work is not defined as a complete form of work.[33]

---

[18] Thus we see here that Admur rules plainly like the lenient opinion. However one can answer that in truth Admur only holds this way with regards to sending messengers, as one cannot force the community to keep a stringency. However for an individual, there is room to be stringent if he so chooses. [See *Magen Avraham* 251 4 for a similar explanation regarding the day workers who would work until close to sunset.]

[19] 251/3

[20] Seemingly this is the meaning of "Derech Keva" written in 251/3. This wording is written in the Rama 251/1 and is based on a ruling of the Oar Zarua. It however does not mean that it is only forbidden if the work is prescheduled, and is permitted if it happened to come up, as what is the logic to differentiate. Either way if the action takes a lot of one's time there is suspicion that one may not be able to prepare for his Shabbos needs. So also learns SSH"K 42/38-39. Perhaps however one can say it also excludes scheduling oneself to perform a certain work every Erev Shabbos for purposes of making money. So is implied from the wording of Oar Zarua, see there.

[21] As the Sages only prohibited doing work which one settles himself over, in order so one be free to deal with his Shabbos needs. [Ibid]

[22] Mishneh Berurah 251/4; Kaf Hachaim 251/11

[23] This implies that even to sew an entire garment in a professional manner is allowed. This is in contrast to the wording of the Michaber [251/2] which writes "to fix cloths".

[24] As doing so for the sake of a Mitzvah is similar to doing so for the sake of Shabbos. [ibid]

[25] Aruch Hashulchan 251/2

[26] As in truth when payment is taken, it is considered that the activity is being doing merely for the money and not for the sake of Shabbos at all, and since it is likewise not evident to others that one is doing so for the sake of Shabbos, it is therefore not allowed. [251/4] However when done free of charge, since in truth one is solely doing so for the sake of Shabbos, it is allowed to be done even though that this is not evident to others.

[27] This includes if he needs the money merely to buy Shabbos delicacies. [Mishneh Berurah 251/5; Kaf Hachaim 251]

[28] As even on Chol Hamoed one may do all forms of labors in order so he have food to eat. Thus certainly on Erev Shabbos past Mincha, which is a lighter working prohibition, then is Chol Hamoed, one may work for food. [ibid]

[29] Just as is the law on Chol Hamoed. [see 562/2 and Kitzur Hilchos Shabbos 251 footnote 6]

[30] 251/5

[31] Such as if one doesn't do the work now it will cause him a loss. It is beyond the scope of this book to delve into all the detailed laws of those situations in which work is forbidden to be done on Chol Hamoed, and those which are permitted. See Shulchan Aruch chapters 530-548, or Chol Hamoed Kehilchasa.

[32] 251/3

[33] This ruling of Admur follows the ruling of the Magen Avraham 251/1. However the Eliyahu Raba rules that doing business is forbidden from the time of Mincha, and so is implied to be the opinion of the Michaber. [Kaf Hachaim 251/2]

When are businesses to close on Erev Shabbos:[34] Although businesses[35] are permitted to remain open after Mincha, nevertheless it is proper to send someone to close the shops an hour before nightfall [which is about a half hour before sunset-**see footnote[36]**]. The reason for this is because many times [if this is not done] a severe dilemma[37] derives, as at times an important person[38] comes into the shop, and the business negotiations continue until actual night, causing Shabbos to be desecrated.[39]

- **Writing a letter:**

  It is permitted to write a greetings letter to a friend. [The same applies for all writing that may be written on Chol Hamoed, they may likewise be written on Erev Shabbos past Mincha. However those writings forbidden to be written on Chol Hamoed are forbidden to be written on Erev Shabbos.[40]]

- **Haircut:[41]**

  For a gentile: It is forbidden to give a gentile a haircut on Erev Shabbos past Mincha. This applies even if one is giving an amateur haircut, and even if he is doing so free of charge.[42] [See Q&A]

  For a Jew: It is permitted to give a Jew a haircut throughout the entire Erev Shabbos, even past the time of Mincha.[43] This applies even if one is giving a professional haircut and is doing so in exchange for payment[44], as it is recognizable to all that the haircut is being done in honor of Shabbos.

---

[34] 256/1

[35] This refers to stores, or any other job which involves buying and selling. In the previous Halacha the term work is defined as physical labor and not mere buying and selling.

[36] Kuntrus Achron 251/1;

In 256/1 Admur rules "one hour prior to night". This refers to nightfall, Tzeis Hakochavim, of which usually begins 30 minutes after accepting Shabbos, as writes Admur in Kuntrus Achron ibid. Hence we wrote inside that a half hour before sunset, which equals a full hour before nightfall, the stores are to be closed. However this calculation of 30 minutes between nightfall and Kabalas Shabbos is only in accordance to the opinion of Rabeinu Tam. However according to the Geonim, which is the accustomed ruling today, the amount of time between sunset and nightfall, can be anywhere between 15-40 minutes, depending on the country and season. Thus the Ketzos Hashulchan [73 footnote 14] concludes that in Jerusalem businesses must close 40 minutes prior to sunset, being that there is usually 20 minutes between sunset and nightfall. Although Tzaruch iyun, as in the Kuntrus Achron Admur states that there is no power of the Sages to enforce the closing of the stores prior to 30 minutes before Kabalas Shabbos, and thus even in Jerusalem the work is to be stopped only 30 minutes before sunset. Accordingly an area which has a 40 minutes Bein Hashmashos would nevertheless need to close their stores 30 minutes prior to sunset, and each area is to calculate 30 minutes prior to its sunset. Vetzaruch Iyun, as according to this understanding Admur should have stated in 256/1 simply "30 minutes prior to Kabalas Shabbos" and not 1 hour prior to night.

Conclusion: There requires further analysis whether stores are to closed 60 minutes prior to nightfall, or 30 minutes prior to sunset.

Opinion of *Mishneh Berurah*: In Shaareiy Tziyon 256/3 he rules that the stores are to close one hour prior to sunset, unlike Admur which rules one hour prior to nightfall.

[37] Lit. stumbling block. Meaning it causes one to transgress a prohibition.

[38] Lit. an aristocrat

[39] The responsibility of enforcing the close of the businesses prior to Shabbos lies on the heads of the community, as the Sages expounded from the verse, "And I will put it on their necks" [From this verse the Sages learned that the transgressions of the community which can be stopped by the community leaders, give liability to those leaders which did not try to stop them.] [Ibid]

[40] Kaf Hachaim 251/12 in name of Ben Ish Chaiy Lech Licha 20

It is beyond the scope of this book to delve into all the detailed laws of those writings which are forbidden to be done on Chol Hamoed, and those which are permitted. See Shulchan Aruch chapter 545, or Chol Hamoed Kehilchasa.

[41] 251/4

[42] As a haircut is considered a laborious activity which one must settle himself down into doing, and is thus forbidden to be done past the time of Mincha if it serves no Shabbos need. [ibid] However the Magen Avraham [251/5] suggests that it is permitted to give an amateur haircut to a gentile, as it is considered a Maaseh Hedyot.

[43] The Arizal however would not get a haircut past the time of Mincha Gedola [midday], based on Kabalistic reasons. [brought in Magen Avraham 251/5] Admur however omitted this custom of the Arizal. See Shaareiy Halacha Uminhag 1/130 that the Rebbe concludes regarding the time of cutting nails, which is similar to the time of the cutting of the hair, that he did not receive a directive in how to follow.

Opinion of Gr"a: The Gra is stringent against allowing haircuts past midday, although this is not the worldly custom. [Aruch Hashulchan 251/3]

[44] The reason that one may give a haircut past Mincha even in exchange for payment, in contrast to sewing for another past Mincha which must be done free of charge, this is because by a haircut it is clearly evident that it is being done for the sake of Shabbos, even if one receives payment for doing so. However sewing which is done for payment is not currently evident that it is being done for the sake of Shabbos, and is thus only allowed to be done free of charge. (Furthermore, in addition to sewing for payment is not evident that it is being done for Shabbos, when payment is taken, it is considered that the sewer is doing so merely for the money and not for the sake of Shabbos at all.) [ibid] It requires further analysis on what the novelty of Admur is here in the parentheses, is it a totally new reason or is it an explanation of why it is not evident? Seemingly it is an additional reason which without it the law would not be understood. Meaning Admur holds that if either the activity is evident to others that it is being done for the sake of Shabbos [as by a haircut], or is not evident to others, but in truth is being done for the sake of Shabbos [as by sewing for free], it is allowed. Thus he explains why when sewing for payment it is forbidden as it is not evident, and one's intention is not for Shabbos.

Summary:
It is forbidden to do work 2.5 Halachic[45] hours[46] prior to sunset on Erev Shabbos unless:
1. The work being done is for a Shabbos need of oneself, or for someone else and is being done free of charge. This is with exception to one giving a haircut to another Jew, which may be done even for payment.
2. The work is done temporarily and not in way of that one needs to establish himself to do it. Meaning it does not take a long time for it to get done.
3. It is being done for the purpose of a mitzvah and if done for another is being done free of charge.
4. One is poor and is working in order to buy things for Shabbos.
5. The work being done is not real labor. Like a counter salesman in a store.
6. If one does not do the work now it will cause him a loss.
7. Likewise all work that may be done on Chol Hamoed may be done past Mincha.

Until what time on Erev Shabbos may a store be left open?
The stores may be left open until 30 minutes prior to sunset.

List of activities that may be done past Mincha of Erev Shabbos:
- Write Sefarim free of charge.
- Sew a garment for Shabbos free of charge.
- Give a haircut to a Jew even for payment.
- Buying and selling at a store.
- Write a friendly letter to an acquaintance.

Q&A

May an employee work past 2.5 hours before sunset if his boss requests him to do so?[47]
If he has employed himself for that day's work then he is obligated to work the entire day. However initially one should stipulate that he will only work up to 2.5 hours before sunset on Erev Shabbos.

If a gentile pays one a monthly payment in exchange for him receiving a haircut whenever he wishes, may one do so if the gentile desires a haircut on Erev Shabbos within 2.5 hours before sunset?[48]
Yes[49]. However initially one should stipulate with the gentile that he does not give haircuts past 2.5 hours before sunset on Erev Shabbos.

May one begin an activity, such as giving a gentile a haircut, prior to 2.5 hours before sunset, if he knows it will continue into the 2.5 hours?[50]
This matter requires further analysis.

May a Sofer write Mezuzas, Tefillin, or Sifrei Torah past 2.5 hours prior to sunset?[51]
If he is doing so as a hobby, or for personal use then it is allowed. If however he is doing so as part of his income then it is forbidden.[52]

May one perform cleaning help for Shabbos past 2.5 hours before sunset, in exchange for payment?
This matter requires further analysis.[53]

---

[45] The above hours are calculated in accordance to *Shaaos Zmaniyos,* in which one divides the total amount of day hours by 12 in order to calculate the amount of minutes in each hour. One then times that by 2.5 and the result is the amount of minutes prior to sunset that the prohibition begins.

[46] This matter is disputed as mentioned above. The Ketzos Hashulchan [69/6] rules in accordance to the opinion which holds of Mincha Ketana, which is 2.5 hours prior to sunset. Nevertheless one who is stringent from midday, has room for his stringency.

[47] Mishneh Berurah 251/3-Shaareiy Tziyon 4; brought also in Ketzos Hashulchan 69 footnote 117

[48] Ketzos Hashulchan 69 footnote 18

[49] As if one were to refuse the gentile he would cancel the payment arraignment which is considered a matter which would cause him a loss. [ibid]

[50] Ketzos Hashulchan 69 footnote 18

[51] Mishneh Berurah 251/6; Kaf Hachayim 251/17

[52] As rules Admur in 151/3 that even a Mitzvah activity may only be done free of charge.

[53] SSH"K 42 footnote 129 leaves this matter in question as although it is recognizable that it is being done for the sake of Shabbos, nonetheless perhaps the Sages only permitted haircuts in exchange for payment as it is done to the body of the person. Vetzaruch Iyun.

May one work in cleaning Shtreimals for Shabbos past 2.5 hours before sunset?
This matter requires further analysis.[54]

May one work to collect payment for Mikveh past 2.5 hours before sunset?
Yes, as it is similar to business which is allowed.

May one build his Sukkah on Erev Sukkos past the 10th hour?
Ideally one is to complete the building of his Sukkah prior to 2. 5 hours before sunset.[55] If however it is past 2.5 hours before sunset and one has still not built his Sukkah, it may nevertheless still be built.[56]

---

4. Learning and doing other activities on Erev Shabbos:[57]

One is to slightly diminish the amount of his learning on Erev Shabbos. It goes without saying that one is to diminish from doing other activities.[58]

Yeshiva on Erev Shabbos: [Due to the above requirement to diminish in ones learning on Erev Shabbos in order to have time to prepare for Shabbos] the custom in some places is to not have a set Yeshiva learning Seder[59] on Erev Shabbos.[60]

Private learning: One who is accustomed to learn a certain Torah subject daily is not to nullify this session on Erev Shabbos if it is a clear subject that will not lead one into debates and analysis. [If he does not learn this subject on a daily basis then based on the above custom, he is to nullify it.] A subject which is customarily learned on Erev Shabbos, such as the commentary of Rashi on the weekly portion, is allowed to be learned as usual [even if it is not studied on a daily basis].

Shnayim Mikra: Is to be learned on Erev Shabbos. See Chapter 285

Having a Shiur on Erev Shabbos: A Shiur which is given on a regular basis[61], is to likewise be given on Erev Shabbos if it involves a non-complicated subject which has a limit and will thus not be carried into debates and analysis. This allowance applies even if this Shiur is not given on a daily basis. [One however is not, based on the above custom, to give a Shiur on a subject which involves debate and analysis.[62]]

Learning with a Chavrusa:[63] Seemingly this follows the same laws as does a Shiur [explained next] and is to be learned if the subject has a limit.

Going shopping prior to learning the permitted subjects: If one will be unable to purchase his Shabbos needs after his learning Seder then he is not to set his learning [of the permitted subjects] for the morning, which is the time that the items are available for purchase.[64]

If ones Shabbos needs are already cared for: [In all the above cases[65]] if one already prepared all his Shabbos needs on Thursday, or he has someone else who is able to do so for him [on Friday] then there is no need for him to diminish in his learning or other activities.

---

[54] SSH"K 42 footnote 129 leaves this matter in question as although it is recognizable that it is being done for the sake of Shabbos, nonetheless perhaps the Sages only permitted haircuts in exchange for payment as it is done to the body of the person. Vetzaruch Iyun.

[55] Mateh Efrayim 625/9; M"B 625/2 [there he writes past midday it is forbidden, however according to the ruling of Admur one may always be lenient according to the opinion which holds Mincha means Mincha Ketana.]

[56] As a) It is for the need of Yom Tov, and B) It is for the sake of a Mitzvah. Vetzaruch Iyun from the wording of Mateh Efrayim and M"B ibid, although perhaps they were merely referring to by what time should one plan to have it built by, and not Bedieved if one did not yet do so.

[57] 250/2-3.
Vetzaruch Iyun why Admur moved the original place of this Halacha from chapter 251, as written in the Rama, to this chapter 250.

[58] The reason for this is in order so one is available to prepare the Shabbos needs. [ibid]

[59] Whether in the Beis Midrash with Chavrusas, or a Shiur given by a Maggid Shiur. [Kuntrus Achron 1]

[60] As the learning which is done within the forum of a Yeshiva does not have a set time limit being that it is common to enter into long Torah debates and analysis. We thus suspect that these debates will carry on for a long time and they will not be left with any time to prepare their Shabbos needs. [ibid]

[61] From the wording of Admur it implies that it is regularly given, however it does not have to be given daily. However in truth one can say that this includes even a case that the Shiur is set only for Erev Shabbos and is not learned any other day of the week. Vetzaruch Iyun.

[62] Kuntrus Achron 1

[63] So is implied from Kuntrus Achron 1. However Tzaruch Iyun how many people have to be learning together for it to be considered "Public" as is a Shiur. As well Tzaruch Iyun if the learning must be done in a Beis Midrash, as is discussing the case of Admur, in order for it to be defined as similar to a Shiur.

[64] The novelty here is seemingly that in a case that one's set time for learning will not give him enough time to reach the store, then he is not to make his learning Seder earlier in the morning and then go shopping but is rather to first go shopping and then have his set Seder. If however ones set learning time is in the morning with enough time left to make the purchases, then there is no need to delay the learning session. Vetzaruch Iyun.

[65] Admur wrote this allowance in 250/2 and then went on to write the above mentioned limitations in 250/3. There thus requires analysis as to

Summary:

If one's Shabbos needs are being taken care of by others, or he has already prepared them on Thursday, then he may continue his learning sessions as usual, without limitation.

If however one needs to personally prepare for Shabbos then he is to diminish in his learning sessions and is only to learn in the following scenarios:

1) It is a non-complicated subject which he learns daily and does not involve long analysis.
2) It is a public learning session which does not involve long analysis, even if not learned daily.
3) Is a subject which is meant to be learned on Erev Shabbos, like Rashi in Chumash.

The above applies only if one has time to still purchase his Shabbos needs at a store. If however the store will be closed by the time his learning session is complete, then he must first go to the store in the morning prior to learning.

whether the allowance is referring to also all the cases mentioned in 250/3. Logically speaking the allowance does apply, as there is no longer need to worry of not having time to prepare for Shabbos. So seems to learn also the Ketzos Hashulchan 70/5 which does not mention any of these laws and simply states if ones preparations are taken care of, no diminishing of his learning is needed. So is also evident from Magen Avraham 251/6 which mentions this allowance only after mentioning all the learning limitations mentioned above, and then concludes "If one prepared on Thursday he may learn as usual". However Tzaruch Iyun why Admur did not then write this allowance at the end of 250/3, after mentioning all the limitations, as is commonly done in the wording of "Beme Devarim Amurim", and rather chose to mention it in 250/2 in the Halacha discussing diminishing learning and activities.

The Kaf Hachayim 251/22 rules that one who has someone else available to prepare his Shabbos needs for him, then he may continue learning as usual.

Chapter 3: Reading Shnayim Mikra

> **Summary of the laws of Shnayim Mikra which are elaborated below:**
> One is to read Shnayim Mikra Echad Targum on Erev Shabbos [immediately] after midday. Prior to reading Shnayim Mikra one is to cut his nails. One reads each Pasuk twice and then immediately reads its Targum, prior to moving on to the next Pasuk. One is not to interrupt at all, even to talk, until he completes the entire reading. After the reading one is to immediately read the Haftorah of that week and in a case that there are two Haftoras both are to be read. After completing the reading one immerses in a Mikveh.

1. The obligation:[1]

In addition to the obligation to hear the reading of the Torah every Shabbos one is also obligated each week to read to himself the weekly Parsha in the form of *Shnayim Mikra Echad Targum* as will be explained next.

> **Q&A**
>
> **Are women obligated to read Shnayim Mikra?**[2]
> No.
>
> **Is a mourner/Avel allowed to read Shnayim Mikra?**
> Although a mourner is forbidden to learn Torah throughout the seven days of mourning[3], including Shabbos[4], nevertheless he is allowed to recite Shnayim Mikra[5] Echad Targum[6], on Shabbos. He may not read it before Shabbos.[7] Some Poskim[8] rule he may not read the commentary of Rashi or any other commentary. However one may look up a verse in English to understand its meaning. However other Poskim[9] rule he may learn the commentary of Rashi if he is accustomed to do so every Shabbos.
>
> ### *The Reward for reading Shnayim Mikra:*[10]
> All those which fulfill the Mitzvah of reading Shnayim Mikra by its proper time are given long days and years.
>
> ### *Sparks of Kabala*[11]
> Reading Shnayim Mikra merits a person to draw down a spirit of purity and receive the extra soul [which is given on Shabbos]. He is then called an "Adam" which is the highest term used to refer to a human. This is hinted to in the verses "And Adam called Sheimos"[12] Sheimos is also the acronym for Shnayim Mikra Echad Targum.

2. What is one obligated to read?[13]

One is obligated to read all the pesukim[14] in the Parsha two times and to read the entire Targum Unkulus of that Parsha. [**see footnote regarding reading other commentaries instead of Targum**[15]] Likewise every G-d fearing

---

[1] 285/1; Based on Tractate Brachos 8a
[2] Mishneh Halachos 6/60
[3] Yoreh Deah 384/1
[4] Yoreh Deah 400/1
[5] ibid
[6] Shach 400/4
[7] Taz 400/1
[8] Beis Lechem Yehuda 400; Bircheiy Yosef 400;
[9] Lechem Hapanim 400/1; Aruch Hashulchan 400/6
[10] Brachos 8b
[11] Brought in Kaf Hachaim 285/32
[12] This refers to Adam Harishon which gave names to all the animals.
[13] 285/1-2
[14] See Halacha 4 Q&A regarding reading the verse of Shema Yisrael twice.
[15] Regarding if one is to read Targum versus another commentary the following is the ruling of Admur in the Shulchan Aruch [285/2]:
First Opinion: Targum Unkelus explains many matters which cannot be understood from the simple reading of the verses. Hence one cannot replace reading the Targum with reading a translation of each word in his language. Furthermore some opinions [Hagahos Maymanis Tefila 13/300 in name of Geonim] say the reading of Targum Unkelous merited taking precedence over any other commentary being that it [or its language of Aramaic-see L.S. Vol. 21 P. 447] was given to Moshe at Sinai [as is evident from the Torah using the words "Yegar Shadusa" in

Jew is to also read the entire commentary of Rashi of that Parsha[16]. If one does not understand the words of Rashi then he is to read another commentary which is written in his language. [Practically it is the Chabad custom to learn every day the daily Torah portion with Rashi, however not to repeat this learning of Rashi when doing Shnayim Mikra.[17]]

A verse which does not contain a Targum translation: Any verse[18] which does not contain a translation in Targum is to be read three times.

The Haftorah:[19] Although from the letter of the law there is no obligation to read the weekly Haftorah to oneself each week, nevertheless the custom is to do so[20]. [On a Shabbos that there are two Haftoras for that week, such as the Shabbos of the 4 Parshiyos, Shabbos Rosh Chodesh, Shabbos Machar Chodesh, Shabbos Chanukah, then one is to read both the Haftorah of the weekly Parsha and the Haftorah which will be read in Shul.[21] **[see footnote]** On

---

Aramaic - Beireishis 31/47], and hence one may only fulfill his obligation through reading the Targum.

Second Opinion: Others [Michaber 285/2] rule that if one reads a commentary on the Torah [irrelevant of language] which explains each and every word of the versus more than does the explanation of Targum, then reading this commentary is better than reading the Targum. Likewise according to this opinion it is better to read the Torah twice and then a third time to read the entire Torah with the commentary of Rashi, then it is to read Targum. The reason for this is because Rashi is based on the fundamentals of the Talmud, and hence explains more than does the Targum. [However even according to this opinion it does not suffice to read the Torah twice and then to go straight to the commentary of Rashi being that Rashi does not explain every verse or word and one is thus lacking the third reading of some words and verses. Hence this option is only valid if one goes back and reads the entire Parsha a third time with Rashi. (Kuntrus Achron 1; however see M"B 285/5)]

Practically the main opinion is like the latter opinion, although a G-d fearing Jew is to read both Targum and Rashi. [285/2]

Summary of ruling of Admur: Based on above it seems that the summary of this Halacha should be as follows: *It is best for one to read the Parsha three times with commentary of Rashi [the main opinion], although a G-d fearing Jew should also read Targum.* So summarizes Kitzur Halachos 285/3. However the Ketzos Hashulchan 72/1 summarizes as written above that first and foremost one is to read the Targum and it is only that a G-d fearing Jew should also read Rashi. Perhaps the reason for this is because according to both opinions one fulfills his obligation with Targum, while with Rashi it is a dispute as explained above. Now, although the main opinion follows that reading Rashi is better, since according to the other opinion one does not fulfill his obligation by doing so, it is ruled that one is to read Targum, and if one is G-d fearing then he should also read Rashi in order to fulfill his obligation the best possible way according to the main opinion. This understanding can also be understood from the wording of Admur in his concluding ruling that "....is to read Targum and also Rashi" hence giving precedence to Targum and making Rashi only secondary. This explanation is unlike the understanding of Kitzur Halachos ibid which gives precedence to Rashi over Targum.

The Kabalistic perspective: Based on Kabala [see below "Sparks of Kabala"] one must read Targum and may not replace it with another commentary. Hence if one does not have time to read both Targum and Rashi he is to read Targum. [Beir Heiytiv 285/2; Shaareiy Teshuvah 285/3 in name of Bircheiy Yosef]

Other Opinions: The Rashal rules that if one is unable to read both Targum and Rashi he is to rather read Rashi. [Brought in Shaareiy Teshuvah ibid]

➢ The practical Custom: In conclusion, practically the Chabad custom is, as written above, to read Targum and only in addition to read Rashi if one so chooses. [Sefer Haminhagim p. 49 [English]; Hayom Yom 30th Sivan]

➢ To summarize the requirements from the letter of the law: From the letter of the law one can either choose to only read Targum [which all agree fulfills one's obligation] or only read a commentary which explains every word, or read the Mikra a 3rd time with Rashi. [As rules the second opinion which is the main opinion.] A G-d fearing Jew is to read both the Targum and Rashi. If one will only be able to read either Targum or Mikra a third time with Rashi, it is better to read Targum [as explained above].

[16] See above footnote for background behind this ruling.

Seemingly Admur singles out learning Rashi over any other commentary due to that Rashi is based on the Talmud and hence is better than other commentaries. To note that according to the opinions which allow reading commentary in place of Targum Admur placed the commentary of Rashi in the plain Halacha and only added other commentaries in parentheses, hence implying that there is room to argue that even according to this opinion which allow other commentaries perhaps they allow only Rashi and not others. To note from Sefer Haminhagim p. 39: The commentary of Rashi on the Torah is the wine of the Torah, it unlocks one's heart and reveals one's innate love and fear of G-d. Studying a section of Chumash with Rashi everyday activates the light within the soul and reveals the soul. This is a glow of the revelation of Moshiach.

[17] So is implied from Sefer Haminhagim ibid that does not mention Rashi as part of being Mavir Sedra. Logically this is because we already fulfill our obligation of Rashi with the reading done during the week. To note however from Igros Kodesh 13 p. 425 that learning the daily Chumash with Rashi is independent of Shnayim Mikra. Perhaps however that means that even without the obligation of Shnayim Mikra it would be done, however once it is done it too counts for one to fulfill the obligation of G-d fearing Jews to learn Rashi.

[18] Such as the versus of the names of the Shevatim.

[19] 285/10;

[20] In order so one be familiar with the Haftorah in case he is called up for Maftir.[ibid] This custom is likewise recorded in Sefer Haminhagim p. 49 [English]; Hayom Yom 30th Sivan.

Nevertheless from the fact that it is our custom to read all the Haftoras of a coming week, even the one which will not be read in Shul such as when Rosh Chodesh falls on Shabbos, makes it evident that this reason alone cannot be the full reason behind reading the Haftorah. This would likewise apply even in accordance to the ruling of Admur in the Shulchan Aruch [see next footnote] that only the Haftorah which will be read in Shul is to be read, as in conclusion Admur rules that when Sos Asis will be read as Haftorah many consecutive weeks one is to read to himself on the second and onward Shabbosim the weekly Haftorah rather than Sos Asis.

Custom to read also the Haftorah with Targum: Some have the custom to read the Haftorah Echad Mikra Vetargum. [M"A 285/8] This is not the Chabad custom.

[21] This ruling follows the custom mentioned in Sefer Haminhagim p. 49 [English]; Hayom Yom 30th Sivan; So rules also Kneses Hagedola; Moreh Betzba

The ruling of Admur in the Shulchan Aruch: In a case that there are two Haftoras that week one is only to read the Haftorah which will be read in public and not the Haftorah of the weekly Parsha. The simple reason behind this ruling is as Admur explained earlier that the entire custom to

Shabbos Chol Hamoed Sukkos and Pesach one is to read to himself both the Haftorah of the Parsha of the coming week and the Haftorah which is read that Shabbos.[22]]

Reading the portions of the Torah prior to a Yom Tov:[23] There is no need to read prior to a Holiday the sections of Torah which will be read on that Holiday.[24]

Reading Vezos Habracha on Erev Simchas Torah:[25] On the eve of Simchas Torah [i.e. Shemini Atzeres in the Diaspora; Hoshana Raba in Eretz Yisrael[26]] one is to read the Parsha of Vezos Habracha, Shnayim Mikra Vechad Targum.[27]

Q&A

Is one who cannot read Hebrew obligated to read Shnayim Mikra in translation to his language?
This matter requires further analysis.[28] [To note however that today there are transliterations available and one is hence to try to read it in transliteration.[29]]

May one read Shnayim Mikra of Vezos Habracha prior to Hoshana Raba?
This matter requires further analysis.[30] Some Poskim[31] have ruled that one does not fulfill his obligation if he did so and he must therefore repeat the reading of the Parsha.

Must one read Shnayim Mikra of the Maftir of the four Parshiyos or Rosh Chodesh?
No.[32] Although some do have a custom to read Shnayim Mikra of the 4 Parshiyos.[33]

Q&A relating to one who traveled from Eretz Yisrael to the Diaspora or vice versa[34]

If one traveled from Eretz Yisrael to the Diaspora in a week that the Diaspora is reading the Parsha that was read the previous Shabbos in Eretz Yisrael, must he re-read Shnayim Mikra[35]?[36]
He is not required to repeat Shnayim Mikra of that Parsha[37], although he is required to hear the reading of the Torah.[38]

---

read the weekly Haftorah is only in order so one be prepared in case he is called up to read it. Hence in a week that it is not being read there is no custom to review it. Nevertheless our custom is to review all the applicable Haftoras. See previous footnote.

[22] Hisvadyus 1985 Vol. 1 p. 351

[23] 285/9

[24] As one has already read, or will read, these portions within their weekly Parsha.

[25] 285/9

[26] After [midday] of Hoshana Raba. We however do not read Shnayim Mikra of Vezos Habracha on the night of Hoshana Raba [after the Tikkun] as is the custom of others. [Sefer Haminhagim p. 145 English, unlike the custom brought in Ketzos Hashulchan 72 footnote 4; So concludes also Peri Megadim A"A 285/10 that although many have the custom to read on the night of Hoshana Raba, it is best to read it on Erev Simchas Torah, and so concludes Ketzos Hashulchan ibid.]
Other customs: Many in Eretz Yisrael are accustomed to read Shnayim Mikra of Vezos Habracha on the night of Hoshana Raba after completing the reading of Mishneh Torah.

[27] As Vezos Habracha is read on Simchas Torah and has not yet been read during the year, hence it is similar to all weekly Torah portions which must be read Shnayim Mikra prior to their being read. [ibid]

[28] Seemingly one is obligated to read the verses in his language, as is the ruling regarding one who does not understand Rashi that he is to read a commentary in the language which he understands. Vetzaruch Iyun as in this case he is still lacking the concept of Mikra, and it is merely like he is reading Targum three times. Vetzaruch Iyun Lemaaseh

[29] Pashut as doing so is no different than reading it in the Hebrew original.

[30] Ketzos Hashulchan 72 footnote 3.
The doubt: Seemingly there is room to say that according to the Poskim which allow completing a Parsha until Shemini Atzeres, the entire year is considered the time for that years Parshiyos, and hence Bedieved one is Yotzei no matter when it was read that year. Vetzaruch Iyun.

[31] Kaneh Bosem 1/16

[32] As is the law regarding the sections read on Yom Tov, being that these sections were, or will be, read in their applicable Parshiyos.

[33] Brought in Piskeiy Teshuvos 285/3

[34] For a thorough analysis on this matter-see Betzeil Hachachmah Vol. 1/2-8

[35] This can occur when the 2nd day of Pesach or Shavuos falls on Shabbos in the Diaspora and hence no Parsha is read, while in Eretz Yisrael the regular weekly Parsha was read. If one travels that week to the Diaspora he will be hearing the same Parsha that he heard the previous Shabbos in Eretz Yisrael.

[36] Ketzos Hashulchan 72 footnote 3

[37] This ruling is evident from Admur 285/9 which does not require one to read Shnayim Mikra of the Yomim Tovim sections prior to each Yom Tov being that it was already read or will be read in its related Shabbos portion. Hence the same logistics apply here and there is no need to repeat Shnayim Mikra.

[38] Piskeiy Teshuvos 285/2

If one will be traveling from Eretz Yisrael to the Diaspora in a week that in Eretz Yisrael the weekly parsha is read while in the Diaspora that Shabbos coincides with Yom Tov[39], is he to read Shnayim Mikra of the Parsha of Eretz Yisrael?[40]
No. One is to do Shnayim Mikra of that Parsha the next week after Yom Tov ends in the Diaspora.

If one traveled to Eretz Yisrael in a week that Eretz Yisrael is reading a different Parsha than the Diaspora[41] which Shnayim Mikra is one to read?[42]
One is to read the Shnayim Mikra of both Parshiyos, the one which he is now missing in the Diaspora and the one which he will now hear in Eretz Yisrael. [If he returns to the Diaspora after Shabbos he is not required to repeat the Shnayim Mikra of the Parsha that was read in Eretz Yisrael and is now being read in the Diaspora.]

Sparks of Kabala-The inner meaning behind reading Targum:
The Shlah Hakadosh [p. 128] writes that on Erev Shabbos the level of Kelipas Nogah requests to be elevated into Holiness. This elevation occurs through the reading of Targum Unkulus. This is because Unkelus was a convert and a convert represents that exact elevation, as a gentile is Kelipa which through conversion entered into holiness.

3. When is one obligated to read Shnayim Mikra?

A. The custom:
The custom is to read the entire Shnayim Mikra Echad Targum after midday on Erev Shabbos.[43] [see footnote]

B. The letter of the law:[44]
The earliest possible to time it is allowed to be read: One is obligated to read the Shnayim Mikra of a specific Parsha during the week that the Parsha is read.[45] Hence each week one is able to fulfill the obligation to read Shnayim Mikra of the upcoming Parsha of that Shabbos beginning from the Sunday of that week. One is not to read Shnayim Mikra of the Parsha prior to that Sunday.
The latest time that it can be read: [For one who did not read Shnayim Mikra on Erev Shabbos[46]] it is a Mitzvah Min Hamuvchar for him to complete the reading of it prior to [Shachris[47] or at the very least prior to] eating the Shabbos morning meal.[48] [See Q&A regarding Kiddush] If one did not complete the reading prior to the meal then it

---

[39] Such as one who travels during Chol Hamoed Pesach, or the week of Shavuos and the second days in the Diaspora coincide with Shabbos.
[40] Piskeiy Teshuvos 285/2
[41] Such as one traveled to Eretz Yisrael the week after a two day Shavuos or Pesach which coincided with Shabbos, in which case Eretz Yisrael is one Parsha ahead in its reading.
[42] Ketzos Hashulchan 72 footnote 3
[43] 285/6 in the first custom mentioned, and so is the Chabad custom as mentioned in Hayom Yom 4th Teveis; Lekutei Sichos 24 p. 342. Beir Heiytiv 285/1 "This is the main Mitzvah". This custom is recorded by the Shalah [p. 128]. Admur writes regarding the reason of this custom "for reasons known to them". The reason recorded by the Shalah is based on Kabala, the reason being due to that on Erev Shabbos Kelipas Nogah requests elevation into Holiness, and the Targum of Unkelus who was a convert represents that exact elevation, hence after midday of Erev Shabbos [when the light of the holiness of Shabbos begins to shine] one is to read Shnayim Mikra Echad Targum and perform the elevation of Kelipas Nogah.
Other Opinions: Others [Arizal brought in Shaareiy Teshuva] are accustomed to read the entire Parsha Shnayim Mikra Echad Targum after prayer on the morning of Erev Shabbos [prior to midday]. [285/6] Although this is the second opinion in Admur and the Rebbe Rashab rules that we always follow the second opinion in a case that no ruling is given [Siddur Im Dach Hosafos p. 12] nevertheless the practical directive is like the first opinion. [L.S. ibid]
The ruling of M"B: The Mishneh Berurah [285/8] brings opinions which say that there is no Mitzvah Min Hamuvchar to read Shnayim Mikra specifically on Erev Shabbos, but rather any day of that week so that it is completed before Shabbos.
[44] 285/5
[45] As one is obligated to read the Parsha simultaneous to when the public reads it, which is only applicable on the week of that Parsha. [ibid]
[46] The Magen Avraham [285/6] rules [in name of Arizal] that one is to only rely on the letter of the law and delay the reading to Shabbos if he was greatly prevented from reading it on Erev Shabbos. He concludes that one is allowed to begin it on Erev Shabbos and then conclude it on Shabbos prior to the morning meal.
[47] M"B 285/9; In Sefer Hasichos 1942 p. 72 it is recorded that one is to try to finish the reading prior to Shachris on Shabbos morning. [See Kitzur Halachos 285 footnote 10*]; Oar Zarua
[48] As so commanded Rabeinu Hakadosh to his children that they should not eat the Shabbos morning meal until they have completed Shnayim Mikra Echad Targum. [ibid]
One is not to delay his meal past midday if he did not yet eat or drink anything at all since the previous night. Likewise one is not to delay his meal to say Shnayim Mikra in a case that he has guests. [M"B 285/9 brought in Ketzos Hashulchan 72 footnote 6]

is an obligation for him to do so after the meal. He must complete the reading prior to [the Shul Minyan[49] of] Mincha.[50] If one transgressed and did not complete the reading prior to the prayer of Mincha then he is to do so prior [to the end of Shabbos[51] and at the very least prior] to Tuesday night.[52] If one did not do so then, he is to complete it until Simchas Torah[53], saying Shnayim Mikra Echad Targum of whatever he missed.[54]

May one read Shnayim Mikra Echad Targum during Kerias Hatorah?[55] There are those[56] which permit to read Shnayim Mikra Echad Targum [to themselves[57]] during the reading of the Torah on Shabbos.[58] [Others[59] however forbid doing so. Practically one is not to do so, as it is proper to listen to the words being read by the Baal Koreh.[60] One may however read along with the Baal Koreh, and doing so is praiseworthy.[61] See next Halacha! It is likewise allowed to read Shnayim Mikra between the Aliyos.[62]]

If one heard Kerias Hatorah prior to saying Shnayim Mikra must he still say each verse twice?[63] In a time of need [such as it is close to Mincha and he does not have enough time to say the Mikra twice[64]] one can rely on the lenient opinion[65] which rules that if one heard the entire Parsha clearly then it counts as one of the two times of reading Mikra and hence he need only read Mikra one time with the Targum [see footnote[66]]. Lechatchilah however if one is

---

[49] As only then does one hear Kerias Hatorah of the next week. [see next footnote] Hence one must finish Shnayim Mikra prior to the last Mincha Minyan in one's town, even if he desires to Daven later alone. Likewise if there are many Shuls and he decided to Daven in an early Minyan, he must finish Shnayim Mikra prior to his Mincha. Vetzaruch Iyun regarding if one's Shul already Davened Mincha and he still did not Daven and has other Minyanim available to Daven with if he follows his personal Shul regarding Shnayim Mikra. [Ketzos Hashulchan 72 footnote 6]

[50] As from Mincha and onwards begins the reading of the next weeks Parsha. This reading thus concludes the final time for being able to read the current weeks Parsha at the same time as is the public. [ibid]
Now, although Admur offers other opinions regarding by when the Parsha must be read, it is only regarding Bedieved if one did not do so that the other opinions rule that one should still read it, however all agree that one is obligated to conclude Shnayim Mikra prior to Mincha as rules the first opinion. [M"B 285/12].

[51] Ketzos Hashulchan 72 footnote 7. This applies even if Shabbos has already ended and one did not yet Daven Maariv, as it still remains Shabbos for the person.
The reason for why one is to read it before he concludes Shabbos: 1) There are opinions which rules one cannot say Havdala until Tuesday. According to this opinion there is likewise no allowance to make up the reading of Shnayim Mikra until Tuesday. However even according to them one may still complete the reading on Shabbos. 2) The Kol Bo rules one may not say the next weeks Parsha past Mincha while still Shabbos. This shows Shabbos still has a connection to the previous weeks Parsha 3) Logically it would be better to make up the reading on a day that is still part of Shabbos itself over a day that just has a connection with the previous Shabbos. [ibid]

[52] This follows the opinion of the Hagahos Maimanis in name of Mahram which rules that Bedieved one has until Tuesday to complete Shnayim Mikra. It is in contrast to the first opinion mentioned by Admur which rules that after Mincha one can no longer fulfill his obligation of Shnayim Mikra. Admur concludes that it is good to suspect for the lenient opinion and still read the Shnayim Mikra by Tuesday if one transgressed.
The reason for having until Tuesday: As until Tuesday the days still carry a connection to the previous Shabbos as is evident from the ruling that Havdala may be said until Tuesday. [ibid]

[53] This follows the opinion of the Hagahos Maimanis in name of Rabbeinu Simcha which rules that Bedieved one has until Simchas Torah to complete it. It is in contrast to the first two opinions mentioned by Admur [see previous footnote] which rule that after Mincha or at the very least by Wednesday the chance is lost. Admur concludes that it is good to suspect to this lenient opinion and still read the Shnayim Mikra before Simchas Torah if one transgressed.
The reason for having until Simchas Torah: As by then the entire congregation completes the entire Torah. [ibid]

[54] This negates the custom of those which only say the Mikra and not the Targum when completing the Parsha past its initial time, prior to Simchas Torah.

[55] 285/8

[56] Michaber 146/2 as rules Murdechaiy; Hagahos Ashriy; Reb Yehuda Hachasid; Terumas Hadeshen.
The Elya Raba rules that not only is this allowed but it is a mitzvah Min Hamuvchar. However the Mamar Murdechaiy argues on the ability to call this leniency a Mitzvah Min Hamuvchar, See Biur Halacha 285 "Yachol".

[57] So as not to disturb the listeners. [Peri Megadim, brought in M"B 146/11]

[58] It is permitted to read even a different section in that Parsha than the section which the Baal Korah is reading. The reason for this allowance is because at the end of the day the reader is involved within the same topic as is the Baal Korah. [Peri Megadim, brought in M"B 146/11] This allowance applies even if he is part of the 10 listeners. [Magen Avraham 146/5 in name of Terumas Hadeshen]

[59] Peri Chadash; Magen Avraham [146/5] in name of Shalah is stringent in this. [M"B 146/15]

[60] Final ruling of Michaber 146/2 as explained in M"B 14 to be referring also to Shnayim Mikra; M"B 285/14

[61] Magen Avraham 146/5

[62] M"B 146/15; 185/14

[63] 285/8

[64] Ketzos Hashulchan 72 footnote 1;
Other cases of need: It is close to Tuesday night and he has not yet said it. It is Simchas Torah and he does not have enough time to say each verse twice of all the versus that he missed.

[65] Some opinions [M"A 285/8; see Shaareiy Teshuvah 285/6] say that one fulfills his obligation of the reading of Mikra one time with hearing clearly the entire Parsha read by Kerias Hatorah. However even according to them this is only Bedieved. However Lechatchilah one is not to rely on his hearing [as perhaps he will become distracted in middle-59/4], rather he is to read it himself [either during the Keria or before or after]. Others however say that one does not fulfill his obligation at all with hearing the reading, as the entire obligation originally was that one read Shnayim Mikra in addition to the Torah reading. Practically Admur rules one may be lenient in a time of need. [ibid]

[66] The Ketzos Hashulchan 72 footnote 1 rules that after Mincha or after Tuesday one is to read the Mikra an additional time in order to fulfill his obligation even according to those which rule that one does not fulfill his obligation with the hearing of the Torah. [This however is not the simple implication from Admur, and so seems to be the logical ruling as Shnayim Mikra is Rabbinical. Vetzaruch Iyun]

holding prior to the reading of the Torah he is not to rely on hearing it, even in a time of need[67], but is rather to read along with the Baal Koreh, and then afterwards read Mikra one time with Targum.

Q&A

Is one to read Shnayim Mikra before or after going to Mikveh on Erev Shabbos?[68]
One is to go to Mikveh only after having first completed saying Shnayim Mikra.

Is one to cut his nails prior to Shnayim Mikra?
Some Poskim[69] rule the proper order is to cut the nails[70], then read Shnayim Mikra and then immerse in the Mikveh. However in *Peri Eitz Chaim* it states to cut the nails after Shnayim Mikra, prior to immersing in the Mikveh.[71]

Is one to begin reading Shnayim Mikra immediately after midday of Erev Shabbos, or may it be delayed?
There is no obligation to begin Shnayim Mikra immediately after midday.[72] Nevertheless it is proper not to delay the reading of Shnayim Mikra once it is past midday. One is thus not to delay reading it due to a private learning session and is rather first to say Shnayim Mikra and then to learn. Nevertheless by a public learning session there is no restraint to delay Shnayim Mikra until afterwards.[73]

May one make Kiddush and eat a snack prior to reading Shnayim Mikra by Shabbos day?[74]
Yes. One may make Kiddush and eat a snack prior to saying Shnayim Mikra on Shabbos day. However one is to refrain from eating a set meal prior to Shnayim Mikra as stated in Admur.[75]

When is the Haftorah to be read?
The Haftorah is to be read on Erev Shabbos [immediately[76]] after reading Shnayim Mikra.[77] At the very least it is to be read before the Haftorah is read in Shul.[78] If one did not read it by this time, he should read it afterwards.[79]

---

[67] This applies even in accordance to the lenient opinion-see previous footnote.

[68] M"A 285/1

This was the custom of the Arizal [Brought in Kaf Hachayim 260/7; M"A ibid] and so writes Shalah p. 138 explicitly in Hagah that one is to read Shnayim Mikra prior to immersing. So rules also Oar Tzadikim 28/18 stating that if one immerses prior to Shnayim Mikra he does not have the ability to receive the holiness of Shabbos.

This is unlike what is written in the Peri Megadim 260 A"A 1 in name of Eliyah Raba [260/4] **in name of Shalah** that one is to immerse prior to Shnayim Mikra. After researching this seeming contradiction the following was discovered: The Eliyah Raba [260/4] himself never makes such a claim and rather simply states in name of Shalah that one is to cut his nails prior to Shnayim Mikra, and does not discuss immersion in that regard. Furthermore, in some prints of the Peri Megadim the entire novelty of immersion after Shnayim Mikra was placed in brackets hence lending suspicion as to the accuracy of what in truth the Peri Megadim wrote. Due to all above seemingly there was a misprint in some versions of the Eliyah Raba or the Peri Megadim. This seemingly occurred due to a misreading of the word "Yitol" [take the nails] which was read "Yitvol" [immerse] and hence this caused the change. In any event the ruling of the Shalah is clear as written in his Sefer Shlah Hakadosh, that one is to immerse after Shnayim Mikra! In light of all the above there is no room for the ruling brought in Piskeiy Teshuvos 260/1 or 285/1. [In the new edition of Piskeiy Teshuvos 260/4 they fixed the ruling and wrote as we stated above.]
Other Opinions: Siddur Yaavetz rules one is to immerse prior to Shnayim Mikra.

[69] M"A 285/1; Shalah P. 138 in the "Hagah"

[70] See Chapter 1 Halacha 17 for all the opinions on this matter.

[71] See Shaareiy Halacha Uminhag 1/130

[72] As from the letter of the law it may be recited up until Mincha, and the Mitzvah Min Hamuvchar is to recite it prior to the morning meal. Thus there is no requirement to recite it immediately after midday on Friday.

[73] See Igros Kodesh 19 p. 370

[74] Ketzos Hashulchan 72 footnote 6

[75] As the reason for why Rabbeinu Hakadosh told his children to finish Shnayim Mikra prior to the morning meal, is so they not become too indulged within the meal and come to forget to say it. [Oar Zarua] This reason is not applicable by a mere snack. Furthermore, it is illogical to say that eating before Shnayim Mikra would be more severe than eating prior to Mincha, in which case eating a snack before Mincha is allowed. [ibid]

[76] See Halacha 4 Q&A

[77] Sefer Haminhagim p. 49

[78] As the main reason behind the custom is so one be prepared to read the Haftorah if he is called up. [285/10]

[79] Ketzos Hashulchan 72 footnote 12, following the ruling of Kneses Hagedola, Moreh Etzba that when there are two Haftoras even the Haftorah which will not be read on Shabbos is to be read for Shnayim Mikra.

May one read Shnayim Mikra of next week on Shabbos after Mincha[80]?
Yes.[81] However some Poskim rule that this matter requires further analysis.[82]

If one read Shnayim Mikra of a Parsha prior to the week of that Parsha must he repeat the reading when that weeks Parsha arrives[83]?
This matter requires further analysis.[84] Some Poskim[85] however rule that one does not fulfill his obligation and he must repeat the reading of the Parsha.

If a certain Parsha will not be read on Shabbos that coming week due to Shabbos coinciding with Yom Tov, when one may begin reading Shnayim Mikra of that Parsha?[86]
Only from the Sunday of the week that the Parsha will be read on Shabbos.

By what time on Simchas Torah should Shnayim Mikra of the previous year's Parshiyos be completed?[87]
One is to complete all the previous year's Shnayim Mikra by Shachris of Simchas Torah.[88] If one did not do so then he may complete it until the end of Simchas Torah.[89] If Simchas Torah fell on Shabbos, as occasionally occurs in Eretz Yisrael, one may in a time of need complete the reading until Tuesday of that week.[90]

When making up Parshiyos of previous weeks should any specific order to be followed?
One is to read it in the order of the Parshiyos.[91] However some Poskim[92] rule the current weeks Parsha is to be read first.
[Seemingly if one will not be able to read up to the currents weeks Parsha in time to finish it by its proper time, then even according to the first opinion he is to say the current weeks Parsha first and then go in order of the Parshiyos he missed.]

If one is in doubt as to whether he said Shnayim Mikra of a certain Parsha must he now say it?
- Example 1: One has to make up a number of Parshiyos from previous weeks and does not recall from which Parsha he has to make up.
- Example 2: One is accustomed to read Shnayim Mikra at the beginning of each week, and now before Shabbos he does not recall if he did so.

By Example 1 there is no requirement for one to read those Parshiyos in which he has doubt[93], however seemingly if possible it is best for one to do so.
By Example 2 this matter requires further analysis as on the one hand it is a doubt in a Rabbinical matter, on the other hand one is easily able to remove himself from the doubt.

---

[80] I.e. If this week is Parshas Lechlecha, may one begin reading Shnayim Mikra of Vayeira beginning from after Mincha of this Shabbos?

[81] M"B 285/7, Shaareiy Tziyon 12

[82] So writes Peri Megadim [A"A 285/5]; Ketzos Hashulchan 72 footnote 3.
Background: The Mordechaiy rules that one who reads from after Mincha of Shabbos the next weeks Shnayim Mikra has fulfilled his obligation. However the Kol Bo rules one has not fulfilled his obligation. [Beis Yosef; Darchei Moshe 1 brought in PM"G ibid]
Ruling of Admur: Admur rules [285/5] that one is to finish that weeks Shnayim Mikra by Mincha of Shabbos, as after the Torah reading of Mincha the new week's portion has begun. This implies that immediately after Mincha one may already begin reading Shnayim Mikra of next week. So implies the Peri Megadim also from similar wording of the Kneses Hagedola. Vetzrauch Iyun why the Ketzos Hashulchan left this matter in question despite Admur's clear wording.

[83] i.e. One read Shnayim Mikra of Vayeira on Erev Shabbos Lech Lecha.

[84] Ketzos Hashulchan 72 footnote 3.
The doubt: Seemingly there is room to say that according to the Poskim which allow completing a Parsha until Shemini Atzeres, the entire year is considered the time for that years Parshiyos, and hence Bedieved one is Yotzei no matter when it was read that year. Vetzaruch Iyun.

[85] Kaneh Bosem 1/15

[86] Kaneh Bosem 1/16

[87] Ketzos Hashulchan 72 footnote 9

[88] As in Shachris one hears the reading of Bereishis which is the start of the new year's cycle and represents the end of the previous year's cycle. [ibid] Kaf Hachayim

[89] Just as is the law after Mincha of Shabbos. [ibid] However the Kaf Hachayim rules after the Torah reading on Simchas Torah Shnayim Mikra of the previous year can no longer be recited.

[90] Similar to the ruling by all Shabbosim. [ibid]

[91] Ketzos Hashulchan 72 footnote 9; See Teshuvahs Mahrsham 213 who brings a proof from Tzemach Tzedek to rule this way. See Ketzos Hashulchan ibid for why there is no problem that one is first reading the Tashlumin and then the Choveh, even though by Davening we rule one must first Daven the Choveh and then the Tashlumin.

[92] Betzeil Hachachma 1/9; See Shut Mahrsham ibid

[93] As even in a case one knows for certain he missed a Parsha it is only "proper" for him to still read it suspecting for the stringent opinion that he can still make it up. Hence certainly here that one is in doubt there is no requirement to read it.

May one read Shnayim Mikra at night?

One is not to read Shnayim Mikra at night[94] with exception to Friday night in which case it may be read[95]. Regarding Thursday night see footnote[96].

One may read Shnayim Mikra at night if he reads it together with a commentary such as Rashi.[97] Nevertheless even in such a case he is not to read Targum at night.[98]

Can one fulfill his obligation of Shnayim Mikra through hearing someone else read it?

Some opinions[99] rule one is able to fulfill his obligation through listening to each and every word being read by another person. Practically one may not initially rely on this.[100]

___

The Custom of the Chabad Rabbeim:[101]

The Rabbeim of Chabad were accustomed to read the first, and at times also the second, section of the weekly Parsha Shnayim Mikra Echad Targum on Thursday night.[102] They would then repeat the entire reading of the Parsha Shnayim Mikra Echad Targum together with the Haftorah after midday Friday. On Shabbos day prior to Shachris they would repeat the seventh section Shnayim Mikra.

4. How is it to be read?

One is to read each verse twice and then immediately read the Targum on that verse prior to continuing on to the next verse. This order is followed throughout the entire reading.[103] Nevertheless, from the letter of the law one may read the verses with Targum in whichever order one chooses. [**see footnote**[104]] Hence if one does not have a Targum available he may read the entire Mikra twice and then read the Targum when it becomes available.[105]

___

[94] Beir Heiytiv 238/2 states in name of Arizal that one is not to learn Tanach at night. This ruling is quoted by many Poskim. So also rules the Rebbe as is evident from Shaareiy Halacha Uminhag 1/24;

Regarding Shnayim Mikra: So is ruled explicitly in Lekutei Mahrich [Seder Kevius Itim Letorah] that Shnayim Mikra is not to be said at night.

Other Poskim: Shaareiy Tziyon 238/1 rules one may read Mikra at night, however it is better to do so during the day.

Regarding if one may read Mikra after midnight: No. This allowance only applies to Tehillim. [Kaf Hachayim 237/9; Ben Ish Chaiy Pekudeiy 7; Lekutei Mahrich ibid; Shaareiy Halacha Uminhag ibid]

[95] Ben Ish Chaiy Pekudeiy 7; Kaf Hachayim 237/9

[96] Some opinions allow reading Mikra on Thursday nights. [Oar Tzadikim] Others go even further to state it is customary to recite Shnayim Mikra specifically on Thursday night. [Machazikei Bracha in name of Rashash] Nevertheless some rule this allowance applies only to Mikra and not Targum. [Machazikei Bracha brought in Lekutei Mahrich ibid] To note however from the custom of the Chabad Rabbeim [Hayom Yom 4th Teves] to read the first and at times also the second portion of the Parsha on Thursday night. It is implied there from the wording [Maavir Sedra] that they also read Targum.

[97] Yesod Veshoresh Havodah Shaar Hanitzutz chapter 2; Shaareiy Halacha Uminhag ibid

[98] Lekutei Mahrich ibid

[99] Machazikei Bracha brought in Shaareiy Teshuvah 285/6

[100] As rules Admur regarding being Yotzei with the Baal Korei.

[101] Hayom Yom 4th Teves [To note this custom was omitted from Sefer Haminhagim, Vetzrauch Iyun if it is to be followed by Chassidim or is within those customs that are specifically designated for the Rabbeim.]

[102] This follows the opinion of the Rashash which states it is customary to recite Shnayim Mikra specifically on Thursday night. [Machazikei Bracha in name of Rashash] Nevertheless some hold this allowance applies only to Mikra and not Targum. [Machazikei Bracha brought in Lekutei Mahrich ibid] However from the wording of Hayom Yom it implies the Rabbeim would likewise read Targum.

[103] 285/3 following the second custom recorded by Admur there. Admur concludes "and this custom is more proper". So is also the practical custom as recorded in Sefer Haminhagim p. 49 [English]; Hayom Yom 30th Sivan. This was the custom of the Arizal. [M"A 285/1]

The reason for why this custom is the most proper: As this follows the same order of the Torah reading of the past which was done by reading the Targum of each verse directly after reading that verse. [ibid]

Other opinions: Some [Shalah; Rashal] have the custom to read a section [of Pesucha/Setuma] twice and then immediately read the Targum of that section prior to beginning the next section. This order is followed throughout the entire Parsha. [First opinion recorded in Admur ibid]

The ruling of the Mishneh Berurah: The Mishneh Berurah [285/2] rules that one may follow whichever opinion he chooses.

[104] 285/3. This implies that one may even read the entire Parsha twice and only then read the Targum, or read an entire Aliyah and then read its Targum etc. This is unlike any of the customs mentioned by Admur, although as he concludes from the letter of the law all methods are valid. See also the next sentence in which Admur rules that in case of need this is the course that one is to follow [reading first the entire Mikra].

Other orders of reading: One fulfills his obligation if he read the Mikra once, then the Targum and then again the Mikra. [285/7] However seemingly this is only Bedieved, as Lechatchila one is always to first read the Mikra twice. [Ketzos Hashulchan 72 footnote 1; Kitzur Halachos 285 footnote 6]

Vetzaruch Iyun if one fulfills his obligation if he reads the Targum **prior** to reading the Mikra even once. [Ketzos Hashulchan ibid; From M"B 285/6 it is implied one does not fulfill his obligation, although perhaps he too meant to leave this matter unresolved. See there.]

[105] 285/6

The last verse: [106] The last verse of the Parsha is to be read a total of three times, twice before saying the Targum, and a third time after the Targum. This is done in order to complete the reading of the Parsha with a Torah verse, as was done in past times when the Targum was read during the public Torah reading, after each verse[107]. [Nevertheless, despite this ruling of Admur in his Shulchan Aruch, it is not the Chabad custom to repeat the last verse a third time.[108]]

May it be read in segments? May one talk in middle or take a break? [109] Some[110] are accustomed[111] not to talk at all, or make any type of interval, throughout the entire reading of Shnayim Mikra. Hence they read it from beginning to end without interruption. [This is a very proper custom, and is followed by those meticulous in Mitzvos.[112] Those which follow this custom must start over again from the beginning if they talked or made an interval in between.[113] See Q&A!] However from the letter of the law there is no requirement to read the entire Parsha Shnayim Mikra in one period, rather one may even read only the Mikra of one section today, the Mikra of another section tomorrow and so on and so forth throughout the week.[114] Hence one who learns the daily Chumash is from the letter of the law considered to have fulfilled the reading of Mikra [up to Shevii] one time and hence must only say the Mikra once with Targum [up to Shevii, while Shevii is said twice]. If he is accustomed to read each verse twice while learning, then he has to only make up the Targum.[115] [Nevertheless the custom as explained above is to re-read the entire Parsha Shnayim Mikra Echad Targum on Erev Shabbos.]

Reading from a Sefer Torah: [116] One who knows by heart the tunes [which mark the end of each verse[117]] in the Torah reading, is proper for him to read Shnayim Mikra from a Kosher Torah scroll on each and every Erev Shabbos.[118] [This however is not the Chabad custom, or the custom of many other Gedolei Yisrael, as by doing so one is unable to read the Targum after each verse.[119] Hence we read it from printed Chumashim which contain Targum.[120] One who does not know the Taamim by heart is not to read from the Torah according to all.[121]]

---

[106] 285/3

[107] Then too the last verse would be repeated after its Targum was read. [Ibid]

[108] Shaareiy Halacha Uminhag Vol. 5/28; However see Ketzos Hashulchan 72/3 and Kitzur Halachos 285/5 that mention this ruling without remark that this is not the followed Chabad custom.

[109] 285/6

[110] Shlah [Torah Oar 138a] in name of Ramak, and so is recorded also in Olas Shabbos 285/2; M"A 285/11; See next footnote. To note the Rebbe in Lekutei Sichos 24 p. 342 does not unequivocally state that it is our custom to follow this opinion and rather uses the wording "those that are stringent to follow this custom". This is in contrast to other matters of Shnayim Mikra mentioned in the above letter in which the Rebbe explicitly states the Chabad custom.

[111] The Beir Heiytiv [285/1] writes "It is a great prohibition to speak in middle of Shnayim Mikra". The M"B in Shaareiy Tziyon 285/11 explains this to refer to speaking in middle of a Parsha [Pesucha/Setuma] as it is considered like one who is interrupting his Torah study for mundane matters. However between Parshiyos everyone agrees that from the letter of the law it is allowed. Admur however makes no mention of there being any prohibition involved and rather simply mentions it as a custom. The M"A 285/11 simply writes it is proper not to talk in-between.

[112] M"B 285/6; So rules also Kaf Hachaim 285/32

[113] Lekutei Sichos 24 p. 342; Kaf Hachaim 285/32

[114] Vetzaruch Iyun from Admur's conclusion "and after that one reads the **Mikra in order**". What is the meaning of this? Is one required to read at least one time the entire Mikra in order? In Ketzos Hashulchan 72/2 and Kitzur Halachos this conclusion is omitted. In Kuntrus Hashulchan p. 31 [of the same author of Ketzos Hashulchan] he edits that the words should read "and after that one reads the **Targum in order**". His basis is that it is untrue to say that one would be required to read the entire Mikra at least one time in order, as such a law does not exist. Hence he edits that it must have said Targum.

[115] Based on 285/7 regarding a Melameid Tinokos.

[116] 285/4

No leniency is however to be learned from this law regarding reading from a Sefer Torah without due reason. See Shach Yoreh Deah 270/5; Nemukei Orach Chayim 669/2 towards end; Shut Marsham 175

[117] Meaning that he knows by which word each verse ends. [Ketzos Hashulchan 72 footnote 1, derived from Admur's additional word "**Piskeiy Taamim**"] The reason for why one must know the end of each verse by heart as a condition to read from the Torah is because it is forbidden for one to stop in middle of a verse that Moshe did not stop by [494/11], and if one does not know the end of each verse certainly he will end up stopping in middle of some of the verses.

[118] This was the custom of the Arizal [Shaar Hakavanos] and of the Taz [Taz 285/1]. The Taz [ibid] rules that each person should read the Mikra at least one time from a Kosher Sefer Torah, as from a mere Chumash one does not properly fulfill his obligation.

[119] The Arizal however would have a student read him the Targum and he would then repeat it after them. [ibid]

[120] Hisvadyus 1988 Vol. 2 p. 167; Lekutei Sichos 24 p. 214 footnote 59; letters printed in Shaareiy Halacha Uminhag 2/189

[121] As he will not know by which word to end each verse. See previous footnotes

Q&A

Is one to read the Pasuk of Shema Yisrael twice?[122]

The verse Shema Yisrael is to be read twice as is the law by all Pesukim. However some Poskim[123] rule one is not to read the Pasuk twice in a row, and is rather to read a few more Pesukim in between. The custom is unlike this opinion.

Is one to read the Parsha with the tune of the Torah reading [Taamim]?

Some Poskim[124] rule one is initially required to read the verses with their tune even when doing so from a Chumash. Practically this is the custom.[125] Nevertheless this is not critical for fulfilling one's obligation.[126] Hence if one does not know the tune of the verses he is to read it without the tune. Likewise if one already read it without the tune, then even if he knows the tune, he is not required to repeat the reading.

Must the verses be read in order?[127]

Yes. One is not to read a later verse prior to reading an earlier verse. Nevertheless, after the fact if one did not read the verse in order he has nevertheless fulfilled his obligation.[128]

Q&A on Interruptions during Shnayim Mikra

May one learn other Mefarshim while saying Shnayim Mikra if he is stringent not to make any interruptions until he completes the reading?

No. Those which are particular not to interrupt when saying Shnayim Mikra are not to learn even other Mefarshim while saying Shnayim Mikra. They are rather to read it straight from beginning to end without any interval at all.[129]

If one used the bathroom while saying Shnayim Mikra is he to say Asher Yatzar after leaving the bathroom if he is stringent not to make any interruptions until he completes the reading?[130]

One is to say Asher Yatzar immediately after leaving the bathroom, and is not to delay it until later on.[131]

May one initially use the bathroom in middle of Shnayim Mikra if he is stringent not to make any interruptions until he completes the reading?

The Ramak[132] writes that one is not to initially use the bathroom until he finishes Shnayim Mikra even if he feels the need to go.[133] However from the Poskim[134] it is evident that one may certainly use the bathroom, even according to this custom.

---

[122] Ketzos Hashulchan 72 footnote 10; Shaareiy Halacha Uminhag Vol. 5/28

[123] Mishmeres Shalom 24

[124] _Machazikei Bracha_, brought in _Kaf Hachayim_ 285; _Ketzos Hashulchan_ 72 footnote 1; _Kitzur Halachos_ 285 footnote 8;
So can also be deduced from the _Peri Megadim_ [285 A"A 9] which rules based on 285/7 that reading the Taamim is not critical to fulfilling the obligation. This implies there is reason to assume that it should be required initially.
So can also be deduced from _Radbaz_ brought in _Magen Avraham_ 285 regarding one who knows the Taamim by heart that he is to read from a Sefer Torah, hence implying that all are to read the Taamim [and hence if one does not know the Taamim by heart it is better to read from a Chumash with the Taamim]. [Ketzos Hashulchan ibid]
<u>Opinion of Admur</u>: From Admur's wording of "**Piskeiy** Taamim" which is in addition to the wording of the Magen Avraham, hence implying that the Taamim themselves need not be read. Perhaps however this is merely coming to teach that it is better to read from a Sefer Torah without the Taamim than from a Chumash with the Taamim, so long as one knows where to stop. Nevertheless even Admur would agree that when reading from a Chumash it is better to do so with the Taamim. [Ketzos Hashulchan ibid]

[125] Ketzos Hashulchan ibid

[126] Peri Megadim 285 A"A 9; Ketzos Hashulchan ibid; M"B 285/17
So is implied from the lack of this requirement or enhancement of the Mitzvah being mentioned in Shulchan Aruch. So is also implied from 285/7 regarding the Melameid who fulfils his obligation of Mikra while teaching without tune. [Peri Megadim 285 A"A 9]
So is also implied from Admur 285/4 which added "Piskeiy Taamim. See previous footnotes.

[127] Ketzos Hashulchan 72 footnote 5; M"B 285/6

[128] As even by the actual Torah reading if read out of order one fulfills his obligation.

[129] So is implied from Poskim brought in Kaf Hachaim 285/32 which write one is not to even interrupt Shnayim Mikra for words of Torah; So is also implied from the wording of the Ramak brought in Shlah 138a. However later on in Ramak he states that one says "Shnayim Mikra Echad Targum with Unkolus **or other translation**". To note however that there he was referring to the Shnayim Mikra of the Haftorah and not of the Parsha.

[130] Piskeiy Teshuvos 285 footnote 30

[131] As he may come to forget to say it later on, as well as that perhaps he may need to go to the bathroom another time prior t completing Shnayim Mikra in which case he enters into a dispute amongst Poskim in whether he may still say Asher Yatzar/ [ibid]

[132] Brought in Shlah 138a; There he writes "After reciting Shnayim Mikra without any interruption, not even for his needs" In general in Halacha the term "Tzrachav, needs" refers to using the bathroom.

[133] Seemingly this does not transgress the prohibition of Baal Tishaktzu as one is allowed to withhold his needs for the sake of a Mitzvah. [See

May one who is thirsty have a drink in middle of Shnayim Mikra if he is stringent not to speak until the end of Shnayim Mikra?
If one is very thirsty some Poskim[135] write that he may drink in middle of the reading and say a blessing before and after.

According to the stringent custom brought above is one to read the Haftorah right after he completes the reading of the Parsha without interrupting in-between?
The Ramak[136] writes that one is to read the Haftorah immediately after finishing the reading of the Parsha without making any interruptions in-between.

Sparks of Kabala
Reason why one is not to interrupt in the midst of Shnayim Mikra:[137]
Reading Shnayim Mikra Echad Targum has the power to create an angle. One who makes an interruption in the midst of reading it enters impurity into this angle.

Admur 3/11 Basra; and Siddur as explained in Ketzos Hashulchan 19 footnote 27 that one may not use the bathroom for a bowel movement in the midst of Davening beginning from Baruch Sheamar.
[134] Lev Chaim 3/23 brought in Kaf Hachaim 285/15 regarding the allowance to drink in the middle
[135] Lev Chaim 3/23 brought in Kaf Hachaim 285/15
[136] Brought in Shlah 138a
[137] Kaf Hachaim 285/32

Chapter 4: Traveling on Erev Shabbos:

1. Traveling On Erev Shabbos:[1]

One must reach his Shabbos destination prior to 4 hours and 48 minutes[2] [see footnote] having passed from the beginning of day.[3] [See Q&A] This is due to concern that if he arrives later than the above time there will not be enough time to prepare food for him for Shabbos. This applies even if one is traveling for Shabbos to his own family[4], as we suspect that perhaps they do not at all know that he is arriving and will thus not have prepared food for him.[5] (This applies whether one is traveling by foot, horse, caravan, [bus, car or train] and thus one must arrive to his destination prior to 4 hours and 48 minutes into the day lest he not have enough time to prepare food for Shabbos.[6])

In the following cases the above obligation does not apply and one may travel to his destination anytime on Erev Shabbos:

1. One has already informed his host, or family, that he will be coming for Shabbos. [One must inform the host prior to 4 hours and 48 minutes passing from the start of the day.[7]]

2. The host has a custom to cook a lot for Shabbos in way there is anyways always enough food for guests to eat even without prior notice. Thus being that today majority of people cook extra food for Shabbos, if one plans to eat by a host or by his own family at that destination, it is no longer the custom to be careful to arrive at his destination prior to the above mentioned time.[8] [Likewise if it is common to sell readymade Shabbos foods at one's destination, he does not need to be careful to arrive prior to the above mentioned time.[9]]

3. If in the area one is now in he is unable to prepare for himself Shabbos food, and is unable to eat as a guest in another's home in that area, then he may travel to the nearest area which has food for Shabbos even if he will only arrive at the end of the day.

4. If the area one is now in is a place of danger then he may travel to the nearest safe area even if he will only

---

[1] 249/1-4

[2] 249/3; Lit. "One may not walk more than 3 Parsaos". The intent of this is to say that one may not arrive past the amount of time it takes to walk this amount of distance. Practically in time amounts, the amount of time it takes to walk 3 Parsaos [12 Mil; 4 Mil per Parsa] is 4 hours and 48 minutes according to ruling of Admur in 459 that a Mil is 24 minutes, and so rules Magen Avraham. However according to those opinions [Michaber and others] which rule that a Mil is 18 minutes the amount of time it takes to walk 3 Parsaos is 3 hours and 36 minutes. According to them one must arrive at his destination within 3 hours and 36 minutes from the beginning of the morning.

[3] So adds Admur [and Mishneh Berurah 249/1] "from the beginning of the day" as is the wording in the Rambam. However the Michaber simply writes not to walk 3 Parsaos" and omits "from the beginning of the day. This can allow one to learn that the Issur is specifically to travel a distance of 3 Parsaos by foot, as by foot one can become tired and will no longer be able to travel. However by caravan or horse it would be allowed to travel any time during the day, and any distance of travel, as learns the Bach. Thus Admur's addition of "from the beginning of the day" negates this explanation. [see Peri Megadim 249 A"A 1 and coming footnotes]
However Tzaruch Iyun why the wording in the Shulchan Aruch is not written as brought above "one may not arrive at his destination past etc" and rather they write simply that it is forbidden to walk more than 3 Parsaos from the beginning of the day. This latter wording [besides for not being a clear definition of the prohibition] can lead one to wrongly deduce that the entire Issur is for one to walk more than 3 parsaos, similar to the way the Bach learns, and not that he must arrive by a certain time. Vetzrauch Iyun. Perhaps however one can say that the Sages wanted to teach us that by walking, he may never walk more than 3 parsaos from daybreak, irrelevant to how long or short it takes him [as rules Admur in 249/3], and thus they did not word the prohibition "one must arrive by this and this time". In any event it remains clear from the Halachas brought in Admur [1-4] that the prohibition applies in all cases, whether by walking, traveling by car or the like, and that its intent is that when traveling by car and the like one may not arrive past the above mentioned time, and not that there is a limit in how much of a distance one may travel.

[4] Lit. Bnei Beiso. So writes Tur/Michaber/Admur.

[5] 249/1

[6] 249/3 Parentheses are in original. When traveling by foot one may not walk more than 3 Parsaos from the beginning of the day [even if he is able to walk more than 3 Parsaos within the above mentioned time]. However when traveling by horse, car and the like then he may travel even many Parsaos, so long as he arrives within 4 hours and 48 minutes from the beginning of the day. [249/3]
Other Poskim: However there are Poskim [Bach, brought in M"A/M"B 249/1; similarly Admur only brings the previous ruling in parentheses thus hinting to the possibility of learning as does the Bach] that rule that when traveling by horse and the like one may travel anytime on Erev Shabbos, even past midday, as they learn that only when traveling by foot does the above suspicion apply, as he may become tired out. [Peri Megadim 249 A"A 1 as he learns Bach]

[7] Pashut, as otherwise it is similar to arriving pass this time.

[8] 249/4. The wording of Admur seems to imply the following:
    A. One may travel anytime on Erev Shabbos even if he does not know for a fact that his potential host in truth makes extra food for Shabbos, being that majority do so.
    B. If one does know for certain that a certain host does not make extra food for Shabbos, he must arrive prior to the above mentioned time, unless the host has been made known of his arrival. [However perhaps one can say that even in such a case one may arrive later as even if his potential host will not have enough food, there are others who will].
    C. If one will be making his own food upon arriving to his destination, he must arrive prior to the above mentioned time.
To note: The Ketzos Hashulchan 69/2 rules plainly based on the above Halacha that whenever one is traveling to his family or a host he may travel any time during the day.

[9] Kaf Hachaim 249/8

arrive at end of the day, as to remain in an unsafe area will make him completely devoid of Oneg Shabbos.

Summary:
In today's times that families generally prepare extra Shabbos food it is permitted to travel to the home of one's host any time on Erev Shabbos, even if the host has not yet been informed of one's intended arrival. [10] It is certainly permitted to travel any time on Erev Shabbos if one has already informed his host of his intended arrival. [11]
Practical application of when the above travel limitation would apply: The application of the above law in light of today's advanced form of communication would be practical mainly in a scenario that one is traveling to a hotel or cabin for Shabbos and will be making his own food upon arrival, in which case he must arrive prior to the above mentioned time. [12] [See Q&A]

Q&A

What is defined as the beginning of the morning from which one begins counting the 4 hours and 48 minutes? The Ketzos Hashulchan[13] questions whether the day begins from sunrise or dawn.[14] Although he leaves this matter without a conclusion, nevertheless he does conclude that according to the Peri Megadim the calculation is started from dawn.[15]

If one does not have a prearranged meal [or a host to eat by] at his destination and it is already past the beginning of morning, how much time does he have to travel?
He may only travel until 4 hours and 48 minutes from morning. If this time has already arrived he may no longer travel at all, and rather is to prepare for Shabbos in his current area.[16]

How close to Shabbos may one travel in a case that he has already informed the host of his arrival?[17]
It is best not to arrive too close to Shabbos as this can lead to Chillul Shabbos.[18] This especially applies when traveling by car, as cars easily break down and may take many hours to fix. It is thus proper not to travel a long distance from home very close to Shabbos.

May one travel on a plane which will be arriving close to Shabbos?
See above Q&A. The Ketzos Hashulchan[19] suggests even regarding cars [of his time] that one should not travel a great distance at all on Erev Shabbos, and certainly not past midday. This obviously would apply tenfold with regards to flying, of which delays are very probable and common.

If one already cooked all his meals, must he still reach his destination prior 5 hours into the day?[20]
If one has readymade food with him, and thus does not need to prepare food for Shabbos upon arriving in his destination, then logically speaking he may travel throughout the day, and so rule most Poskim[21]. However some Poskim[22] rule that even in such a case he must arrive at his destination prior to the above mentioned time.[23]

---

[10] So summarizes Ketzos Hashulchan 69/2 as the final ruling from Admur, and so rules Piskeiy Teshuvos 249/1

[11] In all cases when one informs the host of his arrival prior to 4 hours and 48 minutes into the day then it is not necessary for one to arrive at his destination prior to 4 hours and 48 minutes into the day. Rather he may arrive any time before Shabbos. If however the above conditions do not apply one would have to arrive to his destination within the above mentioned time.

[12] This follows the ruling of Admur that rules even when traveling by car one is to arrive within 4 hours and 48 minutes. However according to the Bach when traveling by car no restrictions apply. Vetzaruch Iyun on Piskeiy Teshuvos 249/1 which plainly rules like the Bach and does not take into account the ruling of Admur.

[13] Ketzos Hashulchan 69 footnote 1

[14] There is a dispute between Rash/Tosafus as to when one is supposed to begin traveling by day. The Torah states that one is to begin traveling only by the time of which it says "Ki Tov" Rashi learns this to be from sunrise while Tosafos learns this to be from dawn. Hence, in our case this dispute would likewise apply. However there is room to say that regarding this matter, the sages began their calculation from dawn, even according to Rashi. [Ketzos Hashulchan ibid]

[15] Vetzaruch Iyun as to his exact reason for learning this way in the Peri Megadim.

[16] Peri Megadim, brought in Ketzos Hashulchan 69 footnote 3, as is the simple understanding of Admur.

[17] Ketzos Hashulchan 69 footnote 5; Mishneh Berurah 249/3

[18] Such as carrying, Muktzah, walking past the Techum Shabbos, Amira Lenachri.

[19] 69 footnote 5

[20] Ketzos Hashulchan 69 footnote 5

[21] Perisha; Eliya Raba brought in Biur Halacha Veyuchal and Shaar Hatziyon 249/9; and so seems to rule Peri Megadim 249 A"A 2; so rules Ketzos Hashulchan 69 footnote 4 in his final conclusion of how to learn Admur.

[22] Olas Shabbos [brought in Mishneh Berurah; Ketzos Hashulchan ibid] as is the simple reading of the Beis Yosef; Levush and Admur in the words "**If one has Shabbos food** then if it is a place of danger he may travel to another place", thus implying that even when one has ready

Regarding the opinion of Admur, see above mentioned footnotes.

If one is traveling with **raw** foods which still require preparation, then according to all the traveling restrictions apply and he must arrive to his destination within 4 hours and 48 minutes from the beginning of the morning.

If one is traveling to a hotel for Shabbos and will be eating his own food, must he arrive at his hotel within 4 hours and 48 minutes from the morning?

Depends; If the traveler is taking readymade Shabbos foods with him, then there is no need to arrive within the above mentioned time.[24] However if he will need to prepare the food upon arrival then all the traveling restrictions apply and he must arrive within 4 hours and 48 minutes into the day.

May one travel close to Shabbos on a bus or taxi driven by a Jew, if doing so may cause him to travel back to his destination on Shabbos?

Many Gedolei Yisrael have advised to only travel on Erev Shabbos with enough time for the driver to return back to his destination before Shabbos.

Shabbos food the traveling restrictions apply. However the Ketzos Hashulchan [ibid] learns that Admur is simply referring to raw foods which still require cooking and preparations and in such a case the traveling decree applies, as one may not arrive with enough time to prepare them. Thus states Admur that in a case of danger even when one has to still cook his food he may travel. However when one's food is already prepared then there is no room to make a traveling decree. See Elyah Raba for an alternative explanation of this wording and the Ketzos Hashulchan's argument against entering this explanation into Admur.

[23] As Chazal made a "Lo Pelug" in their decree of traveling. Meaning that the Sages did not differentiate between travelers on Erev Shabbos and decreed that all must arrive to their destination prior to the given time.

[24] As mentioned in the previous question, in accordance to majority of Poskim.

Chapter 5: Eating On Erev Shabbos:

1. Eating On Erev Shabbos:

A. Arranging a large feast:[1]

It is forbidden for one to establish[2] a large feast on Erev Shabbos, which one is not accustomed to eat during the week if the feast involves drinking alcoholic beverages.[3] It is forbidden to eat such a feast even on Friday morning.[4]

B. The law by a Seudas Mitzvah/Mitzvah meal:[5]

The above prohibition only applies with regards to an optional feast, or a Seudas Mitzvah which is optional in terms of the date in which one must set it for, and it is thus possible for one to delay it to a later date. However a Seudas Mitzvah which has fallen out to be eaten specifically on Erev Shabbos, may be set on Erev Shabbos, even if due to this one will be unable to eat the Friday night meal.[6] In such a case if one is unable to eat the Friday night meal, he is to eat three meals on Shabbos day.

When on Friday should the meal be eaten?[7] When possible, it is a Mitzvah to initially begin the Seudas Mitzvah prior to the [beginning[8] of the] 10th hour [*Zmaniyos*] of the day[9] [or earlier, as much as possible[10]]. [Practically, this is three *Zmaniyos* hours prior to sunset. Thus if there are 60 minutes per *Zmaniyos* hour that day and sunset is at 6:00 P.M. one is to start the feast before 3:00 P.M.] If it is not possible to begin the meal prior to the 10th hour of the day one may begin the meal up until sunset.[11]

How many people may be invited to the Seudas Mitzvah?[12] It is proper[13] not to invite more than ten male guests for the meal. These ten guests are in addition to the invitation of those guests which are personally connected to the Simcha such as the relatives[14] and Shushvinin[15] by a wedding, and the relatives and Baalei Habris by a Bris[16]. Thus

---

[1] 249/5

[2] Vetzaruch Iyun on the wording of "to establish" as opposed to merely saying "eat". Perhaps however one can say that this is going on the wording of the Gemara in Gittin 38b "Two Jerusalem families, one set their meal on Shabbos by time of the weekly Shiur, the other **set** their meal on Erev Shabbos, and both were uprooted". Perhaps their harsh punishment was a result of a premeditated act of setting up the meal during that time, which is a greater effrontery then having simply eaten a large meal spontaneously at that time. Nonetheless even the latter would in truth be forbidden. Alternatively, the Peri Megadim explains [brought in Biur Halacha] that it is coming to teach that even if this meal is a onetime occasion, such as a wedding feast, it is to be avoided.

[3] Lit "Mishteh" The wording in Admur "a great feast that is a Mishteh" implies that he is defining the feast as one which involves drinking wine. However in the Michaber the wording is simply "a great feast and Mishteh" implies that they are independent. Likewise the Levush, which is the source of this additional wording of "Mishteh" at first writes as does the Michaber "and" although then goes on to define it like Admur "that is". Vetzaruch Iyun. To note that the Taz 249/1 learns in Rambam that the entire prohibition of having a large meal is because it contains a set drinking of alcoholic beverages. Hence seemingly Admur is adapting this ruling of the Taz and is defining that a joint of alcoholic consumption is the definition of the forbidden type of meal. Vetzaruch Iyun as accordingly, a large meal without alcoholic consumption would be permitted, as rules the Taz in the Rambam, however Admur states that only a **small** meal that does not contain alcohol is permitted. Thus perhaps one can answer that any meal with alcoholic consumption is forbidden, while all large meals are likewise forbidden according to Admur. Vetzaruch Iyun.

[4] The reason for this prohibition is in order to affirm that one will properly honor Shabbos, as if one were allowed to eat this large meal even in the morning he may satiate himself to the point that he will be unable to properly eat the Friday night meal.

[5] 249/6

[6] As this meal is likewise a Seudas Mitzvah just as is the Friday night meal. [ibid] And hence there is no requirement to push off the Friday Seudas Mitzvah as we why should one delay one Seudas Mitzvah for the sake of another Seudas Mitzvah.

[7] 249/7

[8] 249/9

[9] Other Opinions: The Mishneh Berurah 249/13 rules that the meal should be eaten in the morning [prior to midday]. He basis this ruling on the ruling of the Rama in 695/2 that when Purim falls on Erev Shabbos one is to start the meal prior to midday. The **Ketzos Hashulchan** [69 footnote 8] however argues that one cannot learn from the Purim feast laws that all meals of a Seudas Mitzvah are to be eaten prior to midday as there is much greater of a chance of becoming drunk by a Purim meal, and hence it was initially set to be eaten before midday. However other feast of a Seudas Mitzvah can be eaten even initially up to the 10th hour.

[10] Ketzos Hashulchan 69 footnote 8, as the earlier one can make the meal the more praiseworthy it is for the honoring of Shabbos. Practically it is the custom to make the meal as early as possible.

[11] So is implied from 249/6

[12] 249/7

Other Opinions: The Shulchan Hatahor [Komrana 249/7] rules that until midday one may invite as many guests as he desires, even 1000. This is because he learns the main prohibition is to set a weekly meal for Friday, while by occasional feasts the prohibition is mainly on the Baal Haseuda and not the guests. However clearly this is not the opinion of Admur.

[13] Lit. Tov. In Kuntrus Achron 249/1 Admur explains that the implication from the Rama/Levush is that one may be completely lenient in this regard and invite as many guests as he desires. Thus Admur here simply writes it is proper to be stringent in this and not that it is an actual obligation.

[14] A relative is defined as any relative that is invalid to give testimony regarding the Baalei Hasimcha [the person celebrating the Mitzvah]. [Kuntrus Achron 249/1; Ketzos Hashulchan 69 footnote 9] This includes the following relatives: Siblings and brother and sister in-laws; Parents and step parents; Grandparents and step grandparents; children and their spouses; Grandchildren and their spouses; Uncles and Aunts including great Uncles and Aunts; First Cousins; Nephews. [See Choshen Mishpat 33/2]

[15] The Shushvinin are the escorts of the Chasan and Kalah upon them walking to the Chupa.

[16] Such as the Mohel, and Sandek by a Bris.

one may invite ten more guests besides for the above guests. [By a Pidyon Haben the Kohen which is doing the Pidyon is not included within the ten, and thus ten other guests may be invited other than him and the relatives.[17]]

List of Seudas Mitzvah occasions which may be celebrated on Erev Shabbos:[18]

- *Bris Mila*: Whenever a Bris Mila is performed on Friday, whether it being the 8th day after birth or past the 8th day after birth[19], the festive meal may be celebrated on that day, following the directives given above.[20]
- *A wedding feast*: A wedding[21] may be scheduled for Erev Shabbos[22] and one who does so may celebrate the Seudas Mitzvah that day following the Chupa.[23] However if the wedding took place prior to Erev Shabbos see footnote.[24] [When a wedding takes place on Friday care must be taken that the Chasan and Kalah have fully valid Yichud prior to Shabbos, otherwise they may not be together in private on Shabbos.[25]]
- *Pidyon Haben*:[26] When a Pidyon Haben falls on Erev Shabbos, if it is taking place on its proper time which is the 31st day after birth, then one may have the Seudas Mitzvah on Erev Shabbos, following the laws explained above in terms of its preferred time and number of invitees. If the Pidyon is taking place past its required date, which is more than 31 days after birth, then one may not perform the Pidyon Haben and partake in a festive meal on Erev Shabbos.[27] (Rather he is to do the Pidyon Haben on Erev Shabbos without making a festive[28] meal.)
- *Erev Yom Tov that falls on Shabbos*:[29] When Erev Yom Tov falls on Shabbos one is to start the Shabbos day meal prior to the beginning of the 10th hour of the day, in order to eat the Yom Tov meal with an appetite. If one transgressed or forgot and did not eat prior to the 10th hour, then he may eat a meal past the 10th hour.
- *Yom Tov that falls on Erev Shabbos*:[30] When Yom Tov falls on Erev Shabbos one is to start the Yom Tov day meal prior to the beginning of the 10th hour of the day in order to eat the Shabbos meal with an appetite. If one transgressed or forgot and did not eat prior to the 10th hour, then he may eat a meal past the 10th hour.[31]
- *Yom Tov Sheiyni*[32] When there is a two day Yom Tov the day meal of the 1st day of Yom Tov is to begin prior to the 10th hour of the day in order to eat the night meal of the second day of Yom Tov with an appetite. If one transgressed or forgot and did not eat prior to the 10th hour, then he may eat a meal past the 10th hour [with exception to Erev Pesach and Erev Sukkos].

---

[17] Ketzos Hashulchan 69 footnote 10

[18] 249/6

[19] Such as when it had to be delayed due to illness or yellowness of the infant, and now is the first opportunity that they have to do the Mila. Furthermore, even if there was simple negligence involved that delayed the Bris, such as the parents were irreligious, and now on Friday the opportunity to do the Bris has presented itself, the Bris is nevertheless performed on Friday.

[20] Since one may not leave a Jewish child uncircumcised even one day, the day that the Bris is performed is considered its proper time, as it is forbidden to be delayed. Therefore the Seudas Mitzvah is also considered to have fallen on that day. [ibid]

[21] This applies to both stages of marriage the Eirusin or Nesuin. Neither should be delayed until after Shabbos. The Eirusin should not be delayed as another person may come to marry the bride in the interim. The Nessuin should likewise not be delayed in order to fulfill the Mitzvah of Peru Urevu. [ibid]

[22] This matter is disputed amongst Rishonim. The Rambam rules that it is forbidden to make a wedding on Friday due to fear that one may come to transgress Shabbos. The Tur and Rosh however rule that it is permitted. The Michaber in Even Haezer 64/4 brings both opinions and concludes that the custom is to be lenient. This was the custom of many of the Rabbeim, which married on Erev Shabbos and was a very common occurrence amongst the general public. Today however Friday weddings are less common. A possible reason for this is because the Friday weddings which took place in past times usually had the wedding feast celebrated on Friday night. Today however Friday weddings are commonly celebrated with their feast on Erev Shabbos, and thus people are more apprehensive in scheduling a wedding for such a date. In addition being that many people have non-religious relatives, making a wedding of a Friday may cause them to transgress Shabbos in terms of traveling back from the wedding. In any event it remains permitted for one to arrange a wedding on Erev Shabbos if he so chooses.

[23] 249/6

[24] When just the Eirusin has taken place before Erev Shabbos, while the Nessuin has been pushed off to a later date [as was the custom in previous generations] then the Seudas Eirusin may not take place on Erev Shabbos. When however the Nessuin has taken place prior to Erev Shabbos, then if Erev Shabbos is still within 7 days of the wedding, the feast may still take place on Erev Shabbos. [249/8] [This however is only allowed if one has not yet had a wedding feast prior to Erev Shabbos, and possibly only if Erev Shabbos is the last of the 7 days. See Ketzos Hashulchan 69 footnote 7].

[25] 339/8 As there are opinions which rule that Nessuin only takes place upon having complete Yichud, and one cannot make an acquisition on Shabbos. [ibid]

[26] 249/8

[27] As since the Mitzvah has already been pushed off from the 31st day, it is befitting to push it off from Erev Shabbos out of honor of Shabbos. [Ibid]

[28] Lit. Mishteh

[29] 291/4; 529/2

[30] As learned from 291/4 brought next, and so rules Kitzur Halachos 249 footnote 10.

[31] 529/2

[32] 529/2

- *Purim that falls on Erev Shabbos*:[33] When Purim falls on Erev Shabbos the meal is to [initially] take place in the morning due to Kavod Shabbos. [This applies even according to Admur which generally requires a Seudas Mitzvah to take place prior to the 10th hour and not in the morning.[34]] If one is unable to eat the meal in the morning, then it is best to start it before the 10th hour of the day.[35] If this too is not possible, one may start it up until sunset.[36] Regarding entering Shabbos in the midst of the meal [Pores Mapa] see next Halacha.

C. Pores Mapa Umikadeish-Continuing the Friday meal into Shabbos:[37]

As explained above when one has a Seudas Mitzvah on Friday it is to be eaten in the morning, and if this cannot be done it may be eaten anytime before sunset. Irrelevant to when the meal was started, it is best to complete the meal and recite Birchas Hamazon prior to sunset.[38] If one did not recite *Birchas Hamazon* prior to sunset, he is not to recite it until he performs *Pores Mapeh Umikadeish*.[39] [However see previous footnote for scenario that one may recite Birchas Hamazon even after sunset.] Poreis Mapa Umikadeish means that at sunset one places a Chalah cover over *Lechem Mishna*, recites *Kiddush* and eats a piece of bread. The following is the order:

1. One first brings *Lechem Mishna*[40] [two whole loaves] to the table and covers it.
2. One then says Kiddush over wine. However if one drank wine during the meal, no blessing of *Hagafen* is said over the Kiddush. Rather one says Vayechula and then goes straight to the blessing of Mikadeish Hashabbos. One is then to drink the wine. If there are people listening to the Kiddush which have not drunk wine during the meal, then upon them receiving the wine they are to say a blessing of Hagafen.[41]
3. Immediately[42] after Kiddush, **without washing hands or saying Hamotzi**, one is to cut the bread and **all participants** are to eat a Kezayis/Kebeitza[43] size of bread in order to fulfill their Friday night meal. The

---

[33] Rama 695/2

[34] Ketzos Hashulchan 69 footnote 8, as by the Purim Seuda there is more chance of getting drunk.

[35] As rules Admur here regarding all Seudas Mitzvas

[36] 249/6

One is allowed to start the meal anytime before Shabbos, even past the 10th hour of the day. The reason for this is because a Seudas Mitzvah which has fallen out to be eaten specifically on Erev Shabbos, may be eaten on Erev Shabbos, even if due to this one will be unable to fulfill the Friday night meal, as this meal is likewise a Seudas Mitzvah as is the Friday night meal. [ibid]

[37] 271/9-12

[38] 271/11 in end and 271/12

As if he does not recite Birchas Hamazon before sunset he will be required to begin the next meal and perform Poreis Mapa [271/12 and so is implied from end of 271/11] and the performance of Poreis Mapa involves disputes. Thus one who is meticulous is to avoid it all together. [271/11] The following is the dispute involved: It is disputed whether one has to say another blessing of Hamotzi on the bread that he eats after Kiddush. Some say the saying of Kiddush over wine is considered an interval between the previous blessing of Hamotzi and the bread. Others hold it is not considered an interval and hence a new blessing is not to be said over the bread eaten after Kiddush. Practically we rule leniently when it comes to a questionable blessing. However it is best to avoid the situation all together when possible. [ibid]

[39] The reason why one is not allowed to recite Birchas Hamazon past sunset and must rather follow the order of Pores Mapa is because if one were to recite Birchas Hamazon after sunset it would enter him into a number of disputes. There would be a question as to whether he is to say a blessing over the Kos Shel Bracha after Birchas Hamazon and then say Kiddush, or if he must first say Kiddush on a separate cup of wine, and is then to drink from the Kos Shel Bracha. Likewise if one says Kiddush right after reciting Birchas Hamazon there is a dispute as to whether he must now eat a meal in order so his Kiddush is in a place of a meal. Now if he follows this opinion, which he is to suspect for, and eats another meal after Kiddush, when he says an after blessing it is considered an unnecessary blessing as he could have not recited an after blessing before Kiddush and hence said one after blessing for both meals. Thus it is better for one to be Poreis Mapa and begin his next meal then to recite Birchas Hamazon after sunset and avoid these disputes. [271/12]

Vetzrauch Iyun if one is allowed even initially to recite Birchas Hamazon after sunset without a Kos Shel Bracha and then begin his Shabbos meal later at night. Seemingly one who does so does not enter himself into any disputes, as it is then not considered an unnecessary after blessing. This is also implied from the wording of Admur "if he were to say Kiddush **immediately** after Birchas Hamazon this would enter into the following dispute" thus implying that delaying the Kiddush does not involve any disputes. So also writes Admur explicitly in 271 KU"A 4 that if one delays the Kiddush and Friday night meal there is no prohibition of an unnecessary blessing taking place. Thus seemingly there is no restriction for one to recite Birchas Hamazon after sunset if he wishes to not begin his night meal right away.

In summary: If one is does not plan to have a Kos Shel Bracha after Birchas Hamazon and he does not plan to begin his Friday night meal until later on, then he may recite Birchas Hamazon even after sunset. In such a case it is better for him to recite Birchas Hamazon than to perform Poreis Mapa as doing so involves a dispute regarding the blessing over Hamotzi as explained above. To note that the Rebbe and the Previous Rebbe would not perform Poreis Mapeh after sunset and would rather not eat or drink anything and then recite Birchas Hamazon later on into the night. Some Chassidim based on this are also particular to not perform Poreis Mapah. [See Oatzer Minhagei Chabad Rosh Hashana 372; Sichos Simchas Torah 1957; Sefer Hasichos 1944 Simchas Torah footnote 25.]

[40] The concept of bringing Lechem Mishneh to the table when one performs Poreis Mapa is not mentioned in Shulchan Aruch or later Poskim. However so concludes Piskeiy Teshuvos 271 footnote 146 see there.

[41] 271/11; Sichas 1957 Simchas Torah 3

[42] As Kiddush is required to be Bemakom Seuda.

[43] See Piskeiy Teshuvos 271/14 which rules that one only needs to eat a Kezayis even though in general one needs to eat a Kibeitza of bread during the Shabbos meals.

blessing of Hamotzi is **not** said over the Lechem Mishna as one has already said Hamotzi in the beginning of his meal.[44]

4. If one planned to recite Birchas Hamazon prior to sunset and has already washed Mayim Achronim, and then sunset arrived prior to him beginning to recite it, then he is to be Pores Mapa as explained above and say a blessing over both the wine in Kiddush and Hamotzi over bread.

5. *Birchas Hamazon-Does one say both Al Hanisim and Ritzei if Erev Shabbos is Purim?* [45] One is to say both Al Hanisim and Ritzei in Birchas Hamazon if one ate a Kezayis of bread after Kiddush[46]. If one Davened before reciting Birchas Hamazon Al Hanisim is not said, and thus only Ritzei is said if one ate a Kezayis after Kiddush. [However some Poskim[47] rule Al Hanisim is never to be said together with Ritzei, even if one did not Daven Maariv.[48] Practically it is best to say Al Hanisim in the Harachamans.]

D. Eating a small meal on Erev Shabbos:[49]

A typical meal which is eaten during the week, which refers to a small meal which does not contain consumption of alcoholic beverages, from the letter of the law may be eaten throughout the entire day of Erev Shabbos, even close to sunset.[50] Nevertheless, it is a mitzvah to refrain from setting up such a meal from the beginning of the 10th hour[51] [of Shaaos Zmaniyos[52]] and onwards in order so one enters into Shabbos with an appetite to eat the Shabbos meal[53]. [Furthermore, in light of the above there are those which are meticulous that even prior to the 10th hour they do not eat a typical weekday meal, but rather eat a very small amount, such as mere bread and one dip, and the like.[54] This especially applies in the winter months when the Shaaos Zmaniyos are very short.[55]]

May one eat past the 10th hour if he did not eat prior? [56] If one transgressed or forgot and did not eat prior to the 10th hour, then he may eat past the 10th hour.

---

[44] This matter of dispute has been discussed in previous footnotes. See there!

[45] Based on 188/17 that we say both prayers if Kezayis was eaten at night; Shaareiy Halacha Uminhag p. 211; Sefer Hasichos 5704 p. 40 that even if said Kiddush may still say the previous days prayer and is not considered like Davened Maariv.

[46] If one did not eat a Kezayis of bread after Kiddush then only Al Hanisim is said. In such a case one must still eat a Friday night meal. If this is not possible one is to eat three meals the next day. As already explained above once sunset has arrived one is to do Pores Mapah and is not to bentch prior to eating Kezayis.

[47] Ketzos Hashulchan 47/10-11

[48] As in such a case it is proper to suspect for the opinion of the M"A that both prayers are never said, being that Al Hanisim is not an obligation to mention, as well as that there are opinions which hold we never say the Al Hanisim for the previous day even when there is no contradiction.

[49] 249/9

[50] To note however from Rama 529/1 which rules that it is **forbidden** to eat past Mincha on Erev Yom Tov just like on Erev Shabbos. However here in 249 he brings no gloss on the Michaber which rules as does Admur that it is only a Mitzvah and not obligation. Vetzaruch Iyun. To note from M"B there [529/5] that the Rama's wording is inaccurate.

[51] This is three *Zmaniyos* hours prior to sunset. Thus if there are 60 minutes per *Zmaniyos* hour that day and sunset is at 6:00 P.M. one is not to start a meal after 3:00 P.M.
The Michaber writes the 9th hour and onwards. This is not in contradiction to Admur, as the Michaber is referring to the end of the 9th hour, which is the beginning of the 10th, which is the last 3 hours left in the day. [Mishneh Berurah 249/17]
Other Opinions: Others [Taz 249/1; Ketzos Hashulchan 69 footnote 6-in contradiction to his ruling in 69/3] however mention that the Mitzvah begins from 9 ½ hours into the day. [This seemingly means 30 minutes after the completion of the 9th hour which is in actuality 10.5 hours into the day. Hence they delay the restriction of starting a meal by a half hour. Possibly the reason for this is because that is the time of Mincha Ketana, and in numerous sources [i.e. 529/1] Mincha [Ketana] is mentioned rather than the 10th hour. Nevertheless there still remains a question on the Ketzos Hashulchan ibid, which follows the rulings of Admur, in how he wrote in 69 footnote 6 that we refrain from the 9.5 hours when he himself clearly quoted Admur as ruling from the 10th. To note however from 539/20 which Admur mentions from "Mincha and above". Vetzaruch Iyun as in 249/9 Admur clearly states "from the **beginning** of the 10th hour"

[52] The hours are measured not by 60 minutes but in accordance to how many minutes the day contains. This amount of minutes is then divided by 12. The result is the amount of minutes calculated per hour. Thus in the summer these hours are more than 60 minutes each, while in the winter they are shorter. [M"B 249/16]

[53] The reason that by a small meal it is only a Mitzvah to refrain, while by a large meal with alcohol it is forbidden from the morning, is because a large meal satiates one a lot more, and thus there is suspicion that one may come to completely nullify the Friday night meal or will be unable to enjoy it at all. Likewise alcoholic consumption can also lead to nullifying the meal. However by a small meal without alcohol the only worry is that one may not have such an appetite to eat the meal This explains the contrast of reasoning's mentioned regarding the prohibition of eating a large meal with alcoholic beverages in which Admur states as the reason "one will be unable to properly eat the Friday night meal", and the reasoning mentioned behind the Mitzvah to refrain from eating a small meal from the 10th hour, which is so one have an appetite. [Ketzos Hashulchan 69 footnote 6] To note that the Michaber 249/2 mentions the reason of "so one have an appetite" regarding the prohibition of having a large meal. It is thus understood why Admur did not write this reason and rather wrote it as stated above.

[54] Bach brought in Ketzos Hashulchan 69 footnote 11

[55] M"B 249/16

[56] 529/2 regarding Erev Yom Tov and seemingly the same law applies regarding Erev Shabbos.

E. Eating snacks:[57]

To eat and drink on Erev Shabbos and Erev Yom Tov without making a set meal, [such as one who is eating a mere snack] is permitted to be done up until sunset and there is no need to refrain from doing so.

Erev Pesach: The above rule is with exception to Erev Pesach [in which from the 10th hour and onwards it is forbidden to eat any Matzah, even Matza Ashira, even less than a Kebeitza, or drink wine, even when being eaten as a mere snack and not in a form of setting a meal. However other snacks may be eaten in a limited amount.[58]]

F. Eating on Erev Yom Tov:[59]

The general rule: It is a Mitzvah[60] to refrain from beginning a meal past the 10th hour of Erev Yom Tov, just as is the law regarding Erev Shabbos. This is in order so one be able to eat the Yom Tov meal with an appetite, as eating the meal with a proper appetite is included within the Mitzvah of Kavod Yom Tov. [On Erev Sukkos and Erev Pesach it is not merely a Mitzvah to refrain from eating past the 10th hour but it is an actual prohibition to eat a meal, as will be explained.[61]]

May one eat a meal past the 10th hour if he did not eat prior? If one transgressed or forgot and did not eat prior to the 10th hour, then he may eat a meal past the 10th hour [with exception to Erev Pesach and Erev Sukkos].

May one eat past the 10th hour on the first day of Yom Tov: On the first day of a two day Yom Tov, as occurs by all Yomim Tovim in the Diaspora, and on Rosh Hashana in Israel, one is to begin the Yom Tov meal of the first day prior to the 10th hour in order so one have an appetite to eat the night meal of the second day of Yom Tov. If one did not begin before this time he is to eat the meal even past the 10th hour.

May one have a meal on Erev Shemini Atzeres[62] past the 10th hour?[63] It is a Mitzvah to refrain from beginning a meal past the 10th hour.

May one eat a meal past the 10th hour on Erev Pesach and Erev Sukkos?[64] It is forbidden from the letter of the law to begin a meal past the 10th hour of the day on Erev Pesach or Erev Sukkos[65].

---

[57] 249/9

[58] 471/1-2; so seems to be the intent of Admur here in referring the reader to this chapter.

[59] 529/2

[60] The Rama however states that it is forbidden just like on Erev Shabbos. Vetzaruch Iyun Gadol as by Erev Shabbos itself it is only a Mitzvah and not an obligation. The Mishneh Berurah [529/5] thus concludes that this wording is inaccurate and it really intends to say "a Mitzvah". To note however that also the Magen Avraham [668/1] rules that it is **forbidden** to eat past Mincha of Erev Shemini Atzeres. Vetzaruch Iyun

[61] This is due to an explicit teaching that we have for Erev Pesach and Erev Sukkos which teach that it is forbidden to set a meal past the tenth hour.

[62] Hoshana Raba

[63] 529/2

[64] 471/1-2 regarding Erev Pesach; 639/20 regarding Erev Sukkos

[65] Regarding Erev Sukkos Admur writes "Min Hamincha Ulimalah" which seemingly refers to Mincha Ketana of which we do not eat "Samuch Limincha" which refers to the 10th hour. This explanation that "Min Hamincha" refers to 10th hour is found in Rama 529 which rules that it is forbidden to eat Erev Yom Tov from "Hamincha Ulimala" and the Magen Avraham explains this to refer to the 10th hour and so rules Admur simply [there in 529]. However Tzaruch Iyun as for why Admur here did not also just simply state the 10th hour, as he does there in 529/2, and especially in light of fact that in all the Halachas mentioned of not eating on Erev Chag/Shabbos Admur mentions specifically the 10th hour. [249/9 regarding Erev Shabbos; 471/1-2 regarding Erev Pesach, and 529/2 regarding Erev Yom Tov.]. As well the question intensifies over the fact that the Rama rules it is forbidden from Chatzos and seemingly if Admur were trying to argue on the Rama he should have stated clearly without doubt of its meaning that he holds its from the 10th hour. Thus although we find a source for ruling that Min Hamincha refers to 10th hour, it is puzzling why Admur did not just state this explicitly. Vetzaruch Iyun.

In other Poskim:

Rama 639/3: The Rama rules it is forbidden to eat a meal from midday of Erev Sukkos just as is the law on Erev Pesach.

Magen Avraham 639/12: Asks on Rama that on Erev Pesach it is only forbidden to start a meal from the 10th hour. He answers that bread [which one cannot eat on Erev Pesach] is more filling than other foods, and thus bread which can be eaten on Erev Sukkos we are more stringent and forbid it from midday. However he concludes with asking a) what is the source for such a differentiation, and b) why does the Rama conclude as explained in the laws of Pesach. He thus concludes with a Tzaruch Iyun. Some [Kaf Hachayim 639] learn the Magen Avraham's final stance is to be arguing on the Rama that even bread is only forbidden from after the 10th hour, and others [Kitzur Shulchan Aruch/Chayeh Adam] learn him to accept the differentiation that he made between bread and other foods.

Gr"a 639: **From 10th hour**. Says Rama holds like Rishonim which forbid eating form midday, but that is not how we rule as explained in Hilchos Pesach that we rule it may be eaten until 10th.

Chok Yaakov: Argues on differentiation of Magen Avraham and rather explains that Rama always holds even by Pesach that the prohibition to eat Mezonos or Hamotzi foods begin from midday, and it is just because that eating Mezonos/Hamotzi on Erev Pesach is not done being that we do not eat Matza Ashira anymore, that the Rama did not say so in Hilchos Pesach. [Based on this explanation it is evident that Admur clearly does not rule like Rama being that he clearly states in 471/1-2 that Matzah Ashirah may be eaten on Erev Pesach until the 10th hour, which according to the Chok Yaakov's explanation of the Rama is incorrect.]

Kitzur Shulchan Aruch: Rules that bread may not be eaten from midday while other foods from 10th, and sources it in Magen Avraham.

Chayeh Adam: Rules that bread may not be eaten from midday while other foods from 10th, and sources it in Magen Avraham.

Mishneh Berurah 639: Rules that the Achronim have agreed that it is only forbidden from the 10th hour.

Kaf Hachayim 639: Brings that the Magen Avraham and Admur argue on Rama and the restriction begins from the 10th hour. Although he himself brings other opinions.

Snacks on Erev Yom Tov: See previous Halacha.

Summary of eating on Erev Shabbos:
A large meal: It is forbidden to eat a large meal any time on Erev Shabbos [and Erev Yom Tov] unless it is a Seudas Mitzvah which its date has fallen on Erev Shabbos. In such a case one is to initially begin the meal prior to the 10th hour of the day and should only invite ten people besides for close relatives and the Baalei Hasimcha.
A small meal: One is to refrain from eating a small meal starting from the 10th hour of the day.
Snacks: Snacks may be eaten throughout the day even past the 10th hour.

Q&A on Seudas Mitzvah

May one celebrate a Siyum Mesechta on Erev Shabbos?
Some Poskim[66] rule that a meal celebrating a Siyum Mesechta may be arranged on Erev Shabbos. Others[67] however question this allowance[68] and rule that it may not be set for Erev Shabbos. One is rather to arrange the celebration for another day, or is to serve only light refreshments as opposed to an actual meal.

May one celebrate a Bar Mitzvah on Erev Shabbos?[69]
If the Bar Mitzvah falls on Erev Shabbos[70] then the Seuda may also be celebrated on Erev Shabbos. However one may not arrange the meal for Erev Shabbos if the boy has turned Bar Mitzvah prior to then.

Q&A on a small meal

If one began a small meal prior to the 10th hour may he continue to eat after the 10th hour has arrived?[71]
Yes.

Q&A on eating snacks after the 10th hour

May one eat less than a Kebeitza of bread [less than 55 grams] after the 10th hour?[72]
Yes. Less than a Kebeitza [55 grams] of bread is defined as a snack and not as a set meal.

Is there a limited amount of fruits that one may eat past the 10th hour?[73]
No. One may eat as much fruit as he desires.

May one drink alcohol past the 10th hour?[74]
One may drink up to a Kebeitza worth [55 grams] of alcoholic beverages. [However see footnote[75]]

Mateh Efrayim [625/7] : One is to eat his meal prior to midday, although if one did not yet eat he may nevertheless eat a meal until the 10th hour.

[66] So rules Biur Halacha 249; Shulchan Hatahor [Kamrina] 249/7

[67] Ketzos Hashulchan 69 footnote 7

[68] As there is no obligation for one to finish any Mesechta specifically on Erev Shabbos, as there is no obligation for one to learn this portion of Torah over another. Hence it is no better than a Pidyon Haben which its meal must be pushed off.

[69] Ketzos Hashulchan 69 footnote 7

[70] Meaning that the boy is turning Bar Mitzvah on Erev Shabbos.

[71] Mishneh Berurah 249/16; and so is implied from Admur 249/9 regarding Erev Shabbos and 529/2 regarding Erev Yom Tov as Admur simply writes one is not to <u>establish</u> a meal from that time. This is in contrast to the wording of the Rama in 529/2 as well as Admur in 471/1 which writes "not to eat" a meal from that time. This implies there is no limitation in beginning the meal prior to the 10th hour even if it will continue past the 10th hour. Seemingly the reason for this is because when the meal is started prior to the 10th hour, being it is a small meal, it will not commonly continue long enough for one to still not have an appetite by the time Shabbos comes. However when begun past the 10th hour it is common that it will continue long enough to ruin one's appetite for the night meal. Vetzaruch Iyun

[72] Ketzos Hashulchan 69 footnote 11

[73] Ketzos Hashulchan 69 footnote 11

[74] Ketzos Hashulchan 69 footnote 11

[75] The Mishneh Berurah 249/14 writes that from the beginning of the 10th hour and onwards one is not to drink alcohol to the point that he is satiated, however he does not limit this to a Kebeitza worth. Similarly Admur on 471/2 regarding wine does not limit wine to a Kebeitza worth but rather to either a very small amount or the amount that he can become satiated from it. Vetzaruch Iyun.

2. May one fast on Erev Shabbos:[76]

Setting up a new fast day for Erev Shabbos: One may not initially set up[77] a fast day for Erev Shabbos, unless he eats something prior to the entrance of Shabbos[78]. The reason for this requirement is in order so one not enter into Shabbos in a state of oppression. [As a result of this one may not accept such a fast by Mincha of Thursday, as any fast accepted by Mincha must be completed until nightfall, and as said above one is to eat prior to accepting Shabbos.[79]]

The law by one who is pampered: One who has a very slow metabolism[80] to the point that if he were to eat even a small amount on Erev Shabbos he would no longer be able to eat the Friday night meal with an appetite, then he may fast even up to the entrance of Shabbos.

An accustomed fast day which falls on Erev Shabbos: If the date of a set fast falls on Erev Shabbos [such as the 10th of Teves in certain years and other voluntary fasts[81]], then one may fast on Erev Shabbos and is not required to delay the fast, even if the fast is voluntary[82]. The reason for this is because this prohibition against entering into Shabbos in a state of oppression is a light prohibition, and thus the Sages only decreed against doing so if the fast does not have a set date and may hence be delayed. However when the fast does have a set date, and hence cannot be delayed the Sages did not make issue with one fasting on that date despite it being lax in Kavod Shabbos.

By an accustomed fast day which falls on Erev Shabbos, until when must one fast?[83]

- A public fast day: By a public fast day [such as the 10th of Teves which falls on Erev Shabbos] one must fast until nightfall [Tzeis Hakochavim].[84] This applies even if the congregation has finished *Davening Maariv* prior to nightfall, and even if one had stipulated the day before that he would only fast until after the Maariv prayer[85].

- A voluntary fast day which was accepted the Mincha before: A voluntary fast which falls on Erev Shabbos, then if one accepted the fast in Mincha of Thursday one is obligated to fast until nightfall of Erev Shabbos. However if the congregation has finished *Davening Maariv* prior to nightfall then one is to eat immediately after the congregations prayer.[86] Due to this one is to initially stipulate upon accepting the fast on the Mincha of Thursday that he will only be fasting until after the prayer of the congregation.

- A voluntary fast which was not accepted the Mincha before: A voluntary fast which falls on Erev Shabbos, and was not accepted by Mincha of Thursday, one may continue to fast until nightfall if he so chooses. [However he is not obligated to do so, and may eat after sunset.] However this only applies if one has not entered himself into the status of a vow regarding fasting until nightfall by this fast. If however one is Halachicly deemed to have taken a vow to fast until nightfall by this date, then he is obligated to either fast until nightfall or revoke his vow in the presence of three adult men.[87] [See footnote for cases of vows[88]]

---

[76] 249/12

[77] Meaning that if one decides that he needs to fast for whatever reason, not dependant on any specific date, then he is not to fulfill this fast on Erev Shabbos, as he can simply delay it to a different weekday.

[78] Lit. Kabalas Shabbos, which implies even if he accepts Shabbos early he is to eat prior to accepting Shabbos.

[79] See Admur ibid

[80] Lit. pampered

[81] Such as: Fasts of the Yartzite of a Tzadik; Erev Rosh Chodesh; Aseres Yimei Teshuvah; 20th of Sivan; Yartzite of father or mother; Taanis Chalom; 10th of Teves.

[82] Meaning that it is voluntary as to whether one needs to fast on that date or not fast at all. However the date itself is a set date.

[83] There is a dispute mentioned regarding one who has finished Davening Maariv of Friday night prior to nightfall if he must continue fasting until nightfall. The first opinion rules that one must still continue fasting until nightfall [as all public fasts must be complete fasts]. The second opinion rules that it is forbidden to continue fasting past the conclusion of Maariv, even if before nightfall, as at that time one has already fully accepted Shabbos, and it is forbidden to fast on Shabbos, with intent of fasting, for even one moment. Now, although every public fast must be completed for the entire day [until nightfall], this second opinion holds that after Maariv is already considered a new day and thus there is no need to wait until nightfall out of obligation to complete the fast. [ibid]
Regarding a public fast Admur rules like the first opinion being that it is obligatory for one to fast until nightfall by a public fast. So rules also Rama and Mishneh Berura 249. Regarding a private fast Admur rules like the second opinion.

[84] See previous footnote. Regarding a public fast Admur rules like the first opinion being that it is obligatory for one to fast until nightfall by a public fast. So rules also Rama and Mishneh Berura 249.

[85] As his stipulation is worthless as it is a public fast which is obligated upon all and is not given to individual discretion for stipulation. [ibid]

[86] As by a private, voluntary fast, Admur rules like the second opinion which forbids fasting on Shabbos once Maariv has been concluded by the congregation. Now, although every fast which was accepted the Mincha prior to the fast must be completed for the entire day [until nightfall], this second opinion holds that after Maariv is already considered a new day and thus there is no need to wait until nightfall out of obligation to complete the fast. [ibid]

[87] 249/13

[88] It is considered a vow in the following cases: [ibid]
- One fasted this type of fast once before on Erev Shabbos, until nightfall, and had intent to continue doing so forever.
- One fasted this type of fast until nightfall, three times on Erev Shabbos.

- <u>Taanis Chalom</u>: One who is fasting a Taanis Chalom on Erev Shabbos is to complete his fast until nightfall, even if the congregation has completed the Maariv prayer.[89]

Summary:
One may not initially set up a fast day for Erev Shabbos unless he eats something prior to the entrance of Shabbos However if the date of a set fast falls on Erev Shabbos, then one may fast and it is not to be pushed off. When a set fast day falls on Erev Shabbos [such as the 10th of Teves in certain years] then one must fast until after Tzeis Hakochavim, even if the congregation already Davened Maariv.

- <u>One fasted for the 1st Yartzite of his parents during the week, until nightfall</u>: This matter is a dispute in whether it is considered a vow. Admur concludes that the custom is to be stringent to consider it a vow also regarding Erev Shabbos, although one who is lenient in times of need, may do so.
- <u>By the fast of Tzadikim and Erev Rosh Chodesh</u>: If one fasted one time during the week until nightfall with intent to do so forever, or fasted three times until nightfall, then it is disputed whether this considered a vow also with regards to Erev Shabbos. Admur concludes that the custom is to be stringent to consider it a vow also regarding Erev Shabbos, although one who is lenient in times of need, may do so.

[89] As even on Shabbos itself one may fast a Taanis Chalom. [Ibid]

Chapter 6: Beginning a Melacha before Shabbos which will continue into Shabbos

1. May one begin a Melacha before Shabbos if it will continue into Shabbos?[1]

The rule: It is permitted for one to begin a *Melacha*[2] on Erev Shabbos, up until sunset, even if it will not be completed before sunset, and will thus consequently finish on its own on Shabbos. Furthermore, even if one sets up a situation that the Melacha does not even begin on Erev Shabbos, and rather the entire Melacha is done on Shabbos on its own[3], it is nevertheless permitted to be arranged on Erev Shabbos.[4] The above allowance applies even if a Jew's vessel will be doing the Melacha on Shabbos being that there is no obligation for one to prevent his vessels from doing work on their own on Shabbos.

The Exceptions:

- Noise making Melachas:[5] In a place where there is no accepted custom otherwise, one is to be stringent[6] to forbid starting any Melacha on Erev Shabbos that will continue into Shabbos, if the Melacha will be generating noise on Shabbos.[7] However in a case of loss one may be lenient to begin doing even a noise making Melacha on Erev Shabbos. If the item making the noise does not belong to a Jew, even if the Melacha is being done is on behalf of the Jew, it is permitted to be started on Erev Shabbos even when no loss is involved. Likewise if it is known fact to the public that a certain activity is always begun the day before its noise is heard, even when heard during the week[8], then it may be done on Erev Shabbos even if it makes noise on Shabbos.[9]
- Placing uncooked food on the fire from before Shabbos into Shabbos: Is forbidden due to the Shehiyah restrictions. See "The Laws of Shabbos" Vol. 1 "The Laws of Shehiyah"!
- Placing a vessel of water near a candle to catch its sparks:[10] It is forbidden on Erev Shabbos to place a vessel containing water under a candle in order for it to catch the sparks of the candle on Shabbos.[11] Likewise it is forbidden on Erev Shabbos to place water under a wax candle in order to extinguish the flame when it reaches the water level.[12] It is however permitted to place water in an oil candle in order to elevate the oil.[13] Furthermore the custom is to be lenient to allow one to place water under the oil even if he intends to extinguish the wick, to prevent the flame from damaging the glass of the vessel.[14]

---

[1] 252/1-2

[2] Melacha is the general term used for all activities which are forbidden to be done on Shabbos.

[3] Such as to spread traps on Erev Shabbos to catch wild animals, birds and fish on Shabbos. This is permitted despite the fact that the trap is what is doing the entire action of trapping on Shabbos, as the metal becomes tied and grabs the bird on Shabbos, and similarly the booby-trap which they spread [to catch] wild animals to capture them by their feet, in which when the animal touches [the trap] it jumps and traps it. [ibid] Vetzaruch Iyun from the discussion in Poskim [Piskeiy Teshuvos 252/1; Mishneh Halachos 7/55] regarding if one may cause an entire Melacha to begin on Shabbos, being that from here it is clearly proven that one may, and so rules also Michaber.

[4] The Sages did not suspect that if Melacha which was done before Shabbos is allowed to continue into Shabbos one may likewise think this Melacha is permitted to be done on Shabbos itself, as the concept of not doing Melacha on Shabbos is well known. [265/8]

[5] 252/14-15

[6] It is disputed in Poskim whether or not one may place wheat in a flour mill on Erev Shabbos and have it grind the wheat on Shabbos in a way that generates noise. Some Rishonim rule [as rules Michaber 252/5 and Admur in his 1st opinion, brought as a stam], that doing so is permitted, as they hold that it is always permitted to begin a Melacha on Erev Shabbos even if it will generate noise on Shabbos. Other Rishonim however hold [as brings Rama and Admur as a Yeish Cholkim], that doing so is forbidden, as they hold that all noise generating Melachas are forbidden to be done on Erev Shabbos if they will continue into Shabbos, due to the belittling of Shabbos. Admur concludes as written above that one is to be stringent if there is no explicit custom otherwise. [ibid]

[7] As when the Melacha generates noise, it attracts people's attention and causes a belittlement of Shabbos, as people may say the person began doing the Melacha on Shabbos. [ibid]

[8] Such as an alarm clock which is always set up the day before.

[9] As in such a case there is no belittling of Shabbos apparent.

[10] 265/8-9

[11] 265/8; This is forbidden due to a decree that if it were allowed to do so before Shabbos then one may come to think that it is likewise permitted to do so on Shabbos, as this Shabbos prohibition is not very well known being that people think since the water is being placed before the sparks fall it should therefore be permitted. [ibid]

[12] 265/9

[13] 265/9; The reason for this is because one has no intent to extinguish the flame but rather to raise the oil level and hence there is no reason to suspect that one may come to think that it is also allowed to set up a jar of water to catch sparks on Shabbos. Furthermore in truth the fire would extinguish regardless of the water, as the moment the oil has burnt out the fire extinguishers on its own. Hence adding the water does not proximate the extinguishing of the flame at all and there is thus no reason to suspect that one may come to think that it is also allowed to set up a jar of water to catch sparks on Shabbos.

[14] 265/9; Meaning that one wants to prevent the wick from remaining lit while it is on the bottom of the vessel as the flame can cause damage to the vessel. The reason for this allowance is because in truth the fire would extinguish regardless of the water, as the moment the oil has burnt out the fire extinguishers on its own. Hence adding the water does not proximate the extinguishing of the flame at all and there is thus no reason to suspect that one may come to think that it is also allowed to set up a jar of water to catch sparks on Shabbos.

Examples of cases:

1. Dyes: One may soak dye, herbs and barley in a bucket of water, near the onset of Shabbos, and have them remain there the entire Shabbos.

2. Incense: One may place fragrance under clothing over coals close to sunset, consequently having it give off fragrance into the clothing throughout the entire Shabbos.[15] [However to place plain fragrance over coals, having it give off good smell throughout Shabbos, is forbidden due to suspicion that one may come to stoke the coals.[16]]

3. Traps: One may set up an animal trap on Erev Shabbos for it to trap animals on Shabbos.

4. Dying wool: One may leave wool in a sealed[17] pot of boiling dye which is off the fire[18] in order so the wool absorb the dye throughout the entire Shabbos.

5. Sprinklers:[19] One may turn on his sprinklers before Shabbos, having them hose his garden throughout the entire Shabbos.

6. Medicine:[20] One may place a medicinal bandage, or any other medical item, on a wound before Shabbos[21] even though it will continue curing the wound throughout Shabbos.

7. Alarm Clock:[22] One may set up an alarm clock on Erev Shabbos, having it detonate on Shabbos.[23]

Summary-Doing Shabbos prohibited work on Erev Shabbos which will continue into Shabbos:

It is permitted to begin a Shabbos prohibited activity on Erev Shabbos even if this activity will continue into Shabbos. This is with exception to:

1. One may not place food to cook on Erev Shabbos if it will only become half cooked after the entrance of Shabbos as is explained in Vol. 1 "The Laws of Shehiyah".

2. One is to be stringent not to arrange before Shabbos that a Melacha which generates noise be activated on Shabbos, being people will suspect that the Melacha was done on Shabbos. In any of the following cases however even a noise generating Melacha remains permitted to be arranged on Erev Shabbos:

   A. It is known that this type of activity is always set up the day before.

   B. The noise making object is not known to be owned by a Jew.

   C. A case of loss: Being that there are opinions which say that in all cases it is permitted to set up even noise making Melachas, therefore if one will incur a loss by being stringent in the above, he may be lenient like these opinions.

   D. A community which has an accepted custom to be lenient may do so.

Q&A

May one light incense before Shabbos having its smell burn on Shabbos?[24]

No as we suspect that one may come to stoke the flame.

---

[15] Even if the fragrance is resting within a vessel this is permitted, as even though the work is being done on Shabbos with the vessel of a Jew, this is Halachicly meaningless, as a person is not commanded that his vessels rest from doing work on Shabbos on its own [consequently of an action started from before Shabbos]. [ibid]

[16] Based on Bach 252, brought in Kaf Hachaim 252/52. The Bach explains that when fragrance is placed under clothing we do not suspect that one will come to stoke the coals as doing so will bring up smoke which will ruin the clothes. This implies that when there are no clothing over the fragrance that doing so would indeed be forbidden due to the above suspicion. Accordingly it is also understood why the Michaber/Admur specifically mentioned this case involving clothing.

[17] If however the pot cover is not sealed shut then it is forbidden due to suspicion that one may remove the lid and come to stir the wool, which contains a cooking and dying prohibition. [The mixing of uncooked food within a Keli Rishon is forbidden due to the cooking prohibition, as is explained in the laws of cooking.] If however the wool is already fully cooked then mixing it only contains the dying prohibition. [ibid. and 318/30. Vetzaruch Iyun as for why in 318/30 Admur writes "dying prohibition" in parentheses.]

[18] If however it is on the fire, doing so is forbidden due to suspicion that one may come to higher the flame. [ibid]

[19] 252/14

Although the original Halacha in Admur is referring to digging a channel from a spring to a garden, seemingly today's sprinklers systems would have the same law. [Piskeiy Teshuvos 252/4] However some question the comparison saying that sprinkler systems, in contrast to a channel, make noise of which the ruling is that it may not be done before Shabbos, as explained above. Vetzaruch Iyun as to the amount of noise that can be defined as problematic.

[20] 252/14

[21] However on Shabbos it is forbidden to medically treat oneself with exception to the cases that are explained in Vol. 2 "The laws of Medicine".

[22] 252/15

[23] This applies even if one desires it to ring for the remainder of the day. [336/4] As although it is a noise making Melacha, of which one is to be stringent against doing even before Shabbos, nevertheless since it is common knowledge that alarms are set up the day before they ring, there is therefore no applicable suspicion that people may think it was set up on Shabbos which is prohibited to be done. [252/16]

[24] Based on Bach 252

May one place water under his candles to prevent the possibility of a fire occurring on Shabbos?
If there is suspicion of danger then one may place water before Shabbos near the candles in a way that if the candle were to fall it would extinguish.[25] If however there is no fear of danger it is forbidden to do so.[26]

May one close the water of his sprinklers on Shabbos?[27]
Yes. However if one is only closing an individual sprinkler while leaving other sprinklers on, then one must verify that doing so will not cause an increase in water pressure to come out from the other sprinklers. There are opinions however which do not allow this to be done even in such a case.

May one arrange for his sprinklers to go off on Shabbos?
Yes.

May one place clothing in the washing machine or dryer before Shabbos, having them be washed or dried into Shabbos?[28]
No, as the washing machine and dryer generates noise. If however it is a case of great need, such as one is traveling on Motzei Shabbos, then one may be lenient to do so.[29] Nevertheless even in such a case one may not make use of these clothes on Shabbos.

May one arrange that his Shabbos clock turn on a radio, television, or tape on Shabbos?
The Halachic aspects involved in doing so is discussed amongst Poskim. [see footnote[30]] In any event it is a widespread custom to forbid doing so, as regardless of the Halachic discussion, doing so breaks the Shabbos spirit. However in a time of great need such as in times of natural disasters or war in which case one must hear news directives, one may certainly be lenient to do so, [leaving the radio on a low volume].[31]

May one leave a radio, television, or tape on into Shabbos?
This follows the same ruling as the previous Q&A.

May one listen to the radio of a neighbor which is on?
If the neighbor is Jewish or the radio broadcast is being done by a Jew then it is forbidden to listen as one is benefiting from the Melacha done by the Jew on Shabbos.[32] If however it is a gentile neighbor and the show is broadcasted by gentiles it is permitted from the letter of the law to listen, although it is best to avoid doing so being it breaks the spirit of Shabbos.

May one have a wake up service[33] call on Shabbos?[34]
So long as the actual call is automated[35], as opposed to having an actual receptionist calling, then it is allowed[36].

---

[25] Elya Raba 265/10 in name of Issur Viheter 59/45; M"B 265/6; Now although the Peri Megadim 265 M.Z. 3 argues on the law stated by the Issur Viheter, and the M"B ibid concludes that one is to only be lenient in a time of need to do so through a child, nevertheless perhaps this applies only on Shabbos, although on Erev Shabbos everyone agrees that one may place water under it to prevent danger. [see Piskeiy Teshuvos 265/6 and footnote 45] To note that the Daas Torah 265 and Kaf Hachaim 365/26 does not record the stringent ruling of the Peri Megadim even regarding Shabbos.

[26] As one may not place water under a candle to catch its sparks. [265/8]

[27] Piskeiy Teshuvos 252/4

[28] SSH"K 42/43

[29] As this is similar to a case of loss in which one may be lenient.

[30] Some Poskim [Mahrshag 2/118; Shulchan Melachim 6/72] rule that there involves no prohibition in leaving the radio on into Shabbos, or having a timer activate it on Shabbos. However the majority of Poskim [Beis Yitzchak 2/31; Mishpitei Uziel 2/52; Rav SZ"A brought in Shearim Hametzuyanim Behalacha 80/39; Minchas Yitzchak 1/107; Igros Moshe 4/60 regarding the prohibition of having a timer do any Melacha on Shabbos] have prohibited it for various reasons. These include: 1) Listening to business related items which is forbidden; 2) playing music through the radio 3) Benefiting from hearing a Jewish talk show, of which the Jew is desecrating Shabbos; 4) It falls under the category of Melachas which make noise, similar to a flour mill, of which it is initially forbidden to arrange before Shabbos to continue into Shabbos. 5) It is belittling to Shabbos.

[31] Piskeiy Teshuvos 252/6
Regarding leaving the radio on for a sick person in order to calm him down, Chelkas Yaakov 1/61 rules that it is allowed while in 3/98 he retracts that ruling and forbids it.

[32] Har Tzevi 1/183

[33] Wake up service is a service offered by companies in which they call a person's phone as a wake up reminder, in accordance to the preferred time that he gives them. The question thereby lies in whether or not one may allow on Shabbos for this phone call to be made by the service provider.

[34] Beir Moshe 7/56 Kuntrus "Koach Electri"

[35] Meaning that the service provider has an automated phone service which daily calls the customers without the need of a human to dial the

However in such a case one is to make reminders[37] as a precaution that he not lift up the phone to answer it in the midst of awakening.

There are opinions[38] however which are stringent against having even an automated call due to that they view this as a belittling of Shabbos[39].

May one set up a recorder from before Shabbos to record on Shabbos?[40]
No.[41]

May one leave a microphone on into Shabbos and use it?[42]
No. Doing so is a sever prohibition.[43]

May one leave his answering machine active on Shabbos?
For commercial use:[44] Some Poskim[45] rule that it is permitted to leave an answering machine on for clients and customers to leave messages and receive information. Others[46] however forbid doing so due to a variety of factors.[47] If majority of one's clients or customers are Jews, then it is forbidden to leave on the answering machine according to all.

For home use: It is permitted according to all opinions for one to leave his answering machine active on Shabbos.

Voicemail: The above discussion refers to landline answering machines. However electronic voicemail systems which are provided by phone companies are permitted according to all to be left active on Shabbos[48], especially if one is merely leaving a recorded message of the business opening hours.[49] However according to the above Poskim which are stringent it would be forbidden to leave a recording on the voicemail referring the clients to a gentile worker of the business.

May one leave his fax machine active on Shabbos?[50]
This follows the same ruling as does an answering machine which was explained in the previous question. Thus in accordance to the stringent opinion one is to unplug the machine before Shabbos. In the event that a fax arrived on Shabbos it is forbidden to be read on Shabbos.[51]

May one set up a timer to activate machines which work on electricity?[52]
No.[53]

- **May one set up a timer to activate or shut off his lights at home?**
  Yes.[54]

---

numbers or do any other form of intervention.

[36] As this is similar to a Shabbos clock which is set to turn on electricity, which is permitted.

[37] Such as to cover the phone as a reminder, or before Shabbos move it to a different area.

[38] See Piskeiy Teshuvos 252/7

[39] The Beir Moshe ibid negates this issue for a number of reasons.

[40] Mishneh Halachos 7/55; Beir Moshe 7/77 [Electricity]; Igros Moshe 4/60

[41] As the actual recording is forbidden to be done on Shabbos. See the above mentioned Poskim and their reasons.

[42] Shaareiy Halacha Uminhag 2/167, as rule all Poskim today.

[43] As the speaking into the microphone itself causes a prohibition to be transgressed.

[44] Such as for customers to leave messages for the business, or to be told that the office is closed etc. The question involved in doing so is if this transgresses placing a stumbling block in front of a non-religious Jew who may call, as well as if this involves doing business on Shabbos.

[45] Beir Moshe 6/50 Kuntrus Electri

[46] Minchas Yitzchak 5/14; Chelkas Yaakov 3/94

[47] Such as: 1. Arranging for business to be done on Shabbos; 2. Perhaps a Jew may call and one causes him to desecrate Shabbos, as leaving a message causes the machine to turn on and off, as well as it writes the message on the recording tape which is like writing on Shabbos; 3. One must protest a gentile doing Melacha with a Jews items, of which in this case is the answering machine which turns on and off upon his call.

[48] As by voicemail the Melacha is not being done with the Jews machine or any machine for that matter. As well no extra Melacha is being done by a Jew calling the number and having the voicemail activate, as opposed to getting a busy signal. Likewise the issue of setting up business for Shabbos was only forbidden by the Minchas Yitzchak in the scenario that one leaves a message for the client to call another person to finalize the business.

[49] Minchas Yitzchak ibid

[50] Kinyan Torah 6/17

[51] Piskeiy Teshuvos 252 footnote 20

[52] Igros Moshe 4/60

[53] As doing so is a belittlement of the Shabbos day, even if it itself involves no transgression. The Igros Moshe likewise discusses whether this falls under the prohibition of Amirah Leakum.

[54] As these matters are needed for Oneg Shabbos, as well as that it has even been accepted to ask a gentile to do so prior to the times of electricity.

- **May one set up a timer to activate a fan or air conditioner?**
  Yes.

May one on Erev Shabbos place food on his electric plate which is not yet on but will later turn on with the timer?[55]

If the food is not fully cooked, or is but contains liquid and has fully cooled down, it is forbidden.

If the food is fully cooked but the electric plate is not covered: Then if the electric plate has more than one heat setting and is not covered, it is forbidden to place food there before Shabbos if the food is cold. However if the food is still hot, there is a dispute amongst Poskim and it is proper to be stringent.

Food is fully cooked and electric plate is covered: If the electric plate is covered, or has only one setting it is allowed to place on it before Shabbos fully cooked food [which will still be warm by the time the clock turns on if the food contains liquid].

Practically, due to the above one may not leave a boiler attached to the Shabbos clock being that by the time the clock turns back on, the water has completely cooled off and will become re-cooked on Shabbos.

There is thus no room to be stringent under the claim that it belittles Shabbos.

[55] Shabbos Kehalacha Vol. 1 pages 244-247.

This question is dealt with extensively by many different Poskim of the previous and current generation. Some, including the Munkantcher permit it entirely. Others, including the Minchas Yitzchak and Sheivet Haleivi rule that [Lechatchilah] this is completely forbidden, for the reason that it appears like belittling of Shabbos. Others, including the Chazon Ish, Igros Moshe, and Rav Shlomo Zalman Aurbauch rule that if the food is fully cooked and the flame is covered, it is allowed. The ruling here is based on this latter opinion.

The Laws and Customs of Motzei Shabbos

Based on Shulchan Aruch Chapters 293-300

Table of Contents

Chapter 1: The leave of Shabbos and Maariv

1. **When is the conclusion of Shabbos and hence Melacha is permitted?**
A. At what time is Shabbos over?
B. Saying Baruch Hamavdil or Havdala prior to doing Melacha:
C. Delaying Melacha until after Maariv:
D. May one who has not yet said Hamavdil ask another Jew to do Melacha for him?

Q&A

Practically how much time after sunset is the conclusion of Shabbos?
What is one to do if he does not know what time Shabbos is over?
May one who follows the time of Rabbeinu Tam change his custom to follow the earlier time?
May one who follows Rabbeinu Tam ask another to do Melacha for him?
May one who follows Rabbeinu Tam Daven Maariv prior to the leave of Shabbos of Rabbeinu Tam?
How does one fulfill the Mitzvah of Tosefes Shabbos?
How much time of Tosefes Shabbos is one to add after Shabbos?
Is there a maximum amount of time that one can add to the Mitzvah of Tosefes Shabbos?
Does one fulfill his obligation if he thought the words of "Baruch Hamavdil" without verbalizing them?
If one is in the bathroom by the leave of Shabbos and needs to cut toilet paper may he say "Baruch Hamavdil" in that area?
If a woman lit Yom Tov candles on the second night of Yom Tov and after saying the blessing remembered that she did not yet say Baruch Hamavdil, what is she to do?
If one recited "Baruch Hamavdil Bein Kodesh Lechol" instead of "Bein Kodesh Lekodesh" on Motzei Shabbos which is Yom Tov has he fulfilled his obligation?
If a Jew did Melacha prior to saying Baruch Hamavdil, may another Jew benefit from that Melacha?
May one smoke cigarettes before Maariv after saying Baruch Hamavdil?
May women do Melacha prior to the conclusion of Maariv in Shul?
If the electricity went out on Shabbos may it be turned on before Barchu of Maariv?

2. **Maariv**
Q&A
Is one who has a Yartzite the coming week to Daven for the Amud on Motzei Shabbos?
If one has not yet recited Birchas Hamazon and the Minyan has already begun Maariv, what is he to do?

3. **"Ata Chonantanu": Saying Havdala in Shemoneh Esrei:**
Q&A
If one did Rabbinical Melacha prior to saying Baruch Hamavdil or Havdala, must he repeat Shemoneh Esrei?
If one ate or drank after Shabbos prior to Maariv and then Davened Shemoneh Esrei without Ata Chonantanu, must he repeat Shemoneh Esrei?
If one forgot to say Ata Chonantanu in Maariv and then said a Bracha on a food is he to eat the food, and must he repeat Shemoneh Esrei?
If one forgot to say Ata Chonantanu in his second Shemoneh Esrei which he had to repeat due to eating or Melacha, what is the law?
If one forgot Ata Chonantanu in Maariv of Motzei Yom Tov what is the law?
prior to saying Hamavdil, must he repeat Shemoneh Esrei?
If one forgot Ata Chonantanu and did Melacha prior to Havdala, and then forgot to repeat Shemoneh Esrei at night, is he to repeat Tashlumin after Shacharis on Sunday?
What if in the above case he only remembered past midday of Sunday? Is he to say Ata Chonantanu in Mincha or a later Davening?

If one said Havdala over wine before repeating Shemoneh Esrei in a scenario that he was required to do so must he still repeat Shemoneh Esrei?

If one must repeat Shemoneh Esrei of Maariv such as due to forgetting Yaleh Veyavo on Chol Hamoed, or Vesein Tal Umatar, and the like, must he also recite Ata Chonantanu because in his second Shemoneh Esrei?

If one did not Daven on Motzei Shabbos due to being an Onein, but is Davening on Sunday, is he to say Ata Chonantanu in his Davening?

If one forgot to say Vetodieinu in Shemoneh Esrei of Yom Tov which is Motzei Shabbos may he add it in when he remembers?

4. Vayehi Noam:

Q&A

Is the Chazan to recite Kadosh, Kadosh, Kadosh and Baruch Kevod out loud when he recites the prayer of Ata Kadosh?

If Pesach falls on Shabbos, is Vayehi Noam recited on the Motzei Shabbos prior to it?

What is the law if the Chazan absentmindedly said Kaddish Shalem with Tiskabel before Vayehi Noam, is he then to say half Kaddish after Vayehi Noam instead of Kaddish Tiskabel?

If one began saying Tiskabel before Vayehi Noam and then remembered, is he to complete the Kaddish?

Is Vayehi Noam recited in the house of an Avel?

Does an Avel within Shiva recite Vayehi Noam?

Does a Chasan within seven days of his wedding recite Vayehi Noam?

Chapter 2: Havdala

1. Havdala:

2. Eating before Havdala:

Q&A

If one said Havdala early, before sunset, may he eat after sunset?

From the letter of the law may one drink water based soft drinks before Havdala?

May women eat or drink prior to Havdala?

May children eat prior to Havdala?

If one began eating a meal before sunset may he eat fruits, pastries and the like after sunset even though they will require a new blessing?

If one began eating Mezonos before sunset may he continue to do so after sunset?

If one is reciting Birchas Hamazon after sunset but before nightfall, may he drink the Kos Shel Bracha?

If one made Sheva Brachos for the third meal, what is one to do with the Kos Shel Bracha?

3. The blessings recited during Havdala

Q&A

Are the Pesukim of Hinei Keil Yeshuasi recited on Motzei Yom Tov?

Are the Pesukim of Hinei Keil Yeshuasi recited on Motzei Tishe Beav which falls on Sunday?

Are the Pesukim of Hinei Keil Yeshuasi recited when an Avel says Havdala?

If one skipped the blessing of Hagafen and only remembered after drinking the wine does he fulfill his obligation?

If one said the blessing of Meoreiy Haeish prior to Besamim what is he to do?

What is the law if one said Meorei Haeish and then quickly corrected himself and said Minei Besamim?

If one talked during Havdala must he hear or say it again?

If one accidently drank the wine after saying the blessing of Hagafen, what is he to do?

If one forgot to say the blessing of Hagafen what is he to do?

If one accidently concluded the blessing of Hamavdil with the words "Bein Kodesh Lekodesh" what is he to do?

If one accidently concluded the blessing "Bein Kodesh Lechol" on Motzei Shabbos which is Yom Tov what is he to do?

4. Customs related to Havdala:

5. Laws relating to the cup of wine:

Q&A

If one said Havdala and then realized there was a hole in the cup, does he need to repeat Havdala?

If one said Havdala over wine and then when he tasted it noticed the wine is spoiled or is really colored water, must he repeat Havdala?

If one said Havdala over wine and it spilled prior to having a chance to drink from it what is the law?

6. How to hold the Kiddush cup, Besamim throughout Havdala:

Q&A

How is a lefty to hold onto the Havdala cup?

7. Using beverages other than wine for Havdala:

List of beverages that are considered Chamer Medina and may be used when no wine is available:

8. The law if no wine or other beverages are available:

A. Havdala over bread:

B. Eating prior to Havdala when no beverages are available for Havdala:

C. The blessing of Besamim and Meoreiy Haeish:

9. The laws of Besamim:

A. General Laws:

B. What should one use for Besamim:

Q&A

If one is unsure if he is able to smell may he say the blessing of Besamim in Havdala?

How strong must one's sense of smell be in order to be allowed to say the blessing?

If one said the blessing of Besamim and then realized he does not have a sense of smell must he repeat the blessing of Hagafen?

Until when on Motzei Shabbos may the blessing over Besamim be recited?

If there are many people listening to Havdala should they all smell the Besamim?

May one use an Esrog or Hadassim as Besamim on Shabbos Chol Hamoed Sukkos?

May one use an empty container of Besamim if it has a good smell?

May one use for Besamim a cloth pocket which contains spices?

Must one open the Besamim jar to smell if the smell protrudes from its cover even while closed?

May one use bathroom freshener or bathroom spices for Besamim?

May one use perfume or cologne for Besamim?

May one say a blessing of Besamim on cigarette or tobacco?

May one smell Besamim after Shabbos prior to Havdala?

If one smelled Besamim after Shabbos prior to Havdala may he still say the blessing in Havdala?

If one forgot to say the blessing on Besamim or Haeish before the blessing of Havdala, should he say it after the blessing of Havdala prior to drinking, or after drinking?

Is one to designate a special vessel to hold the Besamim used during Havdala?

Is a mourner to say the blessing over Besamim in Havdala?

When smelling Besamim on Motzei Shabbos outside of Havdala is the blessing of Minei Besamim to be recited even over spices that are Atzei or Asvei Besamim?

10. The laws of Meoreiy Haeish:

A. General Laws:

B. The laws of the candle:

Q&A

Until when on Motzei Shabbos may the blessing over fire be recited?

When is one to place his hands near the flame, before or after the blessing of Meoreiy Haeish?

Does one fulfill his obligation if he did not spread his fingers near the flame?

Are women to say the blessing of Meoreiy Haeish when they say Havdala?

Are women to place their hands by the fire and look at their nails by the blessing of Meoreiy Haeish?

Must one turn off the lights when the blessing of Meoreiy Haeish is recited?

May one benefit from light of a fire prior to saying Borei Meoreiy Haeish?

May one light a match, candle or cigarette from the Havdala candle?

May one say the blessing of Meoreiy Haeish if he can only see the flame through a mirror?

May one use a match to say Meorei Haeish?

May one use an electric light to say Havdala?

May one use the flame of a lighter for Havdala?

May one use the flame of a gas stove to say Meorei Haeish?

If one does not have a match can he ask a gentile to light his Havdala candle?

May one use candles lit by an Avel for Havdala?

May one use a Yartzite candle for Havdala?

May one wear eyeglasses during the blessing of Meoreiy Haeish?

Must one open a window if it is separating between himself and the flame?

11. Hearing Havdala from another person:

Q&A

Is it better to personally say Havdala rather than hear it from another?

May one stipulate at the time of hearing Havdala that if he later decides to say Havdala himself he will not be Yotzei with the current Havdala that he heard?

If one cannot hear the person saying Havdala due to being hard of hearing, or due to his distance from him, may he say the words of Havdala to himself?

If one entered in middle of Havdala is he still Yotzei?

May one repeat Havdala for himself if he was already Yotzei with the Havdala of another person?

If one is in middle of Maariv and hears Havdala is he Yotzei?

Can Havdala be said over loud speaker or Telephone?

May one hear Havdala from a child?

If there are many people listening to Havdala should they all smell the Besamim and place their fingers by the candle?

12. Havdala in Shul:

13. Repeating Havdala for others:

14. May one say Havdala and have another person drink the wine?

Q&A

If one is unable to drink wine is it better for him to say Havdala and have another person drink the wine rather than have someone else repeat Havdala for him?

If one cannot drink wine and there are other Chomer Medina drinks available should he say Havdala over the wine having another person drink it, or should he simply use other beverages and drink it himself?

15. Are women obligated in Havdala?

Q&A

Are women to say the blessing of Meoreiy Haeish when they say Havdala?

Are women to place their hands by the fire and look at their nails by the blessing of Meoreiy Haeish?

May women drink from the wine of Havdala?

What is a woman to do if she cannot say Havdala over wine?

May male children be Yotzei Havdala from a woman?

May women eat or drink prior to Havdala?

16. Are children obligated in Havdala?

Q&A

If the child did not hear Havdala on Motzei Shabbos is he to hear Havdala on Sunday?

If the children will be sleeping by the time Havdala is said what is one to do?

If a boy turned Bar Mitzvah on Motzei Shabbos may he say Havdala for others that Motzei Shabbos?

May children eat prior to Havdala?

17. Havdala during the nine days:

18. Havdala when Tishe Beav falls on Motzei Shabbos:

Q&A

Who is to drink the Havdala wine in the above scenario?

Havdala for an Avel:

19. May one say Havdala early before Shabbos is over if he will be unable to say it after Shabbos?

Q&A

If someone said or heard Havdala before Shabbos is over, prior to Bentching is he to say Ritzei in Bentching?

20. If one did not say Havdala on Motzei Shabbos:

Q&A

May one who did not say Havdala on Motzei Yom Tov say it the next day?

What is one to do if he forgot to say Havdala in Kiddush of Yom Tov which falls on Motzei Shabbos?

If one forgot to say Havdala on Motzei Rosh Hashana and then remembered on Tzom Gedalia what is he to do?

Is one who is saying Havdala on Sunday or onwards to still say the verses of Hinei Keil Yeshuasi?

If one accidently recited the blessing of Besamim and Haeish while saying Havdala on Sunday –Tuesday is it considered an interval between the blessing of Hagafen and drinking the wine?

21. One who is washing on bread directly after Havdala:

Q&A

If one has Mezonos foods on the table when he says Havdala, are they to be covered?

If one had drinks on the table while saying Havdala is he to say a blessing prior to drinking them after Havdala?

22. Vayiten Lecha:

Q&A

Is Vayiten Lecha recited on Motzei Yom Tov?

Is Vayiten Lecha recited on Motzei Shabbos Chol Hamoed?

Is Vayiten Lecha recited on Motzei Shabbos which coincides with Yom Tov?

Is Vayiten Lecha recited on Motzei Shabbos which coincides with Tishe Beav?

May an Avel recite Vayiten Lecha?

Learning Torah directly after Havdala:

May one recite Pesukim from Tanach on Motzei Shabbos?

Chapter 3: Melaveh Malka

1. Mentioning Eliyahu Hanavi:

2. Melaveh Malka:
A. Setting the table:
B. The Menu
C. Singing:
D. Lighting candles:
E. Not to do Melacha until after Melaveh Malka:

Q&A

The source behind Melaveh Malka:
When should one eat the Melaveh Malka?
Are women obligated to eat Melaveh Malka?
If one's third meal continued until after Shabbos, must he still eat Melaveh Malka?
Is it a Chabad custom to recite the Zemiros or Piyutim for Motzei Shabbos?
How is one to fulfill Melaveh Malka when Yom Tov falls on Motzei Shabbos?
The Seder of Melaveh Malka in accordance to the Kabalists:
Drawing the holiness of Shabbos into the weekday:
The Luz Bone:
Chibut Hakever:
Preventive Medicine for the healthy:
Segula for an easy birth:
Segula to prevent Atzvus:
Segula for Parnasa:
Saves one from heresy and murder:
The Neshama Yiseira:
Tikkun for the third meal:
The feast of David Malka Mashicha:

3. Drawing water

Q&A

How is one to fulfill the above Segula if he does not have a well or spring available to draw water from?
Does it suffice to simply open the faucets?

4. Folding ones Tallis:

5. When after Shabbos may one remove his Shabbos clothing?
Giving charity and spending money on Motzei Shabbos
Not to get angry on Motzei Shabbos:

6. Kerias Shema Sheal Hamita
Traveling on Motzei Shabbos

Chapter 1:
The Leave of Shabbos &
Maariv

1. When is the conclusion of Shabbos and hence Melacha is permitted?[1]

The conclusion of Shabbos which allows one to perform Melacha is dependent on three factors:

- A. The time of the night.
- B. Saying Havdala or Baruch Hamavdil.
- C. Conclusion of Maariv in Shul.
- Some are accustomed to further delay doing Melacha until Havdala or Melaveh Malka.

A. At what time is Shabbos over?

Shabbos ends at night after three small stars are able to be seen.[2] One must delay doing Melacha until he sees three small stars <u>consecutively in one line</u>. It does not suffice with three small stars which are scattered.[3] [The amount of time between seeing three <u>scattered</u> small stars and three small stars <u>consecutively</u> is four minutes. Hence once three small scattered stars can be seen one is to wait four minutes and may then do Melacha.[4] However see Q&A for other opinions.]

If it is a cloudy day and one cannot see the stars, he is to delay doing Melacha until he knows for certain that the stars are visible. [Likewise if one is in doubt if the stars are small he is to wait until he knows for certain that they are small.[5]]

Melacha during Bein Hashmashos:[6] In all circumstances that Rabbinical Melacha is permitted during Bein Hashmashos, it is permitted by both Bein Hashmashos of Erev Shabbos and <u>Motzei Shabbos</u>.[7] [For a list of circumstance in which Rabbinical Melacha is allowed during Bein Hashmashos-see chapter 261 or "The Laws of Bein Hashmashos" which will IY"H be available in one of the coming volumes.]

Large, medium and small stars

Orion Belt-Three medium consecutive stars

---

[1] 293/1

[2] Although night time is generally defined as when three medium stars are able to be seen, nevertheless since people are not expert in the difference of size between a large and medium star, therefore one is required to wait until three small stars are seen. [ibid; Beis Yosef in name of Rabbeinu Yonah]

<u>Biurim:</u> Regarding the fact that in the Shulchan Aruch Admur rules like Rabbeinu Tam that Tzeis Hakochavim begins only 72/96 minutes after nightfall, while here it is omitted and only the sign of stars is mentioned, M"B 293/6 asks this same question on the Michaber. He explains the calculation of stars is only given when one cannot calculate the time, such as he does not know when sunset occurred and he thus cannot calculate the 72 minutes. Ideally however if one could calculate the 72 minutes, he is to delay 72 minutes according to Rabbeinu Tam. However in the Biur Halacha "Ad" he brings from the Minchas Cohen that even according to Rabbeinu Tam once three small stars can be seen there is no need to wait any longer. [See however Piskeiy Teshuvos 293 footnote 21 for those which argue on this conclusion]

[3] Ideally Shabbos is over once three small stars can be seen, even if they are scattered. However it is a positive command to add onto Shabbos, and this measurement of time is a minimum of waiting until three small stars can be seen in one row. [ibid]

<u>Other Opinions:</u> The Digul Merivav rules it suffices to wait a slight amount of time after one sees three small stars, even if they are scattered. Others hold one is to wait until the entire sky is filled with stars. [See Kaf Hachaim 293/4]

[4] Ketzos Hashulchan 93 footnote 1. It is not mentioned in Poskim the definition of consecutive stars. Thus one is to wait four minutes, as the reason for waiting to see three small consecutive stars is for Tosefes Shabbos, and since 4 minutes is the minimum amount of time needed for Tosefes Shabbos, therefore once three small stars are visible one is to wait four minutes and do Melacha.

<u>Other Opinions:</u> The above ruling is based on the understanding of the Ketzos Hashulchan ibid and Avnei Nezer 498/3 in the Seder Hachnasas Shabbos of Admur, that the time of Tosefes Shabbos is 4 minutes. Eretz Tzevi 60 however negates their proofs and rules one cannot learn from the above area in Admur anything with regards to the minimum Shiur of time, and rather even waiting one moment is valid.

[5] Ketzos Hashulchan 93 footnote 2

[6] 342/1

[7] Although there is an opinion [M"A 342] which doubts whether the allowances of Bein Hashmashos of Erev Shabbos apply equally to Bein Hashmashos of Motzei Shabbos, as perhaps due to the doubt of Bein Hashmashos the holiness of the essence of the day of Shabbos does not leave, (nevertheless one may be lenient). [ibid] So rules also Bircheiy Yosef and Beis Meir that there is no differentiation. [M"B 342/2], and so seems to be the opinion of the M"A himself in 623/4 which allows blowing Shofar by Bein Hashmashos of Yom Kippur, as explains the Peri Megadim there.

<u>Other Opinions:</u> The Chayeh Adam [brought in M"B 342/2 concludes that one is to be stringent.

<u>Opinion of the Mishneh Berurah:</u> In Biur Halacha 342 "Bein Hashmashos" he concludes to be stringent by Bein Hashmashos of Motzei Shabbos as in addition to the doubts of the M"A ibid, there are also many doubts involved with when is Bein Hashmashos.

Practically how much time after sunset is the conclusion of Shabbos?

In Eretz Yisrael:[8] One is to wait a minimum of 34-35[9] minutes after sunset[10] during the summer months[11], and a minimum of 28-29 minutes after sunset in the winter months.[12] [Others[13] rule one is to wait 32 minutes past sunset in the winter months and 38 minutes past sunset in the summer months.[14] Others[15] rule one is to wait between 45-50 minutes after sunset.]

Diaspora: The amount of time one needs to wait after sunset fluctuates according to each region. The custom in New York is to wait 50 minutes from sunset.[16] [In general the custom is that each country calculates the leave of Shabbos based on when the sun reaches eight degrees below the horizon.[17]]

Zman Rabbeinu Tam:[18]

It is not the Chabad custom [or the custom of majority of world Jewry[19]] to delay the exit of Shabbos until after the Zman Rabbeinu Tam. Nevertheless many meticulous Jews are accustomed to be stringent in this matter.

How long after sunset is Zman Rabbeinu Tam:[20] Those which follow Rabbeinu Tam wait 72 minutes[21] [or 96 minutes[22]] past sunset in all areas of the world[23], [besides for those areas in which the time of Geonim is later than Rabbeinu Tam]. There is dispute amongst Poskim if the Zman of Rabbeinu Tam fluctuates between the winter and summer months or remain a literal 72 minutes throughout the year.

---

[8] The first calculation brought [not in brackets] is based on Ketzos Hashulchan 93 footnote 2; Shiureiy Tziyon of Grach Naah p. 76 and Kitzur Halachos Shabbos Miluim p. 92-100. This calculation follows the amount of minutes needed to wait after sunset as ruled by the Ketzos Hashulchan, and includes the novelty of Admur that sunset begins only 4 [5] minutes after the visible sunset which is recorded on calendars.
Biurim: Regarding the fact that at the mentioned times small stars are not yet visible in the sky, see M"B 293/6; Kitzur Hilchos Shabbos Miluim p. 100-101 for an explanation on this matter. There he explains that in truth the stars are visible under proper weather conditions, and that the main calculation is based on time, and the calculation of stars is only given when one cannot calculate the time, such as he does not know when sunset occurred.

[9] See Kitzur Hilchos Shabbos Miluim p. 99 that in Eretz Yisrael there are 5 minutes between the Shekia Haniris and the Shekia Haamitis. Thus we wrote 34-35 minutes taking into account this extra minute.

[10] This refers to Shekia Haniris, which is the sunset written in calendars.
Shekia Haniris "the visible sunset" is 4/5 minutes before the Shekia Hamitis "the true sunset". Hence from the true sunset one must only wait 20/21 minutes in the winter and 26/27 minutes in the summer. [Kitzur Hilchos Shabbos 293 based on Admur in Seder Hachnasas Shabbos]

[11] Bein Hashmashos in Eretz Yisrael varies between the summer and winter months.

[12] **Background of above calculation:**
1. Sunset begins 4-5 minutes after the visible sunset recorded on calendars. [See Seder Hachnasas Shabbos of Admur, and Kitzur Halachos ibid]
2. After 4-5 pass and sunset begins Bein Hashmashos lasts between 15-26 minutes depending on the time of year. It lasts between 15-20 minutes in the winter and 20-26 minutes in the summer. [See Ketzos Hashulchan and Shiureiy Tziyon ibid]
3. One is to add 4 minutes for Tosefes Shabbos.

Grand Total: Based on the above calculation in order to be sure it is always past the amount of time needed to wait one is to always wait during the winter months a minimum of 29 minutes after the recorded sunset in calendars and in the summer he is to wait 35 minutes from the recorded time in the calendar.

Ruling of Harav Hagaon Avraham Chaim Naah in Ketzos Hashulchan ibid and Shiureiy Tziyon ibid:
One is to wait a minimum of 30 minutes after sunset during the summer months [Nissan-Tishreiy], and a minimum of 24 minutes after sunset in the winter months [Tishreiy-Nissan].
VeTzaruch Iyun in Ketzos Hashulchan if this refers to the Shekia Hamitis or Shekia Haniris which is a 4 minute difference. No mention is made what Shekia he is referring to neither in Ketzos Hashulchan or in Shiureiy Tziyon. Kitzur Halachos Admur Miluim p. 104 learns in the Ketzos Hashulchan that we measure from the Shekia Haniris. Although he himself argues on this premises concluding it must refer to the Shekia Haamitis.

[13] Sefer Bein Hashmashos of Rav Yechial Michel Tuchensky brought in Piskeiy Teshuvos 293/4. There he also records the opinion of Grach Naah which we wrote above.

[14] They checked and found that three small consecutive stars cannot be seen prior to this time in summer and winter. At this time the sun is 8 degrees below the horizon.

[15] Piskeiy Teshuvos ibid in name of Chazon Ish and Rav Aron of Belz

[16] Igros Moshe 4/62; However the Rebbe [Shaareiy Halacha Uminhag 155] after bringing the custom expressed himself there "I am not responsible for this calculation." See there that some wanted to suggest that based on Admur one must always wait 72 minutes. However the Rebbe negated this logic.

[17] See Piskeiy Teshuvos 293/4; Sefer Biur Halacha [Zilber] 293

[18] Ketzos Hashulchan 93 footnote 2; See Piskeiy Teshuvos 293/4 for a summary of all the opinions regarding Rabbeinu Tam after Shabbos.

[19] Piskeiy Teshuvos ibid

[20] Ketzos Hashulchan 93 footnote 2

[21] See 261/5. However based on the calculation of 24 minutes per Mil, Zman Rabbeinu Tam is 96 minutes after sunset, and so is the custom of some communities. [Beis Avi 3/117; Beis Yisrael 1/180; Piskeiy Teshuvos ibid]

[22] So is the custom of some communities as mentioned in the Poskim in previous footnote.

[23] It is interesting to note that in many European countries [and Russia] the time of Rabbeinu Tam is very close in time to the time of the exit of Shabbos which we follow. [sometimes even only one minute apart] Absurdly in certain Northeast countries the time of Rabbeinu Tam actually falls earlier than the time we follow based on the Geonim!

The more one delays the end of Shabbos, so is his time in Gehenim delayed:[24]
It is written in the name of Tzadikim that based on how long one delays his leave of Shabbos will be the delay of his leave from Gehenim on Shabbos, as on Shabbos the souls are freed from Gehenem.

What is one to do if he does not know what time Shabbos is over?[25]
If he cannot tell the difference between medium and small stars, then he is to wait until the sky is filled with stars and he may then do Melacha.

Q&A on Zman Rabbeinu Tam

May one who follows the time of Rabbeinu Tam change his custom to follow the earlier time?[26]
Yes although he must first do Hataras Nedarim. If this is the custom of one's forefathers, he is not to change his custom.

May one who follows Rabbeinu Tam ask another to do Melacha for him?
No.[27] If however one follows Rabbeinu Tam only regarding Shabbos in order to delay Shabbos as much as possible, while regarding other matters [such as Taanis] he follows the Geonim, then he may ask others to do Melacha for him.[28]

May one who follows Rabbeinu Tam Daven Maariv prior to the leave of Shabbos of Rabbeinu Tam?[29]
Yes. Although some[30] write that if one follows Rabbeinu Tam regarding all matters he is to refrain from doing so unless it is a time of need.

Q&A On Tosefes Shabbos

How does one fulfill the Mitzvah of Tosefes Shabbos?[31]
Upon the conclusion of Shabbos, which is defined as the visibility of three small stars, one fulfils the Mitzvah of Tosefes Shabbos until he says Havdala over wine, or in Maariv, or says Baruch Hamavdil, [or does Melacha[32]]. This applies even if he does not consciously intend to fulfill the Mitzvah, nevertheless so long as he has not said Hamavdil and has not done Melacha his Shabbos is still continuing. There is thus no need to consciously have in one's mind or verbalize that he desires to continue the Shabbos past nightfall, although some suggest doing so.[33]

How much time of Tosefes Shabbos is one to add after Shabbos?
Once three small scattered stars can be seen one is to wait four minutes and may then do Melacha.[34]
Some[35] however write the custom[36] is to wait fifteen minutes from after three small stars become visible.[37]

---

[24] See Piskeiy Teshuvos 256 footnote 12
[25] Piskeiy Teshuvos 293/5
[26] Piskeiy Teshuvos 293/4
[27] Sheivet Haleivi 1/53; Minchas Shabbos 263/7; Piskeiy Teshuvos 263/44 and 293
[28] Teshuvos Vehanhagos 1/234
[29] See Piskeiy Teshuvos 293/6
[30] Divreiy Yatziv 1/1134; However see SSH"K 59 footnote 17 which is lenient even in such a case.
[31] See Piskeiy Teshuvos 293/2 footnote 5
[32] Seemingly once one does Melacha, even if it is prior to saying Hamavdil, his Tosefes Shabbos is now over, as this action itself proves that he has now ended his Tosefes Shabbos. We do not say that it is still Tosefes Shabbos and he has thus done a prohibition of Melacha during his Tosefes Shabbos. [Accordingly this would answer the questions posed in Ashel Avraham Butchacher 299] It is nevertheless forbidden to do Melacha until one says Hamavdil due to the obligation to escort the king with Hamavdil prior to Melacha. See next Halacha. [So writes also Piskeiy Teshuvos 293/2 footnote 10]
[33] Piskeiy Teshuvos ibid suggest doing so, even though this concept is not brought anywhere in Poskim. In Mishmeres Shalom 29/6 he brings that one is to verbalize his acceptance of Tosefes Shabbos, although this is with regards to Erev Shabbos and not Motzei Shabbos as is implied from there.
[34] Ketzos Hashulchan 93 footnote 1. It is not mentioned in Poskim the definition of consecutive stars. Thus one is to wait four minutes as the reason for waiting to see three small consecutive stars is for Tosefes Shabbos, and since 4 minutes is the minimum amount of time needed for Tosefes Shabbos, therefore once three small stars are visible one is to wait four minutes and do Melacha.
Other Opinions: The above ruling is based on the understanding of the Ketzos Hashulchan and Avnei Nezer 498/3 in the Seder Hachnasas Shabbos of Admur, that the time of Tosefes Shabbos is 4 minutes. Eretz Tzevi 60 however negates their proofs and rules one cannot learn from the above area in Admur anything with regards to the minimum Shiur of time, and rather even waiting one moment is valid.
[35] Toras Shabbos 293/1; and so writes Piskeiy Teshuvos 293/2
[36] They write there that it is the "custom of Israel".
[37] Piskeiy Teshuvos 293/2

Is there a maximum amount of time that one can add to the Mitzvah of Tosefes Shabbos?[38]
Some[39] rule up to three hours. Others[40] rule one can only add to Shabbos up to 72 minutes from after Shabbos. Others[41] rule one can only add a mere moment. Others[42] rule one can add as much as he desires.

B. Saying Baruch Hamavdil or Havdala prior to doing Melacha:[43]
Even after the time of night that hails the leave of Shabbos has arrived[44] the Sages forbade one from doing Melacha until he escorts the King.[45] This is done through reciting Havdala in prayer or over wine, or through simply saying the words "Baruch[46] Hamavdil Bein Kodesh Lechol"[47].

Performing Rabbinical prohibitions prior to saying Hamavdil: The above prohibition of doing Melacha prior to saying Hamavdil applies likewise to Rabbinical Melacha. Thus one may not even move the Havdala candle until he says Havdala in prayer or says Baruch Hamavdil.[48] (However those Rabbinical prohibitions relevant to speech[49] are permitted even before saying Havdala or Baruch Hamavdil, once Shabbos is over. This however is with exception to asking bodily requests from G-d which is only allowed after one says Hamavdil.[50]) Likewise some permit performing, after Shabbos is over but prior to saying Havdala, all Rabbinical prohibitions which are forbidden simply due to them being a mundane act. Practically the custom is to be lenient on Motzei Yom Kippur.[51]

---

[38] This does not mean to ask "must one must break Shabbos after a maximum amount of time" but rather until how long does he fulfill the Mitzvah of Tosefes Shabbos.

[39] Shulchan Hatahor 188/15

[40] Olas Tamid brought in M"A 188/18

[41] Peri Megadim 188 A"A 18 in his explanation of M"A that after one moment of Tosefes Shabbos, it is now over.

[42] Piskeiy Teshuvos 293/2 based on Peri Megadim and Bach

[43] 299/15-16

[44] Meaning even if three consecutive small stars are visible and it is thus no longer Shabbos, and he has already added Mechol Al Hakodesh, he may nevertheless still not do Melacha. [ibid]

[45] Thus the reason behind this prohibition has nothing to do with the Kedusha of Shabbos, but due to it being forbidden for one to do his own matters prior to escorting the king. This follows the ruling of the Taz 263/3
Vetzaruch Iyun why this is not forbidden due to Tosefes Shabbos in which case one cannot do any Melacha until he concludes Shabbos? Seemingly one must say that that as soon as one does Melacha after Shabbos, that itself is an action which says "my Tosefes Shabbos has concluded" and hence only due to this new prohibition of escorting the king is it forbidden to do Melacha. [See also Kitzur Halachos Miluim p. 123 for a similar explanation; Piskeiy Teshuvos 299 footnote 103; See also Other Opinions below.]
Other Opinions: The M"B [299/33] rules one must say Havdala prior to doing Melacha because the holiness of Shabbos partially continues until Havdala and therefore the Sages forbade it in Melacha. This follows the ruling of the Levush 263. The Ashel Avraham Butchatcher 299 seems to learn that the prohibition applies due to Tosefes Shabbos.

[46] This ruling of Admur follows the ruling of Levush. The Michaber however rules one simply says Hamavdil Bein Kodesh Lechol, without the word Baruch.

[47] 299/16; These words serve as recognition of escorting the king. [ibid]
Other Opinions: The above wording follows the opinion of Rashi and the Beis Yosef which argue there is no need to say Hashem's name in the blessing. Others however rule one must say Baruch Hamavdil with Hashem's name. Practically the ruling is that one may not do so. [Kaf Hachaim 299/56] The Kitzur SH"A 96/5 based on Abudarham writes that one is to recite the entire Nusach of the blessing of Havdala recited over wine without Hashem's name. This is not the accepted ruling of Achronim.
Gutt Voch/G-d of Avraham: See Piskeiy Teshuvos 299/16 regarding if saying Shavua Tov or G-d of Avraham is considered as if one said Baruch Hamavdil.

[48] 299/19

[49] Such as talking of business related matters or Amira Lenachri. [Piskeiy Teshuvos 299/13]

[50] Requesting bodily matters is forbidden on Shabbos, and this prohibition extends until Havdala is said. [Ibid; 294/1; Kaf Hachaim 299/51]

[51] With regards to blowing the Shofar after Neila. [623/11]
Other Opinions brought in Admur: There are those opinions [Rabbeinu Yerucham] which rule that only those Melachas which are time consuming and take effort, such as weaving, writing and chopping wood, were forbidden by the Sages before saying Havdala or Baruch Hamavdil. However those Melachas which are performed without any effort, such as lighting a candle or carrying 4 Amos in a public domain, are permitted even if they are of Biblical nature, if the proper time of night has arrived, even if one has not yet said Hamavdil.
Practically however Admur rules [in parentheses, and so is the main opinion-See Kaf Hachaim 299/52] that the above differentiation was only said as a stringency regarding doing Melacha after saying Havdala in prayer but prior to Havdala over wine. As some opinions [Rambam/Rosh] rule that even if one said Havdala in prayer he may still not do any time consuming Melacha until after he says Havdala over wine. However before Baruch Hamavdil or Baruch Hamavdil Havdala in prayer, no Melacha at all may be done. Thus the above differentiation was only given for those which follow this opinion. [In other words there are two disputes: 1. Can non-time consuming Melacha be done before saying Hamavdil? 2. Even if one rules non-time consuming Melacha can be done some opinions rule this is only prior to Havdala over wine and not prior to saying Hamavdil. Meaning they are even further stringent to still forbid time consuming Melacha until after Havdala over wine.]
Practically the main opinion follows that even non-time consuming Melachas are forbidden prior to Havdala or Baruch Hamavdil [unlike Rabbeinu Yerucham], and once Baruch Hamavdil has been said, all Melachos are permitted even prior to Havdala over wine [unlike the opinions which hold time consuming Melacha may not be done prior to Havdala over wine]. Nevertheless one may rely on the first opinion [Rabbeinu Yerucham] regarding not protesting women who are lenient to do non-time consuming Melachas prior to saying Baruch Hamavdil. If however they do time consuming Melachas they must be protested. [299/18]

[According to this opinion one may measure an item once Shabbos is over, even prior to reciting Baruch Hamavdil.[52]]

Performing Melacha prior to Havdala over wine: After Havdala has been recited within prayer, or one has recited the words "Baruch Hamavdil Bein Kodesh Lechol, he may perform all forms of Melacha even prior to saying Havdala over wine.[53] [See next Halacha regarding doing Melacha prior to Maariv or prior to Havdala or prior to eating Melaveh Malka.]

Reminding women to say Baruch Hamavdil:[54] It is of importance to remind women to say Baruch Hamavdil immediately after Shabbos, prior to doing any Melacha. One is to mention this obligation in public gatherings. Those women who do time consuming Melacha prior to saying Baruch Hamavdil are to be protested.[55] Those women who Daven Maariv on Motzei Shabbos are to say Havdala in Ata Chonantanu just like men. They are not required to say Baruch Hamavdil after Davening Maariv unless they forget to say it in Maariv.

Hearing Baruch Hamavdil from another person: Those which do not know to say Baruch Hamavdil are to hear another person say it [and intend to fulfill their obligation through hearing it[56]].

On Motzei Shabbos which is Yom Tov:[57] Based on the above when Yom Tov falls on Motzei Shabbos one may not begin doing any Melacha which is permitted on Yom Tov until he says Havdala, or recites Baruch Hamavdil Bein Kodesh Lekodesh[58], after the conclusion of Shabbos. It is of importance to remind women of this requirement, and have them say Baruch Hamavdil prior to doing any Yom Tov preparations.

Q&A

Does one fulfill his obligation if he thought the words of "Baruch Hamavdil" without verbalizing them?
No.[59] However there are Poskim[60] which write that doing so is valid.

If one is in the bathroom by the leave of Shabbos and needs to cut toilet paper may he say "Baruch Hamavdil" in that area?[61]
Some write one is to think the words of Baruch Hamavdil in his head and then tear the paper with an irregularity if possible.

If a woman lit Yom Tov candles on the second night of Yom Tov and after saying the blessing remembered that she did not yet say Baruch Hamavdil, what is she to do?[62]
Some write she is to think the words in her mind and then light one candle, and then verbalize the Baruch Hamavdil. Afterwards she may light the other candles.

If one recited "Baruch Hamavdil Bein Kodesh <u>Lechol</u>" instead of "Bein Kodesh Lekodesh" on Motzei Shabbos which is Yom Tov has he fulfilled his obligation?
Some[63] rule that he has fulfilled his obligation, although seemingly he should repeat the correct Nusach.[64]

If a Jew did Melacha prior to saying Baruch Hamavdil, may another Jew benefit from that Melacha?[65]
Yes. There is no prohibition of benefiting from such Melacha being that Shabbos was already over. For this reason it is permitted to enter a bus driven by a Jew which has not said Baruch Hamavdil.

---

[52] 306/18 as measuring is only forbidden due to Uvdin Dechol.

[53] See previous footnote that some opinions forbid time consuming Melacha until Havdala is said over wine.
Other opinions: Some rule one may not do Melacha until he says Baruch Hamavdil even if he said Havdala in prayer. They also rule it is best to be stringent not to do any Melacha until Havdala over wine. [Chesed Leavraham brought in Kaf Hachaim 299/59; Ben Ish Chaiy Vayeitzei 22]

[54] 299/18

[55] See previous footnotes regarding the difference between time consuming Melacha and Melachas that can be performed without delay.

[56] Piskeiy Teshuvos 299 footnote 101, Upashut!

[57] 299/17-18

[58] Other Opinions: The Elya Raba rules it does not suffice on Motzei Shabbos which is Yom Tov to simply say Baruch Hamavdil Bein Kodesh Lekodesh. Rather one must say the entire blessing of Hamavdil without Sheim Umalchus. [Brought in Kaf Hachaim 299/58]

[59] Admur 299/15 writes "to say" Baruch Hamavdil.

[60] Ashel Avraham Butchacher 299 writes that if one thinks the words of Baruch Hamavdil he ends his Tosefes Shabbos [and can then do Melacha. See Piskeiy Teshuvos 299 footnote 101.

[61] See Piskeiy Teshuvos 299 footnote 101

[62] Sheivet Hakehasy 6/153

[63] Piskeiy Teshuvos 299 footnote 102

[64] Based on M"A 299/9 that one who says Bein Kodesh Lekodesh when he is meant to say Bein Kodesh Lechol is saying a lie.

[65] Piskeiy Teshuvos 299/13; Tzitz Eliezer 11/34

C. Delaying Melacha until after Maariv:[66]

In addition to waiting until three small consecutive stars are visible and saying Havdala in prayer or saying Baruch Hamavdil, every meticulous[67] person is to delay doing any [Biblical[68]] Melacha until the congregation has recited the Seder Kedusha after Maariv.[69] [One who is Davening in private at home is to wait until the congregation which he Davens at finishes the Seder Kedusha.[70]] Any person who does Melacha before this time does not see a good omen from this Melacha. Even a candle should not be lit until this time, unless it is being used for a Mitzvah purpose, (in which case it may be lit after Barchu[71]). [However today the custom is no longer to delay until Barchu is recited, and rather one may do Melacha for the sake of a Mitzvah even prior to Barchu.[72]]

Rabbinical Melacha prior to Seder Kedusha: One may move a candle and do [any Rabbinical[73]] Melacha of the like prior to Seder Kedusha if the time of night for the leave of Shabbos has arrived and one said Baruch Hamavdil.

Additional customs of delaying Melacha:

Delaying Melacha until after Havdala: Some Poskim[74] write that those which are meticulous are to delay doing Biblical Melacha until after they hear Havdala over wine.[75] Others[76] rule that from the letter of the law one may not do any time consuming Melacha until Havdala. Thus according to them one must avoid writing, sewing and laundry until after Havdala. However one may wash dishes and sweep the floors and the like.[77] According to Admur there is no need to suspect for these opinions.

Not to do Melacha until after Melaveh Malka: Some[78] write since the extra soul does not leave until after Melaveh Malka, it is therefore proper to delay doing Melacha which is unconnected to food preparation until

---

[66] 299/20; brought in Darkei Moshe in name of Oar Zarua, and so writes Zohar

[67] Lit. Baal Nefesh

[68] As will be explained below.

[69] This is based on the Zohar which is very stringent on this matter. [see M"A 299/17; Piskeiy Teshuvos 299/15] The Zohar [brought in Kaf Hachaim 293/7] that doing Melacha before Kedusha Desidra is repelling to Hashem.

[70] Ketzos Hashulchan 95 footnote 5. Vetzaruch Iyun if majority of the city has completed Maariv if one is still to wait on his congregation. [ibid] See Piskeiy Teshuvos 299/15 which suggests based on the above Ketzos Hashulchan that one does not need to wait for his congregation if majority of the city already finished Maariv.

[71] Parentheses are in original. However before Barchu it may not be lit. The source for this ruling is in the Rama 299/10; Ketzos Hashulchan 95 footnote 6 explains the reason for this ruling of the Rama is because in times of the Rama they would not say Baruch Hamavdil and hence Barchu would represent the leave of Shabbos. Thus they would delay until then. Now although according to this reason one who says Baruch Hamavdil should not be limited to wait until Barchu, nevertheless we do not desire to swerve from this custom of waiting until after Barchu. [This ruling of Admur to wait until Barchu even after saying Baruch Hamavdil is an original ruling not brought in other Poskim, and hence perhaps for this reason it is written in parentheses.]

Alternatively Piskeiy Teshuvos 299 footnote 132 explains the reason is because according to the Rama the holiness of Shabbos extends until after the recitation of Barchu as is evident from the ruling that one is to lengthen Barchu [Admur 293/4]. Thus one is to delay Melacha until after Barchu.

Alternatively Kitzur Halachos p. 121 explains the reason for waiting until Barchu is because Admur rules one is not to do Melacha in front of the congregation prior to Shabbos being let out with the saying of Barchu. Since this ruling is a novelty that has not been brought in other Poskim, therefore he writes it in parentheses. [See there in length for the basis of this explanation.]

[72] Ketzos Hashulchan in 95/2 completely omits the need to wait until Barchu, and in footnote 6 he explains it is no longer the custom to do so. So concludes also Piskeiy Teshuvos 299/17

Similarly today the custom of all is to remove their shoes at home when Tishe Beav falls on Motzei Shabbos, and they do not delay to remove his shoes after Barchu, despite this being the clear ruling of the Rama in 553/2.

To note that this was likewise the custom of the Rebbe to enter Shul for Maariv wearing non-leather shoes, despite the Rama's ruling to delay until after Barchu. [See Hiskashrus 950]

[73] Machatzis Hashekel end of 299, ruled also in Piskeiy Teshuvos 299/15; as Rabbinical Melacha some even allow to be done during Bein Hashmashos regularly, and certainly it may be done now before Seder Kedusha.

[74] Toras Shabbos 299/15; Chesed Leavraham brought in Kaf Hachaim 299/59; Ben Ish Chaiy Vayeitzei 22

[75] The reason for this is because according to the Zohar one is not to do Melacha until after Havdala. Likewise according to the Rambam and Rosh one may never do Melacha until after Havdala over wine. Hence although this is not the ruling opinion, one who is meticulous is to suspect for it. [See however Admur 299/18 which brings that Rabbeinu Yerucham rules that even according to the Rambam/Rosh the prohibition applies only to time consuming Melacha while those Melachas which can be done without effort, such as lighting a candle, may be done before Havdala. Admur concludes that we do not rule like the Rambam/Rosh altogether.]

Who lights the Havdala candles according to this meticulous opinion? The Toras Shabbos ibid rules a woman or child is to light the candles and not an adult. The Aruch Hashulchan 299/23 however rules one may light the candle even according to the Zohar.

[76] In Shaareiy Tziyon 299/51 he brings the Derech Chaim which rules one may not do time consuming Melacha until after Havdala. So rules also Siddur Yaavetz in order so one not come to forget to say Havdala. Admur clearly does not suspect for this opinion, as explained in the previous footnote.

[77] See Piskeiy Teshuvos 299 footnote 148

[78] Shaareiy Teshuvah brought in Ketzos Hashulchan 100 footnote 8

after one finishes eating Melaveh Malka. Others[79] write one is not to do any time consuming Melacha until this meal. Based on Kabala[80] one is to avoid even learning Torah until this Seuda.

Q&A

May one smoke cigarettes before Maariv after saying Baruch Hamavdil?[81]
It is improper to smoke cigarettes after Shabbos until the congregation has completed Maariv.[82]

May women do Melacha prior to the conclusion of Maariv in Shul?[83]
Yes. The above restriction against doing Biblical Melacha prior to the recital of Seder Kedusha after Maariv is only relevant to men. Women may begin doing Melacha once the proper time has arrived and have said Baruch Hamavdil.

If the electricity went out on Shabbos may it be turned on before Barchu of Maariv?
Yes.[84] It may be lit after reciting Baruch Hamavdil Bein Kodesh Lechol.

Is a mourner to delay lighting candles for the Amud until after he says Barchu?
There is no need to do so, as long as he says Baruch Hamavdil prior to lighting the candles.

May a Shul begin setting up the accustomed video of the Rebbe after Shemoneh Esrei of Maariv but prior to Ata Kadosh being recited?
No. They are to delay doing so until after Ata Kadosh.

D. May one who has not yet said Hamavdil ask another Jew to do Melacha for him?[85]

One who has not yet said Hamavdil[86] on Motzei Shabbos, in which case he still may not perform Melacha, is nevertheless permitted to ask a Jew which has already said Hamavdil [either in Maariv or on its own] to do Melacha on his behalf.[87] Thus one who continues the third meal into Motzei Shabbos may ask a Jew which has already said Hamavdil to do Melacha on his behalf, and benefit from it at that time, even though he will still mention Shabbos within his Birchas Hamazon.

General Summary:
In order to be allowed to do Melacha after Shabbos one must wait until a row of three small stars are visible, and is to then say Havdala in Davening or over wine or is to say Baruch Hamavdil Bein Kodesh Lechol. From the letter of the law once any of the above have been done he may then do Melacha. However those which are meticulous avoid doing any Biblical Melacha until the congregation has concluded Seder Kedusha in Maariv. [Furthermore there are those which avoid doing Melacha until Havdala over wine. Others avoid Melacha until after eating Melaveh Malka.]

---

[79] Yaavetz, brought in Ketzos Hashulchan ibid

[80] Peri Eitz Chaim; Mishnas Chassidim, brought in Ketzos Hashulchan ibid

[81] Piskeiy Teshuvos 299 footnote 125 quotes this ruling in name of Kaf Hachaim 299/65, although in truth one who looks there sees he never discussed smoking before Maariv but rather before Havdala. In any event the ruling stands true based on the ruling above.

[82] As it is best not to do Melacha until after Seder Dekedusha, as stated above.

[83] Toras Shabbos brought in Piskeiy Teshuvos 299/15

[84] See above in C and the footnotes there.

[85] 263/25; 299/21

[86] In Maariv or on its own. This commonly occurs when one delays Davening Maariv or continues Seudas Shlishis [or Seder Niggunim] past nightfall. [ibid]

[87] It is even permitted for one to benefit from this Melacha before he says Hamavdil. [ibid] See Kuntrus Achron 263/8 for a lengthy discussion in why this is permitted. In short the reason is because the time before and after Shabbos which is considered still as Shabbos for oneself is called Tosefes Shabbos and one only accepts upon himself by Tosefes Shabbos to avoid doing Melacha himself, and not to avoid someone else doing Melacha for him.

Maariv [Halachas 2-5]

2. Maariv

When to Daven Maariv:[88] It is accustomed to delay the Davening of Maariv [past the time of Tzeis Hakochavim[89]] in order to delay the leave of Shabbos.

May one say Havdala and do Melacha prior to Maariv?[90] Once Shabbos has ended, which is when a row of three small stars are visible, it is permitted to say Havdala and do Melacha even prior to Davening Maariv. [Nevertheless it is proper to delay doing any Melacha until the congregation has concluded Vayehi Noam, as explained above in 1C.[91] Some Poskim[92] rule it is always proper to first Daven Maariv and then do Havdala in order to follow the set order that the Sages established.]

Saying Barchu in length:[93] It is accustomed to lengthen the saying of Barchu with a pleasant hymn in order to delay the end of Shabbos and hence add Shabbos into the weekday. [Doing so is a Segula for success and to be saved from injury during the coming week.[94] Likewise it delays the souls from returning to Gehenim.[95]]

May one Daven Maariv early before Shabbos is over:[96] If one will be unable to Daven Maariv and say Havdala after Shabbos, such as he must travel immediately after Shabbos for the purpose of a Mitzvah[97] [or another purpose[98]] he may Daven Maariv and recite Havdala on Shabbos after Plag Hamincha prior to the conclusion of Shabbos.[99] In such a case he does not say a blessing over fire in Havdala, and remains forbidden to do Melacha until a row of three small stars become visible. He likewise must repeat Shema after nightfall. Nevertheless he does not need to repeat Havdala even if the opportunity presents itself after nightfall. If he is traveling for the purpose of a Mitzvah he may choose to only Daven Shemoneh Esrei while it is still Shabbos, and after Shabbos, while traveling, he is to say Shema and its blessings.[100]

Despite the above allowance, some opinions[101] state it is proper for one to refrain from doing the above [i.e. saying Havdala and Maariv while still Shabbos] as it is a puzzling matter to the public.[102]

Are women obligated to Daven Maariv on Motzei Shabbos?[103] Women are not obligated to Daven Maariv on Motzei Shabbos, as is the law regarding Maariv of every night.

Davening Maariv with concentration:[104]
One is to Daven Maariv on Motzaei Shabbos with special concentration, as at that time the Kelipas are reenergized and receive back their power.

---

[88] 293/1

[89] Seemingly this refers to that even after three consecutive small stars are visible the custom is to delay Maariv even longer, to add even more time to Tosefes Shabbos. [See Kitzur Halachos 293 footnote 5] However Piskeiy Teshuvos 293/1 explains that it is coming to say that one is not to Daven Maariv prior to Tosefes Shabbos, and not that one must add more time past Tosefes Shabbos. See Shaareiy Halacha Uminhag 1/155 that one is not to delay Maariv more than the congregation is able to handle.

[90] 293/1

[91] 298/18

[92] Tehila Ledavid 293/1; see Kitzur Halachos Shabbos p. 119;
In however the Sefer Pear Yisrael 1/207 he writes that the Alter Rebbe at times would say Havdala prior to Maariv.

[93] 293/4

[94] Rav Chaim Vital in name of Rav Haiy Gaon. [Kaf Hachaim 293/11]

[95] Rokeiach brought in Kaf Hachaim 293/12. Based on this one must say there are many levels of returning to Gehenem. [Piskeiy Teshuvos 293 footnote 3

[96] 293/2

[97] Admur brings that one has already began walking on Shabbos to the end of the Techum. Vetzaruch Iyun the necessity to say this.

[98] Kaf Hachaim 293/8

[99] See Nemukei Orach Chaim 293/1 regarding how this does not contradict the ruling that one may not ask for his bodily needs on Shabbos itself.

[100] As since he is traveling for a Mitzvah he is allowed to separate Geula from Tefila. [ibid]
However based on Arizal one is to always say Shema before Shemoneh Esrei. [Kaf Hachaim 293/10]

[101] Bach in name of Rashal brought in Magen Avraham 293/4

[102] 293/3

[103] 106/2; 299/18
However in 296/18 Admur writes in the first opinion there that according to those which hold Havdala is a Biblical obligation then also women are obligated to say Havdala in Maariv! Perhaps however this means that if they Daven Maariv then according to this opinion they must say Havdala in Maariv, although they are not in truth obligated to Daven Maariv. In any event Admur concludes there that the main opinion is like the opinion which holds Havdala is Rabbinical. See Piskeiy Teshuvos 299/16

[104] Moreh Betzbah 5/162

Q&A
Is one who has a Yartzite the coming week to Daven for the Amud on Motzei Shabbos?[105]
Many have the custom to Daven for the Amud on Motzei Shabbos if they have a Yartzite that week. This however is not the Chabad custom, unless of course the Yartzite falls on Sunday.

If one has not yet recited Birchas Hamazon and the Minyan has already begun Maariv, what is he to do?[106]
He is to Daven with the Minyan and recite Birchas Hamazon afterwards. In such a case he does not recite Ritzei in Birchas Hamazon.

---

3. *"Ata Chonantanu": Saying Havdala in Shemoneh Esrei:[107]*

Within the prayer of Shemoneh Esrei recited on Motzei Shabbos one is obligated to recite Havdala.[108] This prayer of Havdala is referred to as "Ata Chonantanu" in name of its beginning words. It is recited within the blessing of "Ata Chonein" as printed in Siddurim.[109]

If one forgot to say Ata Chonantanu:[110] If one forgot to say Ata Chonantanu then if he remembered prior to saying Hashem's name in the end of the blessing of Ata Chonein, he is to say it then and continue with "Vichaneinu Meitcha" and finish the blessing.[111] If he remembered only after he already finished the blessing of Chonen Hadaas, or after having already said Hashem's name in the end of the blessing[112], he is to continue with Shemoneh Esrei as normal.[113] He may not go back and repeat the blessing of Ata Chonein.[114] Likewise he is not to add Ata Chonantanu anywhere else in the prayer[115] [although some[116] write to say it in Elokaiy Netzor prior to the second Yehiyu Leratzon]. Nevertheless he is to beware to say Havdala or say "Baruch Hamavdil Bein Kodesh Lechol" prior to doing any Melacha, as will be explained.[117] In a case that one forgot Ata Chonantanu, if he desires, he may repeat

---

[105] Sefer Haminhagim p. 67

[106] Beir Moshe 3/53

[107] Shulchan Aruch Chapter 294

[108] Originally when the Anshei Kneses Hagedola instituted the recital of Havdala together with the other prayers, blessings and Kiddushim, they did not obligate Havdala to be said over wine, but rather within the prayer of Shemoneh Esrei. The reason for this is because when the Jews returned from exile in Babylon they were destitute and could not all afford wine for Havdala. [ibid 294/1] After the Jewish people became more financially stable the Sages instituted for Havdala to be said over wine. Later they once again became destitute and the Sages returned Havdala to be said only in Shemoneh Esrei. Now, in order to prevent Havdala from being constantly moved from the prayer to wine and from wine to prayer based on the Jewish economic state, the Sages instituted that in addition to reciting Havdala within prayer, one is also obligated, if wine is available, to also say Havdala over wine. If however there is no wine available one fulfills his obligation of Havdala within Havdala said in prayer. [ibid 294/2]

[109] The Sages instituted for Havdala to be recited within Ata Chonantanu for two reasons:
1. The ability to distinguish between Shabbos and weekday is a wisdom, and therefore it was established to be said in the blessing of wisdom "Ata Chonantanu".
2. It is forbidden for a person to request mundane matters from G-d on Shabbos. Similarly it is forbidden to request matters from G-d after Shabbos until he says Havdala. Therefore the Sages instituted Havdala in the blessing prior to the requests one asks in Shemoneh Esrei. [294/1]

Where within Ata Chonein is the prayer to be recited? Shaar Hakolel [9/13] learned in Admur in the Siddur that one is to begin saying Ata Chonantanu as soon as he reaches the 4th blessing of Ata Chonein, and the sentence of Ata Chonen is to be omitted. However the custom is to first recite the sentence of Ata Chonein and only then to add in the paragraph of Ata Chonantanu. [Ketzos Hashulchan 93 footnote 4 in name of Radatz Chein; Sefer Haminhagim p. 67]

[110] 294/7

[111] 294/7

[112] One is not to conclude Lamdeini Chukecha in such a case. [Tehila Ledavid 294/7]

[113] He is not required to repeat Shemoneh Esrei or go back being that he will in any event say Havdala over wine and will hence fulfill his obligation then. [ibid]

[114] This applies even if one wants to be extra stringent as it is forbidden to say an unnecessary blessing [Bracha Sheiyno Tzericha]. [294/7] This is because he anyways fulfills his obligation of Havdala over Havdala said over the wine that night or the next day, and thus saying Ata Chonein is now deemed unnecessary.

[115] He may not add it in when he remembers as doing so is considered a Hefsek [interval] within the prayer. This applies even if he remembers right after concluding Chonein Hadaas, prior to beginning the blessing of Hashiveinu. [294/7] Likewise in such a case one is not to say Ata Chonantanu within Shema Koleinu, as the main Halacha follows those opinions which rule only requests may be recited within Shema Koleinu which is itself a request, and Ata Chonantanu is not a request. Nevertheless, this only applies if one expects to do Havdala over wine that night or on Sunday. If however one does not have wine or expect to receive wine until after Sunday, he is to recite it within Shema Koleinu, as will be explained later. [294/5]

Other Opinions: There are Poskim which rule one may say Ata Chonanatanu after Chonein Hadaas before beginning Hashiveinu. [see Kaf Hachaim 294/18; Siddur Yaavetz]

[116] Kaf Hachaim 294/17

[117] 294/3; As it is forbidden to do any Melacha prior to saying Baruch Hamavdil.

Shemoneh Esrei as a Tefilas Nedava following its relevant laws[118]. [Likewise one is to repeat it in a case that one did not say Ata Chonantanu and does not expect to have wine to say Havdala until Sunday night, as will be explained next.]

If one did Melacha prior to Havdala and did not say Ata Chonantanu in Davening:[119] If one (did Melacha of Issur[120] [prior to saying Baruch Hamavdil and [121]]) prior to saying Havdala over wine, he must repeat Shemoneh Esrei with Ata Chonantanu, and then say Havdala over wine.[122] [Some Poskim[123] learn one is not required to repeat Shemoneh Esrei if he did a Melacha which does not take much effort to do, such as lighting a candle and the like. However from Admur[124] here it is implied all type of Melacha requires the repetition of Shemoneh Esrei. See Q&A regarding Rabbinical Melacha!]

If one ate prior to Havdala and did not say Ata Chonantanu in Davening:[125] If one ate [any amount of food or drink with exception to water[126]] prior to saying Havdala over wine, he must repeat Shemoneh Esrei with Ata Chonantanu, and then say Havdala over wine.[127]

Due to the above in a case that one does not have wine to say Havdala and he does not expect to have wine until after Sunday[128], he must immediately repeat Shemoneh Esrei if he forgot to say Ata Chonantanu and has already finished his prayer.[129] In the above scenario if one finished Shemoneh Esrei but did not yet take three steps back and then remembered that he forgot to say Ata Chonantanu and that he will not have wine, then if he has completed saying the section of Elokaiy Netzor he must repeat Shemoneh Esrei from the beginning. If he did not yet complete Elokaiy Netzor[130], then if he is after concluding the blessing of Shema Koleinu, he is to return to the beginning of the blessing of Ata Chonein. If he remembers prior to finishing the blessing of Shema Koleinu he is to add in Ata Chonantanu within the blessing of Shema Koleinu.[131] [If he remembered prior to concluding the blessing of Chonein Hadaas but after Hashem's name he is to conclude "Lamdeini Chukecha" and restart Ata Chonantanu. If he

---

[118] Tzaruch Iyun as what Admur here is coming to include, as if he is coming to include the necessity to novelize a prayer within Shemoneh Esrei, reciting Ata Chonantanu is itself the novelty. Perhaps then it is coming to add that only one who has meticulous concentration in prayer is to do so [as explained in 107/4] [So writes explicitly Ketzos Hashulchan 93 footnote 7 as the interpretation of Admur here; and so seems to learn Kaf Hachaim 294/17] Some Poskim however learn that saying Ata Chonantanu is not considered enough of a novelty, as it is the regular part of the night prayer of Motzei Shabbos, while the novelty must be recognizable. This however is not the opinion of Admur. [See Ketzos Hashulchan ibid]

[119] 294/3

[120] Parentheses are in original; So rules Rashba; brought in Elya Raba and Rav Akiva Eiger; See Kaf Hachaim 294/8 that Rambam argues that Melacha is not relevant to this law. He explains there that the reason is because since to be allowed to do Melacha one can simply say Baruch Hamavdil without a blessing, therefore it does not belittle the blessing of Havdala if he does Melacha prior to it. [ibid]
Opinion of Admur: See Ketzos Hashulchan 93 footnote 8 regarding this law in Admur being placed in parentheses. The Ketzos Hashulchan ibid concludes one is to repeat Shemoneh Esrei as a Tefilas Nedava. Kitzur Halachos Shabbos 294/8 records this ruling without brackets.
Opinions which rule similar to Admur: So rules also Peri Megadim 294 M"Z 2; Derech Chaim; Kitzur SH"A 96/1; Tehila Ledavid 294/2
Other Opinions: M"B 294 in Biur Halacha "Veim Taam" rules there is no need to repeat Shemoneh Esrei if one did Melacha in the above scenario prior to saying Baruch Hamavdil.

[121] Pashut! So rules Minchas Shabbos 96 footnote 5; See also Piskeiy Teshuvos 294 footnote 38;

[122] In such a case that he omitted Ata Chonantanu in prayer [and then did Melacha] one does not fulfill his obligation by simply saying Havdala over wine as it is unbefitting of Havdala for him to have ate (or done Melacha) prior to it. [ibid]

[123] Derech Hachaim brought in Minchas Shabbos 96 footnote 6; see 299/18

[124] So is implied from Admur 294/3 which writes "Melacha Beiisur" implying any Issur. However see 299/18 regarding different Melachas that are permitted before Havdala according to some opinions. Vetzaruch Iyun.

[125] 294/3

[126] If one drank merely water he does not need to repeat Shemoneh Esrei. [Ketzos Hashulchan 93 footnote 8]

[127] In such a case one does not fulfill his obligation by simply saying Havdala over wine as it is unbefitting of Havdala for him to have ate (or done Melacha) prior to it. [ibid]

[128] If however he expects to receive wine on Sunday, he must fast until then [besides for water] and hence there is no need for him to be required to repeat Shemoneh Esrei. In a scenario that one expected to have wine on Sunday, and hence did not repeat Shemoneh Esrei, and then on Sunday realized he would not receive wine until Sunday night, Tzaruch Iyun if he should repeat Shemoneh Esrei as Tashlumin after Shacharis, or say Ata Chonantanu in his regular Shacharis. [Ketzos Hashulchan 93 footnote 9]

[129] 294/4; As one certainly does not plan to fast until he receives wine after Sunday, and hence since he will eat before saying Havdala over wine, he must repeat Shemoneh Esrei. [ibid]

[130] Meaning he has not yet said the 2nd Yehiyu Leratzon.

[131] 294/5; This is similar to one who forgot to say Vesein Tal Umatar in which case he is to add it in Shema Koleinu. [294/5] Now although there are opinions, and so is the main ruling, which rule Ata Chonantanu is not similar to Vesein Tal Umatar, as it is not a request and only requests may be said within Shema Koleinu being it itself is a request, nevertheless regarding this scenario it is better for the Davener to recite it within Shema Koleinu than to return to Ata Chonein and repeat all those blessings, which according to the second opinion would be blessings that could have been avoided. It is thus better to rely on the second opinion which allows reciting it within Shema Koleinu then to need to repeat blessings of Shemoneh Esrei. [ibid]
One is to say the paragraph of Ata Chonantanu within Shema Koleinu until the words "Umidubakim Beyirasecha". One then continues with Ki Ata Shomeia Tefilas Kol Peh. [Ketzos Hashulchan 93/4]

remembered after concluding Chonein Hadaas prior to beginning the blessing of Hashiveinu, he is to say it then until the words "Umidubakim Beyirasecha".[132]]

Forgot Ata Chonantanu on Motzei Shabbos which is Tishe Beav: [133] If one forgot to say Ata Chonantanu on Motzei Shabbos which coincides with Tishe Beav, he does not need to repeat Shemoneh Esrei, as in any event he will not be eating until he says Havdala over wine on Sunday night. [He must however say Baruch Hamavdil prior to doing Melacha.] [In the event that one broke his fast on Motzei Shabbos prior to saying Havdala he must repeat Shemoneh Esrei. Some however rule this is not necessary.[134] If he ate on Sunday prior to saying Havdala it is unclear if he should recite Ata Chonantanu the next time he Davens Shemoneh Esrei.[135]]

If one said Havdala on wine prior to Davening Maariv does he still say Ata Chonantanu?[136] Even in the event that one said or heard Havdala over wine prior to Maariv he is still required to say Havdala in Shemoneh Esrei.[137]

If one forgot to Daven Maariv does he say Ata Chonantanu in Tashlumin the next day?[138] If on Sunday morning one realizes he forgot to Daven Maariv and is therefore after Shacharis going to Daven Tashlumin of Maariv, then in his second Shemoneh Esrei he is to recite Havdala of Ata Chonantanu as he usually does by Maariv of Motzei Shabbos.[139] [If he recited it in his first Shemoneh Esrei, he has fulfilled his obligation, so long as he did not do so with intention to Daven the Maariv Shemoneh Esrei with this first prayer.[140]]

If one did not Daven Mincha on Shabbos and is Davening Tashlumin on Motzei Shabbos in which Shemoneh Esrei does he recite Ata Chonantanu?[141] He is to recite it only in the first Shemoneh Esrei. If he recited it in both Shemoneh Esrei or omitted it in both Shemoneh Esrei he has nevertheless fulfilled his obligation. If he recited it only in the second Shemoneh Esrei, then if he omitted it from the first Shemoneh Esrei intentionally, he must repeat the Tashlumin for Mincha. If he simply forgot to say it, he has fulfilled his obligation.[142]

Are women who Daven Maariv on Motzei Shabbos obligated to say Ata Chonantanu?[143] Yes.

Summary:
If one forgot to say Ata Chonantanu within Shemoneh Esrei he may not do any Melacha until he recites Havdala or says Baruch Hamavdil. If he did Melacha prior to saying Baruch Hamavdil he must repeat Shemoneh Esrei with Ata Chonantanu. Likewise if he ate or drank liquids other than water prior to Havdala he must repeat Shemoneh Esrei.

Q&A Related one who forgot Ata Chonantanu and did Melacha or ate
If one did <u>Rabbinical</u> Melacha prior to saying Baruch Hamavdil or Havdala, must he repeat Shemoneh Esrei?
Seemingly he is required to repeat Shemoneh Esrei.[144] Although some[145] learn he is not required to repeat Shemoneh Esrei for Rabbinical Melacha. Thus if one moved a Muktzah item he is not required to repeat Shemoneh Esrei. [In a case of doubt one is to simply Daven again in a Toras Nedava.]

If one ate or drank after Shabbos prior to Maariv and then Davened Shemoneh Esrei without Ata Chonantanu, must he repeat Shemoneh Esrei?[146]
Yes.

---

[132] Ketzos Hashulchan 93 footnote 11
[133] 294/6
[134] See Piskeiy Teshuvos 556/3 footnote 16
[135] See Ketzos Hashulchan 93 footnote 9. SSH"K 62 footnote 95 rules if he ate on Sunday he is not to recite Ata Chonantanu or repeat Shemoneh Esrei. See Piskeiy Teshuvos 556/3
[136] 294/2
[137] As the main institution of the Sages was to say Havdala in Davening. [ibid]
[138] 294/2
[139] This applies even if one already said Havdala over wine as the main institution of the Sages was to say Havdala in prayer. [ibid]
Other Opinions: Others [Ridbaz] however argue that Ata Chonantanu is not to be recited in Tashlumin, and so concludes Kaf Hachaim [294/3; 108/50]; Mishneh Berurah 294/2
[140] Tehila Ledavid 294/1
[141] 108/16
[142] Vetzaruch Iyun if in such a case he should initially recite Ata Chonantanu in his second Shemoneh Esrei.
[143] 299/18; 296/18
[144] So is implied from Admur 294/3 which writes "Melacha Beiisur" implying any Issur. However see 299/18 regarding different Melachas that are permitted before Havdala according to some opinions. Vetzaruch Iyun.
[145] Derech Hachaim brought in Minchas Shabbos ibid
[146] Tehila Ledavid 294/4

If one forgot to say Ata Chonantanu in Maariv and then said a Bracha on a food is he to eat the food, and must he repeat Shemoneh Esrei?

He must eat the food so it not be a blessing in vain. Based on this some Poskim[147] write in such a case he does not need to repeat Shemoneh Esrei as he was Halachicly required to eat.

If one forgot to say Ata Chonantanu in his second Shemoneh Esrei which he had to repeat due to eating or Melacha, what is the law?[148]

He must repeat Shemoneh Esrei a third time. If he remembers prior to concluding Shemoneh Esrei, it follows the same law as stated above.

If one forgot Ata Chonantanu in Maariv of Motzei Yom Tov what is the law?[149]

It follows the same ruling as one who forgot to say it on Motzei Shabbos. Thus if he ate or drank [liquids other than water] or did Melacha before saying Hamavdil, he must repeat Shemoneh Esrei.

If one is in doubt as to whether he said Atah Chonantanu, and then accidently did Melacha prior to saying Hamavdil, must he repeat Shemoneh Esrei?

Seemingly one is to repeat Shemoneh Esrei as a Tefilas Nedava.[150]

If one forgot Ata Chonantanu and did Melacha prior to Havdala, and then forgot to repeat Shemoneh Esrei at night, is he to repeat Tashlumin after Shacharis on Sunday?[151]

Yes. In such a case he must recite Ata Chonantanu in his Tashlumin.

What if in the above case he only remembered past midday of Sunday? Is he to say Ata Chonantanu in Mincha or a later Davening?

This matter requires further analysis.[152]

If one said Havdala over wine before repeating Shemoneh Esrei in a scenario that he was required to do so must he still repeat Shemoneh Esrei?

Some[153] write it is questionable whether he must repeat Shemoneh Esrei. Others[154] rule he must still repeat Shemoneh Esrei. Some[155] conclude based on this dispute that one should not repeat Shemoneh Esrei as Safek Brachos Lehakel. The Ketzos Hashulchan[156] rules one is to repeat Shemoneh Esrei as a Toras Nedava if he already said Havdala over wine.

---

[147] See Oar Letziyon 2/22-10; Piskeiy Teshuvos 294/3

[148] Piskeiy Teshuvos 294/4

[149] Piskeiy Teshuvos 294/4

[150] On the one hand Admur writes [in 108/18] that whenever there is doubt as to whether one is to pray again he should just pray a Tefilas Nedava. On the other hand the law of repeating Shemoneh Esrei when one did not say Ata Chonantanu and then did Melacha is brought by Admur in parentheses, and thus the Ketzos Hashulchan does not even rule this way in his summary, but rather brings it in the Badei Hashulchan and concludes that although the Biur Halacha rules that by Melacha one does not need to repeat Shemoneh Esrei, nevertheless one should Daven as a Nedava. However in a case that one is even in doubt if he perhaps did in fact say Ata Chonantanu, then there is room to learn that even to pray a Nedava is not required. As it is a double doubt. Perhaps however one can say that we follow one's usual recital of Shemoneh Esrei which omits Ata Chonantanu, as is the law by a doubt of other additions, and hence we consider him to have certainly omitted it if he is in doubt, and it is hence not considered a doubt at all. See however Rama 422/1 that when in doubt if one recited Yaleh Veyavo in Shemoneh Esrei he does not need to repeat. The Levush [brought in M"A 422/4] explains this to be the case because one does not pass 30 days without saying Yaleh Veyavo and hence we cannot assume with certainty that he did not say it. The same would apply to Ata Chonantanu. And even more so, of which we do not pass 7 days without saying it. Now, although most Poskim argue on this conclusion of the Levush [see M"A and M"B ibid] perhaps it is enough of a doubt to not require one to repeat Shemoneh Esrei as a Nedava if he did Melacha. Practically since there still remains a doubt and one may always repeat a Nedava, one is to do so.

[151] Kaf Hachaim 108/50; 294/10

[152] See Ketzos Hashulchan 93 footnote 9

[153] Peri Megadim in 294 M"Z 2

[154] Derech Chaim, brought in Biur Halacha 294 "Tzarich"

[155] SSH"K 59 footnote 6

[156] 93 footnote 8

If one must repeat Shemoneh Esrei of Maariv such as due to forgetting Yaleh Veyavo on Chol Hamoed, or Vesein Tal Umatar, and the like, must he also recite Ata Chonantanu in his second Shemoneh Esrei?[157]

This matter is disputed in Poskim and does not have a final ruling.

If one did not Daven on Motzei Shabbos due to being an Onein, but is Davening on Sunday, is he to say Ata Chonantanu in his Davening?[158]

No.

If one forgot to say Vetodieinu in Shemoneh Esrei of Yom Tov which is Motzei Shabbos may he add it in when he remembers?

Some[159] rule once he has begun saying "Vatiten Lanu Hashem" he is not to go back to say Todieinu and is rather to continue with Shemoneh Esrei as usual.[160] In such a case he must beware to say Baruch Hamavdil prior to doing any Melacha which is permitted on Yom Tov.

Others[161] however rule that one who does go back to say it has upon whom to rely so long as he has not yet finished the blessing of Mikadeish Yisrael Vehazmanim.

---

[157] Piskeiy Teshuvos 294/6
[158] Kaf Hachaim 294/5
[159] Mateh Efrayim 599/7
[160] His reasoning is because doing so would require the person to repeat Hashem's name in the blessing of Vatiten Lanu.
[161] Sheivet Halevy 9/23

4. Vayehi Noam:[162]

The prayer of Vayehi Noam[163] is recited on Motzei Shabbos after Shemoneh Esrei of Maariv.[164] It is not recited when a Yom Tov falls out within the week as will be explained next.

Omitting Vayehi Noam the Motzei Shabbos before a Yom Tov:[165] When Yom Tov or Yom Kippur falls on a weekday, including if it falls on Erev Shabbos, the entire[166] prayer of Vayehi Noam is customarily omitted on the Motzei Shabbos directly prior to the Holiday.[167] If however the Holiday [or Yom Kippur] falls on Shabbos, Vayehi Noam is recited the previous Motzei Shabbos.[168] [It goes without saying that Vayehi Noam is omitted on Motzei Shabbos Chol Hamoed.[169] Vayehi Noam is recited the Motzei Shabbos which precedes Chanukah and Purim.[170] Vayehi Noam and Yosheiv Beseiser are omitted on Motzei Shabbos which coincides with Tishe Beav. One is to begin from Ata Kadosh.[171]]

Standing:[172] Some are accustomed to stand for the reading of the verse Vayehi Noam.[173]

---

[162] 295/1

[163] This prayer consists of the last verse of Psalm 90, the entire psalm 91 "Yosheiv Beseiser", and the Seder of Kedusha found in the prayer of Uva Letziyon. Nevertheless we do not begin reciting from Uva Letziyon but rather from Veata Kadosh. The reason for this is because the Geula cannot arrive during the night, therefore we omit this verse of Uva Letziyon which mentions Moshiach coming. [ibid] We also do not say the verse of Vaani Zos Berisi as this verse is only said together with the previous verse of Uva Letziyon. [Taz 295/1]

Repeating Orech Yamim: We repeat the verse of "Orech Yamim Asbieihu" in order to complete the name of G-d which derives from this verse. [Admur ibid] This is calculated as follows: Hashem's name Yud Kei Vav Kei when written in full [Miluiy] is the Gematria of 130, which is the number of letters in the verse when it is repeated. Likewise when the verse is repeated there are a total of 130 words in the Mizmor. [Magen Avraham 293/1; Machatzis Hashekel there] The Tashbatz explains this to mean that there are 130 letters in total when the verse is repeated, and this is the numerical value of Hakohanim, as the Kohanim of the Hashmonaim would say this verse 7 times and win the war. [M"A ibid; Kaf Hachaim 295/1]

[164] The general reason for saying these prayers is to lengthen the stay of the Reshaim outside of Gehenim, as they do not return to Gehenim after Shabbos until the last community finishes the end of Vayehi Noam. In particular the prayer of Vayehi Noam is said because it is a prayer of blessing which Moshe blessed the Jewish people after the Mishkan was completed. [ibid; See Piskeiy Teshuvos 195/1 for a full analysis on this subject]

The reason for why we specifically mention the Seder Kedusha is because it has the ability to cool off the flames of Gihenim which are relit after Shabbos. [Mateh Moshe in name of Rokeiach brought in Shaar Hakolel 31/1]

Other reasons:
- On Motzei Shabbos the forces of evil are aroused and swerve around the world/ We therefore recite the verses of Yosheiv Biseiser as a protection against these spirits. For this reason we do not say it when Yom Tov falls during that week as the Yom Tov itself protects one from these forces and there is thus no need for an extra prayer. [Yavetz brought in Taamei Haminhagim 402]
- The paragraph of Yosheiv Biseiser with Vayehi Noam includes 248 words when repeated twice which corresponds to the 248 limbs By repeating the last versus twice it is considered as if we have repeated the entire prayer. This helps protect the limbs for the coming week. [Abudarham brought in Taamei Haminhagim 405]

[165] 295/3

[166] This includes also the prayer of Ata Kadosh. The reason it is accustomed to omit also Ata Kadosh is because the prayer of Ata Kadosh is said as a result of saying the prayer of Vayehi Noam. As once the Shechina resides below, as is stated in the prayer of Vayehi Noam which discusses the Mishkan, it is then fit to sanctify it with the prayer of Ata Kadosh. Thus since Vayehi Noam is omitted, [for the reason to be explained in the next footnote] so too we omit Ata Kadosh. [ibid]

Other Opinions: The above follows the Ashkenazi custom, as brought by the Tur. However the Sefardi custom is to only omit Vayehi Noam and Yosheiv Neseiser and they begin from Orech Yamim, and then say Ata Kadosh. [Tur] Some however say the Sefaradi custom is to recite it entirely, as rule the Sefaradi sources brought in the next footnote. [Piskeiy Teshuvos 294/2]

[167] The reason for omitting Vayehi Noam is because within the prayer we say twice "And the work of our hands", hence all the days of the coming week have to be fit for work. If not then we simply omit the prayer. [ibid; See Piskeiy Teshuvos 294/2 for a thorough analyses on this subject]

Other Opinions: Some, based on Kabala of Arizal, always recite the prayer of Vayehi Noam on Motzei Shabbos, even when a Holiday falls that week, and even on Motzei Shabbos Chol Hamoed. Nevertheless in such circumstances they recite it quietly. Their reasoning is because Vayehi Noam affects the influence of Shabbos on the weekday which is needed every week, without exception. [Bircheiy Yosef brought in Shaareiy Teshuvah 295/2; Kaf Hachaim 295/9-10]

[168] So rules Admur ibid

Other Opinions: Some rule that even in such a case that Yom Tov falls on Shabbos, Vayehi Noam is omitted the Motzei Shabbos prior to it. [See Kaf Hachaim 295/6]

[169] Kaf Hachaim 295/7

[170] Shaareiy Teshuvah 295/2; Kaf Hachaim 295/8

As these days are not days of a prohibition in doing Melacha.

[171] 559/2

[172] 295/2

[173] For reasons known to them. [ibid] The reason is based on Kabala, to draw down from Oar Chozer of Bina. [see Kaf Hachaim 295/1; Peri Eitz Chaim Shaar Shabbos 24]

Q&A

Is the Chazan to recite Kadosh, Kadosh, Kadosh and Baruch Kevod out loud when he recites the prayer of Ata Kadosh?

Some[174] write this is not required to be done on Motzei Shabbos. Others[175] are accustomed to never recite it out loud even during the week.[176]

If Pesach falls on Shabbos, is Vayehi Noam recited on the Motzei Shabbos prior to it?

Yes.[177] However some Poskim[178] rule it is not recited.

What is the law if the Chazan absentmindedly said Kaddish Shalem with Tiskabel before Vayehi Noam, is he then to say half Kaddish after Vayehi Noam instead of Kaddish Tiskabel?[179]

One is to say Kaddish Shaleim without Tiskabel after Vayehi Noam. However some allow repeating Tiskabeil also in the second Kaddish.

If one began saying Tiskabel before Vayehi Noam and then remembered, is he to complete the Kaddish?

This matter requires further analysis.

Is Vayehi Noam recited in the house of an Avel?

Some[180] write in the house of a mourner one is to skip Vayehi Noam, and Yosheiv Beseiser and is rather to start from Veata Kadosh. Others[181] write one is to skip Vayehi Noam[182] and begin from Yosheiv Beseiser. Others[183] rule one is to say Vayehi Noam as usual, and so seems to be the opinion of Admur.[184]
Practically the widespread custom is to recite it.[185]

Does an Avel within Shiva recite Vayehi Noam?[186]

This receives the same dispute as the one mentioned above. The widespread custom however is for the Avel to recite it.[187]

Does a Chasan within seven days of his wedding recite Vayehi Noam?[188]

Yes.

---

[174] Piskeiy Teshuvos 295/1

[175] This is a widespread Chabad custom in various Shuls. It however is not all inclusive. See next footnote.

[176] However the Rebbe's custom when he was Chazan, as heard on audios of the Rebbe's Davening, was to recite it out loud during the week by Shacharis, and so is implied from 59/2.

[177] So is implied from Admur 295/3, and so rules: Peri Megadim 295 M"Z 2; Poskim brought in Sharreiy Teshuvah 295/2; M"B 295/3;
The Chabad Custom: Rav Yaakov Landau writes in his diary that the Rebbe Rashab would recite Vayehi Noam in such a case, and so is recorded to be the custom of the Rebbe. [Kitzur Halachos 293 footnote 9] However in the Luach Kolel Chabad they write that it should not be said. See Nitei Gavriel Pesach 1, and Otzer Minhagei Chabad Nissan.

[178] Sheialas Yaavetz 19 brought in Shaareiy Teshuvah 295/2; Kaf Hachaim 295/7; Minchas Shabbos 96/7; Luach Tuchinskiy writes that so is the custom in Eretz Yisrael; They say that it should not be said when Pesach falls on Shabbos, as Erev Pesach is considered a holiday, being that its forbidden to do work from Chatzos.

[179] Mishneh Halachos 6/16; See Piskeiy Teshuvos 295/2

[180] Kaf Hachaim 295/3 in name of Kneses Hagedola
Vetzaruch Iyun as the source of the Kaf Hachaim is from the Kneses Hagedola, which is the same source as the M"A and they both say different customs. After researching within the text of the Kneses Hagedola [295] the following was discovered: The Kneses Hagedola first records a custom of a community to omit both Vayehi Noam and Yosheiv Beseisar in the house of a mourner, and they would begin from Orech Yamim. He then concludes that he accustomed his community to omit only Vayehi Noam and not Yosheiv Beseiser. Hence both customs are written in the Kneses Hagedola.

[181] Kneses Hagedola brought in M"A 495/1 [This was the personal opinion of the Kneses Hagedola, as explained in previous footnote]

[182] The reason for skipping Vayehi Noam is because it mentions work, and a mourner is forbidden in work.

[183] Ketzos Hashulchan 93 footnote 15

[184] From the fact that Admur omitted this ruling of the M"A in name of the Kneses Hagedola. [ibid]

[185] Piskeiy Teshuvos 295/3

[186] See Piskeiy Teshuvos 295 footnote 26

[187] As although an Avel is forbidden in Melacha nevertheless it is permitted for others and hence is not to be omitted. [Piskeiy Teshuvos ibid]

[188] Lehoros Nasan 13/119 Brought in Piskeiy Teshuvos 295/3

List of Holidays that fall in middle of week and the relevant status of recital of Vayehi Noam

Holiday	Status of Prior Motzei Shabbos
Chanukah	Recited
Chol Hamoed Motzei Shabbos	Omitted
Pesach	Omitted
Purim	Recited
Shavuos	Omitted
Sukkos	Omitted
Tishe Beav	Recited, unless falls on Motzei Shabbos in which case only Ata Kadosh is recited
Yom Kippur	Omitted

Sparks of Kabala

The Kabalistic reason for saying Vayehi Noam and Ata Kadosh on Motzei Shabbos is as follows:

The above prayer has the ability to draw down the G-dliness of the world of Atzilus into the world of Beriyah. This ability is only available when reciting Ata Kadosh on Motzei Shabbos.[189]

---

5. Kiddush Levana:[190]

See the section "The Laws & Customs of Kiddush Levana"

The order of the prayer for Maariv on Motzei Shabbos:
1. Vehu Rachum and Shir Hamaalos[191]
2. Half Kaddish
3. Barchu
4. Birchas Shema/Shema
5. Half Kaddish
6. Shemoneh Esrei
7. Half Kaddish [Full Kaddish if is week Vayehi Noam is omitted]
8. Vayehi Noam [if is week that is said]
9. Full Kaddish with Tiskabel
10. During Sefira, Sefiras Haomer is now recited.
11. Aleinu
12. *Kiddush Levana when applicable*

---

[189] Kaf Hachaim 295/5

[190] Shulchan Aruch 426

[191] See Sefer Haminhagim p. 67; Eliyah Raba 54/4; Shaar Hakolel 17/2; Piskeiy Teshuvos 293/7 for a summary and explanation of the different customs which exist in whether to say Vehu Rachum, or Shir Hamaalos on Motzaei Shabbos.

Chapter 2:
The Laws and Customs of Havdala

Havdala [Halachas 1-17]

The greatness of Havdala

Pirkeiy Derebbe Eliezer

ר' צדוק אומר כל מי (מו) שאינו סביל על היין במתאי
שבתות או אינו שומע שומע מן המבדילין אינו רואה סימן ברכה
לעולם . (מז) וכל מי שרוא שומע מן המבדילין או מבדיל
על היין הקב"ה קונה אותו לסגולתו (מח) שנאמר (ויקרא ך)
ואבדיל אתכם וגו' (שמות יט) והייתם לי (מט) סגולה • בא'

Shavuos 118b

אבל מ׳ דתהי' לא דריש, דהא איצטריך 26 ראויין לְהוֹרָאָה, דְּכְתִיב: "לְהַבְדִּיל וּלְהוֹרוֹת". אָמַר רַבִּי
לכדדריש ב׳החלץ (יבמות מט, ב) דאפילו 27 חִיָּיא בַּר אַבָּא אָמַר רַבִּי יוֹחָנָן: כָּל הַמַּבְדִּיל עַל הַיַּיִן
בשעת נדתה קדושין תופסין בה. לֹא תעשה 28 בְּמוֹצָאֵי שַׁבָּתוֹת - הָוְיָן לוֹ בָּנִים זְכָרִים, דְּכְתִיב: "לְהַבְדִּיל
מנא לן – דלא מיחייב חטאת אלא אם כן יש בה 29 בֵּין הַקֹּדֶשׁ וּבֵין הַחֹל", וּכְתִיב הָתָם: "לְהַבְדִּיל בֵּין הַטָּמֵא
לאו, מידי דהוה אפסח ומילה. 30 וּבֵין הַטָּהוֹר", וּסְמִיךְ לֵיהּ: "אִשָּׁה כִּי תַזְרִיעַ". רַבִּי יְהוֹשֻׁעַ
מדבעי בֶּן לֵוִי אָמַר: בָּנִים רְאוּיִן לְהוֹרָאָה, דְּכְתִיב: "לְהַבְדִּיל וּלְהוֹרוֹת". אָמַר רַבִּי בִּנְיָמִין בַּר יֶפֶת אָמַר רַבִּי

Sayings of the Sages:

Rav Tzadok stated:[1] Whoever does not say Havdala over wine on Motzei Shabbos or does not hear Havdala from others does not see a Siman Bracha. However one who does say Havdala over wine on Motzei Shabbos Hashem calls him Kadosh and calls him a Segula, and separates him from the other nations.

Rebbe Yochanan states:[2] Three inherit the world to come; one who lives in Eretz Yisrael; one who brings up his children to Torah; one who says Havdala over wine.

Rebbe Chiya Bar Rebbe Aba stated in the name of Rebbe Yochanan:[3] Whoever says Havdala over wine on Motzei Shabbos merits having male children. Rebbe Yehoshua Ben Levi says he merits children which are fit to be Rabbis.

---

[1] Pirkeiy Derebbe Eliezer 20, brought in Tur 296
[2] Brought in Tur 296
[3] Shavuos 18b

The Havdala Checklist:[4]

1. Clean the Havdala cup from any wine residue left over from Kiddush.
2. Pour wine in a way it slightly overflows onto a dish.
3. Light the candle and prepare the Besamim.
4. Lift the cup with your right hand, pass it to your left hand and then place it back in your right hand.
5. Lift the cup three Tefach from the table.
6. Recite Hinei Keil Yeshuasi [The listeners say it quietly to themselves] and the blessing of Hagafen.
7. Place the cup down and lift the Besamim with the right hand and then say the blessing of Besamim.
8. Place the Besamim down and then say the blessing of Meorei Haeish.
9. Fold your fingers over your thumb into the palm and place them near the flame. Then turn over your hand, open the four fingers leaving the thumb still hidden, and look at the back of the fingers towards the nails.
10. Recite the concluding blessing of Hamavdil and drink the entire cup of wine while sitting.
11. Dip the Havdala candle in the spilled wine and spill some wine onto the flame.
12. Recite an after blessing and say Vayiten Lecha
13. Have Melaveh Malka

---

[4] All details mentioned here are based on the Halachas, and customs explained and elaborated in this section. See there for the sources.

1. Havdala:

The Sages instituted that in addition to reciting Havdala in Shemoneh Esrei one must likewise recite Havdala over wine, if wine is available.[5]

Is Havdala of a Biblical or Rabbinical origin?[6] Some Poskim[7] rule the words recited in Havdala are of Biblical origin. Others[8] rule it is of Rabbinical origin.[9] [According to all however the obligation to say Havdala twice, once in Davening and another time over wine, is Rabbinical. Thus if one already said Havdala in Davening saying Havdala over wine is only a Rabbinical obligation.[10]]

When after Shabbos is Havdala to be recited?[11] One is to recite Havdala as close to the leave of Shabbos as possible.[12]

May one recite Havdala in middle of a meal prior to Bentching?[13] It is proper to initially avoid saying Havdala prior to Birchas Hamazon if one drank wine during the meal, or is saying Havdala over other beverages.[14] If one desires to say Havdala over wine and did not drink wine during, or before, the meal, he may say Havdala prior to Birchas Hamazon according to all.[15] If one chooses to say Havdala during the meal despite having drunk wine during that meal, see Halacha 2 for the relevant details.

May one say Havdala and do Melacha prior to Maariv?[16] Once Shabbos has ended, which is when a row of three small stars are visible, it is permitted to say Havdala even prior to Davening Maariv. [Some Poskim[17] however rule it is always proper to first Daven Maariv and then do Havdala in order to follow the set order that the Sages established. In a case that one recited Havdala prior to Maariv it is nevertheless permitted to eat those foods that are permitted to be eaten before Maariv.[18]]

---

[5] It is an obligation to search for wine for Havdala just as is required to fulfill any other Mitzvah which is an obligation for one to fulfill. [ibid] Originally when the Anshei Kneses Hagedola instituted the recital of Havdala, together with the other prayers, blessings and Kiddushim, they did not obligate Havdala to be said over wine, but rather within the prayer of Shemoneh Esrei. The reason for this is because when the Jews returned from exile in Babylon they were destitute and could not all afford wine for Havdala. [294/1] After the Jewish people became more financially stable the Sages instituted for Havdala to be said over wine. Later they once again became destitute and the Sages retracted that Havdala is to be said only in Shemoneh Esrei. Now, in order to prevent Havdala from being constantly moved from the prayer to wine and from wine to prayer based on the Jewish economic state, the Sages instituted that in addition to reciting Havdala within prayer, one is also obligated, if wine is available, to also recite Havdala over wine. If however there is no wine available one fulfills his obligation of Havdala within Havdala said in prayer. [294/2]

[6] 296/19; See Lekutei Sichos 31 p. 99 for a thorough analysis on the opinion of the Rambam in what is the essence of the Mitzvah of Havdala. The Rebbe there gives three possible options for the reason behind the obligation, and explains the practical ramification between each approach.

[7] Some Poskim [Rambam; Chinuch] rule Havdala is a Biblical obligation which is learned from the words Zechor...Lekadsho. They expound this verse to mean one must mention Shabbos both by its entrance and by its leave. [ibid]

[8] Rabbeinu Tam; Shivlei Haleket

[9] They rule the words Zachor only refers to remembering Shabbos when it enters and not when it leaves. [ibid]
Regarding the opinion of Admur: In 296/19 Admur does not side like either opinion, and rather suspects for both regarding women saying and hearing Havdala. In however 271/1 he brings the first opinion that Havdala is Biblical as the Stam opinion, while the second opinion which holds it is Rabbinical he brings as "Yeish Omrim".

[10] Kaf Hachaim 296/1; See Piskeiy Teshuvos 296/1

[11] 271/9; Kuntrus Achron 299/2; Based on M"A 235/4; so brings Kaf Hachaim 299/5 from Magid Meisharim; Piskeiy Teshuvos 295/5

[12] As it is a Mitzvah for Kiddush and Havdala to be recited at the first opportunity. Hence by Kiddush one is to recite it as close as possible to the entrance of Shabbos, and by Havdala one is to recite it as close as possible to the leave of Shabbos. [ibid] It is for this reason that the Sages forbade eating and drinking prior to Havdala so one not come to delay making Havdala due to this eating. [Kuntrus Achron 299/2]
See Kaf Hachaim 299/5 which brings the Yalkut Reuveini in name of the Maggid Meisharim that says based on Kabala one is to say Havdala immediately after Maariv in order to distance oneself from the Kelipos which desire to attach to oneself after Shabbos.

[13] 299/4

[14] Admur records a dispute on this matter:
The first [stam] opinion rules one may say Havdala prior to Birchas Hamazon, and if he drank wine during the meal he omits the blessing of Hagafen. The same applies if he is saying Havdala over other beverages, that he omits the blessing of Shehakol. Others however rule one is to always say the blessing over the cup used for Havdala. Practically Admur rules the main opinion is like the first opinion, although it is best to initially avoid the dispute and hence say Birchas Hamazon prior to Havdala. [ibid]

[15] So rules Admur in 299/4 Kuntrus Achron 3, and so also rules Chayeh Adam 8/19 brought in Kaf Hachaim 299/17; M"B 299/10. The reason is because the dispute was only relevant in a case one already drank wine during the meal and it hence exempts the blessing over wine in Havdala according to the first opinion.
Other Opinions: Some Poskim rule one is not to initially say Havdala during the meal even if he did not drink wine during or before the meal as by doing so one enters himself into a dispute if he may continue eating without a Bracha or he must say Hamotzi again. [Elya Raba 299/8; Siddur Yaavetz; Tosefes Shabbos 299/6] Admur in Kuntrus Achron 299/3 negates these opinions.

[16] 293/1

[17] Tehila Ledavid 293/1; see Kitzur Halachos Shabbos p. 119;
In however the Sefer Pear Yisrael 1/207 he writes that the Alter Rebbe at times would say Havdala prior to Maariv.

[18] Pashut. See Piskeiy Teshuvos 299/14
Other Opinions: The M"B 299/35 rules one may not eat or drink until after Havdala. Many Poskim have left this ruling of the M"B with a Tzaruch Iyun. [See Tzitz Eliezer 16/17; Sheivet Haleivi 9/63]

May one place the Havdala wine on the table prior to the leave of Shabbos?[19] No. One may only bring the Havdala wine to the table when Shabbos is over.

2. Eating before Havdala:[20]

It is forbidden to eat, drink or even taste any amount of food or beverage prior to saying or hearing Havdala over wine or other valid beverages[21]. This however is with exception to water which is allowed to be drunk prior to Havdala.[22] [Nevertheless our custom is to avoid drinking even water prior to Havdala.[23]]

May one eat after sunset before nightfall?[24] It is forbidden to eat or drink anything other than water after sunset[25] until one says Havdala. [Furthermore, the custom is to avoid drinking even water from after sunset until one says Havdala.[26]] If one began eating or drinking after sunset he must stop as soon as he remembers even if he had begun eating a meal with bread after this time. Nevertheless those which are accustomed to begin large meals after sunset [but before nightfall[27]] are not to be protested as they have upon whom to rely.[28] According to all once nightfall has arrived it is forbidden to eat or drink, and if one began eating or drinking at this time he must stop as soon as he remembers.

The third meal: [The above restrictions apply even regarding the third meal of Shabbos [i.e. Shalosh Seudos]. Hence one must begin his third meal prior to sunset. Once sunset has arrived he may no longer eat the third meal.[29]

---

[19] 254/10: "*It is forbidden to prepare on Shabbos for a weekday, even in a situation that [doing so] does not involve even a remote similarity to a Shabbos prohibition, but rather only [to simply] move an object, such as [for example when one wants] to bring wine from the cellar to the house on Shabbos to use for Havdala after Shabbos, [this is nevertheless prohibited,] and [so too] anything similar to this [is also prohibited], as will be explained in chapter 503, with regards to Yom Tov, see there.*"

[20] 299/1

[21] This applies even if one recited Havdala within Maariv Shemoneh Esrei. [Ibid]

The Reason: The reason for this prohibition is because one is supposed to say Havdala close to the leave of Shabbos without delay. Thus although in general the Sages only forbade a meal from being eaten prior to fulfilling a Mitzvah while snacking prior to the Mitzvah was allowed, nevertheless here even merely snacking or tasting food was forbidden as Havdala is to be said close to the leave of Shabbos and thus even snacking will cause one to delay saying it within this time. [271/9; Kuntrus Achron 299/2]

Severity of eating prior to Havdala: One who eats before Havdala is liable for death through the illness of Askara. [Pesachim 105a]

[22] This ruling of Admur follows the ruling of the Michaber 299/1

Other Opinions: However the Geonim, and Midrash Talpiyos rule even water is forbidden to drink, and so is the ruling of the Arizal. [Kaf Hachaim 299/6; Ketzos Hashulchan 94 footnote 1; See Maggid Meisharim Vayeishev] and so is the Chabad custom as recorded in Hayom Yom [brought next].

[23] Sefer Haminhagim p. 68; Hayom Yom 3rd Iyar and so brings Ketzos Hashulchan 94 footnote 1 based on Arizal.

[24] 299/2; See Kuntrus Achron 271/3

Background of this ruling in Admur:

It is disputed in Rishonim [Raza/Rosh/Rambam/Rif] and Poskim [Bach/Magen Avraham 1; Taz 1] if the prohibition of eating and drinking before Havdala begins from nightfall or from Bein Hashmashos, which is after sunset [according to our custom]. Admur [ibid] records this dispute in regards to eating during Bein Hashmashos. His first [and main/stam] opinion is that it is forbidden. The second opinion rules it is permitted until nightfall. Admur in his final ruling rules that the main opinion follows the stringent opinion, and one is thus to be stringent, although those which are lenient are not to be protested.

Other Opinions: This stringent ruling of Admur is based on the ruling of the Bach and Magen Avraham 299/1. However the Taz 299/1 rules that one may be lenient to eat and drink until nightfall and so he learns is also the opinion of the Michaber/Rama.

The Mishneh Berura [299/1] rules like the Magen Avraham that the prohibition begins from after sunset however he then concludes that one may be lenient if he is hungry or thirsty until 30 minutes prior to nightfall [in countries that there is more than 30 minutes between sunset and nightfall]. The basis of this ruling [as learns the Ketzos Hashulchan 94 footnote 6] is that one may be lenient like the opinion of Rabbeinu Tam regarding Bein Hashmashos in this situation. The Ketzos Hashulchan [94 footnote 6] however question this ruling concluding that one who does not follow Rabbeinu Tam for the time he lets out Shabbos is not to be lenient in this at all.

The Ashel Avraham Butchather 299 rules that one may eat even a meal after sunset [even not Shalosh Seudos] so long as there is someone who is not eating who will remind them to do Havdala.

[25] As once sunset has passed it is Bein Hashmashos which is questionably considered night time, and at night it is forbidden to eat or drink prior to Havdala. [ibid]

Prior to sunset it is permitted to begin the meal even if it is within 30 minutes to nightfall. This does not pose a prohibition of eating a meal within 30 minutes before Maariv. [See Ketzos Hashulchan 94 footnote 6]

[26] Hayom Yom 3rd of Iyar and so brings Ketzos Hashulchan 94 footnote 1 based on Arizal.

[27] However if they begin after nightfall then they are certainly to be protested.

[28] So explains also Biur Halacha 299 "Mishetechshach" that those which are accustomed to begin large wedding meals after sunset have upon whom to rely. His reasoning there is because it is a Seudas Mitzvah and perhaps by a Rabbinical prohibition we are not stringent to force one to avoid fulfilling a Seudas Mitzvah and one thus can rely on the lenient opinions mentioned above. In the Kuntrus Achron [271/3] Admur explains that since one is unable to make Havdala until after nightfall therefore there is more room to be lenient, as opposed to Kiddush which can be made by Bein Hashmashos.

Furthermore, the Biur Halacha is lenient to allow one who is thirsty or hungry to eat or drink up to 30 minutes before Tzeis Hakochavim, even if it is after sunset. His reasoning is because one may rely on the opinion of Rabbeinu Tam regarding this matter that Bein Hashmashos does not begin until this time. The Ketzos Hashulchan [94 footnote 6] however questions this ruling of the M"B based on that today we do not follow Rabbeinu Tam regarding Melacha. [See Az Nidbaru 13/22; Piskeiy Teshuvos 299/3]

[29] Pashut from Admur, as no differentiation was made. See Piskeiy Teshuvos 299 footnote 31 that Chazon Ish did not allow people to wash for the third meal after sunset.

However there are Poskim[30] which are lenient to allow the third meal to be eaten even past sunset, until nightfall, if one did not eat it before hand.[31] Many are accustomed to be lenient like this opinion.[32] In such a case it is disputed amongst Poskim whether one is to say Ritzei in Birchas Hamazon.[33] According to all once nightfall arrives it is forbidden to begin eating the third meal, even if he is still within the time of Tosefes Shabbos.[34]]

If one already said the blessing over food and then remembered the prohibition:[35] In the event that one said a blessing over food after sunset, or even after nightfall and then prior to eating the food remembered the above prohibition, he is to taste[36] the food and then say Havdala.[37] [If however one merely washed for bread and did not yet say Hamotzi, and then remembered the prohibition, he is to say Havdala right away and then say Hamotzi.[38]]

If one began eating bread before sunset:[39] If one began eating a meal [that consists of bread[40]] prior to sunset he may continue to eat and drink without limit even after nightfall.[41] [This applies even if he has not yet eaten a Kezayis worth of bread prior to sunset, but has said Hamotzi and thus started his meal prior to sunset.[42]] If however one did not begin an actual meal [that consists of bread[43]] prior to sunset but was merely drinking [or eating foods other than bread] he must stop eating and drinking as soon as sunset arrives.[44]

If during the meal, after sunset or nightfall, the group of people eating decided to say Havdala, they may still change their mind and continue eating.[45] [If however they decided to finish the meal and recite Birchas Hamazon they may not continue eating. Furthermore if after sunset an individual decides in his mind to finish his meal, he may no longer continue eating.[46]]

Saying Havdala in middle of the meal, prior to Bentching:[47] In the event that one decides to say Havdala in middle of the meal, prior to Bentching, he is to omit the blessing of Hagafen from Havdala if he drank wine during, or directly before, the meal. Likewise if he is saying Havdala over other beverages the blessing of Shehakol is omitted. Nevertheless it is proper to initially avoid saying Havdala prior to Birchas Hamazon in such a case, as explained above in Halacha 1-See there! [If he said Havdala during the meal and desires to continue eating after Havdala, there is no need to say Hamotzi over the foods and he may therefore continue eating.[48]]

If one Davened Maariv in middle of the meal:[49] In the event that one Davened Maariv [or said Baruch Hamavdil[50]] in middle of the meal, he is forbidden to continue eating or drinking until he says Havdala, even if he washed for

---

[30] M"B 299/1; Ashel Avraham Butchacher ibid regarding if there is someone which is not eating to remind him to say Havdala.

[31] As the eating of the third meal is a Rabbinical command and hence in such a case one may rely on the opinion of the Razah/Taz which allow food to be eaten until nightfall. Furthermore it was already stated above that the custom is to be lenient to begin large meals of weddings after sunset. Furthermore one can say that a Rabbinical command to eat the third meal differs the Rabbinical prohibition of eating after sunset. [M"B ibid; Shaareiy Tziyon 2; Biur Halacha "Mishetechshach"]

[32] Piskeiy Teshuvos 299/3

[33] Some Poskim [Ketzos Hashulchan 92 footnote 8] rule that if one did not eat a Kezayis of bread before sunset he may not say Ritzei in Birchas Hamazon. Others [Ashel Avraham Butchacher 188/19] rule even if he ate a Kezayis of bread after sunset Ritzei is to be recited in Birchas Hamazon.

[34] Piskeiy Teshuvos 299/3

[35] 299/2

[36] One is to swallow the food and not merely taste it and spit it out. [See Admur 167/9; Seder 9/1; Kaf Hachaim 89/6] This is unlike the ruling of Mur Uketzia 210; Shut Kol Gadol 72 that rule so long as one had intent to eat it, if he spits it out it is not a blessing in vain. [See Piskeiy Teshuvos 210/9 Vetzaruch Iyun on his omitting the ruling of Admur brought above.]

[37] The reason he is to taste the food is because otherwise the blessing will be in vain. It does not help to immediately say Havdala and then taste the food after Havdala as this is considered an interval, between the eating and the blessing and a new blessing would be required hence causing the first blessing to be in vain. [ibid]

[38] So is implied from Admur 166/1 in end; Kitzur Halachos 299 footnote 6; Machatzis Hashekel 299/2

[39] 299/2

[40] However eating other foods over which one does not say Hamotzi and Birchas Hamazon is not defined as eating a meal of which its law will be discussed next. [Ketzos Hashulchan 94 footnote 3] Thus even if he ate Mezonos he must stop by sunset. [Aruch Hashulchan 299/5]
Other Opinions: There are Poskim which rule that if one began eating Mezonos prior to sunset for the sake of fulfilling his third meal then he may continue eating after sunset. [See Q&A]

[41] As since he has begun eating his meal at a permitted time he is allowed to continue it past the permitted time, for as long as he desires. [ibid] This follows the custom brought in Rama 299/1 and the first opinion in Michaber ibid. However the second opinion in Michaber rules one is to stop his meal by night and say Havdala and only then continue eating.

[42] Ketzos Hashulchan 94 footnote 4 in name of Peri Megadim.

[43] Ketzos Hashulchan 94 footnote 3; See Q&A

[44] The reason for this is because Havdala is to be said close to the leave of Shabbos and thus there is worry that even snacking can cause one to delay saying it within this time. [Kuntrus Achron 299/2]

[45] 299/3

[46] Ketzos Hashulchan 94/5
Even though in general we rule one may continue eating the meal without a blessing if he later changes his mind, regarding the third meal on Shabbos one is to be stringent due to the severity of eating before Havdala. [ibid]

[47] 299/4

[48] 299/4 Kuntrus Achron 3

[49] 299/5

bread before sunset. This applies even if one Davened Maariv early, prior to dark. [In such a case one is to omit Ritzei from Bentching.[51] Due to this initially one is to avoid Davening Maariv or saying Havdala, or Baruch Hamavdil until after reciting Birchas Hamazon in order for him to be able to recite Ritzei.[52] However there are Poskim which allow doing so even initially.[53] If one answered for Barchu of Maariv prior to saying Birchas Hamazon, he may nevertheless recite Ritzei in Bentching if he recites it prior to Davening Maariv.[54]]

Drinking the Kos Shel Bracha after Birchas Hamazon:[55] One may not drink from the cup of wine used for Kos Shel Bracha during Birchas Hamazon until after Havdala.[56] Thus after Birchas Hamazon one is to leave the Kos Shel Bracha on the table, and not say a blessing over it. The custom is to then Daven Maariv and after Maariv to say Havdala.[57] Unlike the ruling in the Shulchan Aruch, the custom today is to say Havdala over this same cup of wine, as opposed to using another cup of wine for Havdala.[58] [It is best for the person who led the Zimun, or at least participated in Birchas Hamazon, to say Havdala over this cup of wine.[59] In the event that no one will be saying Havdala over the cup of wine, it is nevertheless proper to say Birchas Hamazon over a Kos Shel Bracha.[60]]

---

[50] Ketzos Hashulchan 94 footnote 7 and 6 based on the ruling of Admur that once one has said Baruch Hamavdil he may not say Ritzei in Birchas Hamazon.

Other Opinions: Elya Raba 299 rules one may continue eating after saying Baruch Hamavdil within a meal. So rules also M"B in Shaareiy Tziyon 299/8

[51] 188/17

[52] Based on glosses of Chasam Sofer in end of 263

[53] See Piskeiy Teshuvos 299/4 footnote 41

[54] Beir Moshe 1/5

[55] 299/6-7

[56] Admur 299/6 records a distinction in this matter:

If one is always careful to have a Kos Shel Bracha when he says the grace after meals, then he is to drink from the wine after he finishes Birchas Hamazon, prior to saying Havdala. The reason for this is because according to the opinion which requires Kos Shel Bracha by Bentching, the cup of wine is part of the meal, and the same way one may continue eating a meal past night if he began prior to sunset, so too he may drink this wine. However one which at times says the grace after meals without a [cup of wine], being that he relies on the opinions which say Birchas Hamazon does not require a cup of wine, it is forbidden for him to drink prior to Havdala from the cup of wine used to say Birchas Hamazon. Rather he should immediately after Birchas Hamazon say Havdala on another cup of wine, if available, and have the first cup included in its blessing of Hagafen, and then immediately drink it after drinking the cup of Havdala. [ibid] [Practically today we are no longer accustomed to always have a Kos Shel Bracha when saying the grace after meals. Therefore we must say Havdala prior to drinking the cup.]

Other Opinions: The above distinction in Admur is taken from the Magen Avraham 299/7. However the Elya Raba 299/6 rules one may always drink the Kos Shel Bracha before Havdala even if he is not always particular to say Birchas Hamazon over a cup. The Kaf Hachaim [299/20] rules when one is saying a Zimun with three people he may drink the cup prior to Havdala, immediately after Birchas Hamazon.

[57] Ketzos Hashulchan 94 footnote 9; Tehila Ledavid 299/1; Kitzur Halachos p. 118; Biur Halacha 299 "Mivareich"

Ruling of Admur in Shulchan Aruch 299/7: From the letter of the law, immediately after Birchas Hamazon one is to say Havdala in order not to delay between Birchas Hamazon and the Kos Shel Bracha. The reason for this is because one is required to drink the Kos Shel Bracha immediately after Birchas Hamazon, according to those which rule the cup is an obligation. (Furthermore, even according to those which rule Birchas Hamazon does not require a Kos they nevertheless agree that it is a Mitzvahs Min Hamuvchar to do so, and hence he is to drink it as close as possible to Birchas Hamazon.) [299/7]

Explanation of custom: Tehila Ledavid ibid explains the above ruling of Admur was referring to a person who has already Davened Maariv, in which case we tell him to say Havdala immediately after Birchas Hamazon. If one however has not Davened Maariv he is to first Daven. The reason for this perhaps is because it is better to say Havdala within Shemoneh Esrei before one says Havdala over wine. [Kitzur Halachos ibid]

[58] Ketzos Hashulchan 94 footnote 9; Tehila Ledavid 299/1; Kitzur Halachos p. 118;

Ruling of Shulchan Aruch 299/7: From the letter of the law, immediately after Birchas Hamazon one is to say Havdala on another cup of wine, if available, and have the first cup included in its blessing of Hagafen, and then immediately drink it after drinking the cup of Havdala. The reason for this is because Havdala and Kos of Birchas Hamazon are two separate Kedushos, and hence require two separate cups of wine due to the rule "we do not fulfill Mitzvos in bundles". (This applies even according to the opinion which rules Birchas Hamazon does not require a Kos, as nevertheless it is a Mitzvah Min Hamuvchar to do so, and hence one should not use the same Kos for both Havdala and Birchas Hamazon.) However if one does not have another cup of wine readily available then he should say Havdala on the same cup he used for Birchas Hamazon. He should not delay waiting for more wine as one is required to drink the Kos Shel Bracha immediately after Birchas Hamazon, according to those which rule the cup is an obligation, (and even according to those which hold it is not an obligation it is nevertheless a Mitzvah Min Hamuvchar to do so). [299/7]

Other Opinions: Ashel Avraham Butchacher 299 rules one may always say Havdala over the same cup of wine used for Birchas Hamazon, as since the wine for Birchas Hamazon is no longer an obligation the concept of not doing Mitzvos in bundles does not apply.

Explanation of our custom today: Tehila Ledavid ibid explains the above Halacha in Admur was referring to a person who has already Davened Maariv, in which case we tell him to say Havdala immediately after Birchas Hamazon. If one however has not Davened Maariv he is to first Daven. In such a case there is no longer a problem in using the same cup for Havdala, as there has been an interval between Birchas Hamazon and the blessing over the Kos Shel Bracha. This is based on Admur 299 Kuntrus Achron 4 which rules the rule of "Not to perform Mitzvos in bundle" only applies if there is not a large interval between them.

Others answer that our custom is based on the Rambam which allows and encourages using the same cup for Havdala, and we hence did not accept this current ruling of the Shulchan Aruch. [Ketzos Hashulchan ibid] See Kitzur Halachos ibid

[59] Ketzos Hashulchan 94 footnote 9

As the person who said Birchas Hamazon is to say the blessing over the wine afterwards. Perhaps however today that everyone says Birchas Hamazon quietly to themselves anyone who participated in the meal can say this blessing. [ibid]

[60] Sheivet Haleivi 8/242

Summary:

It is forbidden to eat or drink prior to Havdala. The custom is to avoid even drinking water. The prohibition begins starting from sunset unless one is in the midst of a meal with bread in which case he may continue eating and drinking even past nightfall, until he recites Birchas Hamazon or Davens Maariv or recites Baruch Hamavdil. One must however begin this meal prior to sunset.

Q&A

If one said Havdala early, before sunset, may he eat after sunset?[61]

Yes.

From the letter of the law may one drink water based soft drinks before Havdala?[62]

It is questionable whether soft drinks that are water based are permitted to be drunk before Havdala just as is the law regarding water itself. [Practically the custom is to avoid drinking even water prior to Havdala, and thus certainly water based soft drinks are to be avoided.]

May women eat or drink prior to Havdala?

No.[63]

May children eat prior to Havdala?[64]

Yes. It is forbidden to prevent them from eating if they need to eat.

If one began eating a meal before sunset may he eat fruits, pastries and the like after sunset even though they will require a new blessing?[65]

Yes. Since one is in middle of a meal he may continue to eat all foods that are exempt with his Birchas Hamazon, such as fruits and other desserts.

If one began eating Mezonos before sunset may he continue to do so after sunset?

Some Poskim[66] rule it is forbidden to continue eating past sunset if he did not start a meal which consists of bread beforehand, even if he ate Mezonos. Others[67] rule if he ate Mezonos before sunset he may continue eating it after sunset. Others[68] rule if he intends to fulfill his obligation of the third meal with the Mezonos he is eating then he may continue eating it after sunset.

If one is reciting Birchas Hamazon after sunset but before nightfall, may he drink the Kos Shel Bracha?

Some Poskim[69] rule one may drink from the Kos Shel Bracha even if he is not always particular to have a Kos Shel Bracha while reciting Birchas Hamazon.[70] However seemingly according to Admur it is proper to be stringent to avoid drinking the Kos Shel Bracha in such a case, although those that are lenient have upon whom to rely.[71]

If one made Sheva Brachos for the third meal, what is one to do with the Kos Shel Bracha?

Many Poskim[72] rule one is to say Sheva Brachos over the wine and say the concluding blessing of Hagafen immediately after Birchas Hamazon, before Havdala. In such a case some[73] say the person saying Birchas

---

[61] Peri Megadim 299 A"A 1; Kaf Hachaim 299/4

[62] Piskeiy Teshuvos 299/1 footnote 6

[63] As they are obligated in Havdala.

[64] 269/3 regarding Kiddush

[65] Piskeiy Teshuvos 299/2

[66] Ketzos Hashulchan 94 footnote 3; Aruch Hashulchan 299/5

[67] Oar Letziyon 2/22-8

[68] Sheivet Haleivi 8/36

[69] Chayeh Adam 18/20; M"B 299/14

[70] As in such a case they allow to rely on the Taz/Rosh which rule one may even begin a meal at Bein Hashmashos. However according to the M"A it would remain forbidden to drink the Kos Shel Bracha in such a case even if it is still before nightfall. [Chayeh Adam ibid]

[71] This follows the general ruling of Admur 299/2 regarding eating by Bein Hashmashos, as Admur rules like the M"A although concludes that those which are lenient like the Taz are not to be protested.

[72] Ashel Avraham Butchacher 299; Minchas Yitzchak 3/113; Beir Moshe 4/35-36; Taamei Haminhagim Ishus; Tosefus Chaim 8/14 on Chayeh Adam in name of Achronim

[73] Lekutei Mahrich; Beir Moshe 4/35-36

Hamazon is to drink from the cup. Regarding how much he is to drink some Poskim[74] rule he is to drink a full Revius of the cup. Others[75] rule he is to only taste a small amount. However some Poskim[76] say only the Chasan and Kala are to drink from the cup and not the person who said Birchas Hamazon. For this reason some are accustomed to have the Chasan say Birchas Hamazon. Some only give the Kala to drink from the cup and not the Chasan.[77]

Some Poskim[78] argue on all of the above and rule one is not to say a blessing over the cup of wine until after Havdala.

To note that some have the custom not to make Sheva Brachos at all by the third meal.[79]

3. The blessings recited during Havdala:[80]

The Sages required one to smell Besamim[81] and say a blessing over a candle on Motzei Shabbos. They organized these blessings to be said during Havdala after the blessing over wine, prior to the blessing of Hamavdil. Thus after the blessing over wine the blessing over Besamim is recited, which is followed by the blessing over a candle. The acronym for this order is "YBNH", standing for Yayin [wine]; Besamim [spices]; Neir [candle]; Havdala.[82]

Hinei Keil Yeshuasi:[83] It is customary to recite prior to Havdala the verses of *"Hinei Keil Yeshuasi… Layehudim Haysa Ora…Kos Yeshuos Esa"*. This is said as a good omen and is not obligatory. [It is customary amongst many Chabad Chassidim that those which are listening to Havdala recite these verses quietly to themselves.[84]]

If one did not hear the blessing of Hagafen:[85] If one walked into the room in middle of Havdala after the blessing of Hagafen was recited he nevertheless fulfills his obligation so long as he heard the blessing of Hamavdil. The same applies if he was in the room but could not physically hear the blessing of Hagafen, nevertheless he fulfills his obligation if he heard the later blessing of Hamavdil. Nevertheless in either of the above cases he may not drink any wine after Havdala before saying a blessing of Hagafen. [In such a case if he did not hear the blessing of Besamim or Meorei Haeish he should say the blessings after Havdala.]

Q&A

Savri Maranan:[86]

It was the custom of the Rebbe Rashab to recite Savriy Maranan prior to the blessing of the beverage, even if he was saying Havdala over beer and the like.[87]

Are the Pesukim of Hinei Keil Yeshuasi recited on Motzei Yom Tov?

Yes.[88] Although some[89] have the custom to omit it.

---

[74] Beir Moshe ibid

[75] Zichron Yehuda 87, brought in Minchas Yitzchak ibid

[76] Igros Moshe 4/69

[77] See Minchas Yitzchak ibid; Piskeiy Teshuvos 299/8

[78] Hagahos Chochmas Shlomo 299

[79] See Piskeiy Teshuvos 299 footnote 74

[80] 296/1

[81] This is not done on every Motzei Shabbos, such as when Motzei Shabbos is a Yom Tov. Therefore by Besamim Admur simply writes Motzei Shabbos, while by the blessing over fire he writes "every Motzei Shabbos".

[82] The Rashbatz is quoted to say that the order of the blessings follows the order of one's senses: Taste is the most course of the senses and hence we say the blessing over wine first, then we say the blessing over smell which is a higher sense; then we say the blessing over sight which is a higher sense, and then we say the blessing of Havdala which entails wisdom and is hence the highest of senses. Regarding the four different Havdala mentioned in the blessing of Hamavdil, this corresponds to the four unclean Kelipos which are subdued through this blessing.[Kaf Hachaim 296/3]

[83] 296/3; For a summary of the different customs involved in these verses, see Piskeiy Teshuvos 296/6

Regarding reciting the versus of Hinei Keil Yeshuasi on Motzei Yom Tov: Some Poskim rule it is not to be said. [Mateh Efraim 601/10] Others rule it is to be recited. [Peri Megadim 491 M"Z 1] The Rebbe's custom is to recite it, and so is the Chabad custom.

[84] Shaareiy Halacha Uminhag 5/35 states that the Rebbe Rashab would say "Hinei Keil Yeshuasi" when he was hearing Havdala from another. This custom is also brought in Lekutei Mahrich in Seder Havdala, Luach Dvar Yom Beyomo, Piskeiy Teshuvos 296/6

Practically this is the Chabad custom as heard from numerous Chabad Chassidim, amongst them Rav Chaim Shalom Deutch who testified this was the custom he witnessed in the Chabad Shul since he was a child. This custom was recently footnoted in the new Siddur of Tehilas Hashem published by Kehos Eretz Yisrael.

[85] 296/18

[86] Shaareiy Halacha Uminhag 5/35

[87] This was done in order to complete the amount of words needed to be said during Havdala,

[88] Peri Megadim 491 M"Z 1; and so is the custom of the Rebbe as was witnessed in public.

[89] Mateh Efrayim 601/10; 624/5

Are the Pesukim of Hinei Keil Yeshuasi recited on Motzei Tishe Beav which falls on Sunday?
Yes. [90]Although some[91] have the custom to omit it.

Are the Pesukim of Hinei Keil Yeshuasi recited when an Avel says Havdala?[92]
No.[93] However when others are saying Havdala for an Avel the versus are recited.

If one forgot to say the blessing of Hagafen what is he to do?[94]
If he already drank the wine, see next! If he did not yet drink the wine he is to say the blessing of Hagafen upon remembering. If he remembered after the blessing of Hamavdil he is to say it then. If he remembered prior to the blessing of Hamavdil, he is to say it upon remembering, whether after Meoreiy Haeish or between Besamim and Meoreiy Haeish.

If one forgot to say the blessing of Hagafen and only remembered after drinking the wine does he fulfill his obligation?
Yes.[95] However there are Poskim[96] which leave this matter in question.

If one said the blessing of Meoreiy Haeish prior to Besamim what is he to do?[97]
One is not to correct himself and say Borei Minei Besamim, rather he is to look at his nails and then say the blessing over Besamim.

What is the law if one said Meorei Haeish and then quickly corrected himself and said Minei Besamim[98]?[99]
If one had in mind during the blessing to say Besamim and accidently said Haeish and then quickly said Besamim, he is to repeat the blessing of Haeish. If however he had in mind to say Haeish and indeed said Haeish and then corrected himself to say Besamim, he is to place his hands by the flame, and then repeat the blessing of Besamim.

If one talked during Havdala must he hear or say it again?[100]
At the very least one must pay attention to the last blessing of Hamavdil in order to fulfill his obligation. Thus if he spoke to another person during that blessing, even if he physically heard the blessing, he nevertheless must repeat Havdala. [If he only spoke momentarily during the last blessing and hence heard most of it requires further analysis if he must hear Havdala again.[101]]

---

[90] So writes Hiskashrus 940 footnote 82 to be custom of the Rebbe. This dispute seemingly follows the same dispute regarding if these versus are to be recited on Motzei Yom Tov.
Other Opinions: In Luach Kolel Chabad it states one is to say Havdala like the order of the rest of Jewry which is to skip the verses of Hinei Keil Yeshuasiy. So rules Mateh Efrayim 581/181; SSH"K 62/44

[91] Other Opinions: In Luach Kolel Chabad it states one is to say Havdala like the order of the rest of Jewry which is to skip the verses of Hinei Keil Yeshuasiy. So rules Mateh Efrayim 581/181; 601/10; 624/5; SSH"K 62/44

[92] Piskeiy Teshuvos 296/6

[93] Pischeiy Teshuvah 376/2; 391/1

[94] Piskeiy Teshuvos 296 footnote 20

[95] Admur KU"A 272/2

[96] Tehila Ledavid 271/18 based on Chacham Tzevi which requires the blessing of Hagafen to always be said on a Kos Shel Bracha.

[97] Ketzos Hashulchan 96 footnote 1; Kaf Hachaim 296/9; See Piskeiy Teshuvos 296/2 which rules differently then below, that one is to correct himself within Kdei Dibur if he had in mind to say the blessing of Besamim and then said Haeish. He bases himself on M"B 209/6. Vetzaruch Iyun on his source.

[98] Whether he said Borei Minei Besamim, or simply Minei Besamim has the same law. [SSH"K 58 Footnote 107]

[99] M"A 209/5 brought in Ketzos Hashulchan 96/1; M"B 209/6
Other Opinions: Some Poskim [Kaf Hachaim 296/9] rule in such a case he has fulfilled the blessings of both Besamim and fire and is hence now to smell the spices and look at his nails.
Others rule he is to always smell the Besamim, and then say the blessing of Meorei Haeish. [Kneses Hagedola on Tur; Mishpiteiy Tzedek 2/2 brought in M"A 209/5]

[100] See Piskeiy Teshuvos 296 footnote 142

[101] See Michaber 183/6 and Admur 183/10 that if one talked in middle of Birchas Hamazon which he is hearing from another person, then if he talked in middle of the blessing he does not fulfill his obligation. However the M"B 183/26 limits this only to a case that one did not hear the parts of Birchas Hamazon that are obligatory to be said. Thus seemingly the same would apply here to Havdala that if one did not miss any of the main Nusach he has still fulfilled his obligation. [See Piskeiy Teshuvos 271 footnote 105]

If one accidently drank the wine after saying the blessing of Hagafen, what is he to do?[102]

He is to pour another cup of wine and continue with the blessing of Besamim.[103] However there are Poskim[104] that rule that if there is no more wine in front of him he is to pour himself another cup of wine and say Havdala from the beginning, repeating the blessing of Hagafen.[105] If however there is more wine in front of him he is to pour another cup of wine and continue with the blessing of Besamim even according to this opinion.[106]

In the above case if one did not say Ata Chonantanu in Shemoneh Esrei, he must repeat Shemoneh Esrei.[107]

If one accidently concluded the blessing of Hamavdil with the words "Bein Kodesh Lekodesh" what is he to do?[108]

If he remembers right away, within "Kdei Dibur", he is to correct himself and recite "Bein Kodesh Lechol". If he did not remember within this time he is to repeat the blessing of Hamavdil. If he already drank the wine he is to say Havdala again over wine. Regarding if he should repeat the blessing of the wine, see previous Q&A regarding one who drank the wine prior to saying Havdala.[109]

If one accidently concluded the blessing "Bein Kodesh Lechol" on Motzei Shabbos which is Yom Tov what is he to do?[110]

If he remembers right away, within "Kdei Dibur", he is to correct himself and recite "Bein Kodesh Lekodesh". If he did not remember within this time he is to repeat the blessing of Hamavdil. If he already drank the wine he is to say Havdala again over wine. Regarding if he should repeat the blessing of the wine, see previous Q&A regarding one who drank the wine prior to saying Havdala.[111]

See Halacha 14 Q&A for other related questions!

4. Customs related to Havdala:

Standing:[112] It is accustomed to stand while saying Havdala.[113]

Wearing Shabbos cloths:[114] It is proper to wear at least some of one's Shabbos clothing until after Havdala on Motzei Shabbos. [See Halacha 27 for a full analysis on this subject]

Looking at the cup of wine and candle:[115] While the blessing of Havdala is being recited the listeners[116] are to look at the cup of wine and the candle. [Likewise the person saying Havdala is to look at the cup during the blessing.[117]]

---

[102] See Kaf Hachaim 196/44

[103] This applies whether the bottle of wine is in front of him or not, nevertheless he is not to repeat the blessing of Hagafen, as the wine is the same species. [So rules Admur 206/9; Seder Birchas Hanehnin 9/5;]

[104] Poskim brought in Kaf Hachaim 296/44; 271/96; See Piskeiy Teshuvos 296 footnote 34 that rules if one is not accustomed to drink any more wine after Havdala he is to say another blessing.

[105] His reasoning is because by Havdala one does not have in mind to drink any more wine , and hence even the same species is no longer included within the blessing. [ibid; See Piskeiy Teshuvos 206/18; 296 footnote 34]

[106] Kaf Hachaim 271/96 differentiates between if the wine was in front of him or not. However in 296/44 he makes no differentiation.
The reason: No new blessing is to be said on this wine as all food that is in front of a person is included within his first blessing. [206/9; 212/10; Seder Birchas Hanehnin 1/21; 9/5]

[107] Kaf Hachaim 296/44

[108] Rav SZ"A Maor Hashabbos 2/28; Piskeiy Teshuvos 296/4

[109] Piskeiy Teshuvos 296 footnote 34 rules if one is not accustomed to drink any more wine after Havdala he is to say another blessing.

[110] Rav SZ"A Maor Hashabbos 2/28; Piskeiy Teshuvos 296/4

[111] Piskeiy Teshuvos 296 footnote 34 rules if one is not accustomed to drink any more wine after Havdala he is to say another blessing.

[112] 296/15 as rules Rama 296/6 based on the Igur and Agguda; See Admur 213/5; 298/20
Other Opinions: The Michaber [ibid] rules Havdala is to be said sitting. Likewise all the listeners are to sit. This ruling is based on Tosafus and Moredchaiy which rule one is to sit in order so the blessing over the wine have a Kevius. [Kaf Hachaim 296/39-41; M"B 296/27] So rules also Gra [on Shulchan here and also in Maaseh Rav 150] Aruch Hashulchan 296/17 writes there are Gedolei Yisrael which recite it sitting. The Kaf Hachaim [Rav Falagi] 31/38 rules that based on kabala one is to sit while saying Havdala.
The reason why other Poskim do not require one to sit despite the above need of Kevius to be Yotzei others is because it was only said that one must sit to be Yotzei others in a case of Birchas Hanehin, such as when the listeners will be drinking the wine. It is not required simply to be Yotzei others for a Mitzvah. Thus here since no one else will be drinking the wine other than the person saying Havdala, it is therefore not necessary for them to sit. [Admur 213/5 regarding Haeish and Besamim; Alef Lamagen 625/74] Regarding the blessing of Haeish Admur further added there that no Kevius of sitting is required as Kevius is not needed by those pleasures that all the listeners receive equally. Hence by the blessing of Haeish everyone may stand.
Ruling of Sefaradim: Some Sefaradi Poskim rule like the Rama in this matter that Havdala is to be said standing. [Ben Ish Chaiy Vayeitzei 21] Others rule like Michaber that one is to sit. [Kaf Hachaim ibid; Yechaveh Daas 4/26]

[113] This is done in honor of the king which we are escorting when we say Havdala, and it is customary to stand when escorting the king. [ibid]

[114] 262/3

Sitting while drinking:[118] After completing the recital of the blessing of Havdala one is to first sit down and only then drink the wine.[119]

How much of the wine is one to drink?[120] At the conclusion of the last blessing it is customary that one drink the entire[121] cup of wine himself. It is not distributed to others to drink as is commonly done by Kiddush.[122] [If however one said Havdala over the same cup of wine used for Birchas Hamazon, it may be distributed to others, including women.[123]]

At the very least one must[124] drink a Revius of wine in order to avoid doubt as to whether he is obligated in an after blessing.[125] If one drank less than a Revius, then if he drank the majority of a Revius he nevertheless fulfills his obligation, and is not to say an after blessing afterwards. If he drank less than Malei Lugmav[126], or did not drink wine at all, it is disputed whether he has fulfilled his obligation, and practically he is not to repeat Havdala as Safek Brachos Lehakeil.[127] [Rather he should try to hear Havdala from another person.[128]]

Extinguishing the candle with the Havdala wine:[129] After drinking the wine of Havdala the leftover wine which remains in the cup is customarily poured on the table [or plate, such as the Kiddush plate]. One then uses this wine to extinguish the Havdala candle by dipping the candle into it.[130] [Practically however many have the custom to pour the wine over the candle, and not to first pour the wine onto a plate and then dip the candle into it.[131] Others do both and dip the candle into the wine that is on the plate and then pour wine over it.[132]]

---

[115] 296/4

[116] The reason for looking at the wine and candle is because by a Kos Shel Bracha those listening are to look at the cup as writes Admur in 183/8

[117] 183/8

The person saying Havdala is to look at the cup of wine **and candles**. [Kaf Hachaim 296/8; Kitzur Halachos 296 footnote 12] However this applies only when he says the blessing over the candles. During the blessings of Hagafen and Hamavdil he is to look at the cup. [Kitzur Halachos ibid] and so is the custom of the Rebbe.

[118] 296/15

[119] As it is not proper for Torah Scholars to eat or drink while standing. [ibid] This applies also for those that are not Torah Scholars, and applies by all foods and drink, not just by Havdala. [Elya Raba 296/14; Beir Heiytiv 170/16; Kitzur Halachos 296 footnote 14]

[120] 296/6

[121] Seemingly this applies even if the cup contains more than a Revius, as if it contains exactly a Revius it would be an obligation to drink the entire cup in order not to enter into doubts regarding a Bracha Achrona. Hence from the wording of Admur that doing so is a mere custom it seems he refers even to when the cup holds more than a Revius.

[122] Admur ibid based on Shivlei Haleket brought in M"A 296/4

The reason for not distributing the wine to others: The Seder Hayom writes that he has not heard a reason as for why one drinks the entire cup himself although perhaps it contains some Kabalistic meaning. The M"B 296/6 writes that we do not want one to drink less than a Revius and then enter into a questionable after blessing. Kaf Hachaim of Rav Falagi writes we do not give to other men to drink being that it is customary not to give the women and we do not want to offend the women by singling them out. In Lekutei Torah of Rav M. of Chernobyl he writes that one must be very careful not to drink from the Havdala wine of another person as this causes enmity between them. The Divreiy Yichezkal p. 231 writes similarly that it causes rift in the family. [See Piskeiy Teshuvos 296/8]

The reason why women do not drinking wine of Havdala: In addition to the above reasons for why only the person saying Havdala drinks from the wine there are additional reasons for why women specifically should not drink from the wine. See Halacha 15 Q&A there!

Other Opinions: Some Poskim argue on the above and rule other men on are to drink from the Havdala wine, as is the rule by any Kos Shel Bracha. [Elya Raba, brought in Kaf Hachaim 296/15; See Tur 299; Machzor Vitry 116; Leket Yosher p. 57]

[123] Ketzos Hashulchan 97 footnote 3 and 96 footnote 9 as the wine is considered a Kos Shel Bracha.

[124] So writes Admur in 472/19 "must". However in 190/6 and in Seder he writes "Good" that it is merely proper to do so.

[125] 190/6 Regarding Kos Shel Bracha as there is doubt in whether one must say an after blessing after drinking a Kezayis of wine, or only after a Revius of wine. [Vetzaruch Iyun on this omission from Ketzos Hashulchan 97/3]. So rules Admur also in 472/19 regarding the 4th cup of the Seder and in Seder Birchas Hanehnin 8/1]

[126] The amount of wine to fill one cheek. This is normally the majority of a Revius.

[127] 190/4; Birchas Habayis 47/11; Kaf Hachaim 296/16; Piskeiy Teshuvos 296/11

The first opinion there [190/4] rules it is an obligation to drink the wine of Kos Shel Bracha. The second opinion there rules it is not an obligation to drink the wine, even though one said a blessing over it. Practically Admur concludes Safek Brachos Lehakeil.

Requires further analysis: Tzaruch Iyun Gadol from the ruling of Admur in 295/4 [brought later in Halacha 18] that if one did not have an adult which is fulfilling his obligation drink the Havdala wine, no one has fulfilled their obligation with this Havdala. [Ketzos Hashulchan 97 footnote 6; Tehila Ledavid 295/5; See Kitzur Halachos Miluim p. 109-112, and later on in Halacha 17]

Other Opinions: According to the M"B 296/9 if one did not drink Malei Lugmav of the wine he has not fulfilled his obligation.

[128] Piskeiy Teshuvos ibid

[129] 296/5

[130] The reason this is done is in order to show to all that the candle was lit simply for the Mitzvah of saying a blessing over it and not in order to use its light. (Therefore if one is saying Havdala over a candle which was not lit for this purpose, but for its light, it does not need to be extinguished.) [ibid]

[131] Seemingly the reason for the change of custom is because today we are accustomed to have some of the wine overflow onto the plate before even beginning Havdala, hence there is no need to pour wine onto the plate after Havdala to use to extinguish the candle. Thus they rather pour onto the candle.

[132] See Piskeiy Teshuvos 296 footnote 63

Washing one's eyes with the spilled wine: [133] It is customary to wet one's eyes using the wine which was spilled to extinguish the candle. [134] [The custom is to dip ones fingers into the leftover wine and to then pass them over the external part of the eye. This is a Segula for eyesight. [135] Many have the custom to also pass the wine over the forehead and pockets of their clothing. [136]]

Smelling the candle:
Some [137] have the custom to smell the Havdala candle after it is extinguished in order to show belovedness to the Mitzvah. It is likewise recorded that doing so protects one from evil spirits. [138] It however is not our custom to follow this practice. [139]

The Shabbos tablecloth:
Some [140] write one is not to remove the Shabbos tablecloth until after Havdala.

Blowing out a candle: [141]
One is not to blow out a candle with his mouth. [142] Thus in the event that one is unable to extinguish his candle with the wine he is to extinguish it in another way.

---

5. Laws relating to the cup of wine: [143]
The cup of wine used for Havdala follows all the laws which apply by a Kos Shel Bracha, such as by Kiddush and the cup used for Birchas Hamazon. The following is a summary of the applicable laws: [144]

1. The cup is to be washed inside and outside. [145]
2. The cup may not be damaged.
3. The wine is not to be Pagum. [146]
4. The cup is to be lifted three [147] Tefach from the table
5. The cup is to be received with both hands.
6. The cup is to be held only in the right hand.
7. One's eyes are to be on the cup.

Overflowing the wine: It is customary to pour enough wine so that it **slightly** overflows from the top of the cup. [148] [One is to have an undamaged [149] plate under the cup of wine, having the wine spill onto the plate. [150] One is to throw out the spilled wine after Havdala [151].]

---

[133] 296/5

[134] This is done out of belovedness for the Mitzvah. [ibid]
Other reasons: Using the leftovers of a Mitzvah refrain evil from befalling a person. [Pirkeiy Derebbe Eliezer 20; Gra on Rama 296/1]

[135] Shaareiy Halacha Uminhag 157; See Perisha 269/3
Other Customs: Some have the custom to dip their fingers and place them over the eyes three times. [Mishmeres Shalom Minhagim] Some have the custom to recite the verse "Mitzvas Hashem Bara Meiras Eiyanyim". [Kitzur Shlah in name of Arizal; Siddur Yaavetz] There exists different customs regarding which finger to dip into the wine. Some dip the pinky, others the index finger which is near the thumb. [Piskeiy Teshuvos 296 footnote 65]

[136] Piskeiy Teshuvos 296/7

[137] Siddur Yaavetz; Ketzos Hashulchan 97 footnote 7; Ashel Avraham Butchach 297; Minchas Shabbos in Shiyureiy Mincha 96/5
The Ketzos Hashulchan ibid testifies of the custom of the Sdei Chemed in Chevron to smell the Havdala candle after it was extinguished and he would exclaim "Ah Ah" very loudly. Everyone in the presence would break in laughter.

[138] Minchas Shabbos ibid in name of Sefer Zechariya

[139] Shaareiy Halacha Uminhag 5/35

[140] M"B 262/4 in name of Elya Raba and Aguda

[141] Piskeiy Teshuvos 296 footnote 71 in name of Kaf Hachaim [Falagi] 31

[142] This is said to be of danger to the person. [ibid]

[143] 271/18; 296/2

[144] See Shulchan Aruch Chapter 183. The full details of these Halachos will IY"H be printed in the Volume that contains "The laws of Kiddush".

[145] According to Halacha [183/2] there is no need to wash the cup if it is already clean. Furthermore even if there is leftover wine it does not need to be washed unless it has pieces of bread inside. However based on Kabala one is to always wash the cup before using it for Kos Shel Bracha even when clean. [Kaf Hachaim 183/4]

[146] Being Mitaken the wine with water: Based on Kabala one is never to add water to the wine when the wine is already in the cup. Therefore one is to add the water to the wine while it is still in the bottle. [Ketzos Hashulchan 97 footnote 1 from Shaar Hakavanos and Mishnas Chassidim]

[147] Likutei Taamim Uminhagim, brought in Sefer Haminhagim p. 55 regarding Kiddush; See Shaareiy Halacha Uminhag 1/103 that it is lifted three Tefach as a Hiddur, and so is sourced in different places in Zohar.
Opinion of Admur in Shulchan Aruch: Admur rules [183/8] that one is to lift the cup one Tefach from the table in order so it is visible to all.

[148] 296/5: "It is customary to pour a little wine from the cup onto the floor. It is to be done in a way that one slightly overflows the wine while pouring, and lets it spill to the ground. It is best not to accomplish the above by filling the cup to its top and then spilling some wine from the cup.

Q&A

If one said Havdala and then realized there was a hole in the cup, does he need to repeat Havdala?

Some Poskim[152] rule that if wine was dripping out of the hole then he is required to repeat Havdala. Others[153] however rule that one has fulfilled his obligation, and there is thus no need to repeat Havdala. It appears from Admur like this latter opinion.[154]

[According to all if one had wine on the table at the time of the blessing, aside from the wine in the cup, then he may drink that wine without needing to repeat Havdala or the blessing of Hagafen.[155]]

If one said Havdala over wine and then when he tasted it noticed the wine is spoiled or is really colored water, must he repeat Havdala?

One had a bottle of good wine on the table: If one had a bottle of actual wine on the table at the time of the blessing, then if he had in mind to drink more wine after Havdala he is to drink that wine without needing to repeat Havdala or the blessing of Hagafen.[156] If he did not have in mind to drink more wine after Havdala then although he has fulfilled the blessing of Havdala[157] he is to drink that wine and repeat the blessing of Hagafen.[158]

One did not have any good wine on the table: Most Poskim[159] rule he must repeat Havdala over wine, omitting however the blessings of fire and Besamim. However some Poskim[160] rule he is not to repeat Havdala.[161] According to them he should however try to hear Havdala from someone else.

The reason for this is because if one follows the latter custom he will end up not having a cup filled to its very top as is the commendable practice. Furthermore, he cannot as a result of the above reason say Havdala on a full cup without spilling wine out and then prior to drinking the cup after Havdala spill out some wine. The reason for this is because doing so is a belittlement to the blessing of Hagafen which was said over a full cup, as now when he spills some out it appears like there was something repulsive in the wine which he said the blessing over. Therefore the spillage of wine is to only be done in the above mentioned method." [ibid]

The reason for overflowing the wine: This is done for a good omen, as any house which does not have wine spill like water does not contain a good omen. Therefore we practice an act of good omen in the opening of the week. Doing so is not forbidden due to it being considered a belittling of food, despite that the wine goes to waste, as one is only spilling a small amount of wine. [ibid] This is based on the Magen Avraham [296/3] which explains that on a small amount there is no problem of Bizayon. However the Taz [296/1] explains that in truth there is no good omen involved in wasting wine. Rather the good omen is if wine happens to spill and one does not get angry. Nevertheless he agrees with custom to overflow a small amount of wine.

Other Reasons: Some write one is to pour the wine in order to weaken the Kelipos, as wine is the Gematria of 70 which corresponds to the seventy nations. By spilling the wine one weakens their strength. [Mateh Moshe 504]

Other Opinions: The Rama 296/1 rules one is to pour the wine prior to the blessing of Hagafen.

[149] Shaareiy Halacha Uminhag 5/31

[150] Shaareiy Halacha Uminhag 5/31; This custom is also brought in Minchas Shabbos; Ketzos Hashulchan 97 footnote 2

As for the reason why we do not spill the wine on the ground, as mentions Admur [brought in previous footnotes], perhaps this is because we suspect for those opinions which forbid spilling onto the ground, as well as the opinion of the Mekubalim which negate this custom. Hence we over pour the wine onto a plate which hence is not a belittlement towards it. [See M"A 296/2-3; Taz 296/1; Kaf Hachaim 296/10-11]

[151] It is necessary to spill out the wine as the entire purpose of the spill is so the wine go to waste and be treated like water. [See Shaareiy Halacha Uminhag ibid]

[152] Mishneh Berurah in Shaareiy Tziyon 183/14, as in such a case the cup is not considered to hold a Revius and the holding a Revius is required even Bedieved.

[153] Sheivet Haleivi 9/41; As the law of requiring a vessel is only Lechatchilah, as the Sages only required a vessel by Netilas Yadayim even Bedieved. However by Kiddush and Havdala no such institution was ever made. Thus Bedieved it remains valid.

[154] 183/4 as Admur says that the breaking of vessel is its death, and nevertheless concludes that one is only to be stringent when possible. Thus implying that Bedieved it is valid.

[155] 271/28 as holding the cup of wine in one's hand while saying the blessings is only required initially, while after the fact it is valid even if the cup remained on the table. [ibid]

[156] 271/28 regarding Kiddush. The reason it is valid is because holding the cup of wine in one's hand while saying the blessings is only required initially, while after the fact it is valid even if the cup remained on the table. [ibid]

[157] So rules Piskeiy Teshuvos 296/10 based on Ashel Avraham Butchacher 296

[158] Whenever one did not have in mind to drink more of the wine in front of him then a new blessing must be made if he did not drink the wine in his original cup. [So rules Admur in 206/11; Seder 9/8; Rama 209/2]

Other Opinions: Some Poskim rule that by Havdala one may be more lenient even if he did not have in mind to drink any more wine, as one certainly had in mind to fulfill Havdala as required by the Sages. [Ashel Avraham Butchach 296] The M"B [206/26] rules that whenever one has more wine in front of him even if he did not have in mind to drink any more wine, he does not repeat the blessing of Hagafen.

[159] Based on Admur 271/28 regarding Kiddush and so rule explicitly regarding Havdala: Chida in Chaim Sheal 74/43; Pischeiy Teshuvah 296; Birchas Habayis 46/21; Minchas Shabbos Shiyureiy Mincha 96/3; Piskeiy Teshuvos 296/10

[160] Kaf Hachaim 296/21

[161] As the Tur brings the Pirkeiy Rebbe Eliezer which rules if one does not have wine he may say Havdala without any beverage. Now although we do not rule like this opinion, we should suspect for it to not require a blessing in vain, as is the rule by Safek Brachos Lehakel. [ibid]

If one said Havdala over wine and it spilled prior to having a chance to drink from it what is the law?
If there is even a small amount of wine remaining that he is able to drink then he should drink from it. After drinking this wine he should pour himself another Revius of wine and drink it without saying a blessing.[162]
If there is absolutely no leftover wine that he is able to drink then the following is the law:
One has a bottle of wine on the table:[163] If one had a bottle of wine on the table at the time of the blessing, then if he planned to drink more wine after Havdala, he is to drink that wine without needing to repeat Havdala or the blessing of Hagafen. If he did not have in mind to drink more wine after Havdala then although he does not need to repeat the blessing of Havdala he is to repeat the blessing of Hagafen and drink that wine.[164]
One did not have any wine on the table:[165] He is to pour himself another cup of wine and recite the blessing of Hagafen.[166] He is not to repeat the blessing of Havdala.

May wine which was left open, or left in a cup be used for Havdala?[167]
If it has been left in the open for many hours [3-4 hours] it may not be used for Havdala.

6. How to hold the Kiddush cup, Besamim throughout Havdala:

A. Custom of the Rebbe[168] and today's widespread custom:[169]

1. Lift the cup with your right hand, pass it to your left hand and then place it back in your right hand lifting it three Tefach from the table. Recite until the end of the blessing of Hagafen while holding the cup in the right hand. Do not hold the Besamim while saying this.[170]
2. At the conclusion of the blessing of Hagafen, prior to the blessing of Besamim, place the cup down and hold the Besamim with the right hand. Then say the blessing.
3. After smelling the Besamim place the Besamim down, and say the blessing of Meoreiy Haeish with nothing in the hands. Place both hands by the fire, first one's palm and then one's out fingers
4. Prior to beginning the blessing of Hamavdil hold the cup in the right hand.

B. Ruling of Admur in Shulchan Aruch:[171]

All items of which one is doing a Mitzvah with are to be held in one's right hand. Therefore the following is the order of Havdala. One is to hold the cup of wine in his right hand and the Besamim in his left hand, [while reciting Hinei Keil Yeshuasi and] the blessing of Borei Peri Hagafen. When he reaches the blessing of Besamim he is to switch the cup to his left hand and take the Besamim in his right hand and say the blessing. Likewise for the blessing of Meorei Haeish it is best to continue holding the cup in his left hand so he can place his right hand by the fire.[172] Afterwards he is to transfer the cup back into his right hand and recite the blessing of Hamavdil.

---

[162] See Ketzos Hashulchan 79 footnote 23
One is Yotzei Havdala in such a case as rules Admur in 271/27 regarding Kiddush. One is also does not have to repeat the blessing of Hagafen on the new cup of wine in such a case as rules Admur in Seder 9/5; 206/9
[163] 271/28 regarding finding water or spoiled wine in the cup and the same would apply here that the wine spilled. The reason it is valid is because holding the cup of wine in one's hand while saying the blessings is only required initially, while after the fact it is valid even if the cup remained on the table. [ibid]   See also Ketzos Hashulchan 79/6 which rules this way regarding Kiddush.
[164] Admur rules that even when one has wine in front of him he only saves himself the need to repeat the blessing if he had in mind to drink the wine that was on the table after Kiddush [so is implied from Admur 271/28 from the words "prepared to be drunk" and from the KU"A 8 and so rules Admur explicitly in 206/11; Seder 9/8; Ketzos Hashulchan ibid]
Other Opinions: The M"B [206/26] rules that whenever one has more wine in front of him even if he did not have in mind to drink any more wine, he does not repeat the blessing of Hagafen.
[165] 271/27 and Ketzos Hashulchan 79/6 regarding Kiddush and the same applies for Havdala; So rules Piskeiy Teshuvos 296/11
[166] See however Ketzos Hashulchan 79 footnote 24 that if one has wine in the house and had in mind to drink more after Kiddush [or Havdala] then it is as if it is sitting on the table and one is not required to repeat the blessing of Hagafen.
[167] Biur Halacha 272 Biur Halacha "Al Yayin"; Ketzos Hashulchan 46 footnote 2.
Other Opinions: Rav Akivah Eiger leaves this matter in question. See Biur Halacha there.
[168] As witnessed by thousands of Chassidim in public on various occasions, and as can be viewed from recorded footage.
[169] This custom is prolific amongst Chabad as well as other circles. See Piskeiy Teshuvos 296/15 that the world is no longer careful to follow the order written in Shulchan Aruch. Ashel Avraham Butchacher did not originally follow the custom brought in Shulchan Aruch, although later changed his custom.
As for why the custom today has changed from the custom written in Shulchan Aruch-See Lehoros Nasan 8/17
[170] This matter was also omitted in the Siddur. [Ketzos Hashulchan 96 footnote 4]
[171] 296/16
[172] Rama 298/3

C. Ruling of Admur in Siddur:

When one reaches the blessing of Besamim he is to hold the cup in his left hand and take the Besamim in his right hand and say the blessing. For the blessing of Meorei Haeish one is to switch the cup back to his right hand.[173] [One then places the cup down or into his left hand[174]] and looks at the nails [of his right hand[175]]. Afterwards one transfers the cup back into his right hand and recites the blessing of Hamavdil.

Q&A

How is a lefty to hold onto the Havdala cup?
It is to be held in his left hand.[176] However some Poskim[177] rule that even a lefty is to hold it in his right hand.

---

7. Using beverages other than wine for Havdala:

Using wine over other beverages:[178] One is to say Havdala over wine even if he has other significant beverages available.[179] If one does not have wine at home but has at home other significant beverages, he is not required to purchase wine rather than use the other significant beverages. Nevertheless even in such a case it is a Mitzvah Min Hamuvchar to purchase wine from the store to say Havdala rather than to say Havdala on the other available beverages.

Motzei Pesach:[180] It is accustomed to be lenient to make Havdala over beer on Motzei Pesach even if one has much wine at home available.[181] Nevertheless if the beer is not currently beloved to the person, it is better to make Havdala over wine even on Motzei Pesach. Furthermore the above allowance only applies in those areas that beer is considered a significant drink.

One who does not have enough wine to fill the cup:[182] Even if one does not have enough wine to fill the entire cup, if he has a Revius of wine it is better to say Havdala over this wine than to say Havdala over a full cup of other significant beverages. [If one does not even have a Revius of wine, then he can add water to the wine until it reaches a Revius, so long as the total ratio of water in the wine does not invalidate its Hagafen status.[183] Nevertheless based on Kabala one is never to add water to the wine when the wine is already in the cup. Therefore one is to add the water to the wine while it is still in the bottle.[184]]

If the wine is Pagum:[185] If the wine is Pagum[186] it is possible to be Mitaken the wine by adding even a small amount of water to it[187]. If there is no way to Mitaken it[188] then it is better to say Havdala over other significant beverages than to use such wine.[189] [If there are no other beverages available one may make Kiddush on pagum wine if there is no way to be Mitaken it.[190]]

---

[173] This follows the ruling of the Mordechaiy, brought in Kaf Hachaim 298/21; See Shaar Hakolel 32/3.

[174] Ketzos Hashulchan 96/2 gives both options and so also learns Kitzur Halachos 296 footnote 11; However Shaar Hakolel 32/3 and Kaf Hachaim ibid brings to place the cup in the left hand while using the right hand to place near the flame.

[175] Ketzos Hashulchan 96/2

[176] Based on Admur 183/7; 651/14; Tzemach Tzedek Orach Chaim 5/8 regarding Netilas Yadayim

[177] So is the ruling based on Kabala that one always follows the general right hand of the world. [Kaf Hachaim 183/20]

[178] 296/8

[179] As it is not a Hiddur Mitzvah to say Havdala over other beverages when one has wine available. [ibid]

However based on that which Admur explains next regarding using beer on Motzei Pesach some have learned that even during the year whatever beverage is more beloved to the person may be used for Havdala, even over wine. [Biur Halacha 296 "Im Hu"; Aruch Hashulchan 296/13] Thus there were many Gedolei Yisrael which said Havdala over beer, coffee or tea even initially. [See Piskeiy Teshuvos 296 footnote 89]

The Kabbalistic perspective: Based on Kabala one is to always say Havdala over wine as it has the ability to rejoice the person which is saddened due to the leave of the extra soul which it received over Shabbos. [Tolaas Yaakov brought in Taamei Haminhagim 408]

[180] 296/10

[181] As at that time the beer is more beloved to a person than is wine. [ibid]

Other Opinions: Kaf Hachaim 296/26 rules based on Kabala that one is to always say Havdala over wine rather than other beverages even if the beer is more beloved.

[182] 296/9

[183] Kaf Hachaim 296/7

[184] Ketzos Hashulchan 97 footnote 1 from Shaar Hakavanos and Mishnas Chassidim. See however Piskeiy Teshuvos 296/5 that he brings that even in this method of placing the water in the bottle it is still looked down upon based on Kabala.

[185] 296/9

[186] This means that someone drank from the wine.

[187] Based on Kabala however one is to refrain from ever adding water to his wine. [Kaf Hachaim 296/7]

[188] Such as adding any more water to the wine will invalidate [its taste or Hagafen status]. [ibid]

[189] This ruling of Admur follows the ruling of the M"A 296/5.

Other Opinions: The Rama 296/5 rules even when the wine is Pagum it is better to say Havdala over the wine than over beer. The M"A ibid learns the Rama to only be referring to beer in a country that it is not Chamer Medina. The Elya Raba however argues on this assumption in the Rama. The Kaf Hachaim 296/24 rules like Elya Raba/Rama as based on Kabala it is better to always use wine rather than beer.

[190] Admur 182/6; Kaf Hachaim 296/6

If no wine is available but other beverages are available:[191] If there is no wine available one is to say Havdala over Chamar Medina[192] with exception to water.[193] [These beverages include liquor, beer, tea, coffee. See Q&A for the full details of this subject.]

If one has enough wine for either Havdala or Kos Shel Bracha after Bentching of Melaveh Malka:[194] If one is not always particular to say Birchas Hamazon over a cup of wine, it is forbidden for him to eat before Havdala, and he is thus to rather say Havdala over the wine and not have wine for Kos Shel Bracha. If however one is always particular to say Birchas Hamazon over wine, then if he does not plan to receive more wine until Sunday night[195], he may eat prior to Havdala and then after Bentching use the wine to say Havdala.

List of beverages that are considered Chamer Medina and may be used when no wine is available:[196]

    1. First choice-Alcoholic beverages:[197]

- Beer
- Liquor
- Black beer[198]

    2. Second choice:[199]

- Tea.
- Coffee.

* When using coffee or tea one is to make sure the beverage has cooled down to the point one can drink a Revius of it in a short amount of time.

    3. Third Choice:

➢ Natural pure fruit juice.[200]

❖ *Milk:*
One may not use milk for Havdala.[201] However some Poskim[202] allow using it in a time of need.

❖ *Soft Drinks:*[203]
Soft drinks may not be used for Havdala, and are considered similar to water.

---

[191] 296/8

[192] The defining of a beverage as Chamer Medina is dependent on a number of factors:
1. Wine is not commonly found in the area. If wine is commonly found in the area no other beverage is considered Chamer Medina, and it thus may not be used. [182/2; 272/10; Minchas Shabbos 96/9; Nimukei Orach Chaim 272/1; Piskeiy Teshuvos 296/9]
2. The beverage is commonly drank during meals of majority of that cities populace. [272/10; Ketzos Hashulchan 97/8]
3. The beverage must be considered of significance, and is not just a mere soft drink, and certainly is not water. [182/3]

[193] This means to say that even in a country that plane water is considered Chamer Medina, one may nevertheless not say Havdala over it. [Kaf Hachaim 296/20]

[194] 296/13

[195] So is implied from Admur, although no clear ruling is given regarding if one may be lenient in a case that he will receive wine on Sunday.

[196] It was explained in the previous footnotes that for a beverage to be considered Chamer Medina three conditions must be fulfilled [That wine is not commonly found in the city; majority of people drink this beverage during their meals; it is considered of significance]. Based on the above three conditions there is no beverage today other than wine which can be considered Chamer Medina. [So understands also Piskeiy Teshuvos 296/9; See Ketzos Hashulchan 97 footnote 8] Nevertheless in a time of need the practice is to be lenient on certain beverages. See sources in the following footnotes for more information on this matter.

[197] Piskeiy Teshuvos 296/9; Kitzur Hilchos Shabbos Supplements p. 67; See Admur 182/3

[198] Although black beer is non-alcoholic, it is similar to the relation of grape juice to wine, in which case grape juice has a similar status as does wine even though it is non-alcoholic. See Piskeiy Teshuvos 296 footnote 98

[199] See Kitzur Hilchos Shabbos Supplements p. 66; Piskeiy Teshuvos 296/9; The Alter Rebbe and Rebbe Rashab both made Havdala over coffee prior to their passing away. [Ishkavta Derebbe p. 97] Likewise the Rebbe is recorded to having given instructions to soldiers in the American army to say Havdala over coffee or tea. [Shaareiy Halacha Uminhag 1/140]
Other Opinions: Ketzos Hashulchan 97 footnote 8 rules one may not use tea or coffee for Havdala as these beverages are not considered Chamer Medina, as one never sets a meal with these beverages. Setting a meal with these beverages is defined not as sitting with friends and drinking it, but as a drink which is commonly brought and drank during a meal.

[200] Natural pure fruit juice may be used for Havdala. [Piskeiy Teshuvos 296/9; 272/9; SSH"K 60/5] However see Miluim Kitzur Halachos p. 66 which considers fruit juices an insignificant beverage.

[201] Shaareiy Teshuvah rules one may not use milk for Havdala, and so brings Ketzos Hashulchan 97 footnote 8; So ruled also Rebbe in Shaareiy Halacha Uminhag 1/140

[202] Aruch Hashulchan 272/14

[203] Admur 182/5; Piskeiy Teshuvos ibid

8. The law if no wine or other beverages are available:

A. Havdala over bread:[204]

If there is no wine or Chamar Medina beverages available it does not suffice to say Havdala over bread as is allowed by Kiddush. [205] Rather one is to delay saying Havdala until he receives wine or other Chamer Median as will be explained next.

On Motzei Shabbos which is Yom Tov:[206] If one does not have wine available on Motzei Shabbos which is Yom Tov, the custom is to say Havdala [Yaknahaz] over bread.[207]

B. Eating prior to Havdala when no beverages are available for Havdala:

Wine will be available late Saturday night: [208] If wine or other valid beverages will become available before Sunday morning, according to all it is forbidden to eat or drink until one says Havdala over wine.

Wine will be available on Sunday:[209] If he expects to receive wine or other valid beverages on Sunday during the day, one is to fast until he receives the wine and says Havdala. If one is weak and it is difficult for him to fast until that point, he may be lenient to eat and drink prior to Havdala.[210] [One may however drink water prior to saying Havdala even if he is not weak.[211] Although based on our custom to avoid drinking even water before Havdala seemingly one is to withhold himself from even drinking water if he is able to do so.]

> ❖ Ruling of Admur in Kuntrus Achron: In Kuntrus Achron 296/1 Admur leans to learn that after midday of Sunday one may begin eating if he has still not received wine for Havdala. [Accordingly some[212] learn that if on Motzei Shabbos one knows he will not receive wine or other valid beverages until after midday of Sunday, one may begin eating immediately on Motzei Shabbos, as is the rule in the next case.]

Wine will not be available until after Sunday: [213] In the event that wine or other significant beverages are not available to say Havdala, then if he is unable to receive wine until Sunday night, he is allowed to eat and drink immediately on Motzei Shabbos if he said Havdala in Davening.[214] If he did not say Havdala in Davening he must repeat Shemoneh Esrei prior to drinking.

C. The blessing of Besamim and Meoreiy Haeish:[215]

In the event that one does not have any Halachicly valid beverages available for Havdala he is to nevertheless to say on Motzei Shabbos the blessing over fire as soon as he sees it and the blessing of Besamim if he has spices.

---

[204] 296/7

[205] As Kiddush has a connection to the bread being that Kiddush may only be done in place of a meal. However Havdala is independent of eating a meal and hence has no connection to bread to allow saying Havdala over it. [Ibid]

[206] 296/11

[207] A dispute in this matter is brought in Admur. Some rule [Geonim; 1st opinion in Michaber] since one is allowed to say Kiddush over the bread, and Havdala is secondary to Kiddush on this night, he may likewise say Havdala over the bread. Others [Rosh; 2nd opinion of Michaber] however rule in such a situation it is better to say Kiddush over Chamer Medina than to say it over bread. Practically the custom in these countries is like the former opinion. [ibid] So is the ruling of Rama in our current wording of the Shulchan Aruch, however some prints have written the Rama rules like the latter opinion. [See Kaf Hachaim 296/28]

Other opinions: Michaber, based on Klalei Haposkim rules like the latter opinion. [Kaf Hachaim 296/27]

[208] 296/12

[209] 296/12

[210] Some Poskim [1st opinion in Michaber 296/3] rule if no wine will be available until Sunday morning, from the letter of the law it is permitted to immediately eat and drink if he said Havdala during Davening. It is however an act of piety to fast until he receives wine on Sunday. Others [2nd opinion in Michaber] however rule that if one will receive wine on Sunday it is forbidden from the letter of the law for him to eat or drink until he says Havdala over wine. Practically the Halacha is as stated above that we are stringent unless one is very weak and unable to fast in which case he may be lenient in a Rabbinical matter.[ibid]

So rules also Elya Raba like the latter opinion, and so seems to be the ruling of Michaber based Klalei Haposkim. [Kaf Hachaim 296/30]

[211] 299/1; See Ketzos Hashulchan 93 footnote 8. Vetzaruch Iyun why this ability to drink water was completely omitted by Admur.

[212] Ketzos Hashulchan 94 footnote 10; and so also plainly rules Piskeiy Teshuvos 296/12

[213] 294/2 and 296/12

[214] Even if one expects to receive wine on Monday he is not obligated to fast until then and rather he is allowed to eat immediately if he said Havdala in Davening. [294/2; 296/12]

Other Opinions: Some [Mahram brought in M"A] rule in such a case one is to say the blessing of Havdala without a cup. Practically we do not rule this way. [Kaf Hachaim 296/29]

[215] 298/3

9. The laws of Besamim:[216]

A. General Laws:[217]

The Sages accustomed[218] that one is to smell spices on every[219] Motzei Shabbos in order to comfort the soul which is saddened by the leave of the extra soul[220] which it received on Shabbos.[221]

Motzei Yom Tov:[222] On Motzei Yom Tov however we do not smell Besamim by Havdala as there is no extra soul[223] given on Yom Tov.

Motzei Shabbos which is Yom Tov:[224] When Motzei Shabbos coincides with Yom Tov the blessing of Besamim is omitted from the order of Havdala "Yaknahaz".[225]

Must one search for spices if it is not readily available? One is only obligated to smell Besamim if they are readily available. If however one does not have any Besamim readily available he is not obligated to search for them, [or to go buy them], as is required by other Mitzvos.[226] In such a situation one is to say Havdala and skip the blessing of Besamim. [Nevertheless based on Kabala some write it is proper to always say the blessing over Besamim in Havdala even if he is required to search for Besamim.[227]]

If one does not have a sense of smell:[228] One who does not have the sense of smell [whether due to being born this way or due to a cold or stuffed nose[229]] may not say the blessing of Besamim in Havdala even if there are other adults fulfilling their obligation with hearing his Havdala.[230] If however there are also children who have reached the

---

[216] Chapter 297

[217] 297/1

[218] Thus smelling Besamim was originally enacted as a custom and not as a decree, and so writes Admur in Kuntrus Achron 297/2. Nevertheless in relevance to fulfilling this custom, if spices are available, it is an obligation to fulfill the custom.

[219] This includes even if one fasted on Shabbos, as nevertheless the extra soul which entered on the night of Shabbos does not leave until after Shabbos. [297/2]

[220] See Lekutei Sichos 31 Ki Sisa for a analysis on the meaning of "an extra soul"
In short: According to Nigleh it refers to a state of mood, that on Shabbos one is more relaxed. However according to Kabala it is literally an extra soul. Admur in Lekutei Torah Vayakhel explains it refers to the revelation of the essence of one's soul, the Yechida. This level is revealed on Shabbos and hence gives a person a love and fear which is above intellect.

[221] On Shabbos one receives an extra soul and after Shabbos when this soul leaves the regular soul is saddened. Thus we comfort and rejoice her with a good scent. [ibid]
Other Reasons: The Bach 297 records the reason for the sadness of the soul is both due to the loss of the extra soul and also due to the continuation of the fire of Gehenim which restarts every Motzei Shabbos. Both of these reasons together affect the sadness of the soul. Based on this second reason if Rosh Chodesh falls on Motzei Shabbos there is room to say one is not obligated in Besamim, as also on Rosh Chodesh Gehenim is inactive. [Peri Megadim M"Z 297] Practically however one is obligated even in such a case as the main reason is, as records Admur, due to the loss of the extra soul. [Ketzos Hashulchan 98 footnote 1]
Rabbeinu Bechayeh writes the reason for smelling Besamim is because on Sunday there is always a certain weakness felt being that it is the third day of creation of man, and on the third day one always feels extra weakness.
The Aruch Hashulchan 297/1 concludes that although the above mentioned reasons are all spiritual, nevertheless it is visibly felt every Motzei Shabbos, as is seen from the fact that every person feels different on Motzei Shabbos. As although he may not feel the reason for the change the root of his soul does feel it.

[222] 491/1

[223] "At all" so adds Admur in 491/1. This follows the ruling of Tosafus Pesachim 102a; Rashba 3/290; Radbaz 2/620 that there is no extra soul on Yom Tov. However the Rashbam Pesachim 102b rules there is an extra soul on Yom Tov, and so is the ruling of the Zohar. Vetzaruch Iyun how the above Poskim can go against the Zohar. Perhaps in truth there are many levels of an extra soul, and on Shabbos one receives a higher level than on Yom Tov. However Tzaruch Iyun from Admur which states "on Yom Tov there is no extra soul at all". In truth in the source of Admur from the Magen Avraham and Levush these words "at all" are omitted. Furthermore in certain prints of the Shulchan Aruch of Admur this entire Halacha is missing. It most probably is the case then that Admur did not write this word and it was written by the copier. [Shaar Hakolel 17/22; Lekutei Sichos 31 Ki Sisa] However the Rebbe in Lekutei Sichos 31 Ki Sisa footnote 15 explains that based on Nigleh there is no extra soul at all on Yom Tov, and it is only based on Kabala that there is an extra soul, hence Admur wrote in his Shulchan Aruch which follows the rulings of Nigleh that there is no extra soul "at all".
Regarding the second reason mentioned by the Bach for smelling Besamim due to the return of the fire of Gihenim, the Mordechaiy [Pesachim 105] rules that on Yom Tov Gihenim is not subdued, and thus there is no need for Besamim on Motzei Yom Tov. However Tosafus [Beitza 33b] rules that Gihenim is subdued on Yom Tov and hence the reason for the omission of Besamim is because there is no extra soul.

[224] 473/6

[225] The reason for this is because the entire purpose of smelling Besamim on Motzei Shabbos is to comfort the soul which is saddened due to the leave of the extra soul it received on Shabbos. On Yom Tov the soul is automatically comforted due to the pleasure and joy of Yom Tov, and hence the smelling of spices is unnecessary. [ibid]

[226] The reason for this is because the Besamim are only required in order to comfort the soul [and not due to an innate Shabbos obligation]. [ibid]

[227] Kaf Hachaim 297/13 They write that through the smelling of Besamim one resides upon himself the holiness of Shabbos into the weekday.

[228] 297/7

[229] See Kaf Hachaim 297/34; Halachos Ketanos 2/183

[230] This applies even if the adults do not know how to say the blessings themselves, as all blessings of Birchas Hanehnin may only be said for another person if the person who is saying the blessing is also benefiting from it, and the blessing of Besamim on Motzei Shabbos is included within the blessings of Birchas Hanehnin.
This is thus not similar to the blessing of Hagafen said by Kiddush of which we allow one to say this blessing for another person even if he himself will not be drinking the wine, as the wine of Kiddush is not being brought because of one's benefit from it but rather due to the institution of the Sages to say Kiddush over wine. [Hence it is similar to Birchas Hamitzvos which one can say for another person even if he himself has

age of Chinuch fulfilling their obligation with hearing his Havdala, then he may say the blessing on their behalf and have them smell it. [Some write that even when one does not have a sense of smell it is proper for him to try smelling the Besamim after the blessing is said by others, or on behalf of children, as perhaps his soul feels the smell.[231]]

Is the blessing recited if one is repeating Havdala for one who did not yet hear?[232] In the event that one is repeating Havdala for a person who did not yet hear Havdala and is unable to say it himself[233], one may only say the blessing of Besamim if he also smells the spices.[234] [If however there are children above the age of Chinuch listening to the Havdala one may repeat the blessings of Besamim on their behalf even if he does not smell the spices.[235]]

Should the listeners say their own blessing of Besamim :[236] Those listening to Havdala are to fulfill their blessing with the person saying Havdala[237], and are not to say the blessing over [Besamim or] fire on their own.[238] **See Halacha 11 for further details on this ruling!**

If one will not be saying Havdala on Motzei Shabbos:[239] In the event that one does not have any Halachicly valid beverages available for Havdala, and will thus not be saying Havdala on Motzei Shabbos, he is to nevertheless to say on Motzei Shabbos the blessing over fire as soon as he sees it and the blessing of Besamim if he has spices. [If however one will be able to say Havdala later on at night, it is better to delay these blessings of Besamim and Haeish until Havdala.[240]]

If one is saying Havdala on Sunday or onwards:[241] In the event that one is saying Havdala on Sunday or onwards, he does not recite the blessings of Besamim[242] [irrelevant of whether or not he said these blessings on Motzei Shabbos]. Thus immediately after the blessing of Hagafen he is to begin the blessing of Hamavdil. See Halacha 20 for the full details of this subject.

Q&A

If one is unsure if he is able to smell may he say the blessing of Besamim in Havdala?

If there are other people fulfilling Havdala with him then he may say the blessing of Besamim in Havdala even if he is unsure if he retains a sense of smell.[243] If however he is saying Havdala alone then he may not say the blessing of Besamim if he is unsure of his ability to smell. He may however try to smell the Besamim before Havdala without saying a blessing and if he has a sense of smell then he is to say the blessing in Havdala.[244]

How strong must one's sense of smell be in order to be allowed to say the blessing?[245]

As long as he can smell even a slight scent he may say the Bracha.

---

already done the Mitzvah.] However Besamim on Motzei Shabbos, despite it also being accustomed due to the Sages, it was only accustomed in order to benefit the person to comfort his soul which is saddened due to the leave of Shabbos, and hence its blessing is similar to any other blessing over foods and the like. [Admur ibid based on Taz 8]

Other Opinions: Rama 297/5 rules one may say the blessing of Besamim or those adults which do not know to say it themselves.

[231] Kaf Hachaim 297/36
[232] 297/8
[233] See Halacha 15
[234] It does not suffice for only the listener to smell the spices as one may not say a blessing of Birchas Hanehnin for another unless he too is benefiting. [ibid; M"A 297/5]

Other Opinions: Some rule one is not to repeat the blessing of Besamim in Havdala if he already heard it. Amongst the reasons is because it is considered a Hefsek. [Kaf Hachaim 297/20] Others rule there is no need for the person saying the blessing to smell it himself. [Rama 297/5]

[235] One is not required to smell the Besamim when repeating it for children which have reached the age of Chinuch as explained in 297/7 regarding one who cannot smell. [See 178/23 and 297/7 that one say all the blessings of Birchas Hanehnin for a child in order to educate them in Mitzvos.

[236] 298/10
[237] Now, although the listeners stand for Havdala, and by Birchas Hanehnin one never fulfills his obligation of hearing a blessing while standing, nevertheless this only applies by foods and drinks and not by other blessings. Furthermore these blessings are similar to an obligation and are thus not viewed within the same rules as Birchas Hanehnin. [213/5]

[238] As Berov Am Hadras Melech. [298/10] M"B 297/13
[239] 298/3
[240] Ketzos Hashulchan 99 footnote 2
[241] 299/9
[242] As the Sages only required blessing on the Besamim close to the leave of Shabbos [in order to comfort the soul]. Thus he may not say the blessing now in Havdala, as since it is no longer connected to Havdala it is considered an interval between the blessing over wine and its being drunk. [ibid]

[243] Kaf Hachaim 297/35

As in most cases one does have the sense of smell, and even if he doesn't there are Poskim which rule one may always repeat the blessing for others in Havdala even if he does not smell the spices afterwards. [ibid]

[244] Birchas Habayis 26/36
[245] Birchas Habayis 26/36; Piskeiy Teshuvos 297/7

If one said the blessing of Besamim and then realized he does not have a sense of smell must he repeat the blessing of Hagafen?

No.[246] However there are Poskim[247] which rule it is considered an interval and he must thus repeat the blessing of Hagafen. Certainly if there was another person listening to Havdala there is no need to repeat the blessing.[248]

Until when on Motzei Shabbos may the blessing over Besamim be recited?[249]

The blessing over Besamim may be recited until Alos Hashachar.

If there are many people listening to Havdala should they all smell the Besamim?

Some[250] write it is improper to make a long delay between the blessing of Besamim and the continuation of Havdala, and hence in a case of many listeners they should smell the Besamim after Havdala.

B. What should one use for Besamim:[251]

Preferably one is to use a spice which its blessing is Borei Minei Besamim.[252] Such spices include Mor [clove and cinnamon[253]]. One may add to this spice other spices of a different blessing and say on the entire bundle the blessing of Minei Besamim.[254] It is proper to add to this spice the Hadassim used during Sukkos[255] in order to add another mitzvah to its use.[256] [This however is not the widespread custom.[257]]

If no Minei Besamim spice is available:[258] In the event one does not have a Minei Besamim spice, he is to use a spice of another blessing. Even in such a case he is to say the blessing of Borei Minei Besamim as the custom on Motzei Shabbos is to say the blessing of Borei Minei Besamim on all spices used during Havdala even if they are designated to receive a different blessing.[259] [This applies likewise to one who is using a scented fruit for Besamim.[260]]

---

[246] So is proven from the fact Admur in 297/3 never required one to repeat the blessing of Hagafen if he said a blessing on an invalid spice. See Piskeiy Teshuvos 297 footnote 60; SSH"K 47 footnote 201

[247] Rav Akiva Eiger brought in Biur Halacha 298/5 "Ein"

[248] As brought above from Kaf Hachaim 297/35

[249] Ashel Avraham Butchacher 299 brought in Piskeiy Teshuvos 297/2

[250] SSH"K 61/7; Piskeiy Teshuvos 297/2

[251] 297/3

[252] As today the custom is to always say Minei Besamim on all spices by Havdala. Hence in order to say this blessing on its proper spice, it is best to initially use a spice which receives this blessing. [ibid]

Based on Kabala one is to take three bundles of Besamim for the blessing. [Kaf Hachaim 297/2]

[253] Seder 11/3

There is a dispute as whether the blessing for clove and cinnamon is Asher Nasan Reich Tov Bapeiros, or Borei Atzei Besamim. We therefore say Borei Minei Besamim on these spices to fulfill the obligation according to all. [ibid]

[254] 297/3

[255] See Kaf Hachaim 297/2 and 28 [based on Eitz Chaim] that one should use the Hadassim used on Friday night based on Kabala.

[256] 297/6

Some opinions rule it is a Mitzvah to say a blessing on Motzei Shabbos over the Hadassim used for the Mitzvah [of Lulav], as since one used it for one Mitzvah it is to be used for another Mitzvah. Now although the Hadas by now is dry and hence does not smell very much, nevertheless it still retains some smell.

Others however rule it is better to use other spices which contain strong smell, rather than to use a Hadas which its smell is fading. Practically the custom in these countries is like the latter opinion. Nevertheless it is proper to also place the Hadassim near the other spices of which one says on them Minei Besamim or Atzei Besamim and hence is to smell both of them, fulfilling his duties according to both opinions. [ibid]

Seemingly based on this wording Admur does not hold that these Hadassim lose their Atzei Besamim status, as rules M"A 297/3, Vetzaruch Iyun.

Based on Kabala there is mystical meaning behind using a Hadas for Besamim on Motzei Shabbos. [Brought in Beis Yosef 297] The Hadassim are to be held the way that they grew from bottom to top. [M"A 297]

[257] See Peri Megadim 297 A"A 3 which says not to place the Hadas with the other spices as one is to initially say a designated blessing on each spice.

[258] 297/3

[259] From the letter of the law even during Havdala one is to recite a designated blessing for the spice that he uses. For example, those spices which grow on the ground, if they are from a tree one says Borei Atzei Besamim. If they are herbs, one says Bore Isveiy Besamim. If one smells a fruit he is to say Hanosein Reich Tov Bapeiros [ibid] or Asher Nasan reich Tov Bapeiros [Seder 11/3]. Nevertheless the custom is to say the blessing of Minei Besamim on all spices on Motzei Shabbos. The reason for this is because not all people are expertise in the particular blessings of different spices, and hence it became accustomed to say a blessing which is Bedieved valid for all spices. [ibid] Vetzaruch iyun if one may go against the custom and recite the designated blessing on the spice if he so chooses. From 297/6 there is implication that one may do so

Other Opinions: The Sefaradi custom is to say over each spice its designated blessing. [Kaf Hachaim 297/31] So was also the custom of the Munkatcher. [Darkei Chaim Veshalom 617] So also rule other Poskim. [See Toras Shabbos 297/6; Siddur Yaavetz]

May one use a fruit for Besamim? [261] In the event one does not have a Minei Besamim spice to use one may even use a fruit which has a good scent as Besamim. [In such an event the custom is to still say the blessing of Minei Besamim. [262]]

May one use ground spices for Besamim? [263] One is not to use ground pepper and ginger [and spices of the like [264]] for Besamim even if he enjoys their smell. [If one has no other spice to use it requires further analysis whether one may use it. [265]] One may however use ground cinnamon and clove. [266]

Forbidden spices: [267] All those spices which one may not say a blessing over [268] may not be used for Besamim. If one smelled these spices on Motzei Shabbos, he does not fulfill his obligation and is required to smell other spices with a blessing if they are available.

Spices found in wine: [269] It is permitted to use for Besamim spices which are placed in wine to give the wine a good smell. Nevertheless if the wine is Yayin Nesech or Stam Yayin he is to avoid smelling it on Motzei Shabbos for Besamim. [270]

Summary:
One is to use for Besamim a spice which receives the blessing of Borei Minei Besamim, such as clove or cinnamon. If this is not available one may use any other spice although is nevertheless to say the blessing of Borei Minei Besamim. One may not use any spice which is forbidden to say a blessing over.

Q&A

May one use an Esrog or Hadassim as Besamim on Shabbos Chol Hamoed Sukkos?
If they are being used to fulfill the Mitzvah of Lulav they may not be used. [271]

May one use an empty container of Besamim if it has a good smell?
If there is some residue of leftover spice one may say a blessing. [272] If it is completely empty one may not say a blessing even if it contains a good scent. [273]

May one use for Besamim a cloth pocket which contains spices? [274]
It is best to avoid doing so, if one has revealed Besamim easily available, or is able to easily open the pocket. If this is not easily possible one may use it for Besamim.

---

[260] Kaf Hachaim 297/31

[261] 297/3

See Piskeiy Teshuvos 216 footnote 28 and 297 footnote 38 which tries to learn in Admur in the Seder 11/9 that all fruits which are meant only for eating one is not to say a Bracha over smelling them. However it is very difficult to enter such an interpretation into Admur in Seder 11/3.

[262] As explained above.

[263] 297/4; Seder 11/9

Admur records a dispute in this matter. The first opinion [Shach 108 Yoreh Deah in Nekudos Hakesef] rules one may not say a blessing on ground pepper and ginger even if he enjoys their smell as they are not designated for smelling but rather for spicing food. Others [Taz 297/5; Yoreh Deah 108/10] however rule one may say a blessing over them if he benefits from their smell. Practically Admur rules one is to refrain from smelling them. [ibid] Even the Taz [297/5] agrees one is to refrain from using pepper for Havdala if he has better spices available.

Other Opinions: P"M 297 A"A Hakdama rules one is to say "Hanosein Reich Tov" on pepper.

[264] This refers to all spices which are not commonly smelled for enjoyment.

[265] As Admur rules it is best not to smell them, seemingly leaving room for the opinion which allows smelling them, and hence in a time of need one may be lenient. Nevertheless perhaps the novelty in Admur's words is that one is to avoid even smelling them without a blessing, however to say a blessing is certainly forbidden due to the rule of Safek Brachos Lehakel. See Kitzur Halachos p. 116 for an analysis on this subject. Vetzaruch Iyun on some of his logics.

Other Opinions: Sdei Chemed Mareches Hei 13; Machazikei Bracha 297/5 rule in a time of need one may use pepper for Besamim.

[266] Seder 11/3

[267] 297/3

[268] Whether due to a prohibition, such as spices of idolatry or spices of an Erva; or whether due to the spices not being meant for smelling. [ibid]

[269] 297/5; Michaber Yoreh Deah 108/6 Shach 26

[270] As although it is permitted to smell such spices being one has no intent to benefit from the smell of the wine, nevertheless doing so for the Mitzvah of Besamim is repulsive to G-d. [ibid]

[271] It is forbidden to smell Hadassim which are being used for the Mitzvah during Sukkos. Likewise Mitzvah Esrogim are not blessed over when smelled during Sukkos as rules Admur in Seder Birchas Hanehnin 11/8.

[272] Machazikei Bracha 297/4;

[273] Seder Birchas Hanehnin 11/11; Kaf Hachaim 197/7; M"B 297/7 in name of Taz

The reason for this is because one had no intent to place the spices in the container in order for the container to absorb a good smell. [ibid]

[274] See Ashel Avraham Butchacher 297; Kaf Hachaim 297/7

Must one open the Besamim jar to smell if the smell protrudes from its cover even while closed?[275]

One must open the jar in order to smell the Besamim. It is invalid to smell it externally.[276] If however the cover contains open holes, then it is valid and is not necessary to be opened.

May one use bathroom freshener or bathroom spices for Besamim?[277]

No. If he used it he has not fulfilled his obligation and is to repeat the blessing of Besamim.

May one use perfume or cologne for Besamim?[278]

No.[279]

May one say a blessing of Besamim on cigarette or tobacco?[280]

No.[281]

General Q&A

May one smell Besamim after Shabbos prior to Havdala?[282]

One is to avoid smelling Besamim after Shabbos is over until he says Havdala.[283] Seemingly this applies even if when he says Havdala he will be saying it also on behalf of others.[284]

If one smelled Besamim after Shabbos prior to Havdala may he still say the blessing in Havdala?

If one is saying Havdala on behalf of others as well, it is permitted for him to repeat the blessing of Besamim in Havdala as usual.[285]

If everyone who is hearing Havdala has already smelled Besamim prior to it, or one is saying Havdala only for himself, some Poskim[286] rule one is to nevertheless say the blessing of Besamim in Havdala as usual. Others[287] however rule one is to say the blessing of Besamim prior to saying the blessing of Hagafen, or after drinking the wine.

If one forgot to say the blessing on Besamim or Haeish before the blessing of Havdala, should he say it after the blessing of Havdala prior to drinking, or after drinking?[288]

One is to do so prior to drinking.[289]

---

[275] See Ashel Avraham Butchacher 297

[276] As it is considered like a smell that has no source of which one is not allowed to say a blessing over.

[277] Michaber 297/2; Seder Birchas Hanehnin 11/8; Vetzaruch Iyun why Admur omitted this ruling of the Michaber here but does mention the law of Besamim of an Erva which the Michaber omits. See Kaf Hachaim 297/15.

[278] Piskeiy Teshuvos 297/4

[279] They are invalid for a number of reasons: Being that they are mainly made of synthetic material and thus have no essential smell; perfume of an Erva is invalid.

[280] Piskeiy Teshuvos 297/4

[281] As they do not essentially contain a good scent.

[282] Piskeiy Teshuvos 296/3

[283] As doing so enters into question whether one may say the blessing of Besamim later on when he says Havdala. As perhaps it is considered that he has already fulfilled his obligation and hence cannot make another blessing of Besamim in Havdala due to the prohibition of making an unnecessary interval between the blessing and the drinking of the wine. [Rav SZ"A in SSH"K 61 footnote 17] Others hold one has certainly already fulfilled his obligation, as the reason behind smelling Besamim is to comfort the soul, and what difference does it make if one smelled it before or after. This applies even if one did not have intent to fulfill the Mitzvah. [Mishpitei Tzedek 38 and so is implied from Admur 297/1] Therefore one should not smell Besamim prior to Havdala in order to fulfill his obligation as per the institution of the Sages, which is to do so within Havdala. [296/1]

[284] Based on the second reason mentioned above, seemingly even if one is saying Havdala on behalf of others, although it is permitted for him to repeat the blessing of Besamim in Havdala on their behalf, [so long as he also smells it 297/7], nevertheless it is still proper for him to avoid smelling Besamim prior to Havdala in order to fulfill his obligation of Besamim within the order of Havdala as the Sages established.

This is unlike the ruling of Piskeiy Teshuvos ibid which rules in such a case it is initially permitted to smell Besamim prior to Havdala, since he is allowed to repeat the blessing for others. In any event in such a case the listeners may not say a blessing on the Besamim on their own, even if they are normally accustomed to do so. They are rather to fulfill their obligation with his blessing. Likewise the person saying Havdala must also smell the Besamim.

[285] However in such a case the listeners are not say a blessing on the Besamim on their own, even if they are normally accustomed to do so. They are rather to fulfill their obligation with his blessing. Likewise the person saying Havdala must also smell the Besamim.

[286] Mishpiteiy Tzedek 39; brought in Yabia Omer 4/24

[287] SSH"K 61 footnote 17 in name of Rav SZ"A

[288] Piskeiy Teshuvos 296/3

[289] Shraga Meir 5/51, SSH"K 60/32 in name of Rav SZ"A

Is one to designate a special vessel to hold the Besamim used during Havdala?[290]

It is customary to designate a nice vessel to hold the Besamim which are used during Havdala.

Is a mourner to say the blessing over Besamim in Havdala?

Some Poskim[291] rule a mourner is to omit the blessing of Besamim.[292] Others[293] rule he is to say it as usual. Practically the custom is to recite the blessing on Besamim.[294]

When smelling Besamim on Motzei Shabbos outside of Havdala is the blessing of Minei Besamim to be recited even over spices that are Atzei or Asvei Besamim?

In a case that one was unable to say the blessing of Besamim during Havdala, and is thus saying the blessing after Havdala, some Poskim[295] question whether one is to still say the blessing of Minei Besamim on the spice irrelevant of its species or is to say the proper blessing that its species is to receive, either Asvei, or Atzei, or Minei. Others[296] write one is to recite the spices proper blessing.

---

[290] Kaf Hachaim 297/32 in name of Elya Raba and Taz 297/7; Brought also in Ketzos Hashulchan 98 footnote 4.

[291] Kneses Hagedola

[292] As a mourner does not merit an extra soul on Shabbos due to his state of sadness. [Peri Megadim A"A 297/5]

[293] see Bircheiy Yosef 297/2; P"M 297/5 explains there is no prohibition involved for the mourner to smell it, it is just that he is not obligated to do so.

[294] Piskeiy Teshuvos 297/1

[295] SSH"K 61 footnote 27

[296] Piskeiy Teshuvos 297 footnote 32

10. The laws of Meoreiy Haeish:

A. General Laws:

One is required to say a blessing of Borei[297] Meoreiy Haeish over a candle on every Motzei Shabbos, if he has a candle available.[298]

Should the listeners say their own blessing: Those listening to Havdala are to fulfill their blessing with the person saying Havdala[299], and are not to say the blessing over fire on their own.[300] **See Halacha 11 for further details on this ruling!**

If one does not have a candle by Havdala?[301] If there is no candle readily available on Motzei Shabbos one is not required to search for a candle as is normally required to be done to fulfill other Mitzvos.[302] [In the event that he does find a candle after Havdala he is to say the blessing then up until daybreak.]

Motzei Yom Kippur:[303] If one does not have a candle readily available on Motzei Yom Kippur[304], some say he is obligated to search for one to say the blessing over it.[305] On Motzei Yom Kippur the blessing of Meoreiy Haeish is only said on a candle which has remained lit from before Shabbos.[306]

If one cannot say Havdala on Motzei Shabbos:[307] In the event that one does not have any Halachicly valid beverages available for Havdala on Motzei Shabbos he is to nevertheless say the blessing over fire on Motzei Shabbos, as soon as he sees fire, and the blessing of Besamim if he has spices. [If however one will be able to say Havdala later on at night, it is better to delay these blessings of Besamim and Haeish until Havdala.[308]]

If one is saying Havdala on Sunday or onwards:[309] In the event that one is saying Havdala on Sunday or onwards, he does not recite the blessings of Haeish[310] [irrelevant of whether or not he said these blessings on Motzei Shabbos]. Thus immediately after the blessing of Hagafen he is to begin the blessing of Hamavdil. See Halacha 20 for the full details of this subject.

Repeating the blessing of Haeish for another person:[311] In the event that one is repeating Havdala for a person who did not yet hear Havdala and is unable to say it himself, it is proper not to repeat the blessing of Meorei Haeish for the listener being that he has already fulfilled his obligation.[312] [Rather one is to have the listener say the blessing

---

[297] If one skipped the word "Borei" there is a dispute amongst codifiers in whether he must repeat the blessing. [Kaf Hachaim 298/3]

[298] 298/1; This mitzvah was instituted due to that on Motzei Shabbos fire was first created, as on Motzei Shabbos Adam Harishon rubbed two stones against each other and created a spark of fire. Now although we do not say a blessing over the other creations, nevertheless regarding fire since over Shabbos it was forbidden to light fire, therefore now on Motzei Shabbos it is considered as if it was created anew, and we thus say a blessing over it when it was created. [Admur ibid] For this reason it is permitted on Motzei Shabbos to use a candle which was first ignited after Shabbos as opposed to before Shabbos, as the entire reason for the blessing is the new creation of the fire. This is opposed to Motzei Yom Kippur which requires a candle that was lit before Shabbos. [298/14]

[299] Now, although the listeners stand for Havdala, and by Birchas Hanehnin one never fulfills his obligation of hearing a blessing while standing, nevertheless this only applies by foods and drinks and not by other blessings. Furthermore these blessings are similar to an obligation and are thus not viewed within the same rules as Birchas Hanehnin. [213/5]

[300] As Berov Am Hadras Melech. [298/10; M"B 297/13]

[301] 298/1

[302] As we only say the blessing over fire in commemoration of the creation of fire [and hence if one does not have fire available there is no reason to say the blessing]. [Admur ibid]

Other Opinions: Kaf Hachaim 298/7 rules based on Zohar that one is to always strive to have a candle for Havdala.

[303] 298/2

[304] Even if Yom Kippur falls during the week. [ibid]

[305] As the blessing over fire on Motzei Yom Kippur is similar to the blessing of Havdala which is said to bless Hashem for distinguishing this day of Yom Kippur over other Yomim Tovim, as on this day lighting fire was forbidden until Motzei Yom Kippur. [Admur ibid]

[306] 298/14; see 624/5

[307] 298/3

[308] Ketzos Hashulchan 99 footnote 2

[309] 299/9

[310] As the blessing of fire is only said the time it was first created which was Motzei Shabbos. [ibid]

[311] 297/8-9

[312] 297/9 and so rules Ben Ish Chaiy Vayeitze 15; Kaf Hachaim 298/2

A dispute on this matter is recorded in Admur:

The first [Stam] opinion rules it is permitted to repeat the blessing of Meorei Haeish for the listener even though he has already fulfilled his obligation. Their reasoning is because this is not similar to the blessing over spices of which we require him also to smell, as the blessing said over fire was not established for ones benefit, but rather in memory that fire was created on Motzei Shabbos. It is therefore not similar to Birchas Hanehnin.

Others however rule one may not repeat the blessing. Their reasoning is because even by Birchas Hamitzvos, only by those Mitzvos which are a complete obligation may one repeat the blessing for someone who did not yet fulfill his obligation. However those Mitzvos which are not a complete obligation, such as the blessing over fire on Motzei Shabbos, which one is not required to search for if fire is not readily available, by such Mitzvos one may not repeat the blessing for another.

Practically one is to suspect for the latter opinion in order not to enter himself into a questionable blessing in vain. [ibid]

Other Opinions: Bircheiy Yosef 298/1 and other Poskim rule one may repeat the blessing of Meorei Haeish.

himself[313]. If however there are children above the age of Chinuch listening to the Havdala one may repeat the blessing of Meorei Haeish on their behalf.[314]]

How close must one be to the candle?[315] One may only say a blessing over the flame if he is close enough to the flame to be able to benefit from it. It does not suffice to simply be able to see the flame. Benefiting in this context of Halacha is defined as being close enough to be able to use its light to differentiate between two coins of two different countries. [Thus those listening to Havdala which are a distance from the flame must be close enough to the flame to be able to benefit from the actual flame if the electricity were to be off. Nevertheless there is no need to turn off the electricity.[316] In the event one said the blessing without being close enough to benefit from the flame, as explained above, some Poskim[317] rule that he has nevertheless fulfilled his obligation. Nevertheless, if possible, one is to try to hear the blessing again from another person doing Havdala.]

Looking at ones hands:[318] [After the blessing of Meoreiy Haeish is recited[319]] it is customary to [place ones hands towards the flame] and gaze[320] at ones nails to see if he can benefit from the light and tell the difference between his nail and flesh[321]. It is also accustomed to gaze at the palm of the hands, as the lines of the palm contain an omen of blessing.[322] One is to thus fold his four fingers over his thumb [hiding the thumb[323]] into the palm of his hand, thus being able to see both his nails and palm simultaneously.[324] Some are accustomed [and so is our custom[325]] to then spread open the four fingers and look towards the back of the fingers by the nails. [While doing so the thumb still remains hidden under the four fingers.[326] One first looks at the palm of his hands with his fingers covering his thumb and only afterwards opens his hands and turns them over to see the back of his fingers.[327] It is our custom to place the cup down and look at the nails and palms of **both** hands.[328]]

➢ On Motzei Shabbos which is Yom Tov:[329] When Motzei Shabbos coincides with Yom Tov, the custom is to say the blessing of Meoreiy Haeish over the Yom Tov candles that were lit. We do not place the candles together[330], and nor do we place our nails towards them. Rather we simply look at the candles[331] after the blessing and then continue with Yaknahaz.

---

[313] Kaf Hachaim 693/11

[314] Ketzos Hashulchan 99/7; Kitzur Halachos 298/16 based on 178/23 and 297/7 that one say all the blessings of Birchas Hanehnin for a child in order to educate them in Mitzvos. Seemingly the same would apply here, even though it is viewed as Birchas Hamitzvos and not Birchas Hanehnin.

[315] 298/6

[316] See Q&A

[317] Kaf Hachaim 298/22. His reasoning is because this is not a Mitzvah one has to search for and because the blessing is said over the general creation of fire rather than a specific fire. [ibid]
Vetzaruch Iyun according to Admur which rules one must repeat the blessing when one used a candle lit on Shabbos, perhaps then also here he would require the blessing to be repeated. See also Piskeiy Teshuvos 298 footnote 37 which argues against this ruling of the Kaf Hachaim.

[318] 298/6

[319] Siddur: "After the blessing one looks at his nails" See Q&A for more details.

[320] From the word "Lihistakeil" it is implied one is to concentrate on that area and not merely glance at it, and so is also implied from the reasons for why we look at the nails and palm.

[321] As if he is able to do so he is certainly able to recognize the difference between two coins. Another reason for looking at the nails is because nails are a omen of blessing as they always grow.[Admur ibid]
Other reasons: Based on Kabala one is to look at his nails to weaken the power of the evil forces which are strengthened on Motzei Shabbos. [Tolaas Yaakov brought in Taamei Haminhagim 415]

[322] The Tur 298 writes that the Rishonim were accustomed to stare and contemplate on the lines of the palm

[323] Siddur

[324] One hence sees only the outer side of his fingers where his nails are and not their inner side. [ibid; Machatzis Hashekel 298 on M"A 5; Tolaas Yaakov explains based on Kabala why we do not look at the outer side, see Taamei Haminhagim 415]
This custom follows the custom of the Arizal as recorded in Shaar Hakavanos. Others however bring different testimony of the custom of the Arizal. The Machazikei Bracha 298/2 concludes one is to follow the testimony of the Shaar Hakavanos, which is the first custom recorded in Admur. [See Kaf Hachaim 298/19]`

[325] So is the custom of the Rebbe.
Ruling of Admur in Siddur: One is to look at his 4 fingernails which are folded over the thumb, while the thumb is not to be seen. This is similar to the first custom mentioned above, which do not open their hands afterwards.

[326] Machatzis Hashekel 298 on M"A 298/5

[327] So is implied from Admur, and so is the custom of the Rebbe. So rules Taz 298/2; Mahrahm Meratenberg 538
Other Opinions: The custom of the Rebbe Rashab was to first spread the hands and only after to close the fingers over the thumb. This custom is based on the Teshuvos Hageonim. [Shaareiy Halacha Uminhag 5/35; See Piskeiy Teshuvos 298 footnote 25]
Some have the custom to first look at the hands with the fingers closed over the thumbs, then they spread the fingers and then they once again close the fingers over the thumb as they did the first time. [See Piskeiy Teshuvos ibid] This was not the Rebbe's custom.

[328] Custom of Rebbe
Opinion of Admur in Shulchan Aruch: One is to continue holding the cup in his left hand and look only at the nails of his right hand. [298/6]

[329] Sefer Haminhagim p. 76 [English]

[330] Some suggest this is due to that separating the candles from each other afterwards is similar to extinguishing. [see 502/7; Kitzur Halachos 298 footnote 4]

[331] See Piskeiy Teshuvos 298 footnote 59 for a discussion amongst Poskim in how one is allowed to say the blessing of Haeish over the candle lit

If one cannot see the flame:[332] One must be able to see the actual flame when he says the blessing. Thus if the candle is covered or one is looking from an angle that does not allow him to see the flame [or someone is standing in front of him which is blocking the flame from being seen], he may not say the blessing even if he can fully benefit from the light of the candle.

The candle is in a glass covering:[333] If the candle is covered by glass, it is nevertheless permitted to say a blessing over it[334] (although there are opinions[335] which forbid doing so). [Hence if possible the glass is to be removed, although if he is unable to do so he may still say the blessing.[336]] See Q&A!

May a blind person say the blessing of Meoreiy Haeish?[337] A blind person may not say the blessing of Meoreiy Haeish in Havdala.[338] He is thus to say Havdala with the omission of this blessing.[339] [Initially one is not to fulfill his obligation with hearing Havdala from a blind person.[340] A blind person may say Havdala together with Meoreiy Haeish for the sake of children which have reached the age of Chinuch.[341]]

Saying Baruch Hamavdil prior to moving the candle:[342] One may not move the Havdala candle until he says Baruch Hamavdil or says Havdala in prayer.

Summary:

If a candle is available during Havdala, one is to say a blessing of Meoreiy Haeish over the candle. It is not necessary to turn off the lights during the blessing. One is to be close enough to the candle to be able to benefit from its light. Men are accustomed to place their finger nails near the flame. One must be able to see the actual flame when the blessing is said. Thus the candle may not be covered and people may not block one's view of the flame.

If no candle is currently available he is to say Havdala without the blessing of Meoreiy Haeish. If a candle becomes available later on, on Motzei Shabbos, he may say the blessing of Meoreiy Haeish up until daybreak of Sunday. When reciting Havdala on Sunday or onwards the blessing of Meoreiy Haeish is omitted.

Those listening to Havdala from another person are not to say their own blessing of Meoreiy Haeish. If however one is repeating Havdala for another person then that person is to say the blessing of Meoreiy Haeish.

Q&A

Until when on Motzei Shabbos may the blessing over fire be recited?[343]

The blessing over fire may be recited until Alos Hashachar. Some[344] question whether it may be recited past Alos Hashachar but before the time of Mi Sheyakir.

When is one to place his hands near the flame, before or after the blessing of Meoreiy Haeish?

Some Poskim[345] rule one is to [proximate his nails to the flame and] look at his nails only after the blessing is recited. Other Poskim[346] however rule one is to look at his nails near the flame before the blessing.[347] Other Poskim[348] rule one is to proximate the hands to the flame before the blessing and then look at them after the blessing. Practically Admur in the Siddur rules like the first opinion. The Rebbe was seen placing his hands towards the flame while reciting the blessing although he only fully positioned them by the flame and looked at

---

in honor of Yom Tov. Simply speaking however it is allowed being that Shabbos and Yom Tov candles are lit for the use of their light on the table as well as for Shalom Bayis.

[332] 298/17

[333] 298/17

[334] So rules Rashba; M"A 298/20; Elya Raba 298/25; Chayeh Adam 8/34

[335] Michaber 298/15; Darkei Moshe and so concludes Ben Ish Chaiy Vayeitzei 14

[336] Ketzos Hashulchan 99/4 and footnote 6; Biur Halacha "Veneir Sheyeish Lo Shteiy Piyos"

Other Opinions: Kaf Hachaim 298/71 concludes Safek Brachos Lehakeil and one is thus to be stringent. So rules also Ben Ish Chaiy Vayeitzei 14

[337] 298/19

[338] As even one who can see may only say the blessing if he is close enough to benefit from its light. [ibid[

[339] This follows the ruling of M"A 298/17. However Rashba in the name of Geonim rules a blind person is exempt from Havdala. [See Kaf Hachaim 298/68]

[340] Ketzos Hashulchan 99 footnote 7

[341] Kitzur Halachos 298 footnote 11 based on 297/7

[342] 299/19

[343] Ashel Avraham Butchacher Tinyana 299

[344] Ashel Avraham ibid

[345] Admur in Siddur; Shiyureiy Kneses Hagedola 298/3; Kitzur SHU"A 96/9; Igros Moshe 5/9; Ginas Veradim 2/3-25

[346] M"B 296/31; Mamar Mordechaiy 298/2; P"M 296 M"Z 6

[347] As they hold that by all blessings of praise to Hashem one first is to receive the benefit and then say the blessing. [Mamar Mordechaiy 298/2]

[348] Siddur Yaavetz

them after the blessing was completed.

Does one fulfill his obligation if he did not spread his fingers near the flame?
So long as he was close enough to the flame to benefit from its light he fulfills the obligation.

Are women to say the blessing of Meoreiy Haeish when they say Havdala?[349]
Women are to say the blessing of Meorei Haeish when they say Havdala.[350]

Are women to place their hands by the fire and look at their nails by the blessing of Meoreiy Haeish?[351]
The custom is that women do not look at the nails.[352]

Must one turn off the lights when the blessing of Meoreiy Haeish is recited?[353]
No, as one is not required to actually benefit from the light, but rather to be close enough to potentially benefit from the light.[354]

May one benefit from light of a fire prior to saying Borei Meoreiy Haeish?
Yes.[355] However there are Poskim[356] which are stringent in this matter.[357]

May one light a match, candle or cigarette from the Havdala candle?[358]
It is forbidden to use the flame of the Havdala candle to light any other item until the blessing is said over it. Once the blessing of Meoreiy Haeish has been recited one may use it to light.

May one say the blessing of Meoreiy Haeish if he can only see the flame through a mirror?[359]
No. It is considered as if he cannot see the flame.

B. The laws of the candle:
What type of candle is one to use for Havdala?[360] It is a Mitzvah Min Hamuvchar to use a torch for Havdala.[361] A torch is defined as any double wicked candle.[362] It is valid even if the two wicks of the candle do not touch each other. Thus if one braded two candles together into one candle it is defined as a torch (even though their wicks remain separated). (In the event that a double wicked candle is not available, one is two light two separate candles and have their flames touch each other when the blessing is recited.[363]) If this is not possible, or only one candle is available, one is to nevertheless say the blessing over a single wick candle.[364]

---

[349] Ketzos Hashulchan 96 footnote 12; So rules also Daas Torah 296; Ben Ish Chaiy Vayeitzei 24; Kaf Hachaim 296/54; Igros Moshe 2/47; Kinyan Torah 1/88; Beir Moshe 4/28; Kaneh Bosem 3/17; Sheivet Haleivi 6/42; Yechaveh Daas 4/27

[350] So is proven from Admur which does not mention anywhere any differentiation regarding women in the blessing of Meoreiy Haeish. Furthermore, even according to those Poskim [M"B in Biur Halacha 296 "Lo Yavdilu Leatzman"] which side women are exempt from the blessing of fire, they are nevertheless permitted to say the blessing as is the law by all Mitzvos that they are exempt from. [Ketzos Hashulchan 96 footnote 12]

[351] Ketzos Hashulchan 96 footnote 12

[352] The Ketzos Hashulchan ibid suggests the reason for this is because before the sin of the tree of knowledge Adam was clothed in nails, and the sin which was caused by Chava caused him to lose these nails and have them remain only on the fingers, therefore they do not look at them.

[353] Kitzur Halachos 298 footnote 7; Piskeiy Teshuvos 298/5

[354] Tehila Ledavid 298/4

[355] M"B 298/4

[356] Ashel Avraham Butchach 298

[357] Kaf Hachaim 693/10 states that this matter is disputed in Poskim and concludes that each person is to follow his custom. See Piskeiy Teshuvos 298/1

[358] Biur Halacha 154/14 "Shedolkin Limitzvasan"

[359] Shalmas Chaim 253

[360] 298/4

[361] The reason for this is because a torch contains many pieces of wood and many different flames, and the simple wording of the blessing of Meoreiy Haeish is referring to many flames. [Admur ibid]

[362] An actual torch is made up of many pieces of wood. Nevertheless included within this definition regarding Havdala is any candle that contains two wicks. Hence an oil candle which has two wicks that protrude from the same exit hole is considered a torch. Similarly a wax candle which has two wicks come out from its top is a torch. [Admur ibid]

[363] As when the flames are joined it is considered a torch as there are many colors of flame joined together. If however the flames do not touch each other, then even if they are very close to each other, it is not defined as a torch. [Admur ibid]
This ruling has not been found in earlier Poskim, and is seemingly a novelty of Admur. This has become the widespread custom. [Kitzur Halachos 298 footnote 3] In truth however seemingly Admur learned this way from the Magen Avraham 298/4 [towards end] which gives room

One may use two pieces of wood as a candle for Havdala, and place them together in a way they touch each other. Some[365] have the custom for reasons known to them to only use double wicked **bees wax** candles for Havdala, and not other types of candles or wood. [They designate this candle to be used only for Havdala.[366]]

It is proper to avoid using for Havdala, candles[367] which give off a bad odor, if it is possible to use other candles.[368]

Using a candle which was lit on Shabbos:[369] It is forbidden to say Meorei Haeish over a flame which was lit on Shabbos, even if it was lit by a gentile[370], unless it was Halachicly allowed for the candle to be lit.[371] This applies even if many hours have passed from after Shabbos.[372] If one said the blessing over such a candle [immediately[373]] after Shabbos, he must repeat the blessing over a valid candle, if it is available.[374] If however time has passed since the leave of Shabbos and he then said the blessing over the candle, he has fulfilled his obligation.[375]

It is however permitted to use for Havdala a candle which was lit before Shabbos and remained lit until after Shabbos.[376] It is likewise permitted for a Jew to light a candle on Motzei Shabbos from a candle which was lit on Shabbos, and use that candle for Havdala, even though the original flame is invalid as explained.[377] It is however forbidden for a gentile to light a candle from this candle which was lit on Shabbos and have a Jew use it for Havdala.[378]

Using a candle lit by a gentile:[379] One may not say a blessing over a candle that was lit by a gentile, even if it was lit after Shabbos[380], unless it was lit from a pre-existing flame which had originally been lit by a Jew[381]. In the event that one said a blessing over a flame lit by a gentile after Shabbos, he has nevertheless fulfilled his obligation.[382]

---

for such an explanation, and so learn other Poskim, as brought in Tehila Ledavid 298/2, see there.

[364] As even a single fire contains many colors, red, white and yellow, and it hence falls under the term Meoreiy Haeish said in the blessing. [Admur ibid]

[365] This opinion brought in Admur is of the Arizal, brought in Kaf Hachaim 298/12

[366] Mishnes Chassidim brought in Ketzos Hashulchan 99 footnote 3

[367] In Admur this is mentioned regarding cane wood torches, although seemingly it would apply to all types of bad smelling candles.

[368] As on Motzei Shabbos we need to comfort the soul with a good smell. [Admur ibid]

[369] 298/7

[370] As one can only say a blessing over fire which was not lit through forbidden Melacha. Thus even if a gentile lit it on Shabbos for his own use it cannot be used as nevertheless this lighting is a forbidden Melacha for a Jew.

[371] Such as for the sake of a Yoledes or a dangerously ill person, or a gentile did so for a one who is bedridden even if he is not dangerously ill. [ibid]

Other Opinions: Some [Rame brought in M"A 298/10] rule one may not say a blessing over a candle lit by a gentile on Shabbos, even if it was lit for the sake of an ill person, as one may never say a blessing on a candle lit by a gentile. [See Kaf Hachaim 298/27-28]

[372] 298/9; Due to a decree one may come to say a blessing on this flame immediately after Shabbos prior to it having ability to spread on the candle. [ibid]

[373] 298/9 and 11

[374] Other Opinions: Kaf Hachaim 298/25 rules one never repeats the blessing Bedieved if he used an invalid candle.

[375] 298/11; As since the flame has further spread after Shabbos it is only forbidden to use it for Havdala due to a decree, and in such a case Bedieved one is not required to repeat the blessing. [ibid]

Regarding the amount of time the candle has to be lit after Shabbos Admur [298/9] writes "immediately" regarding the time of Issur, hence implying after this immediate time it is only forbidden due to a decree. Vetzrauch iyun!

[376] As there was no forbidden Melacha done to this candle on Shabbos itself. [ibid]

[377] 298/9; As although this newly lit candle contains the original flame it also contains a new flame of its own which spread from the old flame, and it is on this new flame that was now lit on Motzei Shabbos that the blessing is covering. It however remains forbidden to say a blessing over the original candle even if much time passed after Shabbos and hence a new flame has been added to the original flame. This is due to a decree one may come to say a blessing over the original flame, immediately after Shabbos prior to it having the ability to further spread. This suspicion that one may come to say a blessing over the original flame right after Shabbos does not apply when a Jew lights a candle from a candle that was lit on Shabbos, as usually a flame which was lit on Shabbos was lit by a gentile, and we do not make decrees that if we allow one to say a blessing on the candle of a Jew he may come to say a blessing over the candle of a Gentile.[ibid]

[378] So is implied from Admur in previous footnote. Seemingly however if the candle was lit by a Jew on Shabbos and then a gentile lit a candle from it after Shabbos it is valid, as we do not make decrees of coming to confuse a gentile for a Jew. Vetzaruch Iyun as perhaps it is only the opposite, that we do not confuse a Jew for a gentile in decrees. Vetzaruch Iyun.

[379] 298/9-10

[380] A dispute on this matter is recorded in Admur 298/10:

Some [M"A in name of Rameh] rule that if the gentile ignited a flame on Motzei Shabbos, such as through matches or a lighter, or lit a candle from a flame lit before Shabbos [by a gentile], or from a flame lit on Shabbos [by a gentile] in a permitted way, it is forbidden to say a blessing over this flame. It is however permitted to say a blessing over a second candle which was lit from this candle, if the same gentile lit the second candle as well. [If however another gentile lit this candle it is forbidden, as explained in 298/9.]

Others however rule the opposite of the above opinion that the original candle lit by the gentile after Shabbos contains no decree. Thus if he ignited the flame or lit it from a flame lit from before Shabbos one may say a blessing over it. However if a gentile lights a second candle from this flame one may not say a blessing over the second candle as the Sages invalidated all candles lit by a gentile if they were not lit from a candle that was originally lit by a Jew [unless they are being ignited for the first time] due to a decree one may come to use a candle that was lit on Shabbos.

Practically, Admur concludes one is to suspect for both opinions and hence not say a blessing over the original candle or second candle lit by the gentile, rather a Jew is to light another candle from that candle.

Other Opinions: The M"B 298/23 rules that only the second candle lit by the gentile from the candle of a gentile is invalid while an original

Using a candle which was not lit for the sake of its light:[383] The blessing over fire is only said over a flame which is meant to be used for its light, as opposed to a fire lit for its heat or for purposes of respect. Therefore a blessing is not said over coals unless their intent is to give light, and they are so hot that one can ignite a twig from them.[384] Likewise a blessing is not said over a candle lit for prayer in Shul.[385] [One may however extinguish the candle and then light it for the purpose of Havdala.[386]] See Q&A Regarding Yartzite candles, candles of the Amud.

Summary:

It is best to use for Havdala a beeswax candle which contains at least two wicks. If one does not have a two wicked candle it suffices to light two candles and proximate their flames to the point that they merge. If only one candle is available, it may nevertheless be used.

It is forbidden to use a candle which was lit on Shabbos, although one may use its flame to light another candle.

It is forbidden to use a candle lit by a gentile although one may use its flame to light another candle.

One may not use a candle which was lit for non-light purposes. Thus flames that were lit to transmit heat or for decor purposes are invalid.

Q&A

May one use a match to say Meorei Haeish?

Yes. One is to light two matches and hold their flames towards each other. [He is not however to place two matches adjacent to each other and then light it as this is considered like only one wick.[387]] If one only has one match it is permitted to say Havdala over a single lit match.

May one use an electric light to say Havdala?[388]

One is to initially only use the flame of a candle for Havdala. If a candle is not available the following is the ruling regarding if one may use an electric light:

Some Poskim[389] rule it is allowed. Others[390] rule it is forbidden[391]. According to all one may not use electric lamps or bulbs if the filament [wick] of the bulb cannot be seen, such as florescent lights, or lamps which are colored to the point they block vision of the filament.[392] Some[393] rule that all flash lights are invalid for Havdala even in a case of need.

May one use the flame of a lighter for Havdala?[394]

Yes.

---

candle lit by a gentile is valid.

[381] If however it was originally lit by a gentile, one may not say a blessing over it due to a decree one may come to say a blessing over a candle which was lit on Shabbos by a gentile, and he will say the blessing over it immediately after Shabbos prior to the candle having a chance to spread its flame. If however the gentile lit the candle from a candle which was lit by a Jew after Shabbos, then even if the Jew himself had lit his candle from the candle of a gentile, it is valid for the blessing, as any time there is a Jew in the middle the decree that one may come to use the original flame does not apply. It goes without saying that one may say a blessing over a candle which was lit by a gentile if the gentile himself lit the candle from a candle which was ignited by a Jew on Motzei Shabbos, or on Erev Shabbos and has remained lit until after Shabbos. [298/9]

[382] This applies even if the candle was lit from another candle of a gentile, being such a candle is only invalid due to a decree. [298/11] It certainly applies if the candle was the original candle was lit by a gentile, as explained above that some opinions rule even initially such a candle may be used. [298/10]

[383] 298/15-17

[384] 298/15

[385] 298/17; As such candles are lit for the respect of the Shechina and not for their light. If however in truth the candles were lit due to lack of light in Shul, they may be used. [ibid] Likewise, in the event that one did say Havdala using the Shul candles, he has nevertheless fulfilled his obligation, as these candles are also lit for their light, as we Daven with their light. [624/8] Perhaps however today that we Daven with electric light, and hence the Shul candles do not add much light, one would be required to repeat the blessing. So rules Piskeiy Teshuvos 298/8 footnote 54 that one must repeat the blessing of Haeish .

[386] Kaf Hachaim 298/54

[387] See M"B 298/8; Piskeiy Teshuvos 298 footnote 15

[388] Kitzur Halachos 298 footnote 2; Piskeiy Teshuvos 298/10

[389] Nachalas Shimon 15 in name of Rav Chaim of Brisk; Kochavei Yitzchak 1/11 in name of Rav Chaim Ozer Goredansky; Shearim Hametzuyanim Behalacha 96/6 in name of the Darkei Teshuvah; Har Tzevi 2/114 in name of the Ragitchaver Gaon; Mishpitei Uziel 9

[390] See Mahrshag 2/107; Har Tzevi 2/114; Meoreiy Haeish 5; Yabia Omer 1/17

[391] As the Havdala candle must contain a flame and wick of which an electric current is lacking.

[392] Meoreiy Haeish ibid

[393] Piskeiy Teshuvos ibid

[394] Piskeiy Teshuvos 298/10

May one use the flame of a gas stove to say Meorei Haeish?
In a time of need one may turn on the fire of a stove and use its light for Havdala.[395] One may not use the fire if it was turned on for cooking purposes.[396] Rather he is to extinguish the flame and then relight it for the purpose of using for Havdala.[397]

If one does not have a match can he ask a gentile to light his Havdala candle?
Yes. However the Jew himself is to place the candle by the flame rather than give it to the gentile to light.

May one use candles lit by an Avel for Havdala?[398]
Once Maariv has concluded one may do so.[399]

May one use a Yartzite candle for Havdala?[400]
No.[401]

May one wear eyeglasses during the blessing of Meoreiy Haeish?[402]
Yes. Although if the glasses are shaded, like eyeglasses, and hence change the shade of the light which one sees, it is best to remove them by the blessing of Meoreiy Haeish.

Must one open a window if it is separating between himself and the flame?[403]
It is best to do so.[404]

---

[395] SSH"K 61 footnote 87
[396] Ketzos Hashulchan 99 footnote 8
[397] Kaf Hachaim 298/54
[398] Kaf Hachaim 298/65
[399] As they are no longer being used for their purpose.
[400] M"B 298/30
[401] As it has been lit for the soul of the departed and not for light.
[402] Ketzos Hashulchan 99 footnote 6
[403] See Ketzos Hashulchan 99 footnote 6
[404] Biur Halacha 298 "Oa Besocho" requires the window to be opened. However Ketzos Hashulchan ibid leaves doubt in this matter.

11. Hearing Havdala from another person:

Having in mind to be Yotzei: One who desires to fulfill his obligation through hearing someone else's Havdala must have in mind to do so. The person saying Havdala must likewise have in mind to fulfill the obligation for the listeners.[405] If one heard Havdala without any particular intent[406] then it is disputed whether he has fulfilled his obligation.[407] Practically he may not say Havdala himself although is to try to hear it from someone else.[408] If however one specifically had in mind to not fulfill his obligation with that hearing of Havdala then he may choose to say Havdala himself or hear it from another person.[409] This applies even if the person who said Havdala had in mind not to fulfill his personal obligation and rather said it only for others. In such a case the person who said Havdala would be required to repeat it or hear it from someone else.

Not to answer Baruch Hu Uvaruch Shemo:[410] One who has in mind to fulfill his obligation of Havdala through hearing it from someone else is not to say *Baruch Hu Uvrach Shemo* upon hearing Hashem's name said in the blessing. In the event one said Baruch Hu Uvaruch Shemo he is to hear Havdala again from another person.[411]

If one only had in mind to be Yotzei upon hearing the blessing of Hamavdil:[412] Even if one only had in mind to be Yotzei Havdala upon hearing the last blessing of Hamavdil, he nevertheless fulfills his obligation even though he did not have in mind to be Yotzei the blessing of Hagafen. Nevertheless due to this he may not drink any wine after Havdala before saying a blessing of Hagafen. [If one had in mind to <u>not</u> be Yotzei only upon hearing the blessing of Hamavdil, he is to repeat Havdala with exception to the blessing of Meoreiy Haeish.[413]]

Hinei Keil Yeshuasi: It is customary amongst many Chabad Chassidim that those which are listening to Havdala recite these verses quietly to themselves.[414]

Should the listeners say their own blessings of Besamim and Haeish:[415] Those listening to Havdala are to fulfill their blessing with the person saying Havdala[416], and are not to say the blessing over [Besamim or] fire on their own.[417] [This especially applies if the person saying Havdala has already begun the next blessing of Hamavdil in which case all are obligated to listen.[418] Despite the above some are accustomed to say the blessings of Besamim and Meorei Haeish themselves and not rely on the person saying Havdala regarding these blessings.[419] The Rebbe Rashab was accustomed to say the blessing of Hamavdil himself when hearing Havdala said over beer and the like.[420]]

---

[405] Kaf Hachaim 295/15-16

[406] Meaning he did not have intent neither to be Yotzei nor to not be Yotzei.

[407] 213/4 regarding all blessings; 489/12 regarding Sefiras Haomer

[408] Admur 213/4 brings a dispute in this matter and concludes one is to be stringent not to repeat the blessing. Nevertheless one must try to hear Havdala from another person as according to the first opinion there he has not fulfilled his obligation.

Requires further analysis 1: In 296/17 Admur writes that if one had in mind to not be Yotzei Havdala he is not Yotzei. This implies that to be Yotzei one does not need active intent, and it is only to not be Yotzei that he needs active intent. Based on the above ruling of Admur in 489/12; 213/4 that by Rabbinical Mitzvos there is a dispute if one fulfills his obligation if he does not have intent, the Halacha in 296 is now understood as follows: Initially one must have active intent. However Bedieved if he did not have intent, neither to be Yotzei or to not be Yotzei he should not repeat Havdala, and only if he had intent to not be Yotzei is he to repeat it. [See Kitzur Halachos 296 footnote 30]

Requires further analysis 2: Regarding why in 6/9 Admur rules that one may repeat Birchas Hashachar if he did not have in mind to fulfill his obligation [which is a seeming contradiction to the above ruling which does not allow one to repeat the blessing] see Tehila Ledavid 6/4 which asks this question. Chikreiy Halachos 9/8 explains that by Birchas Hashevach Admur holds one must have in mind in order to fulfill his obligation from another as otherwise it cannot be considered that he praised anyone. However by Birchas Hanehenin or Mitzvos according to one opinion even if he does not have in mind to fulfill his obligation he is nevertheless Yotzei.

Requires further analysis 3: In the end of 296/17 it is implied that if one does not have in mind to fulfill Havdala then he must repeat Havdala later. This seemingly contradicts the ruling that one possibly fulfills his obligation even if he simply heard a blessing without having in mind. See Tehila Ledavid 296/4 which raises this question. However seemingly the meaning here of Admur is as he wrote earlier in that same Halacha that "if one had in mind to not fulfill his obligation" and hence here too in the conclusion of the Halacha Admur's intent is not that one did not have in mind to be Yotzei but rather that he had in mind to not be Yotzei.

[409] 296/17 from the wording in 296/17 "Had in mind to fulfill his obligation"; 489/12 regarding Sefiras Haomer and so applies to all Brachos; Tehila Ledavid 6/4

[410] 124/2

[411] See Admur there that it is possible that even Bedieved one did not fulfill his obligation.

[412] 296/18

[413] Kaf Hachaim 296/47 based on Levushei Serud

[414] Tradition heard from numerous Chabad Chassidim amongst them Rav Chaim Shalom Deutch who testified this was the custom he witnessed in the Chabad Shul since he was a child. This custom was recently footnoted in the new Siddur of Tehilas Hashem published by Kehos Eretz Yisrael. See also Shaareiy Halacha Uminhag 5/35 that the Rebbe Rashab would say "Hinei Keil Yeshuasi" when he was hearing Havdala from another.

[415] 298/10

[416] Now, although the listeners stand for Havdala, and by Birchas Hanehnin one never fulfills his obligation of hearing a blessing while standing, nevertheless this only applies by foods and drinks and not by other blessings. Furthermore these blessings are similar to an obligation and are thus not viewed within the same rules as Birchas Hanehnin. [213/5]

[417] As Berov Am Hadras Melech. [298/10] so rules also M"B 297/13

[418] M"B ibid; See Piskeiy Teshuvos 297/9

[419] Mateh Efraim 600/4 and Aruch Hashulchan 297/7 bring that it is a vintage custom for the listeners to repeat the blessing of Besamim and

Summary:

One who hears Havdala from another person is to have intent to fulfill his obligation. It is our custom for the listeners to recite the verses of Hinei Keil Yeshuasi quietly to themselves. They are not to answer Baruch Hu Uvaruch Shemo. They are not to repeat their own blessing of Besamim and Haeish and are rather to fulfill their obligation with the person saying Havdala. If one only heard the last blessing of Hamavdil he has nevertheless fulfilled his obligation.

If one heard Havdala and did not have intent to fulfill his obligation but also did not have intent to not fulfill his obligation, then he is to hear Havdala again from another person although he may not say Havdala himself. Thus if one desires to say Havdala himself after hearing someone else say Havdala, such as in Shul, he must have intent not to fulfill his obligation with that person.

Q&A

Is it better to personally say Havdala rather than hear it from another?

It was the custom of the Rebbe Rayatz to always try to fulfill his obligation through hearing Havdala from another person. This was with exception to when he distributed Kos Shel Bracha and Motzei Yom Kippur, in which case he would say Havdala personally.[421] Others have a tradition, to always say Havdala themselves.[422] Some[423] write one should try to say Havdala himself as it is better for one to do the Mitzvah himself rather than through a messenger. All in all, the widespread custom is not to be particular to personally say Havdala, as Berov Am Hadras Melech.[424]

May one stipulate at the time of hearing Havdala that if he later decides to say Havdala himself he will not be Yotzei with the current Havdala that he heard?[425]

Yes.

If one cannot hear the person saying Havdala due to being hard of hearing, or due to his distance from him, may he say the words of Havdala to himself?[426]

Yes. In such a case one may look at the cup of wine in the hands of the person saying Havdala and then say Havdala quietly to himself. Nevertheless if one has wine at home it is better for him in such a case to not fulfill his obligation in Shul.[427]

If one entered in middle of Havdala is he still Yotzei?[428]

So long as he heard the entire blessing of Hamavdil, he has fulfilled his obligation and is to say Besamim and Meoreiy Haeish afterwards. [429] If he entered in middle of the blessing of Hamavdil, he should hear Havdala from another person.[430]

May one repeat Havdala for himself if he was already Yotzei with the Havdala of another person?

No. Once one has fulfilled Havdala through hearing it from another person he may no longer say Havdala.[431] Furthermore even if he did not have in mind to fulfill his obligation but simply heard the blessing he may not say Havdala himself and must rather hear it from someone else.[432] If however one specifically had in mind to not

---

Haeish themselves

See Ketzos Hashulchan 96 footnote 8 which explains the reason for this is because according to Tosafus even by Birchas Besamim and Eish the listener must be sitting to fulfill his obligation. Hence to fulfill their obligation according to all, some are accustomed to say it to themselves.

[420] Shaareiy Halacha Uminhag 5/35; See Ben Ish Chaiy Vayeitzei 17 and Kaf Hachaim 295/17 regarding the concept of saying the blessing of Hamavdil on one's own. Vetzaruch Iyun why the Rebbe Rashab did so specifically with beer.

[421] Shaareiy Halacha Uminhag 5/35

[422] See Piskeiy Teshuvos 296/1 footnote 7

[423] Kaf Hachaim 296/48

[424] See Piskeiy Teshuvos ibid; Sheivet Haleivi 10/76

[425] Based on Admur 489/12; See Piskeiy Teshuvos 296/17

[426] Ben Ish Chaiy Vayeitzei 17, brought in Kaf Hachaim 295/17; Ashel Avraham Butchach 295

[427] As initially one is to say Havdala with a cup of wine actually in his hands. [ibid]

[428] See Kaf Hachaim 295/18

[429] 296/18

[430] See Piskeiy Teshuvos 296/4 footnote 31 for a discussion in Poskim in whether the beginning of the blessing is needed to be heard even Bedieved.

[431] So is implied from Admur 213/4 and so rules Rav Akiva Eiger 1/7; Peri Megadim 283 in last M"Z

[432] Admur ibid brings a dispute in this matter and concludes one is to be stringent not to repeat the blessing. Nevertheless one must try to hear Havdala from another person as according to the first opinion there he has not fulfilled his obligation.

fulfill his obligation with that hearing of Havdala then he may choose to say Havdala himself or hear it from another person.[433]

If one is in middle of Maariv and hears Havdala is he Yotzei?[434]

One who stops to listen to Havdala in middle of his Davening Maariv fulfills his obligation even if he is in middle of Shemoneh Esrei. Nevertheless some Poskim write one is not initially to stop to hear Havdala in middle of Shemoneh Esrei.

Can Havdala be said over loud speaker or Telephone?[435]

No. If one heard Havdala over a telephone he does not fulfill his obligation. If he heard it over a loud speaker than if without the loudspeaker he would not have been able to hear the person saying Havdala, he does not fulfill his obligation.

May one hear Havdala from a child?[436]

An adult is not Yotzei if he hears Havdala from a child under Bar Mitzvah. Other children however do fulfill their obligation. Furthermore even if the child is Bar Mitzvah, if he does not yet have a beard, one may not be Yotzei with him unless one knows for certain that the child has already grown two pubic hairs.

May one hear Havdala from a woman?

No. See Halacha 15!

If there are many people listening to Havdala should they all smell the Besamim and place their fingers by the candle?

Some[437] write it is improper to make a long delay between the blessing of Besamim or Haeish and the continuation of Havdala, and hence in a case of many listeners they should smell the Besamim and bless the fire after Havdala. These blessings may be said even before the person who said Havdala finishes drinking the wine.

---

[433] 296/17 from the wording in 296/17 "Had in mind to fulfill his obligation"; 489/12 regarding Sefiras Haomer and so applies to all Brachos; Tehila Ledavid 6/4

[434] See Admur 104/5; Piskeiy Teshuvos 296 footnote 142; 104/15

[435] See Piskeiy Teshuvos 296 footnote 153; 56/3; 689/3; 193/3

[436] Based on Admur 271/7; See Piskeiy Teshuvos 296/19

[437] SSH"K 61/7; Piskeiy Teshuvos 297/2

12. Havdala in Shul:[438]
It is accustomed to say Havdala in Shul over wine in order to be Yotzei those which do not have wine at home to say Havdala over. [If no one is being Yotzei with this Havdala, it is not to be recited.[439]]

Who should drink the wine? (If the person saying Havdala has in mind to fulfill his obligation with this Havdala, he is to drink the wine himself. If he does not have in mind to be Yotzei with this Havdala that he is saying in Shul he may nevertheless say the Havdala for others, so long as another adult is Yotzei Havdala with him and that adult consequently drinks the wine.[440] If however the wine is drank only by children, no one fulfills their obligation with this Havdala.[441]) [The above follows the ruling of Admur in 295/4. In however 190/4 Admur rules the wine may be drank by any Jew. It may thus be drunk by children. This is a direct contradiction to the ruling in 295/4, and so makes mention Ketzos Hashulchan[442] and Tehila Ledavid[443]. Practically they rule like 190/4 that one does fulfill his obligation if the wine was drank by children. Others[444] however conclude based on this contradiction that initially one may only give the Havdala wine to one who is fulfilling his obligation with this Havdala[445], or to a [male] child which has reached the age of **Chinuch for Havdala[446]**. In a case of need or Bedieved, they agree that one fulfills his obligation with a child drinking as written above.]

Should one who has wine at home be Yotzei in Shul?[447] [If one has wine at home, it is better for him to not fulfill his obligation in Shul in order for him to be able to properly say Havdala for his family when he returns.[448]] Thus it is the custom today to have in mind not to be Yotzei Havdala in Shul. Furthermore it is accustomed to say Havdala at home even if all of one's family heard Havdala in Shul as they do not have in mind to fulfill their obligation.

Having in mind to be Yotzei: One who does desire to fulfill his obligation in Shul must have in mind to do so. The person saying Havdala must likewise have in mind to fulfill the obligation for the listeners.[449] If one had in mind not to be Yotzei Havdala in Shul, he must repeat Havdala upon returning home. This applies even to the person who said Havdala that if he had in mind not to fulfill his personal obligation then he must repeat Havdala or hear it from another person.[450] Regarding if one did not have in mind to not be Yotzei, see previous Halacha!

For Q&A related to hearing Havdala in Shul, see previous Halacha Q&A there!

> **Summary:**
> It is customary to recite Havdala in Shul if there are people there which need to be Yotzei. The wine is to be drunk by someone who listened to the Havdala and fulfilled his obligation. In a case of need the wine may be drunk by any Jew, even children. If one desires to say Havdala upon returning home from Shul, he must have intent not to fulfill his obligation with the Shul's Havdala. If he did not have this in mind, see the previous Halacha!

---

[438] 295/4

[439] Ketzos Hashulchan 96 footnote 9

Other Opinions: See Shut Min Hashamayim 25 that even if everyone in Shul will say Havdala over wine when they come home, one is nevertheless to say Havdala in Shul, as Berov Am Hadras Melech.

[440] He however may not drink the wine, as he is still before Havdala. [Ketzos Hashulchan 96 footnote 9] Furthermore he may not drink the wine as one who is fulfilling his obligation with this Havdala is required to drink the wine. [Admur ibid see next footnote]

[441] As no person which fulfills his obligation with this Havdala has drank the wine. [ibid] Vetzaruch Iyun Gadol from the ruling of Admur in 190/4 [brought earlier in Halacha 8] that Bedieved if one did not drink the Havdala wine Safek Brachos Lehakel, and he is not to repeat Havdala. [Ketzos Hashulchan 97 footnote 6; Tehila Ledavid 295/1; See Kitzur Halachos Miluim p. 109-112, and later in Halacha 16 and footnotes there for how some answer this contradiction.]

[442] 97 footnote 6

[443] 295/1

[444] Kitzur Halachos ibid

[445] As rules Admur in 295/4. They explain the contradiction by saying in 295/4 Admur is referring to the law in Lechatchilah, that Lechatchilah only one who fulfills his obligation is to drink it, and this itself he placed in parentheses due to doubt. However Bedieved even in 295/5 Admur agrees one fulfills his obligation, and therefore Admur there wrote the law in a future tense rather than past, as he wrote "one is unable to fulfill his obligation" rather than "one did not fulfill his obligation". [Vetzaruch Iyun on the veracity of this inference]

[446] As opposed to a child which has reached the age of blessings. Vetzaruch Iyun on their source for allowing a child which has reached the age of Havdala, in accordance to Admur in 295/4, as either way such a Katan is not fully obligated as is an adult. Furthermore, in 190/4 Admur differentiates between an older child and younger child, while here in 295/4 he simply writes one may not give it to children, implying any child, even if he has reached the age of Chinuch. Hence seemingly according to 295/4 one may never give it to any child, and one who desires to be stringent like that opinion, is to only give the wine to another adult male which is fulfilling his obligation.

[447] 296/17

[448] Kaf Hachaim 295/15

As if he was Yotzei in Shul he cannot repeat Havdala at home for those that did not hear unless he has children below Bar/Bas Mitzvah that need to hear Havdala. [296/17]

Another reason to not be Yotzei in Shul is because it is better for one to do the Mitzvah himself and not through a messenger. [Kaf Hachaim 296/48]

[449] Kaf Hachaim 295/15-16

[450] 296/17

13. Repeating Havdala for others:

Being Yotzei others Havdala if one already heard Havdala:[451] If one already fulfilled his obligation of Havdala he may not repeat Havdala to fulfill the obligation for other adults, [unless they are unable to say the blessings themselves[452]]. One may however repeat the blessing of Havdala to fulfill the obligation of [male[453]] children[454] [that have reached the age of education[455] and do not know to say Havdala themselves[456]]. Therefore if one heard Havdala in Shul he may still say Havdala for his younger [male] children upon his return home.

Repeating the blessing of Besamim and Haeish:[457] In the event that one is repeating Havdala for a person who did not yet hear Havdala and is unable to say it himself, one may only say the blessing of Besamim if he also smells the spices.[458] It is proper not to repeat the blessing of Meorei Haeish for the listener being that he has already fulfilled his obligation.[459] [Rather one is to have the listener say the blessing himself.[460] If however there are children above the age of Chinuch listening to the Havdala one may repeat the blessings of Besamim[461] and Meorei Haeish on their behalf.[462]]

Repeating Havdala for women:[463] A person [whether man or woman] which has already said or heard Havdala may not repeat Havdala for women that did not yet hear Havdala unless there is a man or male child which is also fulfilling his obligation with this Havdala.[464]

Summary:
One may only repeat Havdala for the sake of another person if one is saying Havdala for male children who have reached the age of Chinuch or an adult male which cannot say Havdala himself. In such an event one must smell Besamim upon saying the blessing of Borei Minei Besamim, and is to omit the blessing of Meorei Haeish having the listeners say it instead. One is not to repeat Havdala for a woman.

---

[451] 296/17

[452] 297/8

[453] See Halacha 15

[454] This applies even if they are not members of his family, and their obligation of education is hence not upon him. [167/23; See Kitzur Halachos Shabbos p. 114]

[455] Ketzos Hashulchan 96/5

[456] 269/3; Kitzur Halachos 296 footnote 32

[457] 297/8-9

[458] 297/8
It does not suffice for only the listener to smell the spices as one may not say a blessing of Birchas Hanehnin for another unless he too is benefiting. [ibid]

[459] 297/9
A dispute on this matter is recorded in Admur:
The first [Stam] opinion rules it is permitted to repeat the blessing of Meorei Haeish for the listener even though he has already fulfilled his obligation. Their reasoning is because this is not similar to the blessing over spices of which we require him also to smell, as the blessing said over fire was not established for ones benefit, but rather in memory that fire was created on Motzei Shabbos. It is therefore not similar to Birchas Hanehnin.
Others however rule one may not repeat the blessing. Their reasoning is because even by Birchas Hamitzvos, only by those Mitzvos which are a complete obligation may one repeat the blessing for someone who did not yet fulfill his obligation. However those Mitzvos which are not a complete obligation, such as the blessing over fire on Motzei Shabbos, which one is not required to search for if fire is not readily available, by such Mitzvos one may not repeat the blessing for another.
Practically one is to suspect for the latter opinion in order not to enter himself into a questionable blessing in vain. [ibid]

[460] Kaf Hachaim 693/11

[461] One is not required to smell the Besamim when repeating it for children which have reached the age of Chinuch as explained in 297/7 regarding one who cannot smell.

[462] Ketzos Hashulchan 99/7; Kitzur Halachos 298/16 based on 178/23 and 297/7 that one say all the blessings of Birchas Hanehnin for a child in order to educate them in Mitzvos. Seemingly the same would apply here, even though it is viewed as Birchas Hamitzvos and not Birchas Hanehnin.

[463] 296/19

[464] See next Halacha and footnotes for the reasons.

14. May one say Havdala and have another person drink the wine?[465]

It is permitted for one to say Havdala over wine and have someone else who listened to the blessing, drink a Revius[466] of the wine.[467]

Giving the wine to drink to a woman: It is best not to give the wine to a woman to drink if other adults are available.[468] If however one did so he has fulfilled his obligation.[469]

Giving the wine to drink to one who has already heard Havdala:[470] One may even initially give the wine to a person who has already heard Havdala. [The above follows the ruling of Admur in 190/4. In however 295/4 Admur rules in parentheses the Havdala wine must be drank by someone who is fulfilling his obligation with this Havdala, otherwise no one fulfills their obligation. This is a direct contradiction to the ruling in 190/4, and so makes mention Ketzos Hashulchan[471] and Tehila Ledavid[472]. Practically they rule like 190/4, as we wrote above. Others[473] however conclude based on this contradiction that initially one may only give the Havdala wine to one who is fulfilling his obligation with this Havdala[474]. In a case of need or Bedieved, they agree that one fulfills his obligation.]

Giving the wine to a child to drink:[475] One may give the Havdala wine even to a child to drink [whether male or female[476]], if the child has reached the age of Chinuch for blessings.[477] The wine however may not initially be given to a child who has not reached the age of Chinuch for blessings.[478] Bedieved if one did so he has nevertheless fulfilled his obligation of Havdala.[479] [The above follows the ruling of Admur in 190/4. In however 295/4 Admur rules in parentheses the Havdala wine must be drank by someone who is fulfilling his obligation with this Havdala, otherwise no one fulfills their obligation. It may thus not be drunk by children. This is a direct contradiction to the ruling in 190/4, and so makes mention Ketzos Hashulchan[480] and Tehila Ledavid[481]. Practically they rule like 190/4, as we wrote above. Others[482] however conclude based on this contradiction that initially one may only give the Havdala wine to one who is fulfilling his obligation with this Havdala[483], or to a [male] child which has reached the

---

[465] 190/4; 271/25

[466] 190/6; In order so he can say a Bracha Achrona however from the letter of the law Metzad Havdala only Maleh Lugmav is required as it says there, and in 271/25

[467] 190/4: By Kiddush and Havdala one may say even the blessing of Hagafen for another person to drink.

271/25: By Havdala one may even initially say Havdala and have another one of the Mesubim drink from it.

So rules also Kaf Hachaim 299/32

Other Opinions: Elya Raba rules one may only say Havdala and have someone else drink the wine if the other person does not know to say the blessing [of Hagafen] himself or for the sake of a child. [Brought in Kaf Hachaim ibid] It is however clear from Admur that it is allowed even for an adult that knows to say the blessing.

[468] As it is accustomed for woman not to drink the Havdala wine. This is besides the fact that in 295/4 Admur requires one who is fulfilling his obligation of Havdala to drink the wine, and it is disputed whether women are obligated in Havdala. [See next two cases for an analyses of this ruling].

[469] As rules Admur in 190/4. See next Halachos.

[470] So is implied from 190/4 that no mention is made that the drinker must be someone who needs to be Yotzei the Mitzvah, as well as that the main issue regarding the Bracha is the Hagafen which one can say for someone else.

[471] 97 footnote 6

[472] 295/1

[473] Kitzur Halachos ibid

[474] As rules Admur in 295/4. They explain the contradiction by saying in 295/4 Admur is referring g to the law in Lechatchilah, that Lechatchilah only one who fulfills his obligation is to drink it, and this itself he placed in parentheses due to doubt. However Bedieved even in 295/5 Admur agrees one fulfills his obligation, and therefore Admur there wrote the law in a future tense rather than past, as he wrote "one is unable to fulfill his obligation" rather than "one did not fulfill his obligation". [Vetzaruch Iyun on the veracity of this inference]

[475] 190/4; See Kitzur Halachos 295 footnote 5 and Miluim p. 109-112 for an extensive elaboration on this subject and its contradiction with 295/4. Some of his conclusions have been brought later on. His conclusion there however does not agree with our first ruling written here.

[476] As the issue here is the child being the age of Chinuch for blessings, and not of him being the age of Chinuch for Havdala, in which case it is questionable whether women or girls are obligated.

[477] From the aspect of Havdala the wine may be given to any Jew, even a one day old baby, and through doing so one has fulfilled his obligation. As the institution of the Sages was that any Jew benefit from the Kos Shel Bracha. Nevertheless initially one is only to give the wine to a child which has reached the age of Chinuch, as the blessing of Hagafen may only be said for a child which has reached the age of Chinuch, according to the first opinion in 190/4. [ibid]

[478] As according to the first opinion in 190/4 the blessing of Hagafen for this child is a blessing in vain. [ibid]

[479] This applies according to all, as all agree so long as a Jew, even a baby, has drunk the wine he has fulfilled his obligation. [See previous footnotes]

[480] 97 footnote 6

[481] 295/1

[482] Kitzur Halachos ibid

[483] As rules Admur in 295/4. They explain the contradiction by saying in 295/4 Admur is referring to the law in Lechatchilah, that Lechatchilah only one who fulfills his obligation is to drink it, and this itself he placed in parentheses due to doubt. However Bedieved even in 295/5 Admur agrees one fulfills his obligation, and therefore Admur there wrote the law in a future tense rather than past, as he wrote "one is unable to fulfill his obligation" rather than "one did not fulfill his obligation". [Vetzaruch Iyun on the veracity of this inference]

age of **Chinuch for Havdala**[484]. In a case of need or Bedieved, they agree that one fulfills his obligation with a child drinking as written above.]

How much does the child have to drink?[485] When giving wine of Havdala to a child, the child must drink Malei Lugmav, which is enough wine to fill one of his cheeks.

Summary
It is not necessary that the person who said Havdala to drink the wine. However the wine is to initially be drunk by someone who listened to the Havdala and fulfilled his obligation. In a case of need the wine may be drunk by any Jew, even children. The wine is not initially to be given to a woman to drink although if one did so he fulfills his obligation.

Q&A

If one is unable to drink wine is it better for him to say Havdala and have another person drink the wine rather than have someone else repeat Havdala for him?
This matter requires further analysis.[486]

If one cannot drink wine and there are other Chomer Medina drinks available should he say Havdala over the wine having another person drink it, or should he simply use other beverages and drink it himself?
It requires further analysis as to what is the better choice. To have someone else drink the wine or that he drink Chomer Medina. Both the saying of Havdala on wine, and the drinking of the wine oneself rather than giving it to another are matters of Mitzvah Min Hamuvchar.[487]

---

[484] As opposed to a child which has reached the age of blessings. Vetzaruch Iyun on their source for allowing a child which has reached the age of Havdala, in accordance to Admur in 295/4, as either way such a Katan is not fully obligated as is an adult. Furthermore, in 190/4 Admur differentiates between an older child and younger child, while here in 295/4 he simply writes one may not give it to children, implying any child, even if he has reached the age of Chinuch. Hence seemingly according to 295 /4 one may never give it to any child, and one who desires to be stringent like that opinion, is to only give the wine to another adult male which is fulfilling his obligation.

[485] 190/4

[486] Perhaps it is better for him to say Havdala and have another drink the wine, than to have someone else do it for him if that other person has already heard Havdala. The reason for this is because one is not allowed to have someone else which already heard Havdala say Havdala for him if he can say the blessings himself. [As rules Admur in 296/17] On the other hand if one gives another person which already heard Havdala to drink he is entering himself into the contradiction between 190/4 and 295/4 regarding if one who is fulfilling Havdala must drink the wine.

[487] As rules Admur in 190/4 (in the first long parenthesize) regarding drinking the wine himself, and as rules Admur in 296/8 regarding Chomer Medinah.
Now, with regards to the ruling of Admur in 272/25 regarding that by all Kos Shel Brachos other than Kiddush one need not drink the wine himself seemingly this is simply coming to say that Bedieved/Shaas Hadchak one is Yotzei even according to the Geonim in these cases and not that there is no inyan at all for the actual person to drink. Rather it still remains a Mitzvah Min Hamuvchar for him to drink it and it is just that if he does not all agree that he is Yotzei. One must say this as otherwise this ruling would be in contradiction to the ruling in 190/4

15. Are women obligated in Havdala?[488]

Women are obligated to hear Havdala.[489] They can either fulfill their obligation through listening to the Havdala of another person, or through saying it themselves[490], just as is the law by men.

Repeating Havdala for women: A person [whether man or woman] which has already said or heard Havdala may not repeat Havdala for women that did not yet hear Havdala unless there is a man or male child which is also fulfilling his obligation with this Havdala.[491]

Hearing Havdala from a woman: A man is not to fulfill his obligation of Havdala from a woman.[492] Although other women may fulfill their obligation through hearing another woman say Havdala.

Summary:

Women are obligated in Havdala just like men. However men are not to fulfill their obligation through hearing Havdala from a woman. A man may not repeat Havdala for the sake of a woman to fulfill her obligation.

Q&A

Are women to say the blessing of Meoreiy Haeish when they say Havdala?[493]

Women are to say the blessing of Meorei Haeish when they say Havdala.[494]

Are women to place their hands by the fire and look at their nails by the blessing of Meoreiy Haeish?[495]

The custom is that women do not look at the nails.[496]

---

[488] 296/19

[489] A dispute in this matter is brought in Admur ibid.

First Opinion: Some Poskim [Rambam; Chinuch] rule Havdala is a Biblical obligation which is learned from the words Zechor…Lekadsho. They expound this verse to mean one must mention the Shabbos both by its entrance and by its leave. Accordingly also women are Biblically obligated in saying the words of Havdala just as women are Biblically obligated in Kiddush. This obligation of women towards positive commands of Shabbos is learned from the words Zachor Veshamor, which is expounded to mean that just like women are obligated in the negative commands of Shabbos so too they are obligated in the positive commands of Shabbos. The Sages therefore also obligated women to say Havdala in Shemoneh Esrei of Maariv and over wine just like the obligation of men, as in this regards both men and women are equally Biblically obligated.

Second Opinion: Others [Rabbeinu Tam; Shivlei Haleket; second opinion in Michaber] rule Havdala is only of Rabbinical origin, as the words Zachor only refers to remembering Shabbos when it enters and not when it leaves. According to their opinion some Poskim [Orchos Chaim; Taz] rule women are completely exempt from Havdala just as they are exempt from all Biblical and Rabbinical positive commands that are time dependent. Now although regarding the laws of Shabbos women are obligated in both Biblical and Rabbinical matters just like men, as since women are Biblically obligated in Shabbos the Sages likewise made them obligated in all the Rabbinical commands related to remembering or guarding Shabbos, nevertheless by Havdala women are exempt as Havdala is not a Mitzvah relating to guarding Shabbos but rather an independent matter which the Sages instituted that one separate between the holy and mundane. They supported their institution on a verse in the Torah which states "And to separate between the holy and the mundane".

Third Opinion: Some [Maggid Mishneh; Meiri; Ritva; First opinion in Michaber] rule that even though Havdala is of Rabbinical origin, women are nevertheless obligated in Havdala. Their reason is because in their opinion Havdala is a Mitzvah relating to the remembrance of Shabbos and its holiness, as in it one mentions the difference between the holiness of Shabbos and the weekday. Therefore women are Rabbinically obligated in Havdala just as they are obligated in all matters which the Sages instituted due to the Holiness of Shabbos, as the Sages instituted that their Shabbos laws have the same status as the Biblical Shabbos laws. Thus just as women are Biblically obligated to remember and guard Shabbos as are men, they therefore are also obligated in all the Rabbinical enactments related to these laws.

The Final Ruling: The main ruling follows the latter [third] opinion although one is to also suspect for the second opinion. Hence one [whether a man or woman] who has already heard Havdala is not to say Havdala for only woman, as according to the second opinion women are not obligated in Havdala and one is hence saying a blessing in vain. Nevertheless the women themselves may say Havdala even according to the second opinion which holds they are not obligated to do so, as a woman may choose to perform with a blessing all positive commands that they are exempt from. [ibid]

[490] This ruling of Admur ibid follows the ruling of the Bach brought in M"A 296/11; So rules also: M"B 296/35; Peri Chadash; Ashel Avraham Butchach; Siddur Yaavetz; Kitzur SH"A 96/3; Aruch Hashulchan 296/5

Other Opinions: The Rama [296/8] rules women may not say Havdala themselves, and are rather to hear someone else say it. So rules also Taz 396/7 and Kaf Hachaim 296/58; Divrei Yatziv 1/135

Custom of Sefardim: Yabi Omer 4/23 rules that according to Michaber women may say Havdala themselves.

[491] See previous footnotes for the reason.

Other Opinions: The Zechor Liavraham and Bircheiy Yosef [brought in M"B 296/36] rule that a man may repeat Havdala for a woman. So rules also Ben Ish Chaiy Vayeitzei 22; Aruch Hashulchan 196/5; Oar Letziyon 2/22-3; Yabia Omer 4/24; Tzitz Eliezer 14/44

[492] In order to suspect for the second opinion which exempt women from Havdala [ibid] as well as due to that they should not come to belittle Mitzvos. [271/6]

[493] Ketzos Hashulchan 96 footnote 12; So rules also Daas Torah 296; Ben Ish Chaiy Vayeitzei 24; Kaf Hachaim 296/54; Igros Moshe 2/47; Kinyan Torah 1/88; Beir Moshe 4/28; Kaneh Bosem 3/17; Sheivet Haleivi 6/42; Yechaveh Daas 4/27

[494] So is proven from Admur which does not mention anywhere any differentiation regarding women in the blessing of Meoreiy Haeish. Furthermore, even according to those Poskim [M"B in Biur Halacha 296 "Lo Yavdilu Leatzman"] which side women are exempt from the blessing of fire, they are nevertheless permitted to say the blessing as is the law by all Mitzvos that they are exempt from. [Ketzos Hashulchan 96 footnote 12]

[495] Ketzos Hashulchan 96 footnote 12

May women drink from the wine of Havdala?
If a woman makes Havdala she must drink the wine. It is however accustomed for women not to drink from the leftover Havdala wine of someone else who made Havdala.[497] The reason for this is because the tree of knowledge was a grape vine, and it is due to Chava eating from it that all women were punished to receive Nida blood. It is therefore improper for women to drink from this wine.[498] This is in addition to the custom that no one drinks from the Havdala wine other than the person saying Havdala.[499] The custom is to allow women to drink from the wine of Kiddush of which Havdala was said over on Motzei Shabbos that coincides with Yom Tov.[500]

What is a woman to do if she cannot say Havdala over wine?
She can say Havdala over grape juice, or warm tea or coffee.[501] Alternatively she can say Havdala over wine and give it to another person to drink, even to a child.[502]

May male children be Yotzei Havdala from a woman?[503]
In a time of need one may be lenient to allow children fulfill their obligation with hearing Havdala from a woman.

May women eat or drink prior to Havdala?
No.[504]

16. Are children obligated in Havdala?[505]
A child who has reached the age of understanding the concept of Shabbos is obligated to hear Havdala. [This is at approximately 5-6 years old.[506]]
Repeating Havdala for a child:[507] One may repeat Havdala to fulfill the obligation of [male[508]] children[509] [that have reached the age of education[510] and do not know to say Havdala themselves[511]]. [One also the blessings of Besamim[512] and Meorei Haeish on their behalf.[513]] Based on this even if one heard Havdala in Shul he may still say Havdala for his younger [male] children upon his return home.
Hearing Havdala from a child?[514] An adult is not Yotzei if he hears Havdala from a child under Bar Mitzvah. Other children however do fulfill their obligation. Furthermore even if the child is Bar Mitzvah, if he does not yet have a beard, one may not be Yotzei with him unless one knows for certain that the child has already grown two pubic hairs.

---

[496] The Ketzos Hashulchan ibid suggests the reason for this is because before the sin of the tree of knowledge Adam was clothed in nails, and the sin which was caused by Chava caused him to lose these nails and have them remain only on the fingers, therefore they do not look at them.
[497] M"A 296/4 in name of Shlah
[498] Shlah ibid
[499] Perhaps this is the reason Admur omitted this custom although it is brought in the Magen Avraham, as it is included within the custom that no one, not even men drink from the Havdala wine.
[500] SSH"K 62/16
[501] See Halacha 7
[502] See Halacha 14
[503] Piskeiy Teshuvos 296/20
[504] As they are obligated in Havdala.
[505] 343/3
[506] SSH"K 58/19
[507] 296/17
[508] See the previous Halacha
[509] This applies even if they are not members of his family, and their obligation of education is hence not upon him. [167/23; See Kitzur Halachos Shabbos p. 114]
[510] Ketzos Hashulchan 96/5
[511] 269/3; Kitzur Halachos 296 footnote 32
[512] One is not required to smell the Besamim when repeating it for children which have reached the age of Chinuch as explained in 297/7 regarding one who cannot smell.
[513] Ketzos Hashulchan 99/7; Kitzur Halachos 298/16 based on 178/23 and 297/7 that one say all the blessings of Birchas Hanehnin for a child in order to educate them in Mitzvos. Seemingly the same would apply here, even though it is viewed as Birchas Hamitzvos and not Birchas Hanehnin.
[514] Based on Admur 271/7; See Piskeiy Teshuvos 296/19-20 regarding women being Yotzei with children.

Q&A

If the child did not hear Havdala on Motzei Shabbos is he to hear Havdala on Sunday?
Yes. The child should make Havdala without the blessing of Besamim or Haeish.[515] However some Poskim[516] argue that there is no need to a child to make up Havdala the next day.

If the children will be sleeping by the time Havdala is said what is one to do?
Some[517] write that in such a case one may be lenient to have them say Havdala after Plag Hamincha on Shabbos.

If a boy turned Bar Mitzvah on Motzei Shabbos may he say Havdala for others that Motzei Shabbos?[518]
It is best to not have others be Yotzei with his Havdala.[519]

May children eat prior to Havdala?[520]
Yes. It is forbidden to refrain them from eating if they need to eat.

---

17. Havdala during the nine days:[521]

When saying Havdala during the nine days [Motzei Shabbos Chazon] one is to give the wine to a child to drink [whether male or female[522], although some rule only male[523]] which has reached the age of Chinuch [of blessings[524] although some say also Chinuch of Havdala[525]] but has not yet reached the age of Chinuch for mourning.[526] If such a child is not available he may drink the Havdala wine himself as usual.

18. Havdala when Tishe Beav falls on Motzei Shabbos:[527]

In the event that Tishe Beav falls on Motzei Shabbos, Havdala over wine is recited on Motzei Tishe Beav, which is Sunday night. The blessings of Besamim and Haeish are omitted from Havdala. One is to say the blessings of Meorei Haeish on Motzei Shabbos upon seeing a candle. The blessing of Besamim is not said at all, not on Motzei Shabbos or Sunday night.
The Nusach of Havdala: On Sunday night one begins Havdala from "Hinei Keil Yeshuasi".[528]
Eating and drinking: It is forbidden to eat and drink after Tishe Beav until one says Havdala over wine, just as is the law on Motzei Shabbos. It is permitted to drink water although our custom is to avoid doing so.

Q&A

Who is to drink the Havdala wine in the above scenario?
Some Poskim[529] rule one may drink the wine of Havdala himself. There is no need to give it to a child to drink. Others[530] however rule wine should not be used, unless it is given to a child, just like on Motzei Shabbos Chazon.

---

[515] SSH"K 58/20

[516] See Piskeiy Teshuvos 296 footnote 182

[517] Piskeiy Teshuvos 296/19

[518] Piskeiy Teshuvos 196/19 based on Ketzos Hashulchan 96 footnote 12

[519] As it is questionable whether he is fully obligated in Havdala being that on Shabbos he was not yet Bar Mitzvah and was thus not yet obligated to keep Shabbos. [Ketzos Hashulchan ibid]

[520] 269/3 regarding Kiddush

[521] Rama 551/10

Other Opinions: Aruch Hashulchan 551/26 rules one is not to say Havdala over wine but rather over beer although some are accustomed to drink wine. Kaf Hachaim 551/152 says Sefardim have the custom to drink the Havdala wine themselves. However by Birchas Hamazon they do as the Rama.

[522] Based on 190/4

[523] Based on 295/4 that only one who fulfills their Havdala obligation may drink the wine, and women and girls are disputed in whether they are obligated in Havdala.

[524] Based on 190/4

[525] Kitzur Halachos 295 footnote 5 based on 295/4 that only one who fulfills their Havdala obligation may drink the wine.

[526] M"A 551/31. This means the child is not yet old enough to understand the mourning period.

[527] Michaber 556/1

[528] So writes Hiskashrus 940 footnote 82 to be custom of the Rebbe. This dispute seemingly follows the same dispute regarding if these versus are to be recited on Motzei Yom Tov.

Other Opinions: In Luach Kolel Chabad it states one is to say Havdala like the order of the rest of Jewry which is to skip the verses of Hinei Keil Yeshuasiy.

[529] M"B 556/3 in name of Degul Merivava; Piskeiy Teshuvos 558/3

> **Havdala for an Avel:**
> An Avel is obligated to recite Havdala or hear it from others. When an Avel recites Havdala he is to omit the verses of Hinei Kel Yeshuasi and rather begin from "Borei Peri Hagafen".[531] The custom is for an Avel to recite the blessing over Besamim as is usually done.[532] It is disputed whether an Avel is to recite Vayiten Lecha.[533]

19. May one say Havdala early before Shabbos is over if he will be unable to say it after Shabbos?[534]

If one will be unable to say Havdala after Shabbos, such as he must travel immediately after Shabbos for the purpose of a Mitzvah[535] [or other purpose[536]] he may say Havdala on Shabbos after Plag Hamincha prior to the conclusion of Shabbos.[537] In such a case he does not say a blessing over fire [or Besamim[538]] in Havdala, and remains forbidden to do Melacha until a row of three small stars become visible. He does not need to repeat Havdala even if the opportunity presents itself after nightfall. [However he is to say the blessing over Besamim and fire after Shabbos.[539] Furthermore, he should repeat the blessing of Besamim after Shabbos even if he already said the blessing over Besamim on Shabbos during Havdala.[540]]

Despite the above allowance, some opinions[541] state it is proper for one to refrain from doing the above [i.e. saying Havdala and Maariv while still Shabbos] as it is a puzzling matter to the public.[542]

> **Q&A**
> **If someone said or heard Havdala before Shabbos is over, prior to Bentching is he to say Ritzei in Bentching?[543]**
> No. This applies even if he recites Birchas Hamazon prior to the leave of Shabbos.[544]

20. If one did not say Havdala on Motzei Shabbos:[545]

The main Mitzvah of Havdala is to say it at night on Motzei Shabbos. If one did not do so, whether due to forgetfulness or advertently[546], he is to say Havdala on Sunday. In such a case it is forbidden for him to eat or drink anything, with exception to water, until he says Havdala. If he began eating or drinking and then remembered, he must immediately stop eating or drinking and say Havdala.[547]

---

[530] Peri Megadim 556 A"A 2; Aruch Hashulchan 556/2; Luach Eretz Yisrael of Harav Tukachinsky

[531] See Halacha 3 Q&A

[532] See Halacha 9 Q&A

[533] See Halacha 21 Q&A

[534] 293/2

[535] Admur brings that one has already began walking on Shabbos to the end of the Techum. Vetzaruch Iyun the necessity to say this.

[536] Kaf Hachaim 293/8

[537] See Nemukeiy Orach Chaim 293/1 which questions this ruling on the basis that how can one say "Hamavdil Bein Kodesh Lechol" if it is still Shabbos.
Perhaps however one can simply answer that Havdala is a praise to Hashem for separating Shabbos from Chol, and is not meant to actually separate.

[538] 299/10, Vetzaruch Iyun why this was omitted in 293/2.
Other Opinions: PM"G A"A 299/1 sides that Besamim is said during Havdala which is done by day, as perhaps the extra soul leaves immediately after Havdala.

[539] 299/10

[540] Peri Megadim brought in Kaf Hachaim 297/23

[541] Bach in name of Rashal brought in Magen Avraham 293/4

[542] 293/3

[543] 188/17; Ketzos Hashulchan 47/8

[544] Tzaruch Iyun, as in actuality it is still Shabbos for him regarding all matters. Hence if he bentches prior to the leave of Shabbos why shouldn't he say Ritzei. If he bentches after Shabbos however it is clearly understood that he is to skip it. As the Havdala he made before Shabbos was over takes effect as soon as Shabbos concludes.

[545] 299/8

[546] Other Opinions: Chasam Sofer 17 rules if one advertently did not say Havdala on Motzei Shabbos he may not make it up on Sunday.

[547] This ruling of Admur follows the first opinion in Michaber 299/6
Other Opinions: Second opinion brought in Michaber [299/6] rules if one ate prior to saying Havdala over wine, then on Motzei Shabbos he may still say Havdala, however on Sunday or onwards he can no longer say Havdala. Admur rules one may say Havdala

If one did not say Havdala on Sunday, he is to do so on Monday prior to eating.[548] If one did not say Havdala on Monday, he is to do so on Tuesday prior to eating. If he did not say Havdala on Tuesday [prior to sunset[549]] he can no longer say it.[550]

Is the blessing of Besamim and Haeish recited?[551] In the event that one is saying Havdala on Sunday or onwards, he does not recite the blessings of Besamim[552] or Meoreiy Haeish.[553] Thus immediately after the blessing of Hagafen he is to begin the blessing of Hamavdil.

If one remembered to say Havdala on Sunday-Tuesday and that day is Yom Tov:[554] [If Yom Tov fell on Sunday, or Sunday and Monday, and one remembered on Yom Tov that he did not say Havdala in Kiddush-see Q&A! If Yom Tov fell on Monday and one remembered on Yom Tov that he did not say Havdala on Motzei Shabbos then some Poskim[555] **(see footnote)** write he is to delay Havdala until Motzei Yom Tov, if Yom Tov will be over Monday night.] If Yom Tov fell on Monday and it is a two day Yom Tov, and hence Yom Tov will conclude on Tuesday night, or if Yom Tov fell on Tuesday and only then did he remember that he did not say Havdala, then if he remembered before Kiddush of the Yom Tov night meal, he is to hear Kiddush from another person[556], and then immediately say Havdala over a cup of wine[557], and then immediately[558] wash for the meal. [If he remembered that he did not say Havdala after he already said Kiddush on Yom Tov night he is to stop and say Havdala as soon as he remembers. If he remembers before Kiddush of Yom Tov day he is to say Havdala over wine and then eat the meal.] In all the above cases that one is saying Havdala on Yom Tov the Nusach is "Bein Kodesh Lechol.[559]

---

[548] This applies even if he transgressed and advertently skipped Havdala on Motzei Shabbos-Sunday. [So is implied from Admur ibid and so rules M"B 299/15]

Background: This ruling of Admur follows the ruling of Rama 299/6 and the first opinion of Michaber ibid.

Other Opinions: The second opinion in Michaber rules one can only say Havdala up to Sunday and not any further. Kaf Hachaim 299/26 and Ben Ish Chaiy Vayeitzei 23 rule Safek Brachos Lehakel, and one may therefore not say Havdala past Sunday. Rather one may say it without Sheim Umalchus.

Difference between Sunday and other days: Some learn that the allowance to make up Havdala on Sunday is not from the laws of Tashlumin, but due to it still being part of the initial time of Havdala, as Motzei Shabbos is the night of Sunday. Their proof is from the fact Admur allows one to say Havdala on Sunday even if he advertently skipped Havdala on Motzei Shabbos. In such a case if Sunday was a status of Tashlumin he would not be able to say Havdala as is always the laws of Tashlumin that the advertent transgressor cannot make it up. [Chasam Sofer 17; **Sdei Chemed** Asifas Dinim Mareches Hei 15] The Rebbe however [Lekutei Sichos 31 Yisro 2 footnote 42] writes according to Admur all the days have the same status, as Admur did not differentiate in the Halacha [that if one missed Havdala purposely he cannot make it up past Sunday]. Thus all the days until Tuesday night are considered the days of Havdala, and not just as Tashlumin. The reason for this is because the entire Mitzvah is to remember Shabbos upon the leave of Shabbos, and the leave of Shabbos reaches until Tuesday night.

[549] Makor Chaim of Chavos Yair 299, brought in Piskeiy Teshuvos 299/10

[550] As the first three days of the week are considered the days after Shabbos, and are included in Motzei Shabbos. The last three days are however considered the days before Shabbos and have no connection to the previous Shabbos. [ibid]

[551] 299/9

[552] As the Sages only required blessing on the Besamim close to the leave of Shabbos [in order to comfort the soul]. Thus he may not say the blessing now in Havdala, as since it is no longer connected to Havdala it is considered an interval between the blessing over wine and its being drunk. [ibid]

[553] As the blessing of fire is only said the time it was first created which was Motzei Shabbos. [ibid]

[554] Based on 299/12

[555] Piskeiy Teshuvos 299/10

The reason for this delay is because there is question as to what should be the Nusach of Havdala on Yom Tov; perhaps he should say "Bein Kodesh Lechol" or perhaps "Bein Kodesh Lekodesh". [M"A 299/9; Biur Halacha 299/6 "Ulikabel Achar Kach"]

However from Admur 299/11 it seems clear that the Nusach is "Bein Kodesh Lechol" and hence in such a case one is to say Havdala on Yom Tov itself being that it is forbidden to eat before Havdala. If he remembered prior to Kiddush of Yom Tov night then it follows the same law as the next case, see there.

[556] It is forbidden for him to say Havdala on the same cup of wine of which he is using for Kiddush as one may not say two "Kedushos" on one cup, as the Kiddush of Yom Tov is one Kedusha and has no connection to Havdala of Motzei Shabbos which enters into a weekday. This is in contrast to when Motzei Shabbos falls on Yom Tov in which case one does say Havdala on the same cup of wine, as since one recites "Bein Kodesh Lekodesh" in the Havdala they have a connection to each other, and are considered like one Kedusha. However in this case one would have to say Bein Kodesh Lechol it has no connection to the Kiddush of Yom Tov and therefore one may not say both of them on the same cup. [299/11]

What is one to do if he has no one else to hear Kiddush from? He is to say Kiddush over wine and then say Havdala over another cup of wine. [Piskeiy Teshuvos 299/10]

[557] He must say Havdala prior to Hamotzi as he may not eat until he says Havdala. [ibid]

[558] He must say Havdala and then wash for bread immediately after hearing Kiddush from another person in order for Kiddush to be followed by a meal within its required time. [ibid]

[559] So rules Admur 299/11 based on M"A 299/9

Other Opinions: The M"B in Biur Halacha "Ulikabel" leaves this matter with a great Tzaruch Iyun.

Q&A

May one who did not say Havdala on Motzei Yom Tov say it the next day?[560]

One who did not say Havdala on Motzei Yom Tov is to say Havdala the next day[561] [until sunset[562]], and is not to eat or drink anything, besides for water, until he does so[563]. If one did not say Havdala the next day [prior to sunset] then he may no longer say Havdala[564], and may thus continue eating and drinking as usual.

What is one to do if he forgot to say Havdala in Kiddush of Yom Tov which falls on Motzei Shabbos?

He is to say Havdala over wine immediately upon remembering, whether he remembers that night or the next day.[565] If he remembered before the Yom Tov day meal, he is to say Havdala over a cup of wine and then eat the meal. If one remembered only on Sunday night which is also Yom Tov, then he is to say Havdala within Kiddush.

If one remembered by Bein Hashmashos on Sunday: If Sunday night is Motzei Yom Tov then he is to wait until then, and when he recites Havdala for Motzei Yom Tov he fulfills Havdala also for Shabbos.[566] If however that night is the second night of Yom Tov then he is to say Havdala by Kiddush of the Yom Tov night meal.

If one forgot to say Havdala on Motzei Rosh Hashana and then remembered on Tzom Gedalia what is he to do?[567]

He should say Havdala on Tzom Gedalia and give the wine to drink to a child which has reached the age of Chinuch.

Is one who is saying Havdala on Sunday or onwards to still say the verses of Hinei Keil Yeshuasi?

Some Poskim[568] bring it is not said in such a case, as it is only meant to be said on Motzei Shabbos. Vetzaruch Iyun

If one accidently recited the blessing of Besamim and Haeish while saying Havdala on Sunday –Tuesday is it considered an interval between the blessing of Hagafen and drinking the wine?

The blessing of Besamim is not considered an interval[569], although there are Poskim[570] which rule that the blessing over fire is an interval.

---

[560] For list of opinions on this question see Sdei Chemed Asifas Dinim Mareches Heim 15; Kaf Hachaim 299/24

[561] So rules Kol Bo 59; Rav Akiva Eiger 299/6; Beis Efrayim; Mishneh Berura 299/15; Piskeiy Teshuvos 299/4; SSH"K and so infers Sdei Chemed [Asifas Dinim Mareches Heim 15] from Admur 299/8 which allows saying Havdala of Shabbos the next day even if one purposely skipped Havdala at night, thus proving that the next say is not a Din Tashlumin, but rather a continuation of the obligation.
Other Poskim: The Sdei Chemed himself [ibid], rules as does the Chida [Bircheiy Yosef 491/1; Machazikei Bracha 491/1], Chesed Leavraham 491/2; Ben Ish Chaiy Vayeitzei 23 and many other Poskim listed by him, that one may not make up Havdala even the next day, as Safek Brachos Lehakel.

[562] However past sunset he is to no longer say Havdala as it is now a question whether or not the next day has begun, and many Poskim even hold that Havdala on Motzei Yom Tov may not be made up even the next day. Thus after sunset one is to be stringent. [So also rules Piskeiy Teshuvos 299/10]

[563] 299/8 regarding Havdala after Shabbos, and the same rule applies to Motzei Yom Tov

[564] So is understood from all the Poskim mentioned in the first footnote which only extend the allowance for the next day.
Other Opinions: The Beis Yehuda 2/28, and other Poskim [brought in Sdei Chemed ibid] rule that one may say Havdala the entire week. We do not rule like this opinion, as brought in Chachma Umusur [see Sdei Chemed] that all the Poskim argued on his ruling. Likewise the Chida [Bircheiy Yosef 491/1; Machazikei Bracha 491/1] argues against his ruling.

[565] As it is forbidden for him to eat until he says Havdala. [Based on M"B 299/16]

[566] Har Tzevi 1/166

[567] Sdei Chemed Asifas Dinim Hei 15

[568] Lekutei Mahrich Seder Havdala

[569] Ashel Avraham Butchacher 299

[570] Rav Akiva Eiger brought in Biur Halacha 298/5 "Ein"

21. One who is washing on bread directly after Havdala:

If one is eating Melaveh Malka directly after Havdala is he to say an after Bracha on the Havdala wine?[571] If one will not be drinking wine during the meal and does not plan on saying Birchas Hamazon with a Kos Shel Bracha[572], then he is to say an Al Hagafen after Havdala.[573] If one forgot to say the after blessing before the start of the meal, he is to say it during the meal when he remembers.[574]

If however he does plan to drink wine during the meal[575], or to have a Kos Shel Bracha after Birchas Hamazon, he is not to say an after blessing after the wine of Havdala. Nevertheless, initially one is to have in mind to not to include the meal wine within his blessing of Hagafen said during Havdala[576], unless he has already set himself on the meal table, and is saying Havdala there.[577] In such a case that he has in mind to not exempt the wine he must say an after blessing after Havdala[578], and Hagafen on any wine he drinks during the meal.[579]

In all cases if he already said Birchas Hamazon, he is not to say an after blessing over the wine he drank for Havdala.

Not to bring the bread to the table:[580] If one desires to eat a meal immediately after Havdala he is to beware not to bring bread to the table until after Havdala. In the event that bread was brought to the table before Havdala it is to be covered.[581] If however one does not plan to eat the meal right away there is no need to cover the bread.

Q&A

If one has Mezonos foods on the table when he says Havdala, are they to be covered?[582]

If one desires to eat the Mezonos directly after Havdala then the Mezonos are to be covered. This especially is relevant on Motzei Yom Kippur and Motzei Tishe Beav that falls on Sunday, in which case many already have the Mezonos on the table prior to Havdala. If however one does not plan to eat the Mezonos right away there is no need to cover it.

If one had drinks on the table while saying Havdala is he to say a blessing prior to drinking them after Havdala?[583]

The person who said Havdala and drank the wine is exempt from saying a blessing on any of the drinks that were in front of him during Havdala, or that he had in mind to drink after Havdala. However those that did not drink from the wine are to say a Bracha prior to drinking the beverages that were on the table.

---

22. Vayiten Lecha:

After Havdala[584] one recites Vayiten Lecha.[585] It is recited even on a Motzei Shabbos that Vayehi Noam is omitted such as when Yom Tov falls during that week.[586] [Our custom[587] is to say it together with another person, possibly in

---

[571] 174/6; 176/2; 299/13

[572] 176/2 Vetzaruch Iyun why Admur omitted this in 174/6.

[573] This is different than Kiddush as Kiddush is connected to the meal, as one may only say Kiddush in Makom Seuda. However Havdala has no connection to the meal and hence requires an after blessing. [Taz 299/7]

[574] If however he has already Bentched he is not to say Al Hagafen on the Havdala wine, as Birchas Hamazon exempts wine Bedieved. [Seder 1/17; 4/12; Unlike the ruling of Piskeiy Teshuvos 299 footnote 94 in Admur, seemingly he forgot the ruling of Admur in the Siddur.]

[575] This ruling of Admur follows the ruling of Taz 299/6 and M"A 299/10 Similarly in 176/2 and Seder 4/12 Admur writes "he did not have in mind at all to drink wine during the meal" hence implying if he had in mind to drink wine during the meal, he does not say an after blessing
Other Opinions: The Rama [299/7] rules one is to say an after blessing after Havdala even if he plans to drink wine during the meal.

[576] 174/5
Admur there brings a dispute as to whether the blessing over Havdala exempts the blessing over wine during the meal. Thus to avoid the dispute one is to have in mind to not exempt the wine and hence say a blessing over the meal wine according to all.

[577] 174/5 According to all when one is already sitting for his meal, he exempts the wine with the Hagafen recited during Havdala.

[578] 174/6
If however he plans on having a Kos Shel Bracha, then he does not say an after blessing after Havdala. [176/2]

[579] 174/5

[580] 299/14

[581] So the bread does not see its shamefulness of being preceded by the wine, as from the laws of precedence of blessings, Hamotzi precedes Hagafen. However now one cannot precede Hamotzi and it is hence an embarrassment for the bread, and is therefore to be covered. [ibid]

[582] Levushei Mordechaiy 1/46

[583] Admur 174/4

[584] See Ashel Avraham Butchacher 298 for why we say it after Havdala as opposed to before. This was also the custom of the Arizal, as mentioned in next footnote.
Other Opinions: Some say Vayiten Lecha before Havdala. [Levush, brought in Biur Halacha 295 "Aval"]

[585] Siddur; Mentioned in 295/3; This was the custom of the Arizal [brought in Shaareiy Teshuvah; Kaf Hachaim 295/12; Shaar Hakolel 32/4] See Piskeiy Teshuvos 295/4 for a thorough analyses on this custom.

order so each one blesses the other.[588] Some are particular to say it together from the same Siddur.[589] Some[590] say one is to recite Vayiten Lecha immediately after Havdala. The Rebbe Rashab however questioned this and he himself was accustomed to at times delay saying Vayiten Lecha after Havdala.[591]]

Q&A

Is Vayiten Lecha recited on Motzei Yom Tov?
No.

Is Vayiten Lecha recited on Motzei Shabbos Chol Hamoed?
Some Poskim[592] rule it is to be recited. Others[593] rule it is to be omitted. The Chabad custom is to recite it quietly.[594]

Is Vayiten Lecha recited on Motzei Shabbos which coincides with Yom Tov?
No.[595]

Is Vayiten Lecha recited on Motzei Shabbos which coincides with Tishe Beav?[596]
No.

May an Avel recite Vayiten Lecha?
Some Poskim[597] rule he may recite Vayiten Lecha. Others[598] rule he may not recite Vayiten Lecha.

If one did not recite Vayiten Lecha on Motzei Shabbos until when should it still be recited?
This matter requires further analysis.

Learning Torah directly after Havdala:[599]
It is a proper custom to begin one's week with Torah learning and hence learn Torah immediately after Havdala. One who does so is assured to be successful in his Torah learning of that coming week.

May one recite Pesukim from Tanach on Motzei Shabbos?
Some[600] write one may read Tanach on Motzei Shabbos until after Melaveh Malka, as the holiness of Shabbos is still upon him. However from the simple wording of the Poskim[601] one is to avoid reading Pesukim of Tanach on Motzei Shabbos just like on any other weeknight.

---

[586] 295/3
[587] So was the custom of the Rebbe Rayatz and other of our Raboseinu Nissieinu. [Shaareiy Halacha Uminhag 5/35]
[588] Shaareiy Halacha Uminhag ibid; Segulos Yisrael 80 likewise brings this custom in name of certain Tzadikim; Some say based on Zohar it is to be said in public. [See Piskeiy Teshuvos ibid]
[589] So is implied to also have been the custom of the Rebbe Rayatz as brought in Shaareiy Halacha Uminhag ibid
[590] The Chassid Rav Munya Munsazen in name of the Rebbe Mahrash of whom he says he heard it from his mouth. Some explain this can be inferred from the Siddur of Admur which states "after Havdala say Vayiten Lecha".
[591] See Migdal Oaz story 174
[592] PM"G 295 M"Z 3; Beir Heiytiv 491/1
[593] Elya Raba 491/2; Aruch Hashulchan 295/3 His reasoning is because Chol Hamoed is forbidden in Melacha, and it is hence a belittling of Chol Hamoed to bless the weeks Melacha.
[594] Hayom Yom 19th Nissan
[595] PM"G 491 M"Z 1
As it is not respectful to bless the weeks Melacha on Yom Tov.
[596] Rama 559/2
[597] Peri Megadim 295 M"Z 3
[598] Gesher Hachaim 20/3-3 based on Rama 559/2; Rav SZ"A SSH"K 62 footnote 155
[599] Seder Hayom Havdala
[600] Zechor Leavraham 3/67; See also Seder Hayom ibid that mentions reading Tanach and the next weeks Parsha and Parshas Vayishlach.
[601] Beir Heiytiv 299/14 based on what he writes in 238/2

Chapter 3:
Melaveh Malka
and
Customs of Motzei Shabbos

1. Mentioning Eliyahu Hanavi:[1]

It is accustomed to mention the name of Eliyahu Hanavi after Havdala on Motzei Shabbos as a prayer that he should come and proclaim the redemption.[2]

Eliyahu Hanavi writes the merits of the Jewish people: [3]

During the time of Motzei Shabbos Eliyahu Hanavi sits in Gan Eden under the tree of life and writes the merits of the Jewish people. It is for this reason that we mention Eliyahu on Motzei Shabbos.

Different Customs in mentioning Eliyahu: [4]

Some have a custom to recite all the verses which mention Eliyahu [see next].

Others[5] write one is to say the name Eliyahu a total of 130 times. Some recite Eliyahu Hanavi 40 times, Eliyahu Hatishbi 40 times, Eliyahu Hagiladi 40 times and then recite again each one three times, concluding with Eliyahu Hanavi for a total of 130 times. They conclude "Bimiheira Yavo Eileinu Im Moshiach Ben David".

Segula to prevent forgetfulness and to bring a successful week:

The Tur mentions the following custom: Some have a custom to recite all the verses that mention Eliyahu and doing so is a Segula for ones memory and to have a successful week

---

2. Melaveh Malka:
A. The Mitzvah: [6]

After Shabbos it is a Mitzvah Min Hamuvchar[7] to have a meal out of respect for Shabbos, to escort it with honor while it is leaving.[8] [This meal is cordially called "Melaveh Malka".]

Setting the table: One is to set his table with a tablecloth, and other normal table settings [such as a lit candle[9]] just like he sets his table for a regular meal.[10] This applies even if one is not currently hungry[11] and only plans to eat a small amount of food, nevertheless he is to set his table as is usually done.[12]

B. The Menu:[13]

One is to wash and eat at least a Kezayis of bread.[14] It is proper to cook meat[15] or another dish in honor of this meal [as opposed to eating mere leftovers].[16] If one is unable to eat much due to still feeling satiated from the Shabbos

---

[1] 295/5

[2] The reason for why he is mentioned specifically on Motzei Shabbos is because Eliyahu could not come on Friday due to it being a disturbance for the Jewish people which are preparing for Shabbos. Likewise he could not come on Shabbos if we hold there is an Issur of Techumin above 10 Tefachim. Therefore after Shabbos we pray that he should immediately come, since Shabbos has passed and he is now able to come. [ibid] See Shaareiy Geula "Haemuna Vehatzefuya" 7

[3] Elya Raba 295/9 brought in Kaf Hachaim 295/19; 300/5

[4] Ketzos Hashulchan 100 footnote 3

[5] Elya Raba 295/7 brought in Ketzos Hashulchan 100 footnote 3; Kaf Hachaim 295/20

[6] 300/1

[7] This meal is not so much of an obligation but rather a Mitzvah Min Hamuvchar. [300/3] See Lekutei Sichos 36 Beshalach that through fulfilling Melaveh Malka one completes the three Shabbos meals, as Melaveh Malka was instituted in memory of the leftover Man which was eaten on Motzei Shabbos, and only when one eats meals in correspondence to all of the Man are all the meals in full commemoration of the Man. Hence the eating of Melaveh Malka completes the commemoration of the Man which was corresponded to in the eating of the first three meals.

[8] See Lekutei Sichos 36 Beshalach that this means that the blessing [as opposed to holiness] of Shabbos remains until the end of the meal, and the meal hence serves to escort the holiness of Shabbos.

[9] M"B 300/3; The Imreiy Eish writes in the name of the Baal Shem Tov that one is to light four candles in honor of the meal

[10] This ruling of Admur follows the ruling of the Taz 300/1. However the Bach rules "setting the table" means to prepare many dishes of food on the table even just as is done for the Shabbos meals, even if he does not intend to eat more than a Kezayis. [See Lekutei Sichos 36 Beshalach footnote 18; Peri Megadim 300 M"Z 1]

[11] Or only has a small amount of food left. [ibid]

[12] See Lekutei Sichos ibid for an analysis on the essence of the Mitzvah of Melaveh Malka. On the one hand it implies from the Gemara and Shulchan Aruch that the main aspect of this meal is not the actual meal but the preparation of the table for the meal, and this preparation is done out of respect for Shabbos, as opposed to Oneg Shabbos, just as is the preparation of the table on Erev Shabbos. Nevertheless from other wordings of Admur it is implied the Seuda itself is part of the Mitzvah and not simply the preparation.

[13] 300/3

[14] M"B 300/1; Biur Hagra 300; Machazikei Bracha brought in Shaareiy Teshuvah 300/1; Rav Poalim 3/35; So is also implied from Admur 300/1 that one is to have a Kezayis of bread, and so is the simple meaning of a Seuda and so is the custom. [However see Lekutei Sichos Vol 36 footnote 22 that does not seem to learn this way in the wording of Seuda.] The Gra was very meticulous to eat bread for Melaveh Malka. The Rebbe was particular to wash for Melaveh Malka and to tell Chassidim to do so. However the Ashel Avraham Butchacher [Mahdurah Tinyana 300] writes it is not necessary to push oneself to eat specifically bread.

meal, he fulfills his obligation even with eating fruits and the like.[17] [Nevertheless if he cannot eat bread he is to initially eat Mezonos bread.[18] If this is not available he is to initially eat another Mezonos food rather than fulfill his meal with fruits and the like.[19] Some[20] say in a time of need, such as if one is unable to eat any food at all, he can fulfill his obligation of Melaveh Malka through having a hot drink such as tea or coffee. If one is unable to eat or drink then he should try to assist others in preparing their Melaveh Malka meal.[21] In any event having a hot drink and bathing in hot water on Motzei Shabbos benefits ones health.[22] The same applies to eating freshly baked bread on Motzei Shabbos after it has cooled down.[23] Some have the custom to eat garlic during this meal.[24] Some write it is proper to serve fish during this meal.[25]]

C. Singing:[26]
Some are accustomed to sing Zemiros and Piyutim after Havdala in order to escort the Shabbos just as is usual to escort the King.[27] [See Q&A regarding the Chabad custom!]

D. Lighting candles:[28]
Some are accustomed to light candles on Motzei Shabbos in order to escort the Shabbos just as is usual to escort the King. [Some are accustomed to light two candles before Havdala.[29] Others are accustomed to light the candles after Havdala. Some light four candles in honor of Melaveh Malka.[30]]

E. Not to do Melacha until after Melaveh Malka:
Some[31] write since the extra soul does not leave until after Melaveh Malka, it is therefore proper to delay doing Melacha which is unconnected to food preparation until after one finishes eating Melaveh Malka. Others[32] write one is not to do any time taking Melacha until this meal. Based on Kabala[33] one is to avoid even learning Torah until this Seuda. [Some[34] suggest to drink something immediately after Havdala and it is hence considered as if he fulfilled Melaveh Malka and he is thus permitted in doing work according to all. Some[35] write it is customary for women to avoid Melacha the entire Motzei Shabbos. This custom was omitted in Admur and is no longer the accepted custom.[36] Some have a custom to avoid writing Safrus on Motzei Shabbos.[37] Others avoid any laborious work done for payment the entire Motzei Shabbos.[38] However according to Admur there is no need to avoid doing so.[39]]

Lechem Mishneh: Some have a custom to have two loaves of bread [Lechem Mishneh] for Hamotzi, although they only hold one loaf when saying Hamotzi. [Peri Eitz Chaim brought in Kaf Hachaim 300/5; Shlah Hakadosh Shabbos "Neir Mitzvah"]

[15] The Ashel Avraham [Butchacher Mahdurah Tinyana 300] writes it is not necessary to eat specifically meat and if one desires to eat dairy for whatever reason he may do so and it is considered as significant as meat.

[16] This is derived from a story in Gemara Shabbos 119 that one is not to suffice with eating leftovers for Melaveh Malka but is rather to cook fresh food for the meal. [Kaf Hachaim 300/8]

[17] It is not required to eat less on Shabbos in order to have ability to eat a full meal on Motzei Shabbos, as this meal is not a complete obligation, as stated above. [ibid] This ruling of Admur was written regarding the third meal, and placed in parentheses. The Rebbe states the reason for the parentheses is because Admur had doubt as to whether the meal of Melaveh Malka is a separate meal of its own, or a Mitzvah Min Hamuvchar which completes all the other three Shabbos meals. [See Lekutei Sichos Vol. 36 p. 74]

[18] Shareiy Teshuvah 300/1 in name of Rame, brought in Ketzos Hashulchan 100 footnote 8

[19] Levushei Serud 300, as is the law by Shalosh Seudos. [ibid] Darkei Chaim Veshalom 473

[20] Ketzos Hashulchan 100 footnote 8; Minchas Shabbos 96/131 in name of Yaavetz.

[21] Shaareiy Teshuvah 300/1 in name of Shlah

[22] Gemara Shabbos 119:

[23] Gemara Shabbos 119: brought in Kaf Hachaim 300/12

[24] Baal Shem Tov Al Hatorah Yisro 51; So is an accepted tradition from the Baal Shem Tov and Gr"a. [Piskeiy Teshuvos 300/1]

[25] Lekutei Mahrich

[26] 300/2

[27] See Piskeiy Teshuvos 300/7 for a full list of Zemiros brought in Sefarim

[28] 300/2

[29] Luach Dvar Yom Beyomo

[30] See previous footnotes

[31] Shaareiy Teshuvah brought in Ketzos Hashulchan 100 footnote 8

Other Opinions: Torah Leshma 79 [of Ben Ish Chaiy] writes there is no Mitzvah or act of piety involved in avoiding work prior to Melaveh Malka.

[32] Yaavetz, brought in Ketzos Hashulchan ibid

[33] Peri Eitz Chaim Shaar Hashabbos 24;; Mishnas Chassidim brought in Ketzos Hashulchan 100 footnote 8

[34] Siddur Yaavetz

[35] M"A 299/15 in name of Abudarham

[36] Aruch Hashulchan 299/22

[37] Based on testimony of Leket Yosher p. 58 in name of Terumos Hadeshen

[38] Tosefes Shabbos 299/18

[39] As Admur 299/20 rules that the statement of the Gemara against doing work on Motzei Shabbos applies only until Maariv is finished in Shul.

The source behind Melaveh Malka:[40]

The scriptural source for fulfilling the Seuda of Melaveh Malka is in memory of the Man which also fell for the Melaveh Malka meal when the Jews were in the Midbar.[41] The blessing of Shabbos was found in the Man[42] and hence since the Man was also eaten on Motzei Shabbos it comes out that the blessing of Shabbos continues into Motzei Shabbos. This is why it states that the Neshama Yiseira [extra soul] remains until after this meal of Melaveh Malka.

Q&A

When should one eat the Melaveh Malka?[43]

One should eat the meal as close to the conclusion of Shabbos as possible.[44] Some[45] rule it should be eaten no later than four hours after Shabbos. Others[46] rule it may be eaten until midnight. Others[47] rule it may be eaten any time throughout the night. Others[48] rule it may even be eaten on Sunday or anytime until Tuesday night, so long as he is making the meal in honor of escorting Shabbos.

Are women obligated to eat Melaveh Malka?[49]

Yes.

If one's third meal continued until after Shabbos, must he still eat Melaveh Malka?[50]

Some Poskim[51] rule if one ate during the third meal at night after Shabbos exited there is no need to make another meal for Melaveh Malka. Other Poskim[52] argue that one is nevertheless to make a separate meal for Melaveh Malka. Based on Kabala one is obligated to do so.

Is it a Chabad custom to recite the Zemiros or Piyutim for Motzei Shabbos?

These Zemiros have been omitted from the Alter Rebbe's Siddur, and [seemingly] one is hence not to recite them.[53] It is likewise not our custom to recite the Piyut of "Al Tira".[54]

Nevertheless some[55] learn these omissions are not because it is not our custom to say it but rather because Admur as a rule did not bring Zemiros, Piyutim, Selichos in the Siddur, being we follow the same Nusach as others in these matters. Nevertheless one is to omit from the Zemiros any versus which mention sadness such as "Yaggon Vaanacha".[56]

How is one to fulfill Melaveh Malka when Yom Tov falls on Motzei Shabbos?[57]

Some write that one is to add an extra dish of food to the Yom Tov meal in honor of Melaveh Malka.

---

[40] See Lekutei Sichos 36 Beshalach in length.

[41] Chizkuni Beshalach

[42] Bereishis Raba expounds the verse "Vayivareich Elokim Es Yom Hashevi" that Hashem blessed the Man.

[43] Ketzos Hashulchan 100 footnote 8

[44] M"B 300/2 and so is evident from sources above that even Torah should not be learned until the meal commences.

[45] Yesod Veshoresh Havoda 8/12; Kaf Hachaim Falagi 31/59

[46] Mishneh Berurah in his understanding of Shaareiy Teshuva 300/1; Ben Ish Chaiy Vayeitzei 23

[47] Chesed Leavraham brought in Ketzos Hashulchan ibid

[48] Ashel Avraham Butchacher 174

[49] Kaf Hachaim 300/2; Peri Megadim 300; Machatzis Hashekel 300

[50] Kaf Hachaim 300/11

[51] Elya Raba 300/1 brought in Beir Heiytiv 300/1; Kaf Hachaim ibid; Mishmeres Shalom 29/2; Mentioned in Lekutei Sichos 36 Beshalach footnote 17

[52] Menorah Hatehorah 300/1; Tehila Ledavid 300/1

[53] See Igros Kodesh Rebbe Rashab 1 p. 19 that all those Pizmonim which were omitted from the Siddur are not to be recited. At the same time however he also mentions that due to this it was not the custom of the Tzemach Tzedek and his Chassidim to recite Selichos or Avinu Malkeinu on public fast days. Now this has certainly become a fully accepted Chabad custom to do so, despite it not being mentioned in the Siddur, and so on and so forth of other examples of prayers not mentioned in the Siddur which we are nevertheless accustomed to say. [See Kitzur Halachos p. 124]

[54] Sefer Haminhagim p. 68; Igros Kodesh 13 p. 361

Other Opinions: In Lekutei Torah [Balak] Admur mentions the custom of saying "Al Tirah Avdi Yaakov" on Motzei Shabbos. Some [Ketzos Hashulchan ibid] have concluded from here that it is Admur's opinion that the Piyut of Al Tirah be sung on Motzei Shabbos. However the Rebbe above says that our custom is not to recite it and the reason it is mentioned in Lekutei Torah is because every custom has a source in Kedusha.

[55] Shaar Hakolel Hakdama; Ketzos Hashulchan 100 footnote 4

[56] Ketzos Hashulchan ibid based on Tzemach Tzedek

[57] Rav Chaim Falagi in Hagada Shel Pesach brought in Piskeiy Teshuvos 300 footnote 10

Sparks of Kabbala & Chassidus regarding Melaveh Malka

The Seder of Melaveh Malka in accordance to the Kabalists:[58]
After Havdala one is to say Hamotzi over two roles of bread, holding on to only one of them. Prior to the meal he is to recite the Psalm of Mizmor Ledavid Hashem Roiy and then say "This is the meal of David Melech Hamashiach" . He is to then say "Lesheim Yichud.. Hareiny Ba Likayeim Mitzvas Seudas Daled DeMotzeiy Shabbos".

Drawing the holiness of Shabbos into the weekday:[59]
The purpose of Melaveh Malka is to draw down the holiness of the Shabbos meals into all the meals of the week.

The Luz Bone:[60]
There is a certain bone in the body called the Luz bone which does not benefit or nurture from any food other than the food eaten during Melaveh Malka.[61] This bone is created from the essence of mans seed and cannot be destroyed, not in fire, nor through a grinder, nor through erosion. It lasts forever and is what Hashem will use to build the body by the resurrection. The reason this bone is everlasting is because it did not benefit from the tree of good and evil.

Chibut Hakever:[62]
In merit of eating Melaveh Malka one is spared from needing to experience Chibut Hakever after his passing.

Preventive Medicine for the healthy:[63]
Even if one is very satiated he should push himself to eat this meal, as it will protect his health and save him from needing to eat medicines.

Segula for an easy birth: [64]
It is said in the name of Harav Elimelech Milizensk that it is a Segula for women to have an easy birth if they eat a food in honor of the Mitzvah of Melaveh Malka. They are explicitly to state they are eating the food out of respect for this meal.

Segula to prevent Atzvus:[65]
Eating freshly baked bread on Motzei Shabbos is a Segula to prevent depression.

Segula for Parnasa:[66]
Eating Melaveh Malka is a Segula for Parnasa.

Saves one from heresy and murder:[67]
The Baal Shem Tov stated that in merit of eating Melaveh Malka one is spared from having thoughts of heresy, and is saved from murder

The Neshama Yiseira:[68]
The extra soul which a Jew receives on Shabbos does not leave the body until after the 4th meal of Melaveh Malka. Upon its [re]turn the soul is asked "What were you fed? What novelty in Torah did you learn?". The soul is then elevated to the Heavenly Yeshiva.

---

[58] Kaf Hachaim 300/5; Kanfei Yonah 2/3
[59] Shaar Hakavanos p. 60
[60] Beis Yosef brought in Kaf Hachaim 300/1; Ketzos Hashulchan 100 footnote 7
[61] See Lekutei Sichos 36 Beshalach for the reason why the Luz bone benefits specifically from the meal of Melaveh Malka
[62] Kaf Hachaim 300/5
[63] Kaf Hachaim 300/4
[64] Orchos Chaim brought in Kaf Hachaim 300/4
[65] Kaf Hachaim 300/12
[66] Mahritz Gais Hilchos Havdala
[67] Minchas Shabbos 85/30
[68] Kaf Hachaim 300/7 and 13

Tikkun for the third meal:[69]
The Zohar states: One who does not fulfill the 4th meal of Melaveh Malka is as if he has not fulfilled the 3rd meal either.

The feast of David Malka Mashicha:[70]
The reason that the meal of Melaveh Malka is referred to as the feast of David is because Davis Hamelech was accustomed to make a large feast every Motzei Shabbos out of celebration that he did not pass away that Shabbos, as David Hamelech knew his day of passing would be on Shabbos.
There are also Kabalistic reasons for referring to the meal as the feast of David.[71]

3. Drawing water:[72]
Some are accustomed to draw water from wells and springs on Motzei Shabbos as a Segula for a cure for all their ailments.[73] [This is helpful for both physical and spiritual ailments and assists in one's understanding of Torah.[74]]

Q&A
How is one to fulfill the above Segula if he does not have a well or spring available to draw water from? Does it suffice to simply open the faucets?[75]
Yes. One can use water drawn from the faucet on Motzei Shabbos, with intent of this Segula. It does not help to use water that was drawn before Shabbos.

Maaseh Shehaya
The Kolbo relates the following incident:[76] There was a certain man which was suffering from leprosy whose wife went out to draw water on Motzei Shabbos. She was delayed at the well and unknowingly managed to draw the water from the well of Miriam. When she came home her husband vented anger at her delay to the point that it caused her to drop the bucket. Drops of water spilled on his skin and immediately cured all the areas they touched. On this the Sages stated the angry man only benefited from the amount of water that remained due to his anger. Based on this it became accustomed to draw water on Motzei Shabbos.

4. Folding ones Tallis:[77]
One is to fold his Tallis on Motzei Shabbos[78] [immediately upon returning from Shul[79]]. [It is proper to personally fold one's Tallis rather than give it to someone else to fold.[80] If one forgot to fold his Tallis immediately on Motzei Shabbos, then the next day prior to wearing the Tallis one is to shake it towards the ground.[81]]

---

[69] Kaf Hachaim 300/15
[70] Taamei Haminhagim 425; Likutei Mahrich
[71] Peri Eitz Chaim 18/17, as there is a ray of David Hamelech revealed by this meal.
[72] 299/20
[73] This is based on the statement of the Sages that the well of Miriam which is found in the sea of Tiberius meets every Motzei Shabbos with all wells and springs, and whoever is able to grab this water and drink it is immediately healed from all ailments. Therefore the custom is to draw water every Motzei Shabbos, as perhaps one will receive the water of Miriam's well. [ibid] The Rama [299/10] adds that he has not seen this custom being followed. Admur however omitted this in his ruling. See Sichos Kodesh 5739 Vol 3 p. 277-279 for an analysis in this subject.
[74] Rav Chaim Felagi in Kaf Hachaim 31/53
[75] Kitzur Halachos Shabbos 300 footnote 9
[76] Brought in Taamei Haminhagim 423
[77] 300/4
[78] In order to begin doing a Mitzvah immediately after Shabbos .[ibid]
See Admur ibid which mentions this in connection with those who are accustomed to have a special Tallis for Shabbos.
[79] Admur [brought in previous footnote] writes "immediately" after Shabbos.
Should one fold the Tallis before or after Havdala? There is a difference of opinion in whether it is to be done before Havdala or after. The Yaavetz in his Siddur as well as Kitzur Shlah write to fold it before Havdala, after Maariv. However the Lekutei Mahrich, Derech Chaim and Darkei Chaim Veshalom 468 record it is to be folded after Havdala.
[80] Ben Ish Chaiy Noach 16; Nemukei Orach Chaim 24
[81] Midrash Talpiyos brought in Taameiy Haminhagim 424; Ketzos Hashulchan 100 footnote 6

Sparks of Kabala
The reason one is required to fold his Tallis immediacy after Shabbos is because the Kelipas attach themselves to the Tallis prior to it being folded, and this is a great danger.[82] This applies even during weekdays after Shacharis that one should fold his Tallis immediately after prayer rather than leaving it rolled up.

Segula for one's wife:[83]
Folding one's Tallis on Motzei Shabbos is a Segula for one's wife to merit long years.

5. When after Shabbos may one remove his Shabbos clothing?[84]

It is proper to wear at least some of one's Shabbos clothing until after Havdala on Motzei Shabbos. [Some however have the custom to not remove their Shabbos cloths until after eating Melaveh Malka.[85] Others only remove them prior to going to sleep.[86] It is told of the Rebbe Rashab that he would remove his Shabbos clothes immediately after Shabbos, not wanting at all to wear them during the weekday. However of the Rebbe Rayatz it is told that his father the Rebbe Rashab told him to follow the custom of Chernobyl to not change his Shabbos clothing on Motzei Shabbos, and so is the custom of the Rebbe.[87]]

Giving charity and spending money on Motzei Shabbos:[88]
It is our custom to avoid giving money or buy items on Motzei Shabbos, as doing so gives nurture to the Kelipas.[89] It is however permitted to distribute charity on Motzei Shabbos, as by doing so there is no better way to drive away the Kelipas.

Not to get angry on Motzei Shabbos:[90]
One is to be extremely beware from strife and anger with his household on Motzei Shabbos as the Satan attempts at this time to stir friction between people, just as he does on Erev Shabbos. His motif for doing so is because after Shabbos one is escorting the King, and causing strife at this time gives the Satan power for the whole week.

6. Kerias Shema Sheal Hamita:[91]

On Motzei Shabbos, Tachanun is omitted from Kerias Shema Sheal Hamita[92] when reciting it prior to midnight.[93] When reciting it past midnight Tachanun is recited.

Traveling on Motzei Shabbos:[94]
One is to avoid flying from Israel on Motzei Shabbos being that the preparations for the flight are usually done by Jews on Shabbos. The same applies for flying Motzei Shabbos using El Al from any destination in the world.

---

[82] Kitzur Shlah; See Tamei Haminhagim 424

[83] Taamei Haminhagim KU"A Ishus p. 7

[84] 262/3

[85] So rules Kaf Hachaim 262/28 as the extra soul does not depart until after Melaveh Malka. [300/106]

[86] Brought in Leket Yosher that so was the custom of his teacher the Terumas Hadeshen.

[87] See Kitzur Halachos Miluim p. 56

[88] Shaareiy Halacha Uminhag 1/160; 5/35

[89] This was the custom of Rebbe Rashab, as revealed by Rebbe Rayatz. See Sichas Motzei Shabbos Vayeilech 5739

Prohibition of Lo Sinacheish: In Shulchan Aruch Yoreh Deah 179/3 the Michaber rules that one who states he will not give money to a collector because it is Motzei Shabbos transgresses "Lo Sinacheish". This raises a question regarding our custom to avoid giving money on Motzei Shabbos. The Rebbe mentions this in Shaareiy Halacha Uminhag 1/160 and concludes that nevertheless this was the custom. To note however from Taz 179/2 and Pischeiy Teshuvah 279/3 that if one does not tell the person why he is not giving the money and simply thinks in his head that it is because of Motzei Shabbos, then no transgression has been done.

[90] Divreiy Torah Munkatch 2/81

[91] Shaareiy Teshuvah 300/1; Shaareiy Halacha Uminhag 1/125

[92] Regarding reciting Yosheiv Beseiser in Kerias Shema Sheal Hamita on Motzei Shabbos, see Shaar Halacha Uminhag 1/125

[93] As until midnight a ray of Shabbos shines, and on Shabbos we do not say Tachanun. [ibid]

[94] See Kfar Chabad 398 p. 31 for an answer of the Rebbe that there is a question involved in flying on Motzei Shabbos; Hiskashrus of Rav Ginzberg

Kiddush Levana

Shulchan Aruch Chapter 426

Table of Contents

1. The Mitzvah
The greatness of Kiddush Levana
The Meaning:
The Reward:

2. From which day of the new month may one begin saying Kiddush Levana?
Must one wait seven complete days from the Molad to say Kiddush Levana?

3. Until what day of the month may Kiddush Levana be said?
Story of Rebbe Rashab from memoirs of Rav Yaakov Landau-Free Translation
Story of the Tzemach Tzedek and Reb Hillel Paritcher
Q&A
What has precedence, Davening Maariv or reciting Kiddush Levana?
What comes first, Havdala in Shul [for those Shuls which say Havdala] or Kiddush Levana?
If the moon became visible during Maariv may one stop in middle to say Kiddush Levana
If the moon became visible during Kerias Megilas Purim may one stop in middle to say Kiddush Levana
May one say Kiddush Levana if there is a Lunar Eclipse?

4. On which night is Kiddush Levana to be said?
Q&A
If delaying saying Kiddush Levana until Motzei Shabbos will cause one to miss saying it with a Minyan should he say it with a Minyan during the week?

5. When at night may Kiddush Levana be said?

6. Reciting Kiddush Levana on Motzei Yom Kippur and Motzei Tishe Beav
Q&A
If eating on Motzei Tishe Beav prior to Kiddush Levana will cause one to miss saying it with a Minyan what is he to do?

7. Saying Kiddush Levana on the night after a fast:
Q&A
May a mourner/Avel say Kiddush Levana?
When a mourner says Kiddush Levana within his seven days of mourning is he to say it outside under the sky or in his house near a window?
Kiddush Levana near a cemetery:

8. Saying Kiddush Levana on Friday night or the night of Yom Tov:
Q&A
If Friday night or the night of Yom Tov is the second to last night to recite Kiddush Levana may one recite it then if the opportunity arrives?

9. Saying Kiddush Levana with nice clothing:

10. Saying Kiddush Levana under the sky?
Q&A
If one said Kiddush Levana under a roof, must it be repeated?
When saying Kiddush Levana indoors must one open the window?

11. If the moon is covered by clouds may one recite Kiddush Levana?

12. What should one do if he began the blessing and a cloud then covered the moon?

13. Saying Kiddush Levana with a Minyan:

Q&A

Should one delay saying Kiddush Levana until he has a Minyan available?

14. Do women say Kiddush Levana?

15. Children:

16. Is a blind man to say Kiddush Levana?

17. How is Kiddush Levana to be said?

Reciting Kiddush Levana slowly with concentration:
A Segula for finding a Shidduch
A Segula for healthy teeth:

18. The Nusach:

19. Singing and dancing by Kiddush Levana?

Practical summary:

❖ *The details of each Halacha listed in this summary is explained below in its proper section. Look there for further details.*

- Every month on Motzei Shabbos between the seventh and 15th night from the Molad one recites Kiddush Levana with a Minyan, while wearing his Shabbos clothing.
- It is said outside under the sky.
- One recites the Nusach printed in the Siddur.
- One says it standing, with his feet together, facing towards Jerusalem.
- One looks at the moon prior to beginning the blessing of Baruch Ata Hashem and then looks down and recites the blessing. One does not look at the moon any longer during Kiddush Levana.
- One rises up on his toes three times when reciting the paragraph of "Baruch Oseich". This paragraph is recited three times.
- One then says Shalom Aleichem three times to a friend. The friend responds Aleichem Shalom.
- One finishes the Nusach printed in the Siddur and then recites Aleinu.
- After Aleinu Kaddish Yasom is recited.
- After Kaddish Yasom one is to shake the corners of his Tallis.

1. The Mitzvah:[1]

[Every month] upon seeing the new moon at night[2] one is to recite the blessing of "Asher Bemamaro Bara Shechakim".

The greatness of Kiddush Levana:[3]
Whoever blesses the moon in its proper time is considered to have accepted the face of the Shechina.

The Meaning:[4]
The moon and stars all express G-d's greatness. His awesomeness and His continued providence and effect in the world. The entire prayer is said only towards G-d and not towards any celestial being, Heaven Forbid. This is the meaning of that we receive the face of the Shechina.

The Reward:[5]
One who says Kiddush Levana does not need to worry that he will die from that day and onwards until the end of the month. This means to say that he will not die an unnatural death that month.

Maaseh Shehaya[6]
It once occurred that a Jew met a gentile late at night, and the gentile desired to murder the Jew. The Jew saw that the moon was shining and he asked the gentile, as a last request, to allow him to do a Mitzvah of Hashem prior to his death. The gentile agreed and the Jew said Kiddush Levana with a great amount of concentration, and with inner desire to give up his soul for the sake of Heaven. A miracle occurred and when he skipped three times, as is the custom to do during Kiddush Levana, the wind carried him away from the gentile. He never met the gentile again and was hence saved from certain death.

When is Kiddush Levana to be recited?
2. From which day of the new month may one begin saying Kiddush Levana?

One should not begin to say Kiddush Levana until seven days have passed[7] from the Molad[8]. [Practically in areas that do not have much visibility of the moon due to cloudy skies[9], as is especially common in the winter months,

---

[1] Michaber 426/1

[2] Rama ibid

[3] Sanhedrin 42a

[4] Peri Megadim 426 M"Z 4

[5] Kaf Hachaim 426/12

[6] Oar Chadash, brought in Yifei Lev 3/2; Elya Raba 602; Kaf Hachaim 426/11

[7] Michaber 426/4; Admur in Siddur based on Kabala [This is based on the Kabalist Rav Yosef Gegetilya, the author of Shaareiy Orah; so is also written in Mishnes Chassidim Miseches Motzei Shabbos; Maggid Meisharim Shir Hashirim; See Hagahos of Rebbe Rashab on Siddur Im Dach p. 321 for other Kabalistic sources, and sources in Chassidus. See Nemukei Orach Chaim 426/4]
Other Opinions:
- The Taz 426/3 brings the Bach who wonders at the above ruling that one must wait until seven days pass. The Bach rather rules, as rules Rabbeinu Yona, that after three days have passed one may say Kiddush Levana. The Bach concludes that practically the custom is to only wait three days, and hence if Motzei Shabbos falls on the fourth day or onwards Kiddush Levana is to be said and the Mitzvah is not to be delayed. The Taz ibid rules, as does the Levush, that if Motzei Shabbos falls after three days have passed then if the moon is already giving much light, Kiddush Levana is to be said, and one is not to delay until the seventh. [Hence the Levush and Taz conclude it is not enough for three days alone to pass but the moon must also visibly be giving much light.]
- The M"A 426/13 brings three opinions on when one may start saying Kiddush Levana: Some [Rambam; Smag; Rashal; Sefer Hakaneh] rule one may say Kiddush Levana even on the first day. Some [Hagahos Maimanis] rule one is to wait seven days. Some [Levush; Bach] rule one is to wait three days. He concludes [so is implied] like the Bach and if Motzei Shabbos falls within the first three days they are to delay until next Motzei Shabbos.
- Final ruling of Achronim-Opinion of M"B: The majority of Achronim [Bach; Taz ibid; M"A ibid; Peri Chadash; Beir Heiytiv 426/10; main opinion in M"B 426/20] dispute the ruling of the Michaber and rather rule that if Motzei Shabbos falls three days past the Molad or onwards one may say Kiddush Levana on Motzei Shabbos even though it is prior to the seventh of the month. The M"B ibid brings that some Achronim, including the Gr"a, rule that one may say Kiddush Levana even before three days have passed, and even prior to Motzei Shabbos. He concludes that one who follows this opinion has upon whom to rely, and in an area of cloudy weather he is praised for doing so.
The Chabad Custom: As stated above, Admur in the Siddur writes that based on Kabala one is to wait seven days past the Molad. So is also written in Torah Oar [109b]. The reason mentioned there is because one can only sanctify the moon after it has received from the seven Midos. Practically however in the winter the Tzemach Tzedek would say Kiddush Levana even before seven days have passed from the Molad. The reason for this is because of the cloudy and rainy weather experienced in the Russian winter which prevents the moon from being seen. Hence delaying Kiddush Levana when the opportunity arises prior to seven days could cause one to not say it at all due to the moon's inability to be

then if Motzei Shabbos falls after three days but prior to seven days it is nevertheless to be recited and is not to be delayed. In cases of question or doubt in this matter one is to follow the ruling of the Rabbinical authority of each community.[10]]

Q&A

Must one wait seven complete days from the Molad to say Kiddush Levana?

Some opinions[11] rule it is not necessary to wait until seven full days have passed since the Molad, rather as soon as six days have passed and one has now entered into the seventh day past the Molad, Kiddush Levana may be recited. Others[12] however rule that based on Kabala one is to wait for a full seven days to pass before saying Kiddush Levana. Practically one may be lenient in this matter.[13]

---

3. Until what day of the month may Kiddush Levana be said?[14]

Kiddush Levana may only be recited within the first half of the month. A lunar month consists of 29 days, 12 hours and 793 Chalakim[15]. Thus it may only be said up to 14 days 18 hours and 396.5 chalakim **past the Molad**[16]. [However there are opinions[17] which allow it to be said until 15 complete days past the Molad. Other opinions[18] allow in a time of need to say Kiddush Levana with a blessing up until the night of the 16th including the night of the 16th. Others[19] allow saying it even past this time up until the end of the month. Practically one should not be lenient

---

seen past the seventh. [Glosses of Rebbe Rashab in Siddur Im Dach p. 321; Shaar Hakolel 33/2; See there [in Shaar Hakolel] that he suggests the reason the Tzemach Tzedek did not wait until seven days is because he found no source in the Kabala of the Arizal or from the Gemara. The Rebbe Rashab however in the glosses ibid negates this remark and brings sources in Kabala, and Chassidus for this practice.]

Other Chassidim: In his glosses of the Siddur [p. 360] Rav Raskin records a tradition of the dynasty of Ruzhin that the Baal Shem Tov was not particular to wait until seven days pass while the Maggid of Mezritch was particular to wait. This is one of the instances that the custom of the Maggid differed from that of his teacher the Baal Shem Tov. See Nemukei Orach Chaim 426/4

[8] Admur in Siddur and Peri Megadim brought in M"B ibid

The Molad is the calculated time that the moon will begin its new cycle.

[9] And hence delaying an opportunity of saying Kiddush Levana could cause one to not say it at all.

[10] Rebbe in Sichas Noach 5752, brought in Shaareiy Halacha Uminhag 2/179; See previous footnotes.

The Rebbe writes as follows: If one is not **stringent** one can say Kiddush Levana on Motzei Shabbos that falls after the 3rd day past the Molad, even though it is before the seventh. This especially applies in cloudy areas and particularly in the winter. The Rebbe concludes that: each community should follow in accordance to his level of cloudiness, and it is given to the discretion of the local Chabad Rav to decide whether to precede the Kiddush Levana to Motzei Shabbos that is before the seventh of the month.

It is implied from the above wording that [even according to the Chabad custom] one may choose to say Kiddush Levana on Motzei Shabbos that is prior to the seventh even if it is not cloudy or rainy. When it is cloudy or rainy one is specifically to do so. However from footnote 14 there it is implied that in a non-cloudy area one is to wait.

[11] Rameh Mepuno 78; Shiyurei Kneses Hagedola; Elya Raba 426/14 [brought in Shaareiy Teshuvah 426/10] that one may say Kiddush Levana on the night of the 7th; Ashel Avraham Butchach 426/2

[12] Bircheiy Yosef 426/4 brought in Shaareiy Teshuvah 426/10; Mateh Efraim 581/10 rules one is to initially say it only after seven complete days have passed, although if he suspects the moon will not be visible again, he is not to delay the blessing.

[13] So concludes Hiskashrus 454 p. 15 and so was the custom of Rav Yaakov Landau.

Seemingly the reason one may be lenient is because even regarding waiting seven days there is a dispute and the Rebbe leaves room to be lenient. See also Sichas 1986 6th Adar Rishon that Kiddush Levana was done that Motzei Shabbos even though seven full days had not passed since the Molad.

[14] Rama 426/3

Ruling of Michaber: Kiddush Levana may be said up to 15 days past the Molad. Once the 16th day past the Molad has begun it may no longer be said. [ibid] These days are calculated as 24 hour days and not by weekdays. [M"A 426/12; M"B 426/17] Thus according to the Michaber one has 6 hours more to say Kiddush Levana past the time of the Rama.

Ruling of Achronim: As rules Rama so rules Bach; Shlah; Chayeh Adam 118/14; Kitzur SHU"A 97/10

Ruling of Kaf Hachaim for Sefardim: The Kaf Hachaim 426/53 concludes that one is to follow the opinion of the Rama in these matters, as Safek Brachos Lehakeil, even against the Michaber.

Ruling of M"B ibid: Rules one may be lenient like Michaber. [Biur Halacha "Velo Tes Zayin Bechlal"]

[15] There are 1080 Chalakim in an hour. [Tur 427]

[16] The month begins at the time of the Molad of that month. Hence one can say Kiddush Levana until the above time passes from the Molad and does not calculate it from Rosh Chodesh. [Michaber ibid]

Other Opinions: Some write one counts the above time not from the Molad but from Rosh Chodesh. [Taamei Haminhagim p. 200; See M"A 426/12]

[17] Michaber ibid; Mor Uketzia, and so concludes Biur Halacha "Velo Tes Zayin Bechlal"

[18] Kneses Hagedola in name of Rabbeinu Peretz; Heishiv Moshe 14; Tzeror Chesed; Shoel Umeishiv Kama 3/151; Chasam Sofer 102 [brought in Alef Lamagen 581/22]

[19] From the testimony of Reb Yaakov Landau recorded below it is evident that the Rebbe Mahrash and Rebbe Rashab allowed to say Kiddush Levana even past the 16th of the month, and even without using a Gemara. The Rebbe Rashab once said Kiddush Levana 17 days past the molad. It was said with a blessing and not from a Gemara. [memoirs of Rav Yaakov Landau, brought in Shemuos Vesipurim p. 184 see below] The

to say Kiddush Levana with a blessing past the first half of the month.[20] However it may be read from the Tur or Gemara any time of the month.[21]]

Maaseh Shehaya

Story of Rebbe Rashab from memoirs of Rav Yaakov Landau[22]-Free Translation
Date: Motzei Shabbos Beshalach 19th Shvat,
A number of members of Anash, myself included[23], had not recited Kiddush Levana, and on Friday night the moon became visible. I entered into the Rebbe Rashab during the Shabbos Friday night meal, after the Chazara on the Mamar "Az Yashir", in order to ask his opinion whether to say Kiddush Levana or not.

The Rebbe Rashab replied to me: There is a lengthy discussion on this matter. Reb Dovid Openhaimer has a lengthy response on this, and he concludes that one is to say Kiddush Levana [on Shabbos]. However the Shvus Yaakov rules one is not to say Kiddush Levana. Reb Dovid Openhaimer discusses these points and he says that there are no Techumin [above ten Tefacim] and that all the prayers are elevated. The Shvus Yaakov however negates this.

Reb Yaakov Landau then asked: The above discussion [mentioned in the Shvus Yaakov and Rav Dovid Openhaimer] is only with regards to saying Kiddush Levana on Shabbos, however today [on the 18th of Shvat] it is also after the time.

The Rebbe Rashab replied: Tonight is already passed the time of Kiddush Levana. (The Rebbe then began calculating the amount of time that had passed since the Molad and the last time for Kiddush Levana had been on Thursday night.) The Rebbe then concluded "if so then it is better to say it tomorrow than to say it tonight." It once occurred by my father [The Rebbe Mahrash] that they recited Kiddush Levana 17 days after the Molad. However on Shabbos I never saw him say Kiddush Levana. This occurred in Lubavitch. After my father [the Rebbe Mahrash] passed away it once occurred that the congregation recited Kiddush Levana on the second night of Sukkos. I said Kiddush Levana earlier. I saw the moon earlier so I already said the Bracha, however the rest of the congregation said it on the second night of Sukkos. (The Rebbe then mentioned to me a certain Rabbi that ruled they should say Kiddush Levana then.) Midmuvsky then reminded me that Reb Yisrael Noach once said Kiddush Levana on the second night of Pesach. Based on this one can also say Kiddush Levana on Shabbos as it is the same reason. Nevertheless I never witnessed anyone saying Kiddush Levana on Shabbos and in truth it is a bit difficult to accept such a practice. In my father's time there were those that said Kiddush Levana after 17 days passed from the Molad. They awoke before daybreak and said Kiddush Levana. My father was always accustomed to awaken before daybreak however us they had to especially awaken for this occasion. That entire night someone stood guard outside to see if the moon would be seen. Feivish was standing guard. Practically it is better [for Rav Landau] to say Kiddush Levana tomorrow night than to say it tonight. Tomorrow is the 17th day past the Molad. The Molad was at 12:00, thus you can say it tomorrow. Regarding saying Kiddush Levana on the 16th such an opinion is recorded in the Heishiv Moshe, however this was seemingly the occurrence with my father [the Rebbe Mahrash].

The Rebbetzin Shterna Sara stated: I remember that at that night they all went outside with Sefarim. [Gemaras?]

Rebbe in 1961 15th Sivan said Kiddush Levana 1.5 hours past the time. The Rebbe stated he relies on the Chasam Sofer ibid.

Taamei Haminhagim p. 199 brings from Derech Pekudecha in name of the Chozeh Melublin that after the time has passed one may nevertheless read the blessing from the Gemara. Alef Lamagen 581/22 concludes from Derech Pekudecha that so is the custom of the world to say it from a Gemara with a blessing after the correct time.

The Chasam Sofer 102 defends saying Kiddush Levana with a blessing even within the second half of the month if one receives much joy from this, such as when the moon had not been seen the entire month and one looks forward to seeing it as a good omen. [See Teshuvah there for the exact case of allowance of Chasam Sofer] His reasoning is because it is a blessing of praise to Hashem for the joy and benefit of the moonlight. Nevertheless he does not permit it unequivocally as is understood there from the Teshuvah.

[20] Hiskashrus 961 writes in the name of the Chasam Sofer that one may say Kiddush Levana up to 18 hours past the time of the Rama, however he may not say anymore once 18 hours have passed. In correspondence with Rav Ginzberg he wrote to me that this was the ruling of Rav Yaakov Landau, as was told to him by his son Rav Eliyahu Landau, that after 18 hours of the time of the Rama one may not be lenient to say it. This is despite the fact that the story mentioned above took place with Rav Yaakov Landau and he received a directive from the Rebbe Rashab to say Kiddush Levana on the night of the 20th. This story has been authenticated by the Rebbe Rayatz and was passed over his holy eyes prior to its publishing. Nevertheless in actuality we are not lenient to rule this way.

In an earlier volume of Hiskashrus [409] as well as in the glosses of Rav Raskin on the Siddur they wrote one may rely on the above story and recite Kiddush Levana even past the above time.

[21] As stated in previous footnotes, see there. See glosses of Rav Raskin on Siddur which writes he recalls a directive of the Rebbe to say it from the Gemara when it is being said past the time.

[22] Brought in Shemuos Vesippurim p. 182; This story was reviewed and authenticated by the Rebbe Rayatz. [See Kfar Chabad 986]

[23] The story was written by Rav Yaakov Landau.

The Rebbe Rashab replied: This occurred very late at night.

Rav Yaakov Landau asked: So it was said without the loophole of using a Gemara or Rif.

The Rebbe Rashab replied: Without using any loopholes. To do loopholes you don't need to wait for the date to be the 17th, you can do it anytime.

Story of the Tzemach Tzedek and Reb Hillel Paritcher[24]

During a certain snowy winter month Reb Hillel visited the city of Lubavitch, the town of residence of the Tzemach Tzedek. The moon had yet to be seen during that month and the last possible day to say Kiddush Levana had arrived. Reb Hillel sent a Pan to the Tzemach Tzedek to receive a blessing that the moon should be seen that night. The Tzemach Tzemach guaranteed Reb Hillel that the moon would indeed appear. Reb Hillel proceeded to station people outside as guard to announce to him when the moon becomes visible. In the midst of the night word came to Reb Hillel that the moon has appeared. Upon going outside he saw that the moon was a bit blurry covered by light clouds. He said that the Tzemach Tzedek said the moon would be seen, and therefore it has to be seen in a clear fashion, so he returned back inside awaiting for a clearer appearance. Slightly prior to day break the moon appeared clearly without any clouds interfering. Reb Hillel immediately went outside and recited Kiddush Levana. He then remarked that it once happened in his younger age that an entire month passed without a visible moon, although back then he was strong enough to handle such an occurrence. However now in his old age he does not know how he would have been able to react if the moon had not been seen.

Q&A

What has precedence, Davening Maariv or reciting Kiddush Levana?[25]

One is to Daven Maariv prior to reciting Kiddush Levana, as Maariv is a more common Mitzvah and hence receives precedence. If however there is suspicion that one will not be able to say Kiddush Levana afterwards that month due to cloudy skies, then one is to say Kiddush Levana prior to Maariv.

What comes first, Havdala in Shul [for those Shuls which say Havdala] or Kiddush Levana?

There are different customs which exist in this matter.[26]

If the moon became visible during Maariv may one stop in middle to say Kiddush Levana?[27]

If one will certainly be unable to say Kiddush Levana after Maariv, such as that by then the time for Kiddush Levana will have expired, then he may stop in middle of Shema or Birchas Shema and recite Kiddush Levana. [In such a case he may only recite the actual blessing and not any of the other verses prior or post the blessing.[28]]

If the moon became visible during Kerias Megilas Purim may one stop in middle to say Kiddush Levana?[29]

If one will certainly be unable to say Kiddush Levana after Maariv, such as that by then the time for Kiddush Levana will have expired, then the congregation may stop in middle of the Megilah reading and recite Kiddush Levana. However an individual is to remain with the congregation for the reading of Megilah even if this will cause him to miss Kiddush Levana.

May one say Kiddush Levana if there is a Lunar Eclipse?[30]

A lunar eclipse can only occur when the moon is full. Thus it is a clear sign that the first half of the month has passed. In such a case one may no longer say Kiddush Levana even if in accordance to our calculation there is time still remaining.

---

[24] Shemuos Vesipurim Vol. 2 p. 57

[25] Machazikei Bracha 426/7; Shaareiy Teshuvah 426/9

[26] See Piskeiy Teshuvos 295/6

[27] Nodeh Biyehuda 41; Machazikei Bracha 426/3; Shaareiy Teshuvah 426/9

[28] Biur Halacha 426 "Velo Tes Zayin Bechlal"

[29] Nodeh Biyehuda 41; Machazikei Bracha 426/4;

[30] Mahril 19 brought in Beis Yosef, Kaf Hachaim 426/60

4. On which night is Kiddush Levana to be said?[31]

[It is a Mitzvah Min Hamuvchar[32]] to recite Kiddush Levana specifically on Motzei Shabbos [or Motzei Yom Tov[33]] as at that time one appears elegant and is wearing nice clothing.[34] [The above time is only with regards to Mitzvah Min Hamuvchar, however from the letter of the law it may be said on any week night.[35]]

If Motzei Shabbos falls past the 10th of the month:[36] One is to only delay saying Kiddush Levana until Motzei Shabbos if Motzei Shabbos falls prior to the 11th of the month. If however Motzei Shabbos falls on the 11th of the month or onwards, then it should be said beforehand [by a weeknight before the 11th].[37] If it falls on the 10th of the month one is to delay Kiddush Levana until Motzei Shabbos which is the 10th.[38] However in a case that the Molad falls out early in a way that the 10th of the month is the 4th night left to say Kiddush Levana [and not the fifth, see previous Halacha], then one is not to delay saying Kiddush Levana until Motzei Shabbos.[39]

Q&A

If delaying saying Kiddush Levana until Motzei Shabbos will cause one to miss saying it with a Minyan should he say it with a Minyan during the week?[40]

If one is unsure whether there will be a Minyan available for Kiddush Levana on the coming Motzei Shabbos then if he has an opportunity to say it during the week with a Minyan he should do so.

---

5. When at night may Kiddush Levana be said?

It may be said any time at night, even past midnight.[41] It may not be said before nightfall, during Bein Hashmashos, even if the moon is visible.[42]

6. Reciting Kiddush Levana on Motzei Yom Kippur and Motzei Tishe Beav?[43]

One does not recite Kiddush Levana prior to Yom Kippur[44] or Tishe Beav.[45] It is rather to be recited on Motzei Yom Kippur[46] [and Motzei Tishe Beav[47]].

---

[31] Michaber 426/2

Other Poskim: The Chayeh Adam 118/14 rules one is not to delay saying Kiddush Levana until Motzei Shabbos, as one is not to delay fulfilling a Mitzvah simply in order to fulfill it in a more enhanced way. [Kaf Hachaim 426/23; See also Admur 25/4 that we do not delay a Mitzvah simply to do it in a greater fashion.] So rules also Bach and Maaseh Rav of Gra. [Brought in Biur Halacha "Motzei Shabbos"; See M"B 426/20]

[32] M"B 426/4

[33] P"M 426 A"A 2; M"B 426/5 in name of Elya Raba; and so is implied from Teshuvos Harameh 78. [Kaf Hachaim 426/22]

[34] Some say the reason for saying Kiddush Levana specifically on Motzei Shabbos is because on Motzei Shabbos the Beis Hamikdash was destroyed and the Shechina exiled. Therefore we say Kiddush Levana on Motzei Shabbos which proclaims the return of the Shechina. [Brought in Kaf Hachaim 426/21 in name of Rav Chaim Vital]

[35] Thus some even say that one should not wait until Motzei Shabbos to say it, but should rather say it as soon as he has a chance. [See M"B 426/20, see previous footnotes]

[36] Rama 426/2

[37] As perhaps there will be cloudy skies on that Motzei Shabbos and a few days onwards, such as two, three or four cloudy nights [depending on when Motzei Shabbos falls, if on the 11th, 12th, or 13th]. Due to this the moon will not be visible and the time for saying Kiddush Levana will pass. [Rama ibid]

[38] M"A 426/3; Brought in M"B 426/6; Kaf Hachaim 426/23

Although the Rama writes "When Motzei Shabbos falls before the 10th of the month" nevertheless based on his reason of suspecting for up to four cloudy nights and not more, it is evident that he means to also include the 10th. [M"A ibid]

[39] M"A 426/3; As according to the Rama one may only say Kiddush Levana up until 14 days 18 hours and 396.5 chalakim past the Molad, hence one must calculate that Motzei Shabbos is not the 4th to last night to say Kiddush Levana, as in such a case we suspect for four cloudy nights.

[40] Shaareiy Tziyon 426/20

[41] Ben Ish Chaiy Vayikra 23

[42] M"B 426/2

[43] Rama 426/2

[44] It is not to be said before Yom Kippur because one is in a state of pain due to it being a time of forgiveness of sin. [M"A 426/5] Others write as follows: It is not to be said as one is in a state of seriousness due to the days of Judgment and he is thus not in a state of joy which is required for the recital of Kiddush Levana. [M"B 426/9]

Other Opinions: The Levush rules one is specifically to say Kiddush Levana prior to Yom Kippur, as perhaps this merit of saying Kiddush Levana will turn the judgment to the side of good. This ruling is likewise the ruling of the Beis Meir. [Biur Halacha 426 "Velo Kodem Yom Hakippurim"] So concludes also Chida in Moreh Baetzba 9/283 and other Poskim brought in Kaf Hachaim 426/27

[45] As one is in a state of mourning. [M"A 426/4; M"B 426/8]

[46] As on Motzei Yom Kippur one is in a state of joy. [Rama ibid; See 623/14; 624/9 that Motzei Yom Kippur is a Yom Tov.]

[47] Custom of Arizal brought in Beir Heiytiv 426/4 and 551/25; so rules Kneses Hagedola [brought in M"A 426/6]; Peri Chadash; Shvus Yaakov 2/11; Aruch Hashulchan 551/22; Elya Raba 551/46; Chida in Moreh Baetzba 8/239; Kitzur Shulchan Aruch 124/19; Ben Ish Chaiy Dvarim 28; Achronim brought in M"B 426/11; Levushei Serud 551; and so is the Chabad custom, and so is the custom of world Jewry. [Kaf Hachaim 551/117; Levushei Serud ibid]

Eating and changing clothing:[48] Prior to reciting Kiddush Levana on Motzei Tishe Beav one is to eat and change his shoes. When reciting Kiddush Levana on Motzei Yom Kippur one does not need to eat prior to saying it as one is already in a joyous mood.[49] However one should switch his shoes beforehand.

Q&A
If eating on Motzei Tishe Beav prior to Kiddush Levana will cause one to miss saying it with a Minyan what is he to do?[50]

He is to say Kiddush Levana with the Minyan rather than first eat as doing so will cause him to miss saying it with the Minyan.

---

7. Saying Kiddush Levana on the night after a fast:

With exception to the above two mentioned fasts of Yom Kippur and Tishe Beav one is not to recite Kiddush Levana on the night after a fast[51], if the fast falls before the 10th of the month.[52] One is rather to delay saying Kiddush Levana until a later time. If however it falls on the 9th[53] or 10th[54] or onwards then one may say Kiddush Levana on the night after the fast.[55] One may certainly recite Kiddush Levana on the night after Taanis Esther, as if he does not recite it then the opportunity may not repeat itself.[56]

A private fast:[57] One who fasts a private fast may say Kiddush Levana with the congregation that night [if he suspects he will not have another Minyan to say it with[58]].

Q&A
May a mourner/Avel say Kiddush Levana?[59]

Some Poskim[60] rule a mourner is not to recite Kiddush Levana during his seven days of mourning if the seven days will end prior to the 10th of the month. If it will end on the 10th of the month or onwards then he is to say it even within the seven days.

Other Poskim[61] rule a mourner may not say Kiddush Levana within the seven days of mourning even if there will only be one night remaining for him to say Kiddush Levana after the end of mourning. If however there will not be any days left after the mourning to recite it, then he is to do so during the seven days.

Other Poskim[62] rule one is only to refrain from saying Kiddush Levana during the first three days of mourning.

Reason: The reason for saying Kiddush Levana specifically on Motzei Tishe Beav is because that is the time Moshiach was born and the renewal of the moon represents that the Jewish people will return to a renewed state. [Kaf Hachaim 426/29 in name of Rav Chaim Vital]

Other Opinions: The Rama [426/2] rules one is not to recite Kiddush Levana on Motzei Tishe Beav, or the Motzei of any fast. The reason for this is because one is not in a state of joy after a fast. [M"B 426/10] In 551/8 the Rama writes one is to say Kiddush Levana after Tishe Beav. The Taz [551/8] explains that the Rama does not mean to say one is to say it immediately after Tishe Beav, as this would be contradictory to his earlier ruling in 426/2. Rather he means that one is to say it the next day. The Kaf Hachayim [551/117] gives an alternative explanation of the Rama that here the Rama is stating the custom, that the custom is to recite Kiddush Levana on Motzei Tisheh Beav while earlier in 426/2 the Rama was ruled based on the letter of the law. Aruch Hashulchan 551/22 rules unlike Rama for the reason that one may not receive another opportunity to say Kiddush Levana if he were to delay it pass Tishe Beav, as well as that one may not delay fulfilling a mitzvah that he was given the opportunity to fulfill.

[48] M"B 426/11

[49] So rules Chayeh Adam 118/15 and M"B ibid

[50] Shaareiy Tziyon 426/9 in name of Elya Raba

[51] Rama 426/2

Other Opinions: The M"A 426/6 records opinions that state the custom is to allow saying Kiddush Levana on the night after a fast. The M"B 426/11 likewise records Achronim that one may say Kiddush Levana on the night after a fast.

[52] Shaareiy Tziyon 426/8 Meaning if the night after the fast is the 10th of the month then one should not push it off. Vetzaruch Iyun

[53] And hence the eve after the fast is the 10th of the month or onwards

[54] Shaareiy Tziyon 426/8 writes "the 9th or the 10th" Vetzaruch Iyun as if he will not delay if it falls on the 9th why does he mention the 10th. Perhaps then the explanation is that it depends on how cloudy one's area is. This perhaps would explain why the M"A 426/6 did not mention any specific date and simply stated if the time will pass one is not to delay.

[55] Shaareiy Tziyon 426/8; The M"A 426/6 rules that if the time is passing one is not to delay it. He however does not mention how many days must be left. In the Shaareiy Tziyon the M"B concludes that if the fast is past the 9th of the month then one should not delay it.

[56] Taz 426/2

[57] M"A 426/6

[58] Shaareiy Tziyon ibid

[59] See Beir Heiytiv 426/4; Shaareiy Teshuvah 426/2; M"B 426/11

[60] M"A 426/4

[61] Shaar Efraim Yoreh Deah 95 and so concludes Biur Halacha "Kodem Tishe Beav"

[62] Shvus Yaakov 2/11

❖ Summary: According to all one may not say Kiddush Levana during the seven days of mourning if the period of mourning will end before the 10th night of the month. According to all one may say Kiddush Levana within the seven days of mourning if the mourning period will end past the 15th night of the month. It is disputed if one may say Kiddush Levana within the seven days if it will end on the 10th night or onwards, prior to the 15th.

When a mourner says Kiddush Levana within his seven days of mourning is he to say it outside under the sky or in his house near a window?
Some Poskim[63] rule the mourner may leave his house to say Kiddush Levana. Others[64] rule it is to be said inside the house near a window if it is possible to see the moon from there. If this is not possible then it may be said outside.[65]

Kiddush Levana near a cemetery:[66]
One may not say Kiddush Levana in a cemetery. Rather he is to distance himself from it in order to say it.

8. Saying Kiddush Levana on Friday night or the night of Yom Tov:

One may not recite Kiddush Levana on the night of Yom Tov even if it falls on Motzei Shabbos.[67] Certainly one may not recite it on Friday night.[68] [See footnote for reasons[69]]
If the last opportunity to say Kiddush Levana is on the night of Shabbos or Yom Tov:[70] If the last opportunity to recite Kiddush Levana falls on Friday night or the night of Yom Tov, it may be recited then. [This applies even if Yom Tov falls on Shabbos in which case one would be saying Kiddush Levana on a night which is both Shabbos and Yom Tov night.[71] In such a case one is to say Kiddush Levana immediately at nightfall and only then Daven Maariv.[72]]

---

[63] Shaar Efraim ibid brought in M"B 426/11

[64] Elya Raba 426/15

[65] Kaf Hachaim 426/26

[66] Kaf Hachaim of Rav Chaim Falagi 35/12, brought in Kaf Hachaim 426/26

[67] Rama 426/2 following the ruling of Mahril end of Hilchos Shavuos and so rules Rameh Mepuno 78; M"A 426/7; M"B 426/12; Kitzur SH"A 97/12;
Other Opinions: The M"A ibid records the opinion of the Mahrash brought in Mahril [he was the teacher of the Maharil] and the Hagahos Maimanis which allows reciting Kiddush Levana on Friday night. So concludes Taz 426/1 to be the main opinion, and so rules Rashba 4/58. [Vetzaruch Iyun Gadol on conclusion of Taz ibid "and therefore the Rama did not record this ruling [of not saying Kiddush Levana on Motzei Shabbos which is Yom Tov]" when in truth the Rama ibid explicitly recorded that it is not to be recited. See Chok Yaakov 494/2 which asks this question on the Taz and concludes the Taz forgot this ruling of the Rama. However see Peri Megadim 426 M"Z 1 which reads the Taz as follows: "and so is the main ruling, **so is the final quote from the Mahril**, and the Rama did not bring the opinion **of the Mahrash which is lenient**". Hence the P"M learns that the Mahril says "and so is the main ruling" and not the Taz. This then leads him to explain that the meaning if the Taz in saying "the Rama did not bring it" is going on the lenient opinion. However Tzaruch Iyun on this explanation of the P"M as the Mahril [as verified after researching his wording in his Sefer] in truth never states "and so is the main opinion", hence it must be the insertion of the Taz, and the question of the Chok Yaakov therefore remains. After writing the above I found the same claim against the P"M in Kaf Hachaim 426/20.

[68] M"A 426/7

[69] The reasons behind the prohibition:
1. There are many reasons based on Kabala for why one should not recite Kiddush Levana on Friday night or the night of Yom Tov. [M"A 426/7; See Teshuvos Rameh 78; Ridbaz 4/133]
2. Some write the reason is because there are Techumin above and one is not to greet the Shechina on Shabbos or Yom Tov outside of the Techum. [Mahril end of Hilchos Shavuos brought in Taz 426/1; Beir Heiytiv 426/5]
3. Kiddush Levana is considered a supplication to Hashem, and one is not to pray supplications, such as Tachanaun on Shabbos and Yom Tov. [Mahril end of Hilchos Shavuos]
4. The honor of the Shabbos queen and the holiness of Yom Tov is greater than even greeting the Shechina and hence we do not mix one joy of a Mitzvah with another joy. [Rameh brought in Chok Yaakov ibid]
5. Through Kiddush Levana one elevates the level of Malchus, and on Shabbos and Yom Tov Malchus regardless has an elevation. [Magid Meisharim Shir Hashirim, brought in Kaf Hachaim 426/31]
6. A simple reason for not doing it then is because the Mitzvah is done with joy and it is thus common to dance, and dancing is forbidden on Shabbos. Now although dancing out of joy of a Mitzvah is permitted to be done on Shabbos, as we see is the custom on Simchas Torah, nevertheless that is because one cannot push off the dancing of Simchas Torah to a different date, as opposed to Kiddush Levana which may be delayed to another date. [Shaareiy Tziyon 426/12]

[70] M"A 426/7 based on Bach which once recited Kiddush Levana on a Friday night that was the last date for it to be recited; So rules also Taz 426/1; Kitzur SH"A 97/12; M"B 426/12;
Chabad Custom: In Shemuos Vesippurim [Vol. 1 p. 182] it is recorded from Rav Yaakov Landau OBM, the previous Chief Rabbi of Bnei Braq and the official Rav of the Rebbe Rashab's courtyard, that he once asked the Rebbe Rashab on Friday night of the 19th of Shevat if he and other members of Anash may still recite Kiddush Levana. The moon had not been seen previously and now it was visible. The Rebbe Rashab replied that since it is anyways past the date of Kiddush Levana it is to be said the next day.

[71] P"M 426 A"A 7; See however P"M 426 M"Z 1 which leaves it as a Tzaruch Iyun if one may also say Kiddush Levana on Friday night.

> **Q&A**
> **If Friday night or the night of Yom Tov is the second to last night to recite Kiddush Levana may one recite it then if the opportunity arrives?[73]**
> Some Poskim[74] rule it may be recited on Friday night even if there is one more day left for it to be said, as perhaps the moon will not be seen the next night. Other Poskim[75] however do not allow one to say Kiddush Levana on Friday night in such a case.

9. Saying Kiddush Levana with nice clothing:[76]

When saying Kiddush Levana during the weeknights one is to [change his cloths and] wear elegant clothing. [However it is no longer the custom to be particular to change clothing when saying Kiddush Levana during the weeknights.[77] Nevertheless, practically one is to follow the above ruling and change to elegant clothing.[78] At the very least one should wear the Shabbos Kapata.[79] The Rebbe[80] in his later years stated that one is to take special care to recite Kiddush Levana with nice, elegant clothing and that doing so is connected with the final and complete redemption.]

10. Saying Kiddush Levana under the sky?

One does not say Kiddush Levana under a roof [even if he is outside].[81] However in a time of need[82] one may say Kiddush Levana even in his house, if he can see the moon through a window or open door.[83] [See Q&A if one may say it through a closed window]

> **Q&A**
> **If one said Kiddush Levana under a roof, must it be repeated?[84]**
> If one said Kiddush Levana under a roof he nevertheless fulfills his obligation.
>
> **When saying Kiddush Levana indoors must one open the window?**
> In all cases one must be able to see the moon when he says the blessing. Thus a window which is not made of clear glass, or is fogged up due to rain, must be opened to allow one to see the moon. If the window is clear and the moon is visible through it, it is disputed amongst Poskim if the window must nevertheless be opened. Some Poskim[85] rule there is no need to open the window if one can see the moon through it. Others[86] rule one must open the window. Practically one should try to open the window when saying Kiddush Levana.[87]

---

[72] Kaf Hachaim 426/33 in name of Poskim

[73] Shaareiy Teshuvah 426/5

[74] Reb David Openhaimer brought in Shvus Yaakov 3/31

[75] Shvus Yaakov ibid

[76] Admur in Siddur; Rama 426/2; See also Michaber ibid that one is to say it on Motzei Shabbos "when his clothing are elegant".

[77] M"B 426/7 in name of Elya Raba in name of Kneses Hagdola. Likewise many Achronim did not record this ruling of the Rama.

[78] As rules Admur in Siddur; Peri Chadash [brought in Kaf Hachaim 426/24]

[79] Peri Chadash ibid

[80] Sichas Noach 1992 brought in Shaareiy Halacha Uminhag 2/179

[81] Rama 426/4
Some write that the reason behind this custom is not known. The Mahril writes the reason is in order to guarantee that impurity does not hover over anyone. The Bach writes the reason is because it is similar to one who goes outside to greet the king. [M"A 426/14] Meaning that since Kiddush Levana is like greeting the Shechina, it is thus not proper to greet it from under a roof and rather one should go outside. [M"B 426/21]

[82] Such as one is in middle of a festive meal [Rashal] or he is not feeling well, or he is in the midst of gentiles which may harm him [Bach] or there are dirty alleyways outside. [M"A ibid]

[83] M"A 426/14

[84] M"B 426/21 "All this is only initially"

[85] Shvus Yaakov 1/126; Bircheiy Yosef 224/1 brought in Kaf Hachaim 426/19; Shaareiy Teshuvah 426/1; M"B in Shaareiy Tziyon 426/4 and 25

[86] Dvar Shmuel 242 brought in Beir Heiytiv 426/1

[87] Shaareiy Teshuvah ibid. He concludes that so is implied from the story with the Rashal that he opened the window.

11. If the moon is covered by clouds may one recite Kiddush Levana?

The blessing over the new moon may only be said at night when the moon shines and one thus benefits from its light.[88] It must shine to the point that its light is visible on the ground.[89] [see footnote] Thus if it is covered by clouds the blessing may only be said if the clouds are thin enough to still be able to benefit from the moonlight, meaning that one is able to recognize matters which are recognizable due to moonlight.[90]

Bedieved:[91] If one said the blessing while the moon was covered to the point that one could not receive benefit from its light, he must repeat the blessing at another time when the moon shines.

12. What should one do if he began the blessing and a cloud then covered the moon?[92]

If one began the blessing with a clear moon and the moon then became covered by clouds, one is to nevertheless continue the blessing. Initially however if to begin with one knew the moon will become covered by clouds in middle of the blessing, then he is not to say the blessing [and is rather to wait for a more opportune time]. [Some Poskim[93] however rule that even initially one may say the blessing so long as he begins it within Toch Kdei Dibur of it becoming covered by the cloud.[94] Others[95] however argue on their ruling.]

A sign from heaven:[96]

In a month that one is able to recite Kiddush Levana on Motzei Shabbos it is a good omen from Hashem that the month will be successful. A month that one is unable to recite Kiddush Levana that month due to it being covered by clouds , that month will not be successful.

---

13. Saying Kiddush Levana with a Minyan:

It is permitted to say Kiddush Levana in private.[97] Nevertheless initially one is to strive to say it together with a Minyan, as the King is more beautified when his commands are performed in a public forum.[98] Likewise saying it with a Minyan allows Kaddish to be recited after the conclusion of Kiddush Levana.[99]

In a group of three:[100] If one is unable to recite it with a Minyan one should strive to recite it with at least two other people, for a total of a group of three.[101]

---

[88] Rama 426/1

[89] So rules M"A 426/1 that its shine must be apparent from the ground, and so rules M"B 426/3; However some Poskim rule that this is not to be taken literally. Rather so long as one can see the moon light and ray of the moon shining, it is valid to say the blessing. [Birkeiy Yosef 426/4, brought in Kaf Hachaim 426/17]

[90] M"A 426/1 from Radbaz 1/154; M"B 426/3

Other Poskim: Some Poskim rule one is never to say the blessing when the moon is covered even by a thin cloud. [Ben Ish Chaiy Vayikra 23; Chida in Moreh Bietzba 184 brought in Kaf Hachaim 426/18]

[91] Magen Avraham ibid

[92] M"A 426/1 from Radbaz 1/154; M"B 426/2

[93] Reb Chaim Tzanzer brought in Biur Halacha "Vinehnin Meorah".

[94] Meaning they allow one to say the blessing even after it has become covered by clouds, so long as one begins the blessing within Toch Kdei Dibbur of the moon becoming covered. Practically Toch Kidei Dibur is about two seconds and hence the blessing may only be started even according to this opinion within two seconds of the moon becoming covered.

The reason behind their allowance: This opinion views this blessing similar to all other blessings said over sights [such as lightning] in which the ruling is it must only be seen at the moment of the blessing.

[95] Mishneh Berurah in Biur Halacha "Vinehnin Meorah

[96] Magid Meisharim Shir Hashirim, brought in M"A 426/2

[97] Peri Chadash 426 brought in Kaf Hachaim 426/13; Biur Halacha 426 "Ela"

[98] Lit. "Berov Am, Hadras Melech"; Kaf Hachaim ibid; Biur Halacha ibid

[99] Kaf Hachaim ibid

[100] Chayeh Adam 68; Kaf Hachaim ibid; Biur Halacha ibid

[101] As a group of three people is considered partially similar to a public forum, as is the law by Halel that if it could not be said with a Minyan it is to be said with three people. [Rama 422/2]

Q&A
Should one delay saying Kiddush Levana until he has a Minyan available?
Some Poskim[102] rule one is to delay reciting Kiddush Levana without a Minyan if he knows he will have a Minyan later on, prior to the 11th of the month.[103]
Other Poskim[104] however rule if one has a group of three, it is better to say Kiddush Levana at that time rather than delay it until a Minyan is available on a later night, even if the Minyan will be available prior to the 11th.[105]
Other Poskim[106] rule one is not to delay Kiddush Levana at all simply to be able to say it with a Minyan.[107]

---

14. Do women say Kiddush Levana?[108]
Women do not recite Kiddush Levana.[109]

15. Children:[110]
A child which has reached the age of Chinuch is to be educated to recite Kiddush Levana. The age of Chinuch is from the age that the child understands the meaning of Kiddush Levana.[111]

16. Is a blind man to say Kiddush Levana?
A blind person is obligated to recite Kiddush Levana just like others.[112] [However there are Poskim[113] which rule a blind man is not to say the blessing being that he cannot see the moon. Many Poskim[114] conclude that practically the blessing is not to be said.[115] Rather one who is blind is to hear the blessing from another person.[116]]
One who can only see with glasses:[117] One who can only see when using glasses is to nevertheless say Kiddush Levana with a blessing.

17. How is Kiddush Levana to be said?[118]
Straight feet:[119] One recites Kiddush Levana with straightened his feet.
Standing:[120] Kiddush Levana is recited in a standing position. [If one is unable to stand he may lean on another person, or on a cane.[121]]
Looking at moon: Prior to beginning the blessing of "Mechadeish Chadashim" one is to lift his eyes[122] [and look at the moon]. After looking at the moon, before beginning the blessing, one removes his eyes from the moon and does not look at it anymore throughout the prayer.[123]

---

[102] Ashel Avraham Butchacher 426/2

[103] As is the law regarding delaying Kiddush Levana until Motzei Shabbos

[104] 426 Biur Halacha "Ela"

[105] As three people is also considered a public forum, as stated above. This especially applies in the winter rainy months. [ibid]

[106] Kitzur Shulchan Aruch 97/9; Chayeh Adam 118/14 regarding Motzei Shabbos; Kaf Hachaim 426/23

[107] As the Mitzvah of "Zerizin Makdimim" overrides the Mitzvah of "Bero Am" [ibid]

[108] Magen Avraham 426/1 in name of Shlah

[109] Although women are allowed to perform Mitzvos which they are exempt from, nevertheless they should not say Kiddush Levana, being that it was a woman which was responsible for the diminishing of the moon, as it was caused due to the sin of Eve. [Shlah ibid]
Other Poskim: Based on the Gemara in Sanhedrin 42a which implies women would say Kiddush Levana, the Kaf Hachaim 426/1 rules women are to hear the blessing from others. [Practically this is not the custom.] The Peri Megadim 426 A"A 1 writes it is implied that women are not to say Kiddush Levana even without a blessing.

[110] M"B 426/1

[111] 343/3

[112] M"A 426/1; Rashal 76; M"B 426/1 however in Biur Halacha "Vinehnin" the M"B concludes a blind man is to hear the blessing from another person.
The Reason why a blind man may say Kiddush Levana: As a blind person also benefits from the light of the moon as others show him items using the moon light. [ibid]

[113] Mahrikash brought in Kaf Hachaim 426/2; See Biur Halacha "Vinehnin"

[114] Machazikei Bracha 229/6; Ben Ish Chaiy Vayikra 23; Chesed Leavraham 2; Biur Halacha ibid

[115] As Safek Brachos Lehakel. [ibid]

[116] Biur Halacha ibid

[117] Shaareiy Teshuvah 426/1; Ben Ish Chaiy ibid
Other Opinions: The Dvar Shmuel rules one who sees the moon with the use of glasses is not to say a blessing. [Brought in Beir Heiytiv 426/1; Shaareiy Teshuvah ibid] The Shaareiy Teshuvah negates this opinion.

[118] 426/2

[119] Michaber ibid

[120] Brought in parentheses in midst of the words of the Michaber. It is unclear if these words are from the glosses of the Rama.

[121] Biur Halacha "Umivareich Meumad"

[122] Lit. Tole Eiynav [Michaber ibid]

Lifting the feet:[124] One is to lift his feet[125] three times opposite the moon and recite "Baruch Yotzreich[126]...Just like I dance..." [One is to beware not to bend his knees as this appears as if he is bowing to the moon. Rather he is to merely lift his feet through lifting the toes upwards.[127]]

Shaking the Tzitzis:[128] After the conclusion of Kiddush Levana [after Aleinu and Kaddish Yasom] one is to shake the corners of his Tallis Katan.[129]

Reciting Kiddush Levana slowly with concentration:[130]
One is to recite each word of Kiddush Levana slowly and properly, as one is accepting the face of the Shechina with this recital.

A Segula for finding a Shidduch:[131]
It is a Segula for finding a Shidduch to recite Kiddush Levana with intense concentration and with a congregation.

A Segula for healthy teeth:[132]
Saying Kiddush Levana properly is a Segula for having healthy teeth.

---

18. The Nusach:[133]

Halilukah:[134] The Shlah records a tradition to recite the Psalm Halilukah Halilu Keil Bekadsho.

Siman Tov:[135] One recites "Siman Tov Tihyeh Lechol Yisrael, Baruch Yotzreich" three times.

Kisheim Sheani Rokeid:[136] One recites "Ksheim Sheani Rokeid..Tipol Aleihem... One then says it backwards "Kaeven Yidmu". [One recites Baruch Oseich etc corresponding to the three worlds of Asiya, Yetzira and Beriyah. This is done in order to save the worlds from the Kelipas. Between each world there is a skipping of a level, therefore we dance three times.[137]]

Reciting Shalom Aleichem:[138] One is to greet a friend three times with the words Shalom Aleichem[139]. [Meaning one greets three friends with the words Shalom Aleichem.[140] If there are not three people available one is to say it to

---

[123] Siddur Admur; M"A 426/8 in the name of the Shlah rules that one looks at the moon one time and after that it is forbidden to look at the moon any longer.

Other Opinions: The Keneses Hagdolah writes that one should look at the moon until he finishes the entire prayer of Kiddush Levana and that so is the custom. However he writes that he heard the author of Sefer Chareidim says to only look at the moon until the end of the blessing of Michadeish Chadashim, and afterwards it is forbidden to look at it just like it is forbidden to look at a rainbow. The Shlah rules that one looks at the moon one time and after that it is forbidden to look at the moon any longer. The Chida [Moreh Baetzba 6/186] concludes likewise that one is only to look at the moon one time prior to the blessing, as according to Kabala it is forbidden to look at the moon.

[124] Rama ibid; Siddur Admur

This is done as an omen of joy, as since Kiddush Levana is similar to accepting the Shechina one is to rejoice when doing so. In the Siddur Rashash he brings a Kabalistic reason for the above dance. [Levush brought in Kaf Hachaim 426/38]

[125] In the Rama the wording is to dance, which implies lifting the feet from the ground. In however Mishnas Chassidm it states to skip, and so writes Admur in Siddur. [See Shaar Hakolel 33/4]

[126] So writes Admur as is the ruling of Mishnas Chassidim that the three skips are to be done before the words of Baruch Oseich. However the Rama writes it is done before the words Ksheim Sheani. [See Shaar Hakolel 33/4]

[127] M"A 426/9 in name of Shlah and so is implied from Admur

[128] Siddur of Admur; M"A 426/11 in name of Ksavim [Arizal]

[129] This is done in order to banish the Chitzonim which have been created from the prosecution of the moon. [Kaf Hachaim 426/48]

The M"A ibid writes one is to shake the end of his clothing, and does not mention specifically the Tallis Katan. Admur in the Siddur writes one is to shake the bottom of his Tallis Katan, but does not mention shaking the corners. The Shaar Hakolel 33/12 adds from the Peri Eitz Chaim that the custom of the Arizal was to shake the corners of the Tallis Katan.

[130] Moreh Baetzbah 187 brought in Kaf Hachaim 426/9

[131] Sefer Hamidos [of Rav Nachman of Breslov]; Kaf Hachaim 426/11

[132] Taamei Haminhagim p. 203 from Reb Yisrael of Ruzhin; Igros Kodesh 11/150

[133] 426/2

[134] M"A 426/10

[135] Michaber ibid

[136] Rama ibid

[137] Shaar Hakolel 33/5

[138] Rama ibid

The reason for saying Shalom Aleichem: The Perisha 426 states it is because earlier one said "Fear and trepidation shall fall upon you.." therefore one assures his friend that to him there will be peace.

[139] It is said in plural as according to the Mekubalim its intent is towards the angles which escort every person. [Shaar Hakolel 33/7]

[140] See Levush 426/1 "...If there are two or three people saying it together then one greets them with Shalom". Thus the wording of friend is not to be understood to mean one tells the same person Shalom Aleichem three times.

himself.[141]] The person who was asked Shalom Aleichem is to reply Aleichem Shalom.[142] One who answers Aleichem Shalom to his friend is considered as if he asked him Shalom Aleichem.[143]

David Melech Yisrael Chaiy Vekayam:[144] The custom is to recite David Melech Yisrael Chaiy Vekayam. The reason why we mention King David is because his kingdom is a parable of the moon, as just as the moon renews each month, so too his kingdom will become renewed in the future. Now just as the moon each month greets the sun light and hence is renewed, so too the Jewish people will in the future return to attach to G-d.

Kol Dodi:[145] It is a tradition from Rav Yehuda Hachassid to recite "Kol Dodi... until Meitzitz Min Hacharakim".

Shir Hamaalos Esa Eiynaiy:[146] The Shlah records a tradition to recite Shir Hamaalos Esa Eiynaiy, Tana Divei Reb Yishmael and Veamar Abayeiy.

Aleinu Lishabeiach: The custom is to recite Aleinu Lishabeiach after Kiddush Levana[147] to emphasize that we are praying to Hashem and not to the moon.[148]

Kaddish Derabanan: The Shlah[149] records a tradition to recite Kaddish Derabanan at the conclusion of Kiddush Levana.[150] However Admur in the Siddur records to recite Kaddish Yasom and so is the Chabad custom.

Reciting Al Tira:[151]
In certain Chabad Siddurim the verses of Al Tira were placed to be recited after Kiddush Levana. It requires further analysis as to the source for this addition. Many Chabad Siddurim[152] lack this addition. To note the Rebbe did not add the verses of Al Tira in the compilation of the blessing of the sun which follows a similar pattern to that of the blessing of the moon.

Reciting Ana Bekoach:[153]
In the first printing of the Siddur it was written to recite Ana Bekaoch at the conclusion of the Psalm of Lamnatzeiach. In later prints this addition was omitted. The Shaar Hakolel suggests the reason for its omission is because Ana Bekoach is only said to elevate from below to above while Kiddush Levana, which is like receiving the Shechina, is a drawing down from above to below.

---

19. Singing and dancing by Kiddush Levana?[154]

It is customary to dance and rejoice when the new month is sanctified[155] just as one would rejoice by a wedding. The reason for this is because the new moon symbolizes the future redemption, as explained above in connection to David, therefore we dance and are joyous as is the joy of a wedding.

---

[141] Shaar Hakolel 33/7; See however Levush in previous footnote that this is negated.

[142] Siddur Admur
Shaar Hakolel ibid explains one must answer back Aleichem Shalom as the Gemara in Brachos 6b states one who is greeted with Shalom and does not reply it is considered as if he stole the blessing. According to the Mekubalim there is no need for the person being asked to answer back Aleichem Shalom as it is being said towards the angles.

[143] Rama ibid

[144] Rama ibid

[145] Mateh Moshe 541, brought in Kaf Hachaim 426/44

[146] M"A 426/10

[147] Siddur
However some Poskim discourage the saying of Aleinu Lishabeiach after Kiddush Levana. [Moreh Baetzba 190] Others defend the practice. [See Kaf Hachaim 426/47]

[148] Biur Halacha 426 "Umivareich Meumad"
Others mention the reason for saying Aleinu Leshabeiach is because it was authored by Yehoshua which is a parable of the moon. Elya Raba 132/3 brought in Taameiy Haminhagim 463

[149] Shlah Shaar Osiyos Oas Yud brought in Kaf Hachaim 426/44

[150] The reason for saying Kaddish is in order to complete G-d's name which will effect that the light of the moon will be like the light of the sun. [Shlah Shaar Osiyos Oas Yud]

[151] See Glosses of Rav Raskin on Siddur p. 364

[152] Kehos Tehilas Hashem 2004 and many other editions

[153] Shaar Hakolel 33/11; See Igros Kodesh 7/136 where Harav Yitzchak Dubov asked the Rebbe why Ana Bekoach is said by Kiddush Levana, and the Rebbe replied to look in Shaar Hakolel ibid. In any event it is seen that some Chassidim had a tradition to recite Ana Bekoach by Kiddush Levana.

[154] Rama 426/2

[155] Lit. Kiddush Hachodesh. Seemingly in the Rama this refers to in the times of the Temple in which the Kiddush Hachodesh was done by the Beis Din and was followed by a great feast and festivities. Nevertheless today too it is customary to dance and rejoice by Kiddush Levana, as is evident from Shaareiy Tziyon 426/12

The Rebbe's Directives:[156]

Being that Kiddush Levana has a connection with the future redemption[157] therefore one needs to have extra alacrity and be more careful regarding Kiddush Levana. Thus one should wear nice clothing, and have it done on the streets with many people, as Birov Am Hadras Melech. As well it is to be said at its prescribed time.

---

[156] Shaareiy Halacha Uminhag 2/179

[157] As it says in Sanhedrin "Anyone that sanctifies the moon at its time is considered as if he has greeted the face of the Shechina", and as the Mharsha there explains, and as is ruled in the Rama as the reason behind the custom to mention "David King of Israel is alive and established".

Copy of Seder Kidddush Levana from Siddur Im Dach, Kapust Print

קידוש לבנה

סא

וַאֲמַרְתֶּם כֹּה לֶחָי וְאַתָּה שָׁלוֹם וּבֵיתְךָ שָׁלוֹם
וְכֹל אֲשֶׁר לְךָ שָׁלוֹם: יְדָוָה עֹז לְעַמּוֹ יִתֵּן יְדָוָה
יְבָרֵךְ אֶת עַמּוֹ בַשָּׁלוֹם:

כנס יפסס ג״א ודע ג׳ דיונים ואומר מכרוד שוק
וכו׳ עד כאן

סדר קידוש הלבנה

דָוִד מֶלֶךְ יִשְׂרָאֵל חַי וְקַיָם: נ״פ

וע״י הקבלה אין מקדש הלבנה עד אחר ז׳ ימים
למולד ויש לקדש הלבנה בבגדים חשובי׳ וכי
וקודם הברכה יאמר

מאמר להגידו שָׁלוֹם עֲלֵיכֶם מאירין הסי עֲלֵיכֶם שָׁלוֹם
נ״פ ואומרי׳ סימן טוב ומל טוב יהא כן ונכל יׂשׂראל
אמן נ״פ

הַלְלוּיָהּ הַלְלוּ אֶת יְהֹוָה מִן הַשָּׁמַיִם הַלְלוּהוּ
בַּמְּרוֹמִים הַלְלוּהוּ וְכָל מַלְאָכָיו הַלְלוּהוּ
כָל צְבָאָיו הַלְלוּהוּ שֶׁמֶשׁ וְיָרֵחַ הַלְלוּהוּ כָּל כּוֹכְבֵי אוֹר
הַלְלוּהוּ שְׁמֵי הַשָּׁמַיִם וְהַמַּיִם אֲשֶׁר מֵעַל הַשָּׁמַיִם
יְהַלְלוּ אֶת שֵׁם ה׳ כִּי הוּא צִוָּה וְנִבְרָאוּ וַיַּעֲמִידֵם לָעַד
לְעוֹלָם חָק נָתַן וְלֹא יַעֲבוֹר:

קוֹל דוֹדִי הִנֵּה זֶה בָּא מְדַלֵג עַל הֶהָרִים מְקַפֵּץ
עַל הַגְּבָעוֹת דוֹמֶה דוֹדִי לִצְבִי אוֹ לְעֹפֶר
הָאַיָלִים הִנֵּה זֶה עוֹמֵד אַחַר כָּתְלֵנוּ מַשְׁגִּיחַ
מִן הַחַלוֹנוֹת מֵצִיץ מִן הַחֲרַכִּים:

יאמר רגליו ויניע בגופו כ״פ קודם שהברכה וכשיתחיל לברך
גם ירמה בה כלל

שִׁיר לַמַעֲלוֹת אֶשָּׂא עֵינַי כו׳ הכוכבים כולם אל נקדשו ט׳

בָּרוּךְ אַתָּה יְהֹוָה אֱלֹהֵינוּ מֶלֶךְ הָעוֹלָם אֲשֶׁר
בְּמַאֲמָרוֹ בָּרָא שְׁחָקִים וּבְרוּחַ פִּיו כָּל
צְבָאָם חֹק וּזְמַן נָתַן לָהֶם שֶׁלֹּא יְשַׁנּוּ אֶת
תַּפְקִידָם שָׂשִׂים וּשְׂמֵחִים לַעֲשׂוֹת רְצוֹן קוֹנָם:
פּוֹעֵל אֱמֶת שֶׁפְּעוּלָתוֹ אֱמֶת: וְלַלְּבָנָה אָמַר
שֶׁתִּתְחַדֵּשׁ: עֲטֶרֶת תִּפְאֶרֶת לַעֲמוּסֵי בָטֶן:
שֶׁהֵם עֲתִידִים לְהִתְחַדֵּשׁ כְּמוֹתָהּ: וּלְפָאֵר
לְיוֹצְרָם עַל שֵׁם כְּבוֹד מַלְכוּתוֹ: בָּרוּךְ אַתָּה
יְהֹוָה מְחַדֵּשׁ חֳדָשִׁים: ידלג שלשה דלוגים ויאמר

בָּרוּךְ עֹשֵׂךְ בָּרוּךְ יוֹצְרֵךְ בָּרוּךְ בּוֹרְאֵךְ בָּרוּךְ
קוֹנֵךְ: כְּשֵׁם שֶׁאֲנִי רוֹקֵד כְּנֶגְדֵּךְ וְאֵינִי יָכוֹל
לִנְגוֹעַ בָּךְ כָּךְ לֹא יוּכְלוּ כָּל אוֹיְבַי לִנְגוֹעַ בִּי
לְרָעָה: תִּפּוֹל עֲלֵיהֶם אֵימָתָה וָפַחַד בִּגְדֹל
זְרוֹעֲךָ יִדְּמוּ כָּאָבֶן כָּאָבֶן יִדְּמוּ זְרוֹעֲךָ בִּגְדֹל
(שָׁחַד אֵימָתָה עֲלֵיהֶם תִּפּוֹל

תָּנָא דְבֵי רַבִּי יִשְׁמָעֵאל אִלְמָלֵא לֹא זָכוּ יִשְׂרָאֵל אֶלָּא
לְהַקְבִּיל פְּנֵי אֲבִיהֶם שֶׁבַּשָׁמַיִם פ״א בְחֹדֶשׁ
דַיִם אָמַר אַבַּיֵי הִלְכָךְ נֵימְרִינְהוּ מְעוּמָד וְיֹהִי
זֹאת עוֹלֶה מִן הַמִּדְבָּר מִתְרַפֶּקֶת עַל דּוֹדָהּ וִיהִי
רָצוֹן מִלְּפָנֶיךָ ה׳ אֱלֹהַי וֵאֱלֹהֵי אֲבוֹתַי לְמַלֹאות
פְּגִימַת הַלְּבָנָה וְלֹא יִהְיֶה בָּהּ שׁוּם מִעוּט וִיהְיֶה
אוֹר הַלְּבָנָה כְּאוֹר דְּחַמָּה כְּאוֹר שִׁבְעַת מִי בְרֵאשִׁי
כְּמוֹ שֶׁהָיְתָה קוֹדֶם מִעוּטָהּ שֶׁנֶּאֱמַר וַיַּעַשׂ אֱלֹהִים
אֶת שְׁנֵי הַמְּאוֹרוֹת הַגְּדוֹלִים וִיהֻקַיַּם בָּנוּ מִקְרָא
שֶׁכָּתוּב וּבִקְשׁוּ אֶת ה׳ אֱלֹהֵיהֶם וְאֵת דָּוִד מַלְכָּם
אמן ,

ויאמר למנצח בנגינה מ׳ עולם קדש יסוס ויסר
פוני טליח קטן ,

שער הריח

וְהָרֵיחַ מִידֵי חֹדֶשׁ בְּחָדְשׁוֹ וְשַׂבְּתוֹ בְּשַׁבַּתוֹ יָבֹא כָל בָּשָׂר
להשתחוות לפני אחר כי כו״כפי׳ כל סנק׳בּשׂמ
לכבודי נראה לו מ׳פי׳בׂשׂמי נשׂנק׳אדם נחמת אדם
העליון אשר על כוכא כו׳נמ׳ש נעשה אדם כלומם
כדמותינו כו׳ ודיפי הדנדים כנס נמיב
כו׳ונפא אל כמקים אשר נסארות שם ביום המטשׂט׳
וגל צי״ס אית יוס סמטשׂ ונמינ שנת ימים חוסס

Index

Index

A

Answering machine, 77
Ata Chonantanu, 96
  Ate, 97
  Did Melacha, 97
  Doubt if recited, 99
  Forgot to say, 96
  Motzei Yom Tov, 99
  Tashlumin, 98
  Vetodieinu, 100
  Women, 98

B

Baruch Hamavdil Bein Kodesh Lechol, 91
  Bathroom, 92
  Benefiting from Melacha, 92
  Doing Melacha beforehand, 91
  Hearing from another person, 92
  Kodesh Lechol versus Kodesh Lekodesh, 93
  Motzei Shabbos which is Yom Tov, 92
  Said Bracha over Yom Tov candles, 92
  Thinking the words, 92
  Women, 92
Bein Hashmashos, 88
Besamim, 123
  Air freshener, 127
  Cloth pocket of Besamim, 126
  Empty container, 126
  Esrog, 126
  Forgot to say, 127
  Fruit, 126
  If no Besamim are available, 123
  Motzei Yom Tov, 123
  Mourner, 128
  No sense of smell, 123, 125
  Pepper, 126
  Perfume, cologne, 127
  Prior to Havdala, 127
  Unsure if he has sense of smell, 124
  Weak sense of smell, 124
  When saying Havdala on Sunday, 124
  Which Besamim to use, 125

C

Closing sprinkler on Shabbos, 76

D

Davened Maariv in middle of third meal, 110

E

Eating before Havdala, 109
  After sunset, 109
  Began meal before sunset, 110
  Children, 112
  Eating Shalosh Seudos after sunset, 110
  Kos Shel Bracha, 111, 112
  Mezonos, 112
  Not able to say Havdala, 122
  Recited Bracha before Havdala, 110
  Sheva Brachos, 112
  Soft drinks, 112
  Women, 112
Eating on Erev Shabbos, 66
  Bar Mitzvah, 71
  Bris Mila, 67
  Eating on Erev Yom Tov, 70
  Erev Yom Tov that falls on Shabbos, 67
  Fasting on Erev Shabbos, 72
  How many people may be invited to Seudas Mitzvah, 66
  Large feast, 66
  Pidyon Haben, 67
  Poreis Mapa Umikadeish, 68
  Purim that falls on Erev Shabbos, 68
  Seudas Mitzvah, 66
  Siyum Misechta, 71
  Small meal, 69
  Snacks, 70, 71
  Tenth hour, 69
  Tenth of Teves, 72
  Wedding feast, 67

F

Folding Tallis, 156

H

Havdala, 108
  Another person drinking the wine, 142
  Beer, liquor, 121
  Before Maariv, 108
  Before Shabbos is over, 146
  Besamim. *See* Besamim
  Biblical or Rabbinical, 108
  Blessings, 113
  Blowing out a candle, 117
  Candle-Meoreiy Haeish. *See* Meoreiy Haeish
  Chomer Medina, 121
  Children, 144
  Coffee, 121
  Did not hear Hagafen, 113
  Does not have enough wine, 120,121

Index

Drank the wine before saying the last Bracha, 115
Eating after Havdala, 149
Eating before Havdala, 109
Extinguishing candle with Havdala wine, 116
Forgot blessing of Hagafen, 114
Forgot to say on Motzei Rosh Hashana, 148
Forgot to say on Motzei Shabbos, 146
Forgot to say on Motzei Yom Tov, 148
Havdala checklist, 107
Hearing Havdala from another person, 136
Hinei Keil Yeshuasi, 113
Hole in the cup, 118
How to hold the cup, 119
How much to drink, 116
Laws of the cup, 117
Loudspeaker, 138
Learning Torah after Havdala, 150
Looking at wine and candle, 115
Middle of meal, 108, 110
Milk, 121
Mourner, 146
Motzei Pesach, 120
Nine days, 145
No beverages are available, 122
No wine is available, 120
Overflowing the wine, 117
Preparing before Shabbos is over, 109
Said Haeish before Besamim, 114
Said Bein Kodesh Lechol on Motzei Shabbos which is
    Yom Tov, 115
Savri Maranan, 113
Shabbos clothing, 115
Sitting while drinking the wine, 116
Smelling the candle, 117
Standing, 115
Sunday, 146
Talked during Havdala, 114
Tea, 121
Using wine over other beverages, 120
Washing eyes with Havdala wine, 117
When to recite, 108
Who drinks the wine in Shul, 139
Wine is Pagum, 121
Wine is spoiled or is colored water, 119
Wine spilled, 119
Wine was left in the open, 120
Women, 143
Havdala in Shul, 139
Hearing Havdala from another person
    Baruch Hu Uvaruch Shemo, 137
    Children, 139
    Did not have anything in mind, 137
    Entered in middle of Havdala, 137
    Having in mind to be Yotzei, 136
    Hinei Keil Yeshuasi, 136
    In middle of Maariv, 138
    In Shul, 139
    Repeating Havdala after hearing, 139

Saying the words quietly, 136, 137
Should the listeners repeat blessing of Besamim,
    Haeish, 136
Women, 138

K

Kavod and Oneg Shabbos, 22
    Iskafya on Shabbos, 23
    Simcha on Shabbos, 23
    Why is no blessing said, 23
Kiddush Levana, 162
    Before Maariv, 166
    Blind, 172
    Cemetery, 169
    Children, 172
    Covered by clouds, 171
    Friday Night, Yom Tov night, 169
    How is it to be said, 172
    Looking at moon, 172
    Lunar eclipse, 166
    Minyan, 166, 171
    Moon became visible in middle of Maariv, 166
    Motzei Shabbos, 167
    Motzei Tishe Beav and Yom Kippur, 167
    Mourner, 168
    Nice clothing, 170
    Night after a fast, 167
    Nussach, 173
    Seven complete days, 163
    Shaking Tzitzis, 173
    Singing and dancing, 174
    Straight feet, 172
    Under the sky, 170
    Until what time at night may it be said, 167
    Until when may it be said, 164
    When may one begin saying it, 163
    Women, 172
Kos Shel Bracha, 111

L

Laundry
    Erev Shabbos, 41
    Leaving laundry in washer or dryer, 76
Learning on Erev Shabbos, 50

M

Maariv Motzei Shabbos, 95
    Ata Chonantanu. See Ata Chonantanu
    Before Shabbos is over, 95
    Havdala before Maariv, 95
    In middle of Shalosh Seudos, 96
    Vayehi Noam. See Vayehi Noam
    Women, 95
    Yartzite, 96

Melacha during Bein Hashmashos, 88
Melacha using Shabbos clock
    Electric plate, 78
Melacha that will continue into Shabbos
    Alarm Clock, 75
    Answering machine, 77
    Dye, 75
    Fax machine, 77
    Incense, 75
    Microphone, 77
    Recorder, 77
    Sprinklers, 75
Melaveh Malka, 152
    Candles, 153
    Melacha, 153
    Menu, 152
    Setting the table, 152
    Singing, 153
    When to eat, 154
    Women, 154
Meoreiy Haeish, 129
    Benefiting from fire before Bracha, 132
    Blind, 131
    Candle lit by gentile, 133
    Candle was lit on Shabbos, 133
    Candle was not lit for its light, 134
    Cannot see flame, 131
    Electric light, 134
    Forgot blessing, 127
    Gas stove, 135
    How close to be to the candle, 130
    Lighter, 134
    Looking at nails, 130
    Matches, 134
    Motzei Yom Kippur, 129
    No candle is available, 129
    On Sunday, 129
    Single wick, 132
    Torch, 132
    Using flame of Havdala candle, 132
    Women, 132
Mincha Erev Shabbos, 44
Motzei Shabbos
    Anger, 157
    Asking others to do Melacha, 94
    Baruch Hamavdil, 91
    Bedtime Shema, 157
    Candles, 153
    Charity, 157
    Delaying Melacha until after Havdala, 93
    Delaying Melacha until after Maariv, 93
    Delaying Melacha until after Melaveh Malka, 93
    Does not know when Shabbos is over, 90
    Drawing water, 156
    Eliyahu Hanavi, 152
    Folding Tallis, 156
    Havdala. See Havdala
    Maariv, 95

Melaveh Malka. See Melaveh Malka
Rabbeinu Tam, 89
Removing Shabbos clothing, 157
Smoking cigarettes before Maariv, 94
Three small stars, 88
Tosefes Shabbos, 90
Traveling on plane, 157
Turning on electricity before Maariv, 94
When is the conclusion of Shabbos, 88
Women doing Melacha before Maariv, 94

P

Placing water under candles before Shabbos, 76
Preparing for Shabbos
    Avoid quarreling, 44
    Baking Chalas, 26
    Bathing, 30
    Blech, 41
    Borrowing money for Shabbos expenditure, 25
    Checking pockets, 43
    Cleaning the house, 28
    Designating food for Shabbos, 21
    Doing personal preparation, 19
    Food designated for Shabbos, 28
    Haircut, 33
    How much to spend on food, 24
    Kapata of Silk, 40
    Laundry, 41
    Meat and fish, 24
    Mikveh, 32
    Must perform one act, 19
    Nails, 34
    Preparing food enjoys most, 19
    Reminding one's household, 42
    Removing cobwebs, 28
    Separating Chalah, 27
    Setting the table, 29
    Shabbos clothing, 39
    Sharpening knives, 29
    Shopping, 20
    Tasting the foods, 30
    Two cooked dishes, 24
    Using charity money for Shabbos expenditure, 25
    When is one to begin the preparations, 20

R

Rabbeinu Tam, 89
    Asking others to do Melacha, 90
    Changing custom, 90
    Davening Maariv early, 90
Radio
    Listening to neighbors radio, 76
Radio, TV, tape, 76
Repeating Havdala for others, 140
    Repeating Besamim and Haeish, 140

Index

Women, 140

S

Shabbos clock
    Fan or air conditioner, 78
    Lights, 77
    Machines, 77
    Radio, TV, tape, 76
Shabbos Menu, 24
Shnayim Mikra, 52
    Asher Yatzar in middle, 61
    Avel, Mourner, 52
    Cannot read Hebrew, 54
    Cutting nails, 57
    Drinking in middle, 62
    Haftorah, 53, 62
    Hearing Kerias Hatorah, 56
    Hearing someone else say it, 59
    Kabalistic meaning, 52
    Kabalistic meaning of Targum, 55
    Last verse, 60
    Learning Mefarshim during Shnayim Mikra, 61
    Making up Parshiyos, 58
    Mikveh, 57
    Nighttime, 59
    One is in doubt, 58
    Order of reading, 59
    Read Shnayim Mikra a week early, 58
    Reading during Kerias Hatorah, 56
    Reading the verses in order, 61
    Reward, 52
    Sefer Torah, 60
    Shema Yisrael, 61
    Taamim, 61
    Talking in middle, 60
    Targum, 52
    Traveled to Diaspora or Israel, 54
    Verse that does not contain Targum, 53
    Vezos Habracha, 54
    What to read, 52
    When to finish on Simchas Torah, 58
    When to read, 55
    When to read Haftorah, 57
    Women, 52
Sprinklers, 75

T

Tanach on Motzei Shabbos, 150
Tosefes Shabbos, 88
Traveling on Erev Shabbos
    Airplane, 64
    Is arriving with cooked food, 64
    Motel, inn, 65
    Taxi, 65

V

Vayehi Noam, 101
    Avel, 102
    Kaddish Shaleim before Vayehi Noam, 102
    Pesach falls on Shabbos, 102
    Standing, 101
    Yom Tov falls that week, 101
Vayiten Lecha, 149

W

Wake up call service, 76
Working on Erev Shabbos, 46
    Businesses and stores, 47
    Cleaning help, 49
    Cleaning Shtreimals, 50
    Collecting Mikveh payment, 50
    Haircut, 48
    Writing, 48
    Writing Stam, 49

היה קורא פרק שני ברכות יז.

ולא פריה ורביה ולא משא ומתן ולא קנאה ולא שנאה ולא תחרות אלא צדיקים יושבין ועטרותיהם בראשיהם ונהנים מזיו השכינה שנאמר י'ויחזו את האלהים ויאכלו וישתו: גדולה הבטחה שהבטיחן הקב"ה לנשים יותר מן האנשים שנא' י'נשים שאננות קומנה שמענה קולי בנות בוטחות האזנה אמרתי א"ל רב לר' חייא נשים במאי זכין י'באקרויי בנייהו לבי כנישתא ובאתנויי גברייהו בי רבנן ונטרין לגברייהו עד דאתו מבי רבנן. כי הוו מפטרי רבנן מבי ר' אמי ואמרי לה מבי ר' חנינא אמרי ליה הכי עולמך תראה בחייך ואחריתך לחיי העולם הבא ותקותך לדור דורים לבך יהגה תבונה פיך ידבר חכמות ולשונך ירחיש רננות עפעפיך יישירו נגדך עיניך יאירו במאור תורה ופניך יזהירו כזוהר הרקיע שפתותיך יביעו דעת וכליותיך

Rav said to Rav Chiya
"With what do women receive merit [of learning Torah]? Through escorting their children to the Talmud Torah, and assisting their husbands in learning Torah, and waiting for their husbands to return from the Beis Midrash"

This Sefer is dedicated to my dear wife whose continuous support and sharing of joint goals in spreading Torah and Judaism have allowed this Sefer to become a reality.

May Hashem grant her and our children much
success and blessing in all their endeavors

שיינא שרה ליבא בת חיה ראשא
&
מושקא פריידא
שניאור זלמן
דבורה לאה
נחמה דינה
מנוחה רחל
חנה
שטערנא מרים

Made in the USA
San Bernardino, CA
17 November 2016